Zol Zayn Shulem
II: Faroys!

Zol Zayn Shulem II: Faroys!

(May there be Peace)

זאל זיין שלום

Loss, hatred, murder

Questions of identity from an autobiographical perspective over more than three generations

---

Daniel Zylbersztajn-Lewandowski

© 2025 Daniel Zylbersztajn-Lewandowski

All rights reserved.

ISBN: 978-1-78324-381-5

Bibliographic information from the German National Library

The German National Library lists this publication in the German National Bibliography; detailed bibliographic data are available online at *http://dnb.d-nb.de*.

Automated analysis of this work, in particular to obtain information about patterns, trends, and correlations pursuant to Section 44b of the German Copyright Act (UrhG) ("Text and Data Mining"), is prohibited.

Contents

Foreword and Acknowledgements		vii
Chapter 1	The Brit Milah	1
Chapter 2	Funkerstrasse 6	5
Chapter 3	September 5, 1972	7
Chapter 4	Family Memories	11
Chapter 5	"Despite Everything." Childhood Amongst Shoah Survivors	20
Chapter 6	Pizzeria at Harry's	29
Chapter 7	"Dry Bread"	36
Chapter 8	Swastika and Germansin the Pizzeria	40
Chapter 9	Everyday Life	43
Chapter 10	Religions	46
Chapter 11	Jewish Child in German School	54
Chapter 12	On Air	59
Chapter 13	Musical Steps	66
Chapter 14	My Father, the Survivor	68
Chapter 15	"Worse than the Germans"	71
Chapter 16	Dalfsen – Netherlands	75

Chapter 17	At the School of the Germans	80
Chapter 18	Adult?	86
Chapter 19	My Family in Tel Aviv	93
Chapter 20	German School	101
Chapter 21	Love and Deaths	106
Chapter 22	Münchner Freiheiten – Munich Freedoms	108
Chapter 23	Mates	114
Chapter 24	On the Piano	118
Chapter 25	Jewish Awakening	121
Chapter 26	Welcome to the Hotel California!	127
Chapter 27	Jude!	146
Chapter 28	Soweto in Tel Aviv	152
Chapter 29	Model Student	155
Chapter 30	Kafr Qara and Other Forbidden Places	163
Chapter 31	Shir-Lifnei-Ha-Sehara	169
Chapter 32	School in Israel in Retrospect	175
Chapter 33	Lehitraot Israel	179
Chapter 34	Back in Deutschland	181
Chapter 35	The German Test	187
Chapter 36	Fears, Hiding, Running Away	192
Chapter 37	Concerning the First Anniversary of the German Unity	197
Chapter 38	My Father, Not a German!	200
Chapter 39	London	203

Chapter 40	Crooks and Racists	212
Chapter 41	The World is Bigger!	222
Chapter 42	Trip to West Africa	227
Chapter 43	What the Others Might Think	230
Chapter 44	A Dead End – London East End	233
Chapter 45	Hitchhiking to Wales	237
Chapter 46	White Man	245
Chapter 47	Freetown and Fights for Freedom	248
Chapter 48	The Tube Strike Wedding	256
Chapter 49	Brighton's Shadows	259
Chapter 50	Postgrad Avenue	264
Chapter 51	No Work	271
Chapter 52	PTSD – Decades After the Shoah	274
Chapter 53	Power Years!	276
Chapter 54	Radio	278
Chapter 55	Sport as a Way Out	280
Chapter 56	Doctoral Student	283
Chapter 57	"Migrants Excluded!"	286
Chapter 58	Old Hatred in London	290
Chapter 59	Pilates School	294
Chapter 60	PhD 2.0	298
Chapter 61	I Die with the Truth	301
Chapter 62	The Therapy Continues	304
Chapter 63	„Shifrah"	310

Chapter 64	To Live Life!	317
Chapter 65	Nothing to Save	321
Chapter 66	Children Days	324
Chapter 67	Locked Doors	327
Chapter 68	The End	329
Chapter 69	Broken Gravestones	334
Chapter 70	The Key to Tolerance	344
Chapter 71	Screaming Stones: Auschwitz and Auschwitz-Birkenau	351
Chapter 72	The Dream	358
Chapter 73	Grandma!	361
Chapter 74	Return to Journalism	364
Chapter 75	Not Quite German?	373
Chapter 76	Educational Dances	379
Chapter 77	Becoming British	384
Chapter 78	Forty-Five Years to Justice	390
Chapter 79	End of an Era	395
Chapter 80	Bat Mitzvah with a Surprise	397
Chapter 81	German, Jewish, Mizrachi, British, Dutch, Human. Call to Confront Self-Destruction	407
Chapter 82	Epilogue Following the 7th October 2023	412
Literature, Sources and Archives		415
Index		443

לְדוֹר וָדוֹר

Foreword and Acknowledgements[1]

"Nobody can force a goat to walk backwards."

Wolf Zylbersztajn, z"l

"Perhaps the most important form of symbolic memory is the narrative. The person who remembers tries to place in chronological order what happened to him or her. Moreover, the narrative is a conscious and unconscious attempt at sharing and thus has an intersubjective aspect. The narrative reflects the state of the person, but the formation of the narrative helps to restore self-integrity. If an event, even a traumatic one, can be brought into a self-narrative and retold, then this is already an important part of the healing process."[1]

Tihamér Bakó & Katalin Zana in *Transgenerational Trauma and Therapy (2020)*.[2]

What kind of goat is this, a goat that nobody can force to walk backwards. Is that an ordinary goat? Has anyone ever tried and succeeded to make a goat walk backwards? Perhaps it is a scapegoat that was sent to Azazel, and never returned? My father Wolf Zylbersztajn ben-Herszik-we-Szyfra

---

[1] The foreword in part I and II of the book series is the same
[2] Bakó & Zana (2020) p. 26, retranslated from German by author

Zol Zayn Shulem II: Faroys

z"l was mostly thinking of the past whenever he quoted that old saying about that goat you could not force to walk backwards. It is said that the Messiah will one day reunite us living people with those who have gone before us. This may give hope to some, but my father, who lost his faith in a caring G-d during the Shoah, had none of it. Still, today he lies in eternal rest in the divinely blessed Jewish cemetery in Munich, awaiting the arrival of the Messiah, just like all those buried there. His soul possibly also hopes that "die Bayern" (the football team F.C. Bayern Munich) shall be blessed with another good season and that there may finally be peace between Israel and its neighbours.

My parents Wolf and Corrie gifted me the middle name Zwi, following my grandfather Herszl. Grandpa Herszl – I could never call him Grandpa affectionately – died during a typhus outbreak in the forced labour camp in Skarżysko-Kamienna, caused by the inhumane and unhygienic conditions to which "the clean Germans" subjected their enslaved Jewish labourers.[4] Zwi is the Hebrew term for a gazelle, i.e. in the broadest sense a deer or a goat (however, a goat itself is called an *ess* in Hebrew). Despite my name, I am neither able to undo the past nor am I able to reconstruct everything as history. *Zol Zayn Shulem* is only an attempted retrospective that won't be able to change anything about what was. Understanding and reflecting upon the past, however, strengthens our path into the future. It serves to pass it on to the next generation, in keeping with Jewish custom as we say:

Le dor va dor!
From generation to generation!

---

[3] It is not clear if his Hebrew name was ben Herszik, or ben-Zwi. The Munich Synagogue had the first version recorded, but often the Hebrew name was in Hebrew.

[4] I use both Herzl and Herszik to describe my grandfather. The two versions of the name thus refer to the same man.

Dedication

In honour and memory of my dear father Wolf z"l. and for my dear mum, Corrie Zylbersztajn. This book is dedicated to my daughter Shifrah Zylbersztajn, her generation and all those who will follow her, and in blessed memory of all those who accompanied us, those who came before us, in particular those we were never able to meet.

In blessed memory of my aunt Rosza Silberstein *z"l*, who barely survived Bergen-Belsen, and of Abraham Silberstein *z"l*, my uncle, survivor of Skarżysko-Kamienna, Buchenwald and of Terezín (Theresienstadt). In memory of my uncle Moshe Silberstein *z"l* and his wife Chaftje, *z"l*, my aunt, who both escaped the worst by fleeing early. In blessed memory of my murdered grandmother Szyfra, whom I would have liked to have seen and been able to hug, and in blessed memory of my uncle Fiszl, who was murdered as a young boy. In blessed memory of my uncle Dawid, who would experience the joy of liberation, but was unable to survive and live beyond that point and perished as a result of his starvation in Theresienstadt. In blessed honour of my grandfather Gerhard *z"l*: I am still fighting for your rights and against the world forgetting what was done to you, and I would have liked to have met you and talked about your life. Through my research, I learnt that countless family members on my mother's side were murdered in Auschwitz and elsewhere. This book is also dedicated to their blessed memory, whose lives I only learnt about in fragments. May the memory of them all be a blessing.

In blessed memory of my aunt Gerda Cavallini *z"l*. Gerda always tried to answer my curious questions about her childhood and teenage years. She sadly passed away in the middle of the research for this book in August 2020.

Zol Zayn Shulem II: Faroys

In blessed memory of my dear cousin Hanni *z"l*, the daughter of my uncle Moisze and his wife Chaftjie, my aunt. Hanni succumbed to cancer on 1 Inyar 5781 (13 April 2021), one day after my father's Yahrzeit.[5] She tried to always share with me what she knew, even though that was little. Months before she left the world of the living, I was able to send her a Hebrew Google-translation of the then unedited preliminary chapters concerning our family in Szczekociny. Had she lived on, it was always my wish to share this book in its finished form with both Hanni and my aunt Gerda. Writing a book well and thoroughly takes a lot of time, hence I did not manage to finish before they left; however, the two of them are part of this book's *Ruach Ha Nefesh* (Hebrew for wind of the soul), as are all others that left the world of the living.

This book is also intended as a blessed memory to the many Shoah survivors who made the Bavarian capital of Munich their home, and where I grew up. The book is also written in gratitude to my wife Claudia, without whose support I would have struggled over many passages of my life and to the blessed memory of her family and ancestors who once passed through transatlantic slavery and, as soon as they were able, rebuilt their freedom in Freetown, West Africa, their Zion.

The deaths of our two families serve as a warning against overly blind arrogance, self-confidence and over-zealous nationalism.

Yossi and Agnieszka (Aga Piskiewicz) Bornstein (Yossi is the son of a survivor from Szczekociny) have personally campaigned for many years for the remembrance of Szczekociny's Jewish family and history. It is thanks to Yossi's and Aga's initiative that I was able to travel to Szczekociny with my mother in 2011 and join all the other survivors and their descendants in the task of preserving the blessed memory and honour of the local Jewish kehilah (Hebrew community). Thanks also to Yossi and Aga for allowing me to reproduce photos and quotes from the memoirs of Izyk Mendel Bornstein, their father and stepfather, and

---

[5] In the case of relatives, the Jewish year is often given after that of the current general calendar.

for providing me with the Polish translation of the book of remembrance "Pinkes Szczekociny" by the Jewish survivors of the Szczekciny community. I will always be honoured that you named your son Daniel.

Imran Manzoor became an indirect companion of this project, at least for the first part, because it was he who asked me years ago to talk to students in Swindon, England, about my family's experience of the Shoah. I first met Imran through my work for Oasis of Peace UK when I was their education officer. Later he accompanied me to the Jewish cemetery of Sosnowiec, where I recited a private Kaddish for my uncle. Thanks to the Sosnowiec Cultural Office for allowing me access to the cemetery. Thanks also to Imran's wife, Ewelina Chmielik, for her hospitality.

Thanks to the USC Shoah Foundation for interviewing my father and allowing me to use the material for this book and to Le Monde Diplomatique (Germany) for permission to reproduce the chapter "Ich werde Brite" (Becoming British) here, which was the inspired idea of Oliver Pohlisch, a colleague at *taz*.

I would also like to thank Stefan Walter and Wolfgang Heidrich of the "Flößberg gedenkt" (Flößberg Remembers) initiative for their information. Wolfgang walked me through dense bushes and forest to show me left-over traces of the Flößberg forced labour camp as well as its cemetery there, where those who lost their lives in the camp continue to be commemorated. Dr Jürgen Wolf guided me for several hours through the remains of Schlieben, passed on information and helping me with some improvements to the draft of this book without even being asked. Even before this book was published, he arranged for an appropriate memorial plaque to my father and his brothers in the memorial centre of KZ-Schlieben.

Thanks also to Krzysztof Gibaszewski, who not only tried to show me what's left of the Hasag factories in Skarżysko-Kamienna, but also took me to mass graves and execution places in the middle of the dense local forest. Unfortunately, his attempt to also show me the remains of Plant C was thwarted due to the war Russia had started against the

Ukraine, but I must at least thank the Mesko company, which runs the current factory, for the short tour of their exhibition centre.

Pamela Castillo Feuchtmann was kind enough to take me on a tour of the Buchenwald Memorial Complex, where we also had a confrontation with a disrespectful family visiting the camp. Her commitment to education about what happened at Buchenwald is unparalleled. Thanks also to Šárka Neumanová from Památník Terezín, who authorised a tour of Terezín (Theresienstadt) for me.

I am grateful to Beata and Mirek Skrzypczyk for hosting me in their flat in Lelow, the village where my paternal grandmother lived, and showing me around Lelow and Szczekociny.

Thanks to my distant cousins Philipp Lewandowski, Steve Gundel and Frank Jones for their contributions to this book about their side of the Lewandowski family.

Angie Grützner helped with the deciphering of old official handwriting. Thanks also go to *Absolute Medien GmbH* for licences and rights. Many other archives and archivists in Munich, Amsterdam, Dachau and Berlin, as well as the German State Archives in Koblenz, helped to reconstruct parts of my family's history as best they could. Thanks to Thomas Pohl from the administration of the Jewish cemetery in Weißensee, Berlin, for information about those members of my family who are buried there.

Special thanks also go to Libor Schröpfer, who, as mayor of Holýšov, a small municipality in the Czech Republic between Domazlice and Pilzen, spent months trying personally to reconstruct my father's escape route from one of the German death transports by train to the Mauthausen extermination camp. It was important to Libor to honour the dead in this way, and I know that he did much more than was necessary.

Above all, Käthe Fleckenstein for the German edition and Susan Boobis and Kevin Avison for the English edition, but also Hannah Holtschneider and Eva Kollmar, deserve special praise for the final version of this book. They proofread the book page by page and scrutinised

Foreword and Acknowledgements

my lines and thoughts. They worked with love for the subject matter for days, weeks and even months.

I would like to thank once more my wife Claudia, my life companion of many years, and my daughter Shifrah, for their patience, support and love. This book is also their book and would not have been finished without their help.

Without the very generous financial support of the following foundations, for the German edition, this book-series would not be in your hands. May it so honour the founders of the respective foundations.

> Kurt and Hildegard Löwenstein/Losten Foundation
> Irene Bollag-Herzheimer Foundation,
> 2mag AG, Kai Kress, Michael Fischer, Germany

The following amazing individuals supported "Zol Zayn Shulem" in its German crowdfunding drive: Eva Kollmar on behalf of Gregor Kollmar, Katy Elmaliah, Arie Meller, Jackie A. Boronow Danson, Alexander Diehl, Carlos Labraña, Silke Goldberg, Carl-Friedrich Laue, Victoria Hart, Catherine Brusky, Kirsten Wiseman, Gaby Coldewey, Bettina von Borries, Kim Segel, Guido Stefanec, Doo Ri Lichtenberger, Christiana Meredith, Erik Dege, Julia Orth, Kalmon Hener, Cornelia Topf, Josi Rosenfeld, Ina Lober, Rebekka Wedell, George Wilkes, Rena Beck, Margareta Burrell, Isabella Benson, Jan and Joost Gwinner, Michael Zur-Szpir, Tobias Müller, Hazel Seidel, Käthe Fleckenstein, Patricia De Souza, Paul Günczler, Friedrich-Wilhelm Höper, Lea Mühlstein, Joerg Nijmeijer, Marry Abberton, Rabbi Barbara Borts and seven people who wished to remain anonymous.

The following individuals supported the English edition crowd drive. Hazel Seidel, Doo Ri Lichtenberger, Roza Stegmann, Hilary Freeman, Ilana Treister, Steven Derby.Catherine Brusky, Ishmael Abberton.

Thanks to my German publisher BOD.

Much of the music and songs mentioned in this series has been put together on Tidal and on Spotify under Playlist >>Zol Zayn Shulem<<

Zol Zayn Shulem II: Faroys

The future lies on the tracks of the past. It is forged in the fire and nothingness of absolute madness and beaten into a solid sword to fight for justice and humanity. And yet we pray for the time when we were promised by the prophet Isaiah that swords would be turned into ploughshares.

1

The Brit Milah

So that the name Zylbersztajn survives. If I hadn't had a son, the whole family would have been dead. Nobody survived the war. It was good because it meant that things would go on.[6]

Wolf Zylbersztajn

Did fate connect me by my birth with the date of passing of my late grandfather, of blessed memory, thirteen years earlier on 10 December 1956?[7] According to the Gregorian calendar this may appear to be the case. On the other hand, according to the Hebrew calendar, I was born on 1 Tevet 5730 (my Brit Milah date would have been eight days later 9 Tevet, according to Jewish tradition). My maternal grandfather died on 6 Tevet 5717. Thirteen years lie between the two events.

In Judaism the number 13 is considered to be a fortunate number. There are 13 articles of faith in Judaism and the age of maturing into

---

[6] My father, 1995 on the question of what the birth of me meant to him In Zylbersztajn (1995), p. 18

[7] My mother once told me in the summer of 2022 that the The date of death was given incorrectly, and my grandfather died a little earlier, but was officially recorded as 10 December. Unfortunately, I can't say whether this is correct.

adulthood is also 13, adulthood here defined as being mature enough to read from the Torah.

My happy father holding me soon after my birth, back at home in 1969.

There are other numbers: My birth was associated with round numbers, in the Hebrew calendar, 5680, 5700, 5730. Within the Gregorian calendar there were nines: 1919, 1939, 1969. What's more, I was born 50 years after my father's birth, 30 years after the German invasion of Poland, 25 years following the death of my grandfather Herszik, and 27 years since my father last saw his mother and little brother, who he watched being deported to Treblinka, where they were later stripped of their clothes and their hair shaved to be murdered by gas.

It was this last point, that made my birth most significant. Here I was, the long-awaited son in the arms of my father, new life to a Shoah-survivor who had witnessed more violent death and destruction than most people, a man who only narrowly escaped his own death.

The Brit Milah

I was told that just a few days after I was born, at most some weeks, I had started vomiting and would not stop. It wasn't long before my parents rushed me back to hospital. After a thorough examination and consultation with the paediatric team my worried parents were presented with the devastating news that surgery was unavoidable. There was a problem with the exit of my stomach, a condition called pyloric stenosis. Given that I was a tiny infant, this was not without considerable risk back in 1969. Operations on small children were by no means common then, nor were such procedures always successful. My mother must have looked at me, her child, with trepidation. She may have expected anything but not this. After all, when I was born, I appeared to be a healthy "*yingel*," as my father would have described it.[8]

My mother remembered that a young paediatric surgeon performed the operation, less concerned than the others to give it his best shot, whilst others were more hesitant to take the risk.

The fact that I am writing these lines is testimony to the successful outcome of the surgery. Only the scar on my abdomen that grew with me serves as a lifelong reminder of an early trauma worse than any Britmilah incision.[9]

At some stage during my first months of life, that other cut would also be performed on me. My father claimed that several rabbis from different cities would gather for community events like these. Jewish friends of mine from Munich who are of similar age also confirmed this. For example, a mohel or rabbi from Vienna is said to have attended or performed a friend's Brit Milah in the Bavarian city of Augsburg, while another friend's mohel had travelled all the way from Switzerland.[10] These must have been busy days for such people, and I am sure their efforts also increased the costs to each family.

I still haven't found a photo of the ceremony. Perhaps with rabbis and mohels rushing through communities, things were done in a hurry

---

[8] Jingel, yid. boy, boy
[9] *Brithmilah,* Hebrew for circumcision
[10] *Mohel,* traditional religiously authorised person who may perform the circumcision of Jewish boys.

Zol Zayn Shulem II: Faroys

and with little notice in order to complete the formalities. On the other hand, perhaps my parents were not in the mood to celebrate. Mum and Dad would call me Daniel and Zwi. The middle name is symbolic of my grandfather Herszik and I am not the only one who bears my grandfather's name. My cousin, the first son of my uncle Abraham and his wife Ruszke (Rosza), is called Zwika (his sister who followed him was called Bracha, "Blessing").

2

Funkerstrasse 6

"Look Mum, a chimney sweeper!" The man in black was moving around on the roof of the building opposite. He was a frequent visitor on the roof tops of the postwar housing estate opposite from where my parents lived. "They carry with them good luck," my mum explained.

One morning, I tried to reach our blue and black budgie, whose cage was hanging in the living room of my parents' tiny two-bedroom flat next to the window. I rocked my white cot so successfully back and forth, that I made it all the way from the bedroom to that living room, even though it went round two corners, only to meet that feathered friend. Looking back, perhaps that was an early attempt to go my own way, by whatever means.

After getting her own morning routine – my mum usually dressed me perfectly and in best clothes – she would sometimes take me to the Hubertusbrunnen, a fountain near the canal of the Nymphenburg Palace. There, I was always fascinated by the deer sculpture, and just as much by the ducks and swans swimming in the canal.

The flat my parents had lived in since 1961 was situated on the second floor. My mum told me when I was an adult that she wasn't happy with its small size, especially after I was born. Eventually she managed to persuade my father to finally look for a flat that they could buy. It was an excellent time to do so, because at the end of the 1960s a building frenzy had broken out in Munich due to the upcoming Olympic Games. My parents wanted to invest the money they had been saving for years – mum said, they lived on a very tight budget in those years – in the heart of the Olympic Games, on the Olympic Village itself.

The flats in which the athletes were later housed could be purchased in advance. This would finance part of the construction expenses of the Games. Some of the best German architects of the prevailing zeitgeist worked on the designs of both the Olympic Village, as well as the entire Olympic site. It was to conform to utopian ideals and to be built in generous and large-scale fashion.

The village was to be informal, "non-violent," barrier-free and cheerful; with light streaming into the planned high-rise apartments; all car-traffic was banished underground so that pedestrians and residents could live on the upper levels car free. After the Olympic Games, numerous playgrounds would be erected, as well as a kindergarten and a primary school, even a shopping centre with a hairdresser, bank, post office and supermarket, all with access to the newly created Olympic Park. My parents only had to decide which floor they intended to live on. They chose a flat in the middle, not too high and not too low. During a family viewing of the yet unfinished flat, I discovered a black flush button in the toilet-room, the toilet itself still missing. Without my parents or the seller nearby, for the little two-year-old or three-year-old that I was, that button was all too tempting. My action caused a flush of cold water which rapidly expanded over the concrete floor. Given such initiation ritual, Mum and Dad agreed to the purchase.

3

September 5, 1972

There surely must have been a bouquet of pretty colourful flowers hidden in a bucket of water on the balcony of our small flat in Funkerstraße. My father had been preparing for a special day. It was my mum's 35th birthday. The dachshund "Waldi", the Olympic Games mascot decorated with the Olympic rings, was probably resting on the living room sofa. That four legged stuffed soft-toy was a souvenir from a walk my parents had taken with other family members through the crowds on the Olympic site. I can only vaguely remember this visit today, that there were lots of people walking around, the new and wide pavements, the late summer flair, and that we went to see the Olympic flame flickering in a fire-bowl. We took some photos and returned via the south-west exit, passing the Olympic Park tram stop, in order to walk back to my parents' apartment.

Despite it being her birthday, my mum surely would have switched on the radio in the living room to hear the latest news from the Olympic Games. My parents were particularly interested in Mark Spitz, the American-Jewish miracle swimmer, as he had won seven gold medals during the previous days and had set a new world record in nearly every swimming discipline.

Instead of exciting reports of that kind, it was suddenly reported that the living quarters of the Israeli Olympic team had been stormed by a group of Palestinian terrorists and that members of the Israeli Olympic team were now being held as hostages. Some Israelis were said to have been able to escape. Of course, our black-and-white television-set would now also be running, and on it the hostage drama unfolded live on-camera. Demands by the terrorists became known and reports of German officials attempting to negotiate. Also live on TV was the unsuccessful attempt by the Bavarian police to storm the Olympic quarters of the Israeli team and free the hostages. In fact, the terrorist hostage takers managed to follow the TV footage too and reacted accordingly, resulting in the cancellation of the rescue operation. By the end of the day, when I was most likely already in bed, eleven members of the Israeli Olympic team, a German policeman and five Palestinian Black September Movement terrorists, had been pronounced dead (after initial false reports that apparently the Olympic team members had survived).

I certainly had no capacity to understand all of that back then. My recollection is based more on what I know today. However, I can still remember the images of this television broadcast to this day. These images, and the worry and tension of my parents, count amongst the first memories of my early childhood, alongside the deer sculpture at Nymphenburger Palace, and the ducks swimming in the water features and canals of the palace gardens. They ingrained themselves in my memory as early abstract images, so that what happened here would stay with me forever, not least since my parents and I would move less than a year later to the very same location where most of this drama had taken place, the Munich Olympic Village.

For many others, such as Ankie Spitzer, the wife of Olympic fencer Andre Spitzer, one of the murdered athletes, their fight for recognition and later for adequate compensation had only just begun. To them the Olympic Village was now a symbol of the most horrific moments of their lives. It was also a symbol of the defencelessness and failure of the postwar German state against attacks of a terrorist nature. You see, the Olympic Games were meant to showcase a new kind of Germany. Germany was so troubled by the Third Reich images of arms and people in uniform that only civilian and unarmed police forces were allowed to provide protection for the athletes – with unspeakable consequences that caused the opposite of what all had wished and hoped for.

With the flat in the Olympic Village already purchased and contracts signed and exchanged, my parents had no choice but to move in, regardless of what had just occurred. Interestingly, my father even toyed with the idea of buying one of the now hard-to-sell flats in Connollystrasse opposite the place where the terror drama had started. They were now on offer at discount bargain rates. *Davka*![11] This was part of a kind of sarcastic and macabre defiance, and perhaps, in the remotest sense, a sort of compensation for past and possible future disappointments at the hands of Germans.

My uncle Abraham (l.), me (m.) and my father (r.) with me, on a visit to Connollystraße 31 in the Olympic Village in Munich, probably in September 1975.

I assume my father saw no difference between 1972 and the years from 1933 to 1945. In the end, he did not buy another apartment, it

---

[11]   davka, Hebrew for this very reason, out of defiance.

was nothing more than a thought, a fleeting idea, but he enjoyed retelling this anecdote, because people whom he reported it to reacted with confusion and disbelief, which pleased him.

It was disconcerting enough that he now had to justify the flat we had moved into to our Israeli relatives, as if the terrorism attack had been his fault. This planned ascent into something new, something beautiful and good for the family, with its sadly unfulfilled promise of a "new Germany," had led once again to a place where Jewish people bled a violent death. Not only had the "strong Germans", as dad would cynically label them, not been able to prevent all this, but they had planned and executed the liberation of the hostages so poorly and unprofessionally, refusing an offer of a rescue attempt to be conducted by Israeli special forces, that it all ended in a disastrous bloodbath.

The discomfort of postwar Germans when it came to military and uniforms (despite intelligence warnings of possible terrorist attacks planned by the extreme left), as displayed by the outward appearance of a pacifist cheerful Germany, could not have existed without the preceding Hitler years. Visits to the former residence of the Israeli Olympic team in the Munich Olympic Village, in front of which a memorial stone had been erected, became a regular, compulsory trip for our family whenever we had Jewish and Israeli guests visiting us.

4

Family Memories

The place of terror of 1972 would nevertheless soon transform into "my" Olympic Village. This former "stage of terrorist horror" was the very place where I would spend almost my entire childhood. To be honest, I am still not sure if it was right for my father to move to the Olympic Village. However, if the answer to that is that he should not have, the question would certainly have to be extended into whether people like my parents and my maternal grandfather should have considered or reconsidered Munich, indeed Germany itself as their chosen home after Hitler and all?

For my father, Munich and Germany were never a home anyway. In fact, I was surprised that years later he planned to be buried in the Jewish cemetery in Munich after his death, perhaps for my mother's sake so that she would have somewhere to go to, but also because some of his friends who had gone before him were already there. If that would not have been the case, I think he would have chosen Israel as his final resting place.

My father refused to accept German citizenship for much of his life. Only in the 1990s, when he was already well over 70 years old, did he make efforts to apply for German citizenship and get a German passport. Before that, he had travelled the world for decades with his blue passport that declared him as a "stateless person."

Zol Zayn Shulem II: Faroys

His life in Germany he justified as a form of resistance against the Führer's plan for a "judenfreies Deutschland", a Germany "cleansed" of Jews. This lived and rather complex form of "revenge" made neither his life nor mine any easier.

Picture from around the end of the 1960s. L to r. Johanna (nanny), Marcello, Gerda, Louise, my grandmother Maria, Edi.

As far as I was concerned, I had little choice but to learn to deal with the contradictions this position entailed.

In fact, my parents had plans to eventually move to Tel Aviv and to join my father's brothers. Whilst my parents now owned a flat in Munich, and truly lived there, my father continued to refer to most Germans of his generation with utter contempt. He honestly and perhaps understandably wanted nothing to do with them, even the neighbours from our block of flats were shyly avoided, never more than a friendly "good morning" and "hello" with small talk comments about the weather in the elevator, whilst many of them met for regular summer parties or the like. The closest thing to an emotional and actual home to my father was neither Munich or Germany, but Tel Aviv in Israel, a place that was then still a partly Yiddish-speaking country, by which I mean not just Orthodox Jews.

My aunt Gerda and my uncle Marcello Cavallini, on the other hand, had lived for years in in Zorneding, a rural village in the district of Ebersberg in the 1970s, on the outskirts of Munich, that became accessible by regional trains from 1972 onwards. The distance from the centre made accommodation more affordable here. For most of my childhood in the 1970s they lived on the ground floor of a house in one of the main streets. The house had a huge garden, that I appreciated. Zorneding was surrounded by a forest and in the middle of it was a children's playground. My parents would visit Gerda and Marcello often, a journey that took under an hour's drive by car. Together we would go for long walks through the forest, on a lucky day marvelling at wild boars to whom that forest was home. After a few years, my aunt Louise, the youngest of my mother's siblings, and her husband, my uncle Georg Zierer, himself of a Christian Bavarian family background (I saw him more as Bavarian rather than German, as if the things were not the same), would move to the adjacent village of Pöring.

In the Bahnhofstraße (Station Road) in Zorneding, which still had a village like atmosphere back then, my aunt Gerda made her last attempt of running a corset and ladies undergarment shop in line with what she had learned from her father Gerhard Lewandowski. Her uncle Bruno Lewandowski's shop at Munich Sendlinger Tor was by that time no longer owned by anyone of the family, but had been taken over by an employee of her uncle.

Aunt Gerda's shop was final remnant of a family business that once spanned the whole of Germany, with branches in the finest streets of Munich and Berlin. Predictably the shop's location so far from the centre of Munich and of limited use to the few people living in that then still small village and its surrounding area, sealed the faith of that enterprise.

Uncle Marcello, on the other hand, worked for the electrical goods company Siemens in Munich all his life and slowly rose up the company's hierarchy. Yet he remained at a disadvantage until the very end of his employment because he did not have a high school diploma (he only had an apprenticeship diploma as an electrician). Marcello had come to Germany from Verona in the early 1960s to try his luck as a "guest worker." Initially working in a small town in the Black Forest, he soon grew tired of its small-town feel and relocated to Munich. An eternal optimist, he was the only one amongst his siblings who dared to work abroad for a long period. His brother Salvatore Cavallini (1925-2000) stayed in Verona, where he would soon be a much sought after glass artist, producing countless hand-crafted church windows and other artistic works in glass. My uncle's nephew Flavio gifted his life to the Christian Son of G-d and became a priest in the Catholic Church. He is said to have been a kind-hearted man who came to the aid of many people in Albania.

During the summer months, I would sometimes spend the whole day in Gerda and Marcello's garden and later, when I was older, in the aforementioned forest. According to my uncle's humorous and imaginative stories, the woods were the reign of a particular gnome by the name of Michelangelo with a special gift. He knew of all children's misdeeds. I was keen to let my uncle know, that I had nothing to fear, having been a good boy. "Really?", he asked, as if I was hiding something that this gnome would soon lecture me about.

Aunt Gerda and Uncle Marcello would sometimes plan hiking trips for the family, for example, to the Upper Bavarian mountains, or skiing excursions in winter, which my parents would join. They were truly pleasurable highlights for me, and my Aunt Louise and Uncle Georg would join us occasionally too, which increased the fun, as far as I was concerned.

There were also holidays together in the Netherlands. Once, when my parents had won a trip to New York as first prize at a Jewish fund-raising tombola and could not or did not want to take me along with them, I even lived with Uncle Marcello and Aunt Gerda and, important from a child's perspective, their pet rabbit Murmelman. That was long before they had children of their own.

For a few years, everything was as in any "normal" extended family. I would soon get company. Markus, Louise's and Georg's first son, born in 1975, was the first little cousin I was able to play with.[12] When I was seven, Gerda and Marcello were also finally blessed with their own child, my cousin Claudia, as my mother once told me, after several failed attempts. Claudia was, in this sense, a special and eagerly awaited daughter. Later, Aunt Gerda and Uncle Marcello would also adopt a child, Alexander. The boy was two or three years old when he entered their lives and had come from a difficult home. Alexander stayed with them until he was 16 years old. After he left his adoptive parents' home, he was never heard of again. My uncle believes that something may have gone pear-shaped in his later life and that Alexander may have been too embarrassed to make contact.

In the early 1980s, my grandmother also moved from the Netherlands to Munich. She had last lived in Ugchelen, near the Dutch town of Apeldoorn, next to her sister Martha (Margje), but her daughters persuaded her to move to Munich so that they could take better care of her there. It was not until Martha increasingly had to look after Anton, her life partner of later years, after he began to suffer from Alzheimer's Diseases, and had little time left for her sister, that my grandmother finally made the move, this time for good.

A house-share located in Vaterstetten just a 15 minutes' drive from Aunt Gerda and Marcello, was to become her new home. My Oma would occupy the entire first floor, another lady in her 60s the ground-floor. As my grandmother grew older, she would often complain about the stairs. But the proximity of my aunt and uncle also meant that she was very present for my cousin Claudia.

---

[12] Markus Alexander was the first son of Louise and Georg. The couple would go on to have two more children: Franziska Johana Louise, born in 1985, and Dominik Ignaz Georg, born in 1988. Markus had a son together with Dahlia, born 1983 Hummer, in 2005, Maximilian Markus Maria. Franziska and her husband Thomas Böck (born 1975) have two children together: Lukas (2013) and Benedikt. Dominik lives with his wife Ramona, née Eder, 1989.

My grandmother's living quarters, whether in the Netherlands or later in Vaterstetten, always carried a scent of the forbidden. It had unusual odours of polish and tobacco and everywhere were old and fragile objects such as porcelain figurines that I was expressly told not to touch. Unforgettable is her always-ticking wall clock that would chime on the hour and half hour. Come to think of it, I think there were several such clocks. There were also paintings depicting Amsterdam and the Netherlands and sea scenes with ships intermingled with art from Indonesia, where her father had once worked. Some were souvenirs she had brought with her, after she and her sister Martha had travelled to Indonesia for a holiday, perhaps to explore some of the stories they may have picked up from their parents about the time when they had lived there.

In the same way that I was not permitted to touch the figurines or other porcelain, my grandma demanded a certain general distance. She was not exactly the image of a dear huggable granny. However, a few years earlier, when she was supposed to look after me for a few days while my parents were travelling, she also revealed a funnier side. All over sudden, she showed her silly side, making holes in the morning toast, and calling it mouse-bread, much to the delight of the little boy that I was.

After my grandmother became sick and died of pneumonia in 1991, the family had her buried in the Christian cemetery of North-Munich, where her remains lie reunited with her husbands, who had passed away almost three decades earlier. Her funeral was one of the many events that my parents did not allow me to attend. Perhaps my father did not wish me to get too close to the experience of death. He certainly had witnessed more than his fair share of it. Perhaps he also lacked the experience of dealing with normal funerals. The funerals of my uncles Abraham and Moisze and of my aunt Chaftije passed by me in the same way. It was only when I earned enough of my own that I was able to attend funerals. However, let us go back to Munich of the 1970s.

My memories of my mum's brother, Eduard "Eddie" Lewandowski and his family, are less concrete than those already mentioned. All I can remember is a children's birthday party for his daughter Sonia with the cheesy 1970s disco hit "Yes Sir, I can boogie."[13] I haven't heard from that side of the family since that time.¹ In fact, I even thought that Uncle Eddie had disappeared until I realised during the research for this book that he lived in a small community not far from Munich.

As the 1980s progressed, Aunt Louise and Uncle Georg were increasingly plagued by money worries. Georg Zierer was a warm and hearty "Bavarian" and an excellent hairdresser who owned a salon near Gärtnerplatz, a central location in Munich's City Centre with some exquisite shops, near the city's market. Whenever we stayed with Louise and Georg, we were treated to something tasty to eat and drink. Louise herself was the youngest of the Lewandowski siblings. This meant that amongst her siblings, who all were over ten years of age when they moved from Holland to the Bavarian capital, she was the one who was more naturally at home in Munich. In the way I experienced her, her younger age meant higher levels of fun and dynamism. She and Uncle Georg married as Christians, like the rest of the family and I remember attending the wedding. There was no way anyone would have been able to tell that her grandfather had been a Jewish citizen of Munich and her father a victim of the Third Reich. To add to this, she liked to wear Dirndl, traditional Bavarian dress, from time to time. She had tried to establish herself by selling cosmetics, among other things. I remember shelves full of products in her garage, which I assume she was not able to sell as easily as the company had made her believe. That was perhaps an early hint of what was to come for her and my uncle. At some point, when I was six or seven years old, they decided to build a house in Pfaffing (near the Bavarian city of Wasserburg-am-Inn). Uncle Georg now had to travel to Munich by car every single day. While that was not a problem in the summer, early in the morning and late in the evening during the winter months, with snowy and icy roads, the journey to work and back home

---

[13] Dr Sonia Lewandowski, born 1973 in Munich, is the daughter of Eduard Lewandowski and Elisabeth Anna Burda (born 1949 in Augsburg). Sonia now has a daughter, Kristine, with Allan J. Tsemach, born 1967 in Bergen, Norway, who was born in Cape Town in 2005.

could be treacherous. The house in a beautiful rural area was huge. But something seemed to have gone wrong with their planning and the construction costs, even though Georg did a lot of the work himself. Even before the house was finished, it had to be separated into two halves so that one half could be sold. My cousin Markus believes that his father sacrificed his health for this house-building project.

The passing of my grandmother led to a dispute between the siblings, as my grandmother appeared to not have prepared adequately who should get what after her death. Louise, Georg and Markus disappeared from my radar. It wasn't until the unexpected death of my aunt Gerda in August 2020, after she had been diagnosed with late stage cancer, that I would even meet my cousin Markus again for the first time in over three decades and learnt about his wife Dahlia (born Hummer 1975) and his son Maximilian (born 2005). I also learnt that my Uncle Georg was no longer alive.

Survival

Today I lived death just getting up lying there and enduring existence

On my mattress,
TV flickering
in front of me
meaningless
images of wonderful life, trouble free
unknown to me

Was lying
with outstretched arms
staring at the wall
death – not ending
an intolerable situation,
condemning my life.

*That desire sometimes
to be like those figures
just next to me
on screen
-absurd.*

*Nothing
could get me up.
Everything
Surrounding me,
Anything
I could do
reminded me
of the potential of
human hypocrisy
trapped in attitudes
that spelled*

G-E-R-M-A-N-Y

*in capital letters.
Every job
every deed
everyone.*

*Another day
another side of
Jewish survival
overcame me
pulling me to the ground
and then lifting me again
to face another day*

(Daniel Zylbersztajn-Lewandowski,
August 1996, slightly modified for this edition)

5

"Despite Everything." Childhood Amongst Shoah Survivors

> *For survivors of severe social trauma, the post-traumatic intra-subjective world can freeze and become permanent if no integration takes place. The anxiety, fear and pain that were initially associated with the trauma are not past emotions or memories for survivors, but constantly present realities that preserve the experiences of the trauma.*
>
> *In addition, survivors also have a relationship with the outside world and can deal with the here and now. But these relationships are weak, fragile, and cannot be maintained for long. At the slightest sign of real or perceived danger, the survivor steps back into the continuity of his/her traumatic world.*[14]

Despite the shadow of the terrible terror attack that burdened the Munich Olympic Village, this modern 1970s concrete "village" offered quite a few up-sides to its residents, including children. True to its name, the former athletes' centre did possess a village-like atmosphere. Those

---

[14] Bakó & Zana (2020), P. 27, retranslated into English

of us who were children were able to play freely and safely on the many playgrounds of the village. Our homes were out of reach, and playmates of the same age lived everywhere around us. There were many green bushes and imaginative corners inspiring children's fantasies, as well as lawns that enabled the playing of footbal, roller-skating areas, small paths for cycling, climbing frames and adventure playgrounds. In addition, the Olympic Park extended play opportunities further, be it swimming, bike rides or playing cops and robbers or visiting the small artificial lakes with their ducks and geese. As already mentioned, there were no cars on any of the upper levels, and thus, as a four-year-old, I was able to walk to my kindergarten, which was literally three minutes away, by myself. In that sense, my childhood was seemingly worry free, even expressively positive. My primary school was also less than a ten-minute walk away from home and I often went to the supermarket or baker's on my own.

As far as I knew at the time, I was the only Jewish child growing up in this village.[15] Sometimes I even thought I was the only Jewish child in Munich, because I didn't personally know any other children of the same age who were Jewish. My parents decided that I should attend kindergarten and school in the local neighbourhood, rather than attend the one and only Jewish kindergarten and school of Munich that existed back then. This was a somewhat unorthodox decision. I learned later that other Jewish children like me did attend the Jewish kindergarten and school, because their parents not only wanted their children to experience Jewish life amongst Jewish compatriots, but they also hoped that their children would not grow up predominantly amongst non-Jewish German children. On the other hand, it is very probable that my father was not just unwilling to send me to a Jewish kindergarten and school, but also logistically unable, as these were based at least half an hour's drive away from where we lived. Coming home in the early morning hours, my father was also not able to get up at 7.00 am to give me a ride

---

[15] A resident of the village recently wrote to me that she was too but only learnt about it as an adult.

to school, nor was my mother seemingly prepared to take on the journey on public transport, nor with her car, especially given the alternative of a kindergarten and school just around the corner. I am not sure if there were supplementary and compensatory afternoon or weekend classes for Jewish children available; if they were, my parents did not take me to these either.

The consequence of that meant that I lacked the opportunity to acquire any kind of formal Jewish education. My dad made little effort to that effect. Shabbat and kashrut would only become more important in my life after my mother's official conversion to Judaism.[16] For my father, Judaism had other components: the story of his survival, his strong sense of not being German, the festivals of Passover and of Yom Kippur. Amongst Jewish people, such persons are often described as so-called "three-day Jews." Numerous visits to Tel Aviv, where my father's brothers and many other relatives lived, completed what he would see as a Jewish life, beside his Yiddish newspaper.

Whilst I was not exposed to a Jewish kindergarten or school, there were other Jewish people around, amongst them my father's friends. One was Henrik Goldfarb and his wife Edith. The two were a childless couple who I was allowed to call aunt and uncle. Edith and Henrik were my parents' closest friends. Henrik was also a Jewish survivor from Poland, whilst Edith came from Dresden, now Gdansk. Photos of my parents show that they and the Goldfarbs had been friends for a long time, at least since the 1960s, probably even before that.

They lived at the start of my life in the same building complex as my parents in Funkerstrasse, probably not a coincidence. On certain weekends, but especially for birthdays, we would often travel with the Goldfarbs to the countryside for example to Rottach-Egern, or to a Bavarian restaurant called "Sonnenbichl" in Bad Wiessee in the picturesque Southern Alpine Lake region. This always included meals in local restaurants, mostly trout, wiener schnitzel and often – the highlight of

---

[16] Kashrut – diet according to Jewish regulations.

any such trip – apple cake or apple strudel, not to dismiss the extensive walks alongside some of the Alpine Mountain streams. Hungarian and Serbian-Croatian cuisine were favourites of the Goldfarbs for birthdays. On all such occasions I was invariably the only child in the company of adults. I didn't know any different for a long time. On the positive side it meant that I was always spoilt, and it was always special to go somewhere with my father. Henrik and his wife, as well as my parents, would dress up elegantly for these excursions. They carried a spark of life affirmation, that after all, life was good. I should also mention that my parents often participatred in the secular Christian New Year celebrations with the Goldfarbs or with my mother's family. In the Olympic village, you could see fireworks going off from every floor from all sides, and my dad would usually shoot some up as well. They would toast to a happy New Year, while the regular New Year's Eve programme was shown on television. There was less celebration for the Jewish New Year, but during the first ten years of my life, we would spend all Passover Festivals together.

Henrik was first and foremost a cigar-smoking football fanatic, a member of both F.C. Bayern Munich and 1860 Munich. He earned his living as a bar owner or manager. The bar he ran was near Munich's central railway station. There were so-called "*Zugehfrauen*", ladies, probably also topless, who would delight lonely and lust-seeking men's hearts with small-talk and expensive spirits. Whether the male guests also got more, or whether it was just a matter of striptease and a bit of tenderness for hard cash, I don't know, because it was never discussed in my presence. I was only there a few times and still remember the thick curtains at the entrance and the covered windows and the dark red light at the bar. In my childhood innocence, I thought that the bar probably only opened in the evening. Henrik presented himself always as a finely dressed soft spoken gentleman and generous man to me, speaking Yiddish, Polish, Hebrew and German. He would often comb his few remaining hairs neatly back. Apart from football, his other passion was his Ford Granada 3.0 Ghia "with fully automatic transmission", the lack of a manual gear system still something out of the ordinary back then. In it he liked to play music cassettes of famous Jewish synagogue cantors on his top of the range stereo. My father would often compete with Henrik when it came to ties and suits. Dad liked to seek out special offers and remnants, big brand names at low prices; Henrik was more likely to buy them at standard prices, for example at Loden Frey, an upmarket Munich clothing store in the city's centre, not far from the Lewandowskis' former Munich headquarters. Edith's delight was a small Chihuahua which was always bad-tempered and biting and, to my disappointment, could not be persuaded to play with me, but only growled warningly.

The Goldfarbs, my parents told me once, were unable to hold on to their fortunes. As they were childless, there was perhaps little reason to do so. Their flat may have only been a small three-room apartment, but the interior was of the finest quality. Henrik and Edith had the wallpapers, carpets and furniture changed often and regularly. Everything in their lives had to be exquisite. My parents eventually also changed the wallpapers now and again, but not as often as the Goldfarbs, and unlike them, it was my Dad himself, who would fit them.

During Passover Henrik would read the Haggadah quickly in Yiddish-influenced Hebrew. For example, he would pronounce the word for "Lord" Adonei as Adonoy.[17] All the males present, including myself, would put on a "*Käpl*", the women would briefly tie a headscarf or at least a small scarf over their hair, and I was always allowed to look for the afikomen[18]. That said, I can't remember Dad teaching me the Ma Nishtana, one of the first traditional songs, which I later taught my daughter.[19] Later, other acquaintances would join us, especially Oleg and his wife Lisbeth, as well as their son Freddie Maurer, who was about ten years older than I was.

---

[17] *Haggadah*, Hebrew trad. Prayers and stories for Passover
[18] *Afikomen*, a piece of matzo (Passover bread), which is hidden as a "dessert" and must be found by the youngest child.
[19] *Ma Nishtana* is the traditional song, the traditional song of the four questions, sung by the youngest children attending the Seder (the festive dinner): Ma Nishtana ba Leila ha se? What is different about tonight than usual?

This annual get together for Passover was usually held in the Goldfarbs' dining room, if it wasn't at our home. At the Goldfarb's dining room, there was not just fine wallpaper, but I remember a painting of a Jewish and bearded scholar, next to a picture of the laughing wine god Bacchus, and some landscape scene from Israel. The men would often reach for a glass of vodka, Metaxa or expensive whisky to toast and I can still hear their "L'chaim!." We sat around the table listening to Jewish melodies on Henrik's top class radio and cassette recorder. It was the latest Sony model, which made my young heart beat faster. Edith would have spent days preparing all the food in her tiny kitchen. One of the highlights for everyone was "Galle", an abbreviation for the Polish dish Galareta, also known as "p'tcha." The gel like dish was made from veal or beef shank and eggs. Sometimes there was also gefilte fish and "*Lockshen mit Kneidlach.*"[20]

The ingredients for this feast came from Munich's only kosher butcher's shop "Jakobowitz" adjacent to the city's main market, Viktualienmarkt. The little shop was always packed before the Jewish holiday season. Whilst dad took me along, I often had to stay behind in the car to make sure we didn't get a parking ticket, yet another loss of my Jewish experiences, which were already very limited. I cannot remember that I ever shooed away any traffic warden either, so it was pointless and there would have been parking spaces around the corner for a few coins and peace of mind.

But back to the Passover feast. The main course often consisted of boiled or fried chicken with potatoes and sometimes carp. This was accompanied by the traditional symbolic dishes of the Seder[21]. Charoset made of cinnamon, sultanas, nuts and apples, *maror* (bitter herbs), *chaseret* made of hot radish and bitter herbs, usually parsley, and a lamb's bone. *Beitzah* (egg), whereby not only was a symbolically burnt egg placed on the table but also boiled and already peeled eggs for all to eat often combined with salt water for the *karpas* (parsley). Every now and then there was borsht or there were pickled gherkins. As dessert

---

[20] Soup with matza balls
[21] Seder, Passover meal

sweet, tinned preserved fruits would often be served, usually peaches with cream or ice cream and coffee with coconut and almond macaroons.[22] A discussion would often be had about which matzah was the best.[23] After we had eaten and finished and the women had cleaned the dishes, my father would drive us home in the early hours of the morning, often after one o'clock, probably with some alcohol in his blood (In the 1970s, drink-driving behaviour was sadly more casual, but soon enough, legislation would regulate it. As for our drives home, luckily everything went well). I often fell asleep on the journey home.

All that said, it was only decades later, and after Edith and Henrik had passed away, that my mother confided to me that Edith was not Jewish at all but had been born Christian German. Perhaps it was because of this that my parents sometimes discussed the topic of German civilians as victims with Henrik and Edith. Edith's home had not only been totally bombed, but she also had to move after the war to West Germany.

Edith was a warm slender and always elegantly dressed woman, about 10-15 years older than my mother. She made a great effort to settle into "Jewish life", probably out of love for her husband, and even spoke some Yiddish. This is why I was left clueless that she wasn't Jewish. The "big difference" between Germans and Jews as proclaimed by my father was hardly recognisable here. I don't know whether Edith had converted to the Jewish faith like my mother. In the early 1980s, Edith and Henrik welcomed one of Edith's nieces, "Lotte", who had fled communist East Germany. I can still remember Lotte's East German accent, which was unusual for me at the time. She was unfamiliar with Jewish customs and seemed insecure in our presence.

To say it again, Edith's cooking was just as "authentically Jewish" as that of my aunts Ruszke and Chaftje in Tel Aviv. When it wasn't Passover, Edith was, in my view, also a master baker of cheesecakes. What's more

---

[22] In the1970s tinned preserved fruits with fresh ice cream or the like were regarded as part of modern, progressive, even elegant table desserts.
[23] Matzah Hebrew unleavened bread

"Despite Everything." Childhood Amongst Shoah Survivors

Edith would speak in high praise of Israel, Tel Aviv and so many other Jewish things.

Oleg and Lisbeth were also a German-Jewish couple, with Lisbeth having completed Orthodox conversion, as far as I know, and her son Freddy regularly going to *"Dawenen"* in the Orthodox synagogue.[24]

It didn't matter whether "Peepsee," the Goldfarbs' yellow canary, whom I felt drawn to as a child, was Jewish, German or Spanish. Either way, he whistled his beautiful songs every time I visited and even used to eat kosher.

There were other survivors of the Shoah in Munich with whom my father met regularly. There was a Mr Rakotcz, who ran a photography business and "Silberschatz", who owned a shop selling hi-fi and audio equipment. When I was 18 and started to look for jobs, my father tried to arrange a place there, but I declined, it wasn't for me. There was an older Jewish gentleman called Karstan, who had worked with my dad, but he passed away in the 1980s. Another Jewish acquaintance, Natan Lewitan, would take over the restaurant from my father. He was the father of Louis Lewitan, who made a name for himself as a psychologist and journalist in the 1990s. There was also Mr Kucharski and his Swedish wife Karin who visited us for a while. Another acquaintance who later survived my father by a few years was a certain Mr Marian Gross. After Henrik's death, it was he who became my father's best friend, together with his wife Ruth.[25] Dad would argue with him about how peace could be achieved in Israel. There were many more. Whenever I met Jewish residents of senior age, whom I did not know, they would often ask me for my father's name. As soon as I gave the answer, they would reply with a: "Yes, I know him. He has a restaurant in Leopoldstraße!"

Having seen and gone through the gruesome experiences, concentration and labour camps during the Shoah, this generation of survivors

---

[24] *Dawen en*, yid. pray
[25] As I mentioned before, death was always hidden. I wasn't told anything about Edith and Henrik's funerals either. I only found out much later that they had died at all.

Zol Zayn Shulem II: Faroys

always helped each other out whenever there was need. Now almost all of them rest in close proximity to each other in the Jewish cemetery in Munich. One must wonder if calmly at night, they continue to secretly discuss Germany, Israel and above all, the fortunes of their much beloved adopted football club F.C. Bayern München?

Some of them, however, rest alone and separated from their wives, having been faithful to them for decades. The reason for this, just as for my great-grandfather David and my great-grandmother Luise, is, that one of them was not Jewish by birth and, unlike my mother or Lisbeth, had not converted to Judaism. I think this separation has some degree of unfairness to it, because some of these non-Jewish wives (or less often husbands or non-married long-term partners) had to accommodate the emotional turmoil of their husbands and comfort them, when painful thoughts and memories returned unexpectedly. Their souls must now come to terms with having to rest in death separated from these sojourners who loved them. May the almighty El-Shadai resurrect and reunite them, if not soon, when the Messiah will come.[26]

We the younger generations were always looked upon by the survivors with great favour. We symbolised the future for which surviving the Shoah had been worth something. Following a long line of loved ones, who had been torn from them violently, our role as their children could sometimes feel like a heavy a burden. It was impossible to fulfil all their invested hopes or embody a lived form of compensation for the losses.

One of the best things about the generation of survivors was their insistence to a good life "despite of everything." If there was not even a time to enjoy life now, then there would have been little point in surviving. Whilst they were all individuals and different, I feel that I can say with some confidence that I witnessed this attitude repeatedly and that I highly appreciated it. It is something that continues to give me strength until today. I miss many of them dearly.

---

[26] El-Shadai, Hebrew G-d

6

Pizzeria at Harry's

"I was the first to own a pizzeria on Leopoldstrasse, maybe even in Munich," my father used to declare proudly. A Jewish friend of mine from Munich disputed this and claimed that his father was the first. Perhaps they were both among the first in their own right. The important thing is, that in Munich Jewish survivors established livelihoods and businesses that had a direct and fundamental impact on the city and its citizens.

Through hard work these young Jewish men took advantage of any gaps in the market to make a quite successful living. Having survived the Shoah with nothing, the future was up to their investments in sweat and labour.

After having run a few pizzerias with friends, he took over the "Kaffeewirtschaft Lola" at Leopoldstraße 171 in October 1960 and a year later a restaurant at Leopoldstraße 173 called "Bei Harry." The two combined became his "Pizzeria bei Harry." Shortly before or afterwards, he received some reparation payments from the German state.

I imagine that he had invested part of this compensation, which was to give him something for the physical and mental injuries he had suffered in the Shoah, into the restaurant. My father hired Italian chefs, and it was they who taught him how to prepare all the dishes authentically.

Soon enough, never tired to perfect new skills, he himself became an expert chef, without ever having completed a traditional cooking apprenticeship, as far as I know.

Pizzeria at Harry's c.a. 1970s.

Leopoldstrasse is one of Munich's main streets. It stretches from the core shopping district at "Münchner Freiheit" and "Gieselastrasse" and the "Siegestor," past the University of Munich to the "Feldherrenhalle" at Odeonplatz (once a place where Hitler paraded).

The part between "Gieselastrasse" and "Münchner Freiheit" has always been home to Munich's bohemian, self-important and chic crowds. It showcased many boutiques, restaurants, ice cream parlours and pubs. Whoever owns a restaurant in that part of Leopoldstrasse can do little wrong. Whilst my father had chosen the same street for his restaurant, it wasn't situated in this part. Instead "Pizzaria bei Harry" was more than 20 minutes by foot north of "Münchner Freiheit", right at the beginning of Leopoldstraße (at number 17). Like a world apart, here, there were no fancy clothing shops or bohemian city crowds. Instead, the pizzeria had to rely on hungry local residents in the neighbourhood.

Initially, the atmosphere of the restaurant resembled more of an ordinary Munich pub, until my father transformed it with special illuminated views of Venice, interior décor, and toilets. At the front, next to the entrance there were purpose-built fridges, a bar where beer could be pulled and, as long as an Italian waitress called Marica worked there, there were also several posters of her favourite band, The Rolling Stones.

The first table next to the entrance was a "Stammtisch," a reserved table for regulars. Others preferred to sit at the bar counter behind which my father served stronger liquors and spirits. In the back were about a dozen tables. The kitchen was concealed and in a separate large room behind the bar. It was dominated by large work surfaces made of steel and dozens of bowls. There were two large, long pizza ovens, gas cookers and more refrigerators. Cooking utensils would stand around as well as prepared bowls with dough. A variety of sauces and other things like grated cheese and tomato sauce would also to be ready for use. In a separate area there were tins of all sorts, boxes, a dishwasher, a sink that was always full, and in the basement further huge cold stores and a dry store, from where I used to pinch ice-cream waffles. All in all, it was quite a massive operation and a huge challenge for my father. He was in the kitchen day and night, the little window to the rear barely giving enough fresh air to the sometimes hot and steamy room that carried a hundred different aromas and vapours. In the 1970s the main part of the restaurant also carried the scent of cigarette smoke, a by-product of his job that my father much disliked.

Despite not being in the centre of Leopoldstraße, my father made a success of it all and the restaurant was usually packed to the brim, especially during the weekend. It got even busier after my father introduced the possibility to make telephone orders in the late 1970s. The phone number that hungry people used to order their pizzas was also my connection to my parents, who sometimes had to leave me behind and alone at home so that they could both work in the restaurant. This happened especially when a waitress was ill.

Then in 1974 my father was lucky. He was able to open a second restaurant, "Pizzeria im Schwabylon" without even trying too hard.

Zol Zayn Shulem II: Faroys

The "Schwabylon" was an urban project and shopping centre complex erected exactly opposite my father's restaurant. It was a pyramid-like, yellow-orange-red, windowless, utopian, fantastic and gigantic construction, held all in bright colours outside, and inside in orange with black rubber studded floor, very much in the style of the avantgarde of the 1960s and 1970s. The architect Justus Dahinden and his investor Otto Schnitzenbaumer intended to construct an extravagant building that was in line with the futuristic zeitgeist of the time. Visitors to the complex could spoil themselves with whatever Munich's most exclusive boutiques had to offer, swim lengths in the integrated indoor swimming pool, watch an aquarium full of exotic fish, including sharks, relax in saunas and thermal baths, or dance until the early morning hours in its nightclub *Yellow Submarine*. There was also a casino, as well as an artificial ice rink. Long circular ramps connected the multiple levels together. With so much on offer what could go wrong?

Barley five years old I was able to rummage over several floors in search of a young boy's adventure. It was there, where I lost my Mecki hedgehog, a popular German rubbery fully dressed up soft toy of the time – a tragedy that had me in desperate tears. On another occasion, I found myself near the ice rink behind a self-closing door that could only be opened from the other side. I was locked in and trapped. After what appeared to be an eternity to the young boy I was, it was my Aunt Louise, who had been visiting, who came to rescue me, having looked for me everywhere.

But the utopian complex could not meet the expectations of the many business and trades people. "Schwabylon" turned out to be unprofitable, although for my father it was, in his words, "the best business of my life." Inside the complex he had seating areas and a bar where his pizzas and dishes sold like hotcakes.

According to my father, who held out in the building until its bitter end – after more than 100 other shopkeepers had given up – the main problem of the centre was a structural fault. To the investors, giving the complex up seemed a better, perhaps cheaper proposition than conducting the necessary additional improvements. Meant to be a long-lasting architectural masterpiece and a new heart of the town, Schwabylon would soon be largely demolished, with my father making do with a settlement. The "Bomb business," as he often described it, was over as quickly as it had come. Somehow, he also lacked the strength and initiative to try and find a new compensatory venture elsewhere.

At least the large hotel next door and the housing estate opposite continued to provide a continuous flow of hungry customers. During the 1983 Ice Hockey World Championship, my dad's pizzeria was packed with hungry ice hockey teams, and my father brought me a few autographs of the players.

The work in the restaurant was hard. Sweating, my father hurried around the kitchen with his shirt sleeves rolled up. Today, I know that the speed he adopted at work was similar to what was called "the norm" in the Hasag-SS labour camps. Nobody would come close to the speed and effort with which he was able to work. Unlike "in the factories", this time he was paid for his speed and sweat, and there was no life threat, nor shouting or beatings.

Before I was of school age, I often accompanied my father during his shopping rounds for the restaurant. Initially my father occasionally went to Italian food importers at the Munich wholesale market. I also regularly travelled with him to the brewery that supplied the restaurant. He also often went to the "Hurler", the commercial wholesale market, which conveniently was barely five minutes away from the restaurant and located alongside Leopoldstraße.[27] My father bought everything from flour, mushrooms, peppers and salad to cheese and salami and my favourite, very occasionally, he also found toys for me. I came with him to the drink supplier, where I admired the towering colourful crates and sometimes would get a lemonade or a Spezi.[28] For a short time, my father

---

[27] Later also known as IKS and Metro. Today, the area has long been a residential neighbourhood on Johann-Fichte-Strasse.

[28] Spezi is a German drink, where lemonade and cola are mixed.

had meat delivered by a butcher called Herr Sommer. I still remember him today, because what happened to him was something out of the ordinary. One day I was told that Herr Sommer had lost two or three of his fingers whilst pressing meat into an electronic mincer. When I met the butcher, I could not stop my questions, if it hurt. Looking at his finger stubs, Herr Sommer smiled and assured me that he hadn't felt anything whilst it happened. But that was only a small tragedy within the microcosm of the restaurant.

Towards the end of the 1970s life became much darker. Uschi, one of my father's waitresses left the restaurant after her shift in the early morning hours and began to cross the four-lane street in the dark. At that time, the speed limit on Leopoldstraße was still 60 kilometres per hour. Early in the morning and on an empty road, some people may have driven even faster. Uschi ran right into an approaching car, whose driver did not spot her; she lost her life instantly.

My father had reportedly few problems with his employees, that is, so long as they did what they were meant to do. However, one Sicilian cook, a man by the name of Cito, made a name for himself as the laziest employee my father had ever encountered, or so my father described him at home. While my father hurried to prepare the kitchen for a busy evening, Cito reportedly sat down quietly, ate and drank at leisure and then smoked some cigarettes, leaving my father to do everything on his own. To make matters worse, he and a waitress pocketed orders and eventually got caught. It wasn't long before they both faced the sack.

Antonio, another Italian chef, on the other hand, was my father's favourite. He lived with his family not far from the restaurant. One day, at the beginning of the 1980s, he was headhunted by the owner of another Italian restaurant at the end of Maximiliansstraße, a fine address that offered a higher salary. According to my father, Antonio later very much regretted his move. Although he was now earning more, he had much more work to do, less flexibility and a longer journey to and from work. There was also another member of staff who "worked" in my father's the restaurant: me! I would choose music from the jukebox. I remember that I once persuaded my father to ask the supplier of the juke box records to get David Bowie's single "Let's Dance", a big hit in 1983. When I was younger, I also made rolls out of pizza dough and asked all the staff to try these. Of course, they always said they tasted marvellous, and yet, strangely enough, the rolls were always left barely eaten.

There was even a burglary at some point. They emptied the game vending machines and the coins inside the jukebox, but that was about all they got their hands on. My father then had a better door and bars at the window installed.

7

"Dry Bread"

Perhaps this is the appropriate place in this book to address the strongly felt absence of my father. My father, dedicated to his business, worked nearly every day, almost seven days a week from around 3.00 pm (even earlier if he had to stock up on supplies) until 1.00 in the morning or later. When I went to school in the morning, he was fast asleep, and when I came back from school, he was often already gone or about to leave. My parents did not keep Shabbat, at least not until the late 1970s or early 1980s, the time my mum completed her conversion to Judaism. What I could usually count on was that my father was at home on Saturdays. That was not because of Shabbat either, but because of football, his pilgrimage to the Bayern Munich games and then watching the German football Bundesliga on TV. He held an annual season ticket for the Olympic Stadium, where F.C. Bayern was still playing all its home games at the time. But if the pressure was too immense in the restaurant, or a cook or waiter was off sick, or on holiday, my father had no choice but to rush to the restaurant and help out even on Saturdays. Regularly he would bring me a pizza from work, which I would usually have cold for breakfast in the morning. Only during the weekends did I ever get to see him around ten or eleven in the morning. Instead of Jewish morning prayers, he would "religiously" perform a morning routine of rehabilitative exercises. This, he assured us, cured his back, which had been damaged by years of forced labour during the Shoah and caused him problems, especially after getting up. At some point, a physiotherapist had taught him these exercises.

My father breakfasted modestly. A piece of bread with butter, jam or honey and coffee would be plenty. Dad also ate any bread available, even if it was left over and hard as a rock. "*We would have been happy with something like that in the camps, I just can't throw it away,*" he would remark.

I also remember him shaving, lathering up with a brush and soap, almost in a ritual way. He was unconcerned about any religious requirement for Jewish men not to use knives (including razors), but at best scissors or a shaving machine. "Nothing beats a good shave with soap and a razor", as he used to say. I have already written about the fact that shaving was an elementary lifesaver for the men in the camps. My father's morning routine would not be complete without a little sprinkle of hair tonic and a few splashes of "Old Spice" aftershave.

Other daily rituals included the obsessive following of the hourly news and reading the *Süddeutsche Zeitung* and once a week the "*Letzte Naijes*", a Yiddish-language weekly, sent to him from Israel. These newspapers were read from start to end in his living room. He followed the news all day long, whether it was on the radio or on television.

It was as if my father always expected terrible things lurking around the corner. If that was the case, he would be among the first to know and be able to form an opinion too. I would describe it as a type of instinctive defence mechanism. If it were ever 1939 again and the German troops were about to invade, he would be able to run away with his brother Moisze instead of staying where he was. Luckily it would never again be 1939 for as long as he lived.

Often his studies would bring about comment; perhaps somebody exposed to be an antisemite, who should perish, or another was labelled "a *verückter Hund*" – a "mad dog" or "a *Verbrecher*" – a criminal", or should have a "*schwarzen sof*" – a dark ending

Zol Zayn Shulem II: Faroys

My father, circa 2003, reading the German daily newspaper Süddeutsche Zeitung.

On Sundays, my dad also followed the live-televised morning news discussion "*Der Frühschoppen*" which usually had half a dozen international correspondents and journalists as guests, discussing current politics. In my father's gallery of respectable people such persons discussing global politics had a place of honour – that is, if they were not hostile to Jews and Israel.

I wonder these days, if my dad's obsessive news consumption caused me to later become a journalist myself, a foreign correspondent based in London?

If it wasn't one of the normal days, with the aforementioned news consumption, then my father could be mending a variety of things or making himself busy with home improvements. He was a highly talented and experienced craftsman. After all, he had first learnt handcrafts in form of a leather worker from his father and then under the worst possible circumstances in the Shoah. He was able to repair or install anything himself, be it new covers for chairs, shoes with new or better heels, he would wallpaper the walls or cut and lay tiles. He was also the cook at home and would iron all his shirts to place them neatly in his wardrobe. However, in spite of all of that, it never ever occurred to him that he ought to teach me any of these useful life skills. I was destined for a different path: I was to study and escape the supposedly "too difficult" tradition of trade and craftsmanship of both sides of my family. It was my father's dream and idea that it would be better for me to find my career in studies and books.

8

Swastika and Germans in the Pizzeria

Amongst the regulars in my father's restaurant, were an actor and the head of the local Munich city *Abendzeitung* newspaper. With his obsessive pastime of following the news debates and current events my father did not hesitate to share his views with these knowledgeable guests. Whilst doing so, Dad made no secret of his experiences during the Shoah or his position on Germans and Israel.

> *We talked about the Israeli crisis, you know – Dayan – the Six-Day War, the great victory over Egypt. Amongst all these German (guests of the restaurant), it was impossible for me to find a single person who thought positively about Israel. Very few!*

He went on to say:

> *I told those Germans that I had been in a concentration camp and the many things I was involved in, I told them what happened there, what the Germans were like back then. I always told them, for example: 'You were great heroes – it's easy to murder children and*

women. You won't have such an easy game facing the Israeli army. I would like to see what you would do against those armed forces.

He answered the question himself:

You would no longer be heroes, as you were against women and children. You locked us into ghettoes and didn't let us eat, and starved the people. People who don't eat lose their will to live. That's how you did it.[29]

Most people probably had no choice but to swallow such words, out of respect for my father, but there must have been people who did not like everything my father said. One night in the 1970s, a big red swastika was smeared onto the exterior wall of the restaurant. I was still young, but I think it also said "*Juden raus!*" – Jews out. In the 1980s, there was someone who kept calling the phone number of the restaurant, announcing himself with a Hitler salute and then went on to say that the Gestapo would be on their way soon.[30] My father told the caller, if my memory serves me right, he should try saying it to his face, instead of calling him anonymously from a distance. I don't remember whether the police came and investigated any of this. In any case, the graffiti was soon painted over and eventually the phone calls stopped too.

My father had very clear views about his German guests. He believed the majority of his guests edged towards antisemitism or anti-Israelism, intertwined with resentments. During the 1973 Yom Kippur War, just one year after the terror of 1972, German guests in his restaurant were consistently siding with Egypt. Even during the (Six-Day) War in 1967, there already existed such attitudes. My father carried a whole list of people and their comments in his head because they had either relativised the Shoah or compared Israel to the actions of the Germans during the Third Reich.

---

[29] Zylbersztajn (1995), p. 16
[30] Ibid.

Once, in the queue at the post office and out of nowhere, well into the 1990s, a man told him the Nazis had forgotten to gas him during the Second World War.[31] My father came home upset and swearing. It is because of experiences such as these too that I feel that he could never be fully at home in Germany. There existed an unending and unresolvable tension, if not deliberate provocation, and it would emerge suddenly, in moments you did not expect it.

---

[31] Ibid.

9

Everyday Life

I have already mentioned that my father made no effort to pass on his knowledge and skills to me. All my attempts to learn from him were dismissed with the reasoning that I possessed "two left hands." It is an extraordinary way of behaving towards your only son. He truly was unable to demonstrate paternal patience, affection and interest. He hoped that I would become an academic and, so he reasoned honourably, I would not have to work as hard as he did. However, this hope shifted the responsibility for my education outside his sphere of knowledge and control and right into the hands of non-Jewish Germans, for as long as I lived in Germany.

My mother accepted her role of housewife in all of this. She too "shouldn't have to work hard" either, was my dad's stance. Nevertheless, she needed to help out regularly in the restaurant when a waitress was unwell, or the place was overcrowded. On such occasions I was left at home alone in the evenings and got up alone in the morning, with only our budgerigar parakeet for company.

Dad didn't just withhold his manual skills or his football passion from me. There was also that lack of religious Jewish education, the teaching of Yiddish or anything else. That I learnt the basic rules of kashrut, was down to my mother's (re)conversion to Judaism.[32] So for a while we had dishes and pots for milky foods and others for meat-based dishes, and the rabbi put up mezuzot on all door posts.[33]

As a teenager, like so many at that age, I however rebelled against my father by declaring loudly that I didn't want to be a pizza chef. It was my accusation against my absent father and a sign of my frustration. I later felt guilty and sorry about that outburst. In fact, the truth is, that my father had achieved more from a financial perspective as a pizza chef and restaurant owner than I would later with all my academic honours and positions.

That said, I must emphasize that I had no shortage of other childhood wants. I had one of the fashionable high-riser bicycles (with three gears!), an electric car racing track, an electric railway, later a remote-controlled battery car and some of the first computer games, including a Pacman game in 1982, which you held in your hand and operated using a small joystick. As said, my father would only attend synagogue on Rosh Hashanah, the Jewish New Year's Day and on Yom Kippur. I don't think we ever attended synagogue on a Saturday, as I do it myself these days.

Within the narrow, elongated synagogue in Reichenbachstraße, which was situated in the middle of the city centre, near "Gärtnerplatz" and not far from my uncle Georg's hairdressing salon, radiated a mysterious atmosphere that touched me deeply, in spite of the police car that was always parked in the entrance. After you entered the entrance gateway you faced a hall with a special room for Yizkor candles, in which on Yom Kippur, many hundreds of candles were lit, in honour of the memory of thousands of murdered relatives and friends of the congregants, who were all mostly survivors of the Shoah. The lighting of the candles was my father's main act at the synagogue. Afterwards, he stood with one of his prayer books among the praying men for a while,

---

[32] For my mother, it was always a case of "converting back", in the sense of "back to the faith of the grandfather."
[33] Mezuzah – Jewish relig. trad. Doorpost box with the "Hear Israel" (Shema) prayer.

talked to his acquaintances, and usually left the synagogue after no more than an hour. These were brief impressions I never fully understood at the time. There were usually some children about in the forecourt, but I was not familiar with any of them and I was too confused and exposed in this unfamiliar unexplained environment to venture out and conquer my shyness to speak to the kids.

Many years later, despite my father's constant opinion that there had been no sign of any G-d in the camps, he begged me shortly before his death, his only and last request to me, to read an acceptable Kaddish for him, after he had passed away. I even test-read it to him. Not knowing anything about the relationship between my father and my grandfather, I wonder if my grandfather, asked my father to do the same. It is certainly the tradition, passed on from generation to generation for millennia, even though traditionally the mourners' kaddish is recited in attendance of a minyan.[34]

---

[34] Minyan – the prescribed minimum number of attendees for a community prayer

10

Religions

I would not properly understand what goes on inside a synagogue until I was an adult in England, and yet something stuck. When the day of a Jewish holiday had come, dad took the appropriate prayer book and suddenly he read Hebrew and uttered Hebrew words. Dad also usually fasted on Yom Kippur. The sad and poignant melodies of Yom Kippur, the Kol Nidre, Avinu Malkeinu, sung by the men in the Orthodox synagogue of Munich, still resonate in my head today, and they still regularly give me goosebumps on Yom Kippur, especially when they are performed in the same style as back then.[35]

Some people, including my father and his friends, also used the synagogue as a meeting place for chatting and catching up. No wonder the rabbi and others would occasionally bang loudly on the tables and demand "Shhhh!"

When I was young, most of the members of the Munich Synagogue were Shoah survivors, the rest mainly Israelis who lived in Munich for various reasons. Only later did immigrants who escaped the Soviet states increasingly populate the community. All prayed intensely during the

---

[35] This is one of the reasons why I later switched from liberal Judaism to the more traditional Masorti Judaism, because they kept closer to the traditional melodies.

high holidays, with the women watching down from the upper floor gallery. Munich's main synagogue, now relocated inside a stunning new building, remains an Orthodox and conservatively run synagogue with a gender separation to this day.[36]

One of the congregants that my father would usually seek out in the synagogue was his best friend Henrik Goldfarb. He and my father and a few others were, as it happened, worshippers of an additional "alternative" religion. This religion was so potent that it could even interfere with the strength of the meaningfully deep and beautiful Yom Kippur prayers. And so it was, that on one such occasion Henrik surprised my father right in the middle of such a Yom Kippur service. "Oy vey, is mir shleht (oh my G*d, I am feeling terrible)", he uttered quietly in Yiddish. When my father whispered back with worry and concern, what on earth the matter was, Henrik confessed no sins of the soul or heart, but that amid his reflections and atonement concerning the last year, he could not help but worry whether the football team F.C. Bayern Munich would still be able to be victorious, because there was another tough game coming up.

Yes, most of the group of Shoah survivors in my father's circle of friends and their acquaintances did not go to Shul on Fridays, nor on Saturdays, let alone on weekdays.[37] Instead, together with about a dozen others, they made a weekly pilgrimage every other Saturday to that place that was in part symbol of the fate of the Israeli athletes in September 1972, the Munich Olympic Stadium. The reason was the fact, that the

---

[36] Rabbi Herschel Gluck, a well-known Lubavitcher rabbi in London, once told me, that there was a reason why the German communities were all orthodox after the war, in contrast to the years before the Shoah. If you believe Gluck, few Jewish rabbis had any mind to go to Germany after 1945. Gluck told me, that his father however had begun to work for exactly these communities in the name of Lubavitch rabbi Schneerson. It is also true that most Jews from Eastern European countries were Orthodox Jewish rather than reformed or liberal. Since the 1990s, however, Beth Shalom, a liberal community, has established itself in Munich, which was not exactly welcomed by the Orthodox Jewish community of Munich at first.

[37] *Shul*, yid. synagogue

stadium was then the home ground of F.C. Bayern Munich until 2005, when they moved to a purpose-built stadium on the outskirts of town.

Their adopted religion was therefore not based on the five books of Moses, but on the divine fortunes of the German Bundesliga. Not that it would not have been perfectly possible to combine the two – synagogue on Saturday morning, football in the afternoon. Maybe a few amongst them did. Henrik, my father and others, however, avoided the synagogue, except for those major holidays. They would never miss any home games of F.C. Bayern Munich, except for illness, death or, a little less dramatic, the odd holiday abroad (for which one would try to have German TV coverage). It was there in the middle of the roofed area, amongst the best seats the stadium offered, where they kept their weekly minyan, that quorum of adults required for certain prayers. And they prayed a lot, for the Almighty to protect their team and would say Amen to that. Their permanent seats were in the immediate vicinity of the VIP and media lounge, called zone Z. These were, if you like, F.C. Bayern's Jewish rows. As if it was an orthodox synagogue, it was mainly the men who congregated here. At most, there were a few of their older sons, most of them older than me, who would join them there. Henrik was one of the few who even had three religious memberships! He was a member of the 1860 Munich Football club, and of the F.C. Bayern Munich and of course he was member of the Synagogue of Munich.

When they arrived at the stadium, they greeted each other in Yiddish "Nu, was haert sih?"- what's new, followed by long chats and debates about the turns of the game they were about to watch. And just as if they would be going to synagogue, these Jewish men dressed elegantly for their outing, wearing barely a sign of football insignia. In winter, they brought along cushions and warm tea in thermos flasks. One or the other also brought something stronger in smaller flasks. However, you were unlikely to find them at the sausage stand or queuing for beer, not the least because the food there was not kosher. It wasn't about the food or the drink, but purely about the football. These men would follow every kick and step of their chosen eleven prophets on the grass and comment on every move in Yiddish: oy, a Broch, oy gevalt, Mazl gehabt, a zoy a groiser Akrobat, er is gefaerlih, es is geshen a wunder![38]

When I finally started to take an interest in F.C. Bayern Munich myself, my dad agreed to take me. The stadium was but a 20-minute walk from home. Later, when school friends of mine also started going to the stadium – I was about eleven or twelve years old – I preferred to stay with them in the stadium in the cheaper standing rows. Munich fans would be in the "Südkurve," the southern bend, where thousands of ultras were congregated, wrapped in red and white, holding flags. The tickets for this zone were also the most affordable. Here in the cheaper stands exposed to the heavens when it rained, the fans were cut from a different type of wood compared to those in the Z section, where my father and his friends were sitting. Hundreds of fans with denim jackets emblazoned with stitched on Bayern stickers stood here, often rougher types, carrying flags, beer or sausage rolls in their hands.

At some point between 1982 and 1983, I noticed what many fans in the crowd were shouting in addition to "Hey super Bayern" to the tune of "Guantanamera" regular insults for the players of the opposite team. These frequently contained the word "Jude" (Jew) and different added verbal attributes that related to pigs. In Germany the use of such descriptive linguistic oddities had strong association with the years of the Third Reich, its profane use in postwar Germany regarded as absolute and prohibited hate speech. Here I stood in the midst of this cheerful mob, wearing my little gold chain showing my name in Hebrew. As a young, vulnerable and exposed Jewish boy, my enthusiasm for Bayern Munich and for football was not just temporarily disrupted, but after repeated visits extinguished. Unlike my father, I felt that I could not and did not want to be part of the red flagged Bayern-army (yet again red flagged).[39] I felt so betrayed and so personally insulted that my time as

---

[38] Yid. Bad luck, oh my word, that was luck, what a great artist, he is dangerous, a miracle happened.
[39] Many Third Reich flags were red.

a Bayern fan and, when I realised that such jeering also existed among supporters of other clubs, my time as a football fan was buried forever. Decades later, not even an offer from the sports editor of the German *taz* newspaper to report on the British Premier League could get me interested in that sport again.

But as said, none of this seemed to bother the Jewish minyan in area Z of the stadium, and my father and the others continued to frequent the stadium without interruption. Of course, they were neither deaf nor unaware, after all they were survivors of the Shoah. When I asked my father why it did not have the same effect on him, that there were often Nazis and antisemites at football matches, my father simply replied, make of it what you like, "No, football, is football!" That was it! If you ask me what I make of it today? His love for the game came first, you had to live and follow your passions, the rest was full of Jew-hate this way or that way, here or there, inside the stadium, his restaurant or other places anyway. If you allowed antisemitism, hate and racism to determine your likes and passions, there was no hope. Perhaps I made a mistake.[40]

Slowly, with the passing of one or the other members of the minyan, the rows next to my father became thinner. And then arrived the day when the worst happened, nevertheless. At a Bayern game, when my dad was about 80 years old, he found himself without provocation attacked by hooligans after a match against Eintracht Frankfurt.

A group of men had come up to my father, appearing to be jubilant. Then one of them hugged my father and squeezed him hard, allegedly with a piece of steel under his coat. After he had come home in pain and following medical examinations, it was clear that he had sustained two broken ribs. He said he had assumed the men were just happy about their team's success, but there was obviously something much more sinister going on. The perpetrators were the usual type of "German heroes" and on that late afternoon their chosen victim for their dark and sadistic entertainment was an 80-year-old defenceless man. What is it in the

---

[40] Zylbersztajn (1995), p. 15

psyche of some Germans, a country in which relative prosperity prevails, and relatively good education is imparted, that some cultivate such passion for violent sadism as a joke? Incidentally, the scene of this crime was not the stadium but, of all places, the walkway between the stadium and the underground station at the end of the bridge over Munich's urban circular road, in other words, if you are familiar with the geography, in the immediate vicinity of a large memorial to the Jewish-Israeli- Olympic athletes, and one Bavarian police officer, murdered in 1972.

What else can be said about football and my father? Maybe that my father was basically supporting the German national team during international matches because he was familiar with all the players, but it was still difficult for him to grant the ultimate victory of a European or World Cup title to them. When asked who he would support if Germany played Israel, he simply replied: "What kind of a silly question is that, you are asking?"[41] He eagerly followed the German team right up to the finals, in my view, with genuine joy and enthusiasm, even love for many of the individual players, but he preferred it if the ultimate title of European or World Champion went to others. I can understand that. None of us younger children of the Jewish postwar generation felt enthusiasm when crowds of people ran around with German flags and jerseys after successful games. Remember, these were the 1970s and 1980s. It was unthinkable that we would wear emblems of Germany or a German national jersey, and if somebody somewhere did, I was not aware of that person. Those who cheered for Germany had caused our families too much pain in the name of these insignias. Even though Germans had significantly changed, the colours were still the same, and the shouting was still for "Deutschland!" to an unchanged melody with different words. Occasionally, some fans would not bother about the new lyrics, and deliberately recite the old verses and old stanzas, whilst waving historic old pre-1945 flags.

With my mother born in the Netherlands, it was also natural that we supported that country during the 1974 World Cup. In 1982 and

---

[41] Ibid. p. 16

1986, we were glad that there were no nationalistic rumblings on the streets, since Germany did not become champions. The many emerging German flags all around us were enough of an imposition anyway, especially for my father's generation.

My father also disliked the fall of the Berlin Wall. In his opinion, Germans did not deserve the "growing together of what belonged together," as Willie Brandt put it. He saw the division of Germany into an Eastern and Western country as a form of just punishment and a guarantee that Germany would no longer develop into an overly powerful state. And then, in 1990, one year after the fall of the wall, Germans started to talk in tones of "*wir sind wieder wer*" – which meant essentially that we are again a force to reckon with. That made me, and probably some others too, feel quite uneasy.

Football was the only public engagement of my father and of his generation, that took place side by side with non-Jewish Germans. Some may have had work relationships, but most of the group of survivors worked independently or were self-employed. I imagine few had any appetite to serve under a German non-Jewish boss or supervisor. Occasionally some went to a concert, visited a restaurant or a beer garden, but that was it. The fate of ultimately having stayed behind in the Federal Republic of Germany, when others had left a long time ago, meant that they mostly lived in self-imposed seclusion, preferring to stay amongst themselves.

As far as I am concerned, I later learnt that football and sports-enthusiastic nationalism and racism actually attracts the same kind of people in most if not all countries. It was no different when I lived in the Netherlands, England, Scotland or Israel amongst others. For historical reasons, I was more sensitive and critical in Germany, but essentially, it is the same everywhere.

I now always hope that blind, rabid nationalism, based on a particular team of humans winning a ball game, does not emerge in any country I happen to presently live in. The victories often lead to apparent feelings of superiority against people from other countries. What that effectively means for me is that I wish the country I happen to live in every success in all games – but only up until they reach the quarter finals.

In July 2016, I watched the UEFA quarter-final match between Germany and Italy from the German embassy in London, where I had been invited due to my correspondent status. The German team also had many players who were German from a wide variety of backgrounds. I must admit that such a team made it more pleasant to cheer for their 1-0 win.

As my father got older and in retirement, he made fewer pilgrimages to the football stadium and the violent incident, he had experienced did not make it any easier. Instead, he developed an amended form of the Jewish Havdala (end of Shabbat ceremony) custom. His football-related substitute ritual and part of the customary hopes and wishes for a good week was the ARD "*Sportschau*," the sports programme, that showed a summary of the most relevant matches of the day. Dad would sit near to the television screen and follow every movement and every word. You could hardly disturb him or get his attention during the broadcast.

When he was terminally ill in bed in 2011, some four weeks before his death, I tried to lure him out of bed with that sports programme. His Bayern team was playing, so he did come, but due to his condition, he was no longer able to watch and concentrate on the entire sports programme. If there was any indicator at all of how ill my father was at that time, this was it.

11

Jewish Child in German School

Als ich bei meinen Schafen wacht, ein Engel mir die Botschaft bracht, des bin ich froh,
bin ich froh – froh, froh, froh,
Benedicamos Dominio![42]

German Christmas carol ca. 1600, author unknown

My kindergarten was the nearest to to our home, the one run under the auspices of the Catholic Church in the middle of the Olympic Village, located only three minutes from where we lived.[43] As far as I knew at the time, I was the only child there from a non-Christian family. Nevertheless, I took part in the St Martin's, Nikolaus (St Nicholas), Christmas and Easter celebrations like any other child. There was no trace of any attempt of recognising or teaching diversity then. But this soft wrapping into Christian traditions also extended to my family. There were Christmas parties at Aunt Gerda's and Uncle Marcello's home

---

[42] *Translation: As I watched with my sheep, an angel brought me the message. I am glad, I am glad, glad, glad, glad, oh, oh, oh, benedicamus domino, benedicamus domino.)*
[43] A nursery and preschool that runs over three years in Germany for children between three and six years of age,

from time to time. Uncle Marcello even visited me dressed up as Father Christmas on St Nicholas Eve. When it was time for him to redo the trick in the following year, my father's restaurant happened to be very busy, and my mum was once again forced to help him out. It was one of the evenings I had to spend alone. I was probably six or seven years old (leaving a child alone like this today, would be unthinkable). Nobody had confided anything to me about my uncle or any St Nicholas visits, as it was of course meant to be a surprise. When the door-buzzer rang and, checking through the spy hole, I somehow recognised the person standing there, I remembered my mother's explicit and strict instructions, that I was not to let anyone into the apartment. To my mind, the person in front of the door could very well be a trickster, like the wolf in the children's story of the wolf and the seven little goats. I left my uncle standing outside the door until he gave up and left.

Is it possible that there is more to this story? Perhaps the outside world seemed extremely dangerous for my family and no one could be trusted. That was certainly part of my upbringing and, according to psychological studies, that of many other children of survivors. My mother's fear was pronounced throughout her life. And so even that St Nicholas, who looked just like and spoke exactly like my uncle, was not to be trusted. Despite the warm Italian accent I recognised, this dressed up Nikolaus was a potential wolf in sheep's clothing.

On the other hand, perhaps remarkably, I made the journey to kindergarten on my own. The walk there was only a few hundred metres. To be honest, I don't remember much about these kindergarten years, apart from the fact that at some point I imagined I was a "girls' protector", granting protection against nefarious boys in a knightly manner. Did this childish boy's idea that the girls were supposedly not safe and needed to be rescued by me have anything to do with my parents', especially my Mum's, ideas of an unsafe world? A few girls awarded me with the honour, after all it was all play, but it wasn't long before I learnt, from a corner in the kindergarten's outdoor yard where I was trying to do my defending and protecting, that I had nothing more to offer other than my empty words. When other boys arrived, slightly older, stronger, bigger and wilder than myself (we're talking a four year old facing six-year-olds), I totally failed in my task as saviour. My reward was the wounding of my feelings of honour. The two girls looked venomously at me whilst I considered that bad and evil, essentially stronger forces, had won over me. How unfair, it was so well intended imagined! It must have been quite an emotion for the little boy I was, why else can I still remember it today? That I even contemplated such a mission had perhaps also something to do with the many fairytales we are exposed to in Germany, with all those knights that rescue people, usually princesses, from dragons and witches.

That being that, when I tried to learn judo a few years later, a taller girl finally buried the rest of any expressed and misplaced patriarchal concepts I had acquired. She put me over the edge with such a degree of power that I chose to drop judo. I think it was a good lesson, though I should have continued.

In primary school, my world remained relatively safe and intact. In September 1976, I stood in the assembly hall with a school cone that is typical for Germany at the onset of school, full of goodies. The headmistress gave a speech, and we saw our classroom for the first time. To celebrate the day, we watched a film in the series "The Little Mole." I truly loved school and learning. The primary school in the Olympic Village has a large schoolyard and relatively spacious sports facilities up to this present day. The gymnasium and our sports field were probably once used for training the many Olympic teams, our annual sports festival and sports training often took place in the former Olympic grounds, and our swimming lessons were held in the actual 1972 Olympic swimming pool, exactly where Mark Spitz won all his medals. The classrooms of the school had large windows overlooking a generous courtyard. I have never forgotten my first-grade teacher, Frau Zehetbauer. She was a little strict but just as warm and she had those "angel cards" which she handed out as a reward for good behaviour. Ethnically, it was a relatively homogeneous school, although there was a boy from Krakow in

Jewish Child in German School

Poland and Hanako, a girl with a Japanese mother. Maybe there were others, but there weren't many. Nevertheless, there was a noticeable social difference between kindergarten and the primary school. While there were still many children from the immediate Munich neighbourhood in my kindergarten, often from working-class families from the area of Milbertshofen, who spoke in the local Munich dialect, most children in the primary school came from well-to-do middle-class families, of whom almost all were home-owning residents of the Olympic Village. Essentially, unlike the locals from Milbertshofen, they were people who had moved into this area, even if some had lived in Munich elsewhere. Amongst these families, a few were different from the rest, such as the children whose parents were labelled "hippies" by others (it was only the mid-1970s and that lifestyle and philosophy still lingered on – in many ways we were the children of that generation). One of my friends at the time who came from such an anti-authoritarian family was a boy called Dominik Frolic. It was thanks to his parents, who both worked in schools themselves, that I was able to go on a camping trip for the very first time in my life at the age of nine and experience an outing without my parents. Dominik's parents exuded a freedom that was unfamiliar to me and for which I somehow craved, in contrast to my mother, who was always anxious about everything, including appearances.

One of the highlights of the school year was the annual "Kasperl" puppet theatre put on by the traffic police of Munich to teach children safe passage through traffic. There were regular children's church services in the ecumenical church centre of the Olympic village the children would attend. I took part quite a few times but was eventually, perhaps by year three, exempted due to my Jewish religious affiliation making me feel left behind and somehow missing out.

When I was still in the first grade, Frau Zehetbauer once wrote a warning into my exercise book, because I had managed to furnish it with dog-ears. When my mother learned of this comment, she reacted with fear and truly extreme concern. I was given a proper talk down in no unmistakable language that I had to be tidy and not sloppy, "because otherwise the Germans would think we Jews were sloppy and messy." I didn't understand what she was on about at the time and felt unjustly and too harshly done by, but of course, I promised to do better. It was not about me but about deeper fears. That social anxiety and insecurity about being judged by others haunted my mother and to some extend my father their entire lives. There was a direct line between the fear that these dog-ears might lead to an outcome that was similar in its danger to the reasons why my grandfather had to flee Munich in 1934 after his Dachau internment. That said, years later I saw degrees of that behaviour and concern for respectability also in some working-class English families and migrant and black families, as to give no one any chance to think of their children as not being up to the highest standards and demanding respect. The funny thing was, that in wealthy families I would later often frequent, after I became a Personal Pilates teacher, high standards of order and cleanliness were often upkept by employed cleaners and nannies.

12

On Air

It is fair to say, that in spite of such hiccups, I had a good childhood. We, the children of the Olympic Village played extensively after school and visited each other. Often, we played football on a grassy patch in between two of the streets, where the goals were the gaps between two trees. We were also able to immerse ourselves in many fantastic adventures amidst the creative, stimulating playgrounds of the Olympic Village, made up from the leftovers of its construction. There was a "White City", a structure erected out of concrete slabs and pipes, a "Red City", built out of bricks, and there were various other adventure playgrounds, one of them on the Olympiaberg, the "Olympic Hill", under which the remains of the bombed-out Munich of the 1940s are still buried today.

We cycled through the gigantic Olympic Park at free will – not a hint of a car in our way. When we were a little older, one of our frequent games was pretending to be detectives. Another favourite game that we staged especially in the school playground was "moon landing." Don't forget, we were children of the late 1960s and early 1970s with all the moon landings just behind us, elaborated by "Raumschiff Enterprise" as the Star Trek Series was called in German, on our TV-screens.

Star Trek wasn't the only programme we enjoyed, in the ever-increasing range of children entertainment on TV. There was "Lassie,"

"Wickie and the Strong Men," "Pink Panther," "Pumuckl,", a series about a gremlin in a Bavarian Munich-based carpenter's shop, "Pippi Longstocking," "Heidi," "Tom and Jerry" and "Maya, the Bee."

Television expanded in Germany during the 1970s. My parents had only switched from a black and white TV set to a full colour television in the early 1970s. For them and their generation television was still that great, never before seen miracle of live home-entertainment that happened in their life-time. Music programmes such as the German schlager-show "Musikantenstadl" and before that, "Die Hitparade mit Dieter Thomas Heck", and a similar music programme for younger audiences called "Disco" with Ilya Richter (another Jewish person on screen), both featuring top-ten hits, were popular with my parents. One of the great stars my parents loved was Peter Alexander, an Austrian actor, singer and entertainer. The TV-Show "Dalli Dalli" however, was in a special league of its own.

"Dalli Dalli" was a quiz show where participants had to perform a whole array of special tasks. When they performed something well, the presenter Hans Rosenthal (1925-1987, 5685-5747), a short man, with frizzy hair and a pleasant, cheerful voice with a Berlin accent – would jump into the air and shout "Ich bin der Meinung, das war Spitze!" – I am of the opinion, that this was superb, with the whole TV audience cheering along. The entertainment value of Rosenthal was only half the reason why it was considered a special family event, for Rosenthal was one of the few Jewish people on German television screens in those postwar years. What's more, whilst Rosenthal's Jewish parents from Berlin had died before the Shoah, everyone else in his family had been murdered during the Third Reich. Rosenthal himself became a forced labourer enslaved in the service of the Nazis until he took the risk to go into hiding in a garden. Hidden there, he managed to survive the Shoah.

My father regarded Hans Rosenthal as one of his own, alongside the Polish-born Marcel Reich-Ranicki, whom the Germans had crowned literary pope and critic. Reich-Ranicki's fate in the Shoah had been similar to that of my father.[44] In addition, the Dutch show hosts Rudi Carell and Herman van Veen of course spoke to my mother, given her country of her birth.

The annual highlight amongst all those TV-shows was the "Grand Prix Eurovision de la Chanson", which is known today as the Eurovision Song Contest. Again, it was because here we saw Israeli and Dutch artists. In 1978 and in 1979 Israel won, first with Itzar Cohen's "A-Ba-Na-Bi" and then with Gali Atari and the group "Milk and Honey" performing "Hallelujah." Years later, Ofra Haza, Yardena Arazi, Rita and Dana International followed. These were moments when our whole family sat together and celebrated with relatives, usually my aunts and uncles in Israel. It made us proud for the achievement of Jews and of Israel. Other countries in the Middle East supposedly ignored Israel's victories. Paradoxically, some of the Israeli performers were born in some of these Arabic or Persian-speaking countries, that had by en large kicked their Jewish populations out.

The intolerance by some towards Israel and additional antisemitism, but also the flaming up of conflicts there, led to the political penalisation of Israeli contestants from the 1982 Lebanon War onwards upto the present day. The politics of Eurovision were often hotly debated in Munich's Jewish community, while some of my German non-Jewish friends questioned why Israel was involved at all. "Israel is in the Middle East, after all", they would argue. On the contrary, my aunt Ruszke, who was born in Auschwitz, had survived Bergen Belsen and lived in Tel Aviv, was completely delighted by the German entry "Ein bisschen Frieden" – "A Little Bit of Peace" – that won in 1982. For her, there sat a young German woman of the postwar generation who sang "beautiful words" about peace. Why couldn't others have a heart like my aunt?

Television thus had great significance in the family-life. The TV-Set was situated in the centre of the living room, and everything revolved

---

44 Reich-Ranicki (1920-2013, 5680-5774) fought in the Warsaw ghetto underground, while his parents were murdered in Treblinka, as were my father's mother and relatives

around it. As a child, I often had to fall asleep alone because my mum sat spellbound in front of a show. It was incomprehensible to me to only hear the distant sounds of the TV in the darkened children's room instead of having my mum with me until I had fallen asleep.

I believe today that there was also a deeper reason why TV shows took such centre stage in my home: for people who were keeping their distance from German society and who didn't feel comfortable and safe taking part in public German life, television opened alternative ways to still be part of public life in perfect safety and privacy. It was a life-saving window to the outside world. At some stage we even had two large TV-Sets, so that mum and dad could watch different programmes.

My father had another additional obsession that became especially apparent after he retired, and due to the emergence of a newly evolving abundance of television channels. Amongst all the available programmes, he would highlight and intensely study everything he could identify about the Shoah, the Third Reich and the Second World War. He nourished this obsessive habit for two reasons: firstly, so as not to forget anything that he held relevant as evidence concerning the Shoah and secondly, in a desperate attempt to better understand the brutality and tragic losses he had lived through. It did not change his mind, rather was he searching for confirmation that Germans ranked, this being his personal belief on grounds of his own experiences, as the world's greatest criminals ever. The average German person, whether they were guests in his restaurant or others, generally did not watch such programmes. I sometimes heard from acquaintances that they could not and did not want to hear any more about the Holocaust and that included avoiding all those guilt-invoking TV-programmes. "Why should we always feel guilty?", one acquaintance once asked me. He expected me, of all people, to meet his confession with degrees of sympathy. I kept my mouth shut. That was his answer.

The first intense collective confrontation of the nation and much of the television watching world with the horrors of the Shoah via TV was Claude Lanzmann's documentary Shoah, which was broadcasted in Germany in 1985. My family sat fully emotionally charged in front of the TV-set and my father commented without end on the images and statements before him. "*Di verückten Verbrecher, zolln sie alle habn, a shwarzn sof!*", he said in Yiddish (Those crazy criminals, may they all have a black ending), which he attributed not only to Germans, but also to Polish and Ukrainians helpers of the Germans.[45] During one episode my aunt Ruszke and uncle Abraham happened to be visiting from Israel and I remember the despair and condemnation and anger in the living room.

It was not all that grim. My generation was the first generation that was able to enjoy colour television, with an increasing number of children's programmes on offer. I have already listed a few, but I have not given more insight into an important aspect of these. Allow me to tell you about the particularities of German language TV-series such as "Rappelkiste," "Löwenzahn," "Das feuerrote Spielmobil," "Kli Kla Klawitterbus" (with the clown Arminio Rotstein, the child of an Austrian-Christian-Jewish couple) and "Die Sendung mit der Maus" (lit. the Programme with the Mouse): "Löwenzahn" and "Sendung mit der Maus" specialised in explaining how everything works, for example the production of a glass bottle or in depth explanations of parts of the human body. Rappelkiste and "Das feuerrote Spielmobil" offered short and longer dramatized interactions with a pedagogical teaching point that aimed to empowered children. In addition, German stations screened a multitude of Czechoslovak productions, Krtek (Der Kleine Maulwurf – The little Mole), Pan Tau, "Luzie, der Schrecken der Straße", as well as several fairytale film series, above all Arabela (Die Märchenbraut), all produced in co-operation with Western TV-companies across the Iron Curtain. The Czechoslovak productions were not just standard children's programmes, but originated from Soviet-Communist controlled countries, where they were created in

---

[45] 15 years later I would write an essay at Leeds University on this film and on another film by Lanzmann called "Tsahal", which deals intensively with the trauma of military service in Israel.

co-production with Western stations. They contained a particular dose of unspoken magic and that particular subtle hope for a better world which could only arise from a place of strict limitations on thought, art and freedom (some would add the East and West German children programmes "Sandmann" to this, but the story and politics of this children's character is a book in its own right).[46] I think that these programmes had a special relevance for me and probably for many others, Jewish or not. They were the results of thoughtful postwar pedagogy in the spirit of rethinking and in the aftermath of the student revolt in Germany.

As to children, the revolutionary spirit placed them centre stage. They were people to whom adults should listen, not just the other way around. The postwar generation of the 1960s and 1970s also advocated non-violence and how conflict could be positively dealt with and constructively minimised. These series and films were about healing and goodness and justice amongst human society, not just because they were children's programmes, but because the (West) German postwar generation also deeply desired to achieve this as a higher aim. Take the children's presenter Peter Lustig who constantly wore dungarees, who after he passed away, was described as Germany's first Green poster boy, or Michael Habeck and Eberhard Peiker, who played the two characters Oswin and Nickel, and the puppets Ratz and Rübe. They were all the faces of a new attempt to be better German people.[47] Anti-authoritarian, approachable, above all fair, always endeavouring to understand and encourage children and allowing everything to be expressed. To my delight, I also experienced Habeck and Peiker at children's play festivals in Munich. At one point there was even the fiery van from the children series "Das Feuerote Spielmobil" on the streets of the Olympic Village, as well as the set of a windmill from the series "The Strange Adventures of Herman van Veen" that stood on a square of the student quarters of the Olympic Village – Van Veen, another progressive and imagination-stimulating pioneer of his time.

---

[46] See Bundesministerium für Bildung und Forschung (2020)
[47] See Kruse (2016)

When I became a father myself, I ordered the antiquated "Rappelkiste" series on DVD for my daughter without thinking twice, because there existed few programmes of equal quality and pedagogy in England. Children's programmes in the UK were and are rather silly and infantile. Of course that is part of the world of children, but it lacked any explanations and the postwar ethos I had been exposed to in Germany. In terms of diversity, however, the 1970s were not yet that progressive. Children of African or Asian background were nearly absent even in the otherwise progressive programmes. In the "Kik Kla Klawitterbus" series, people talked about children from Italy as "foreigners" because there were prejudices against them at the time. "Rappelkiste" had a series about Children of Colour.

Unfortunately, even in Germany, cheaper animated series have now largely replaced these elaborate efforts. It remains the exception that children are encouraged to defend the world from their point of view in real-life scenes. This postwar awareness of empowerment and democracy was therefore a particular and amazing treasure, and I think it truly influenced me and many others.

Reality was not too far off in Germany. Munich staged a regular "Kinderstadt", a so-called Children's City, which was a holiday programme in which children, in the words of Herbert Grönemeyer, "should be in power." The "Kinderstadt", a project that exists up until today, is an entire city simulation, similar to the adult world, but created, governed and inspired by children. When I was a child in Munich, it always took place in one of the side halls of the Olympic Grounds. That was a good fit, because the Olympic Park itself was of course planned as a "democratic park." There was also a "city of art" for children, which, like the full city simulation, is still held regularly today. Here, artists enable children during the holiday times to try out types of art and as independently and child centred as possible. The public funds that enabled this were indeed an excellent investment into the next generation. For long days and afternoons, we were free under the supervision of qualified youth workers, pedagogues and teachers whose greatest concern was to encourage children to be more proactive, engaged and creative.

13

Musical Steps

I always loved music lessons in kindergarten and primary school. It was all about making music together with instruments. The kindergarten and school were well organised. I wanted to learn the guitar, probably because it was an instrument that frequently accompanied children's music sessions. However, the little children's guitar that my Mum had bought somewhere was regarded as unsuitable by the only available guitar teacher near the Olympic village. My mum didn't want to buy the recommended instrument and that was that.

Piano lessons were offered through a private teacher who rented a room in my primary school, and I was immediately interested. An old second-hand piano would have sufficed for my initial endeavours. Given that the guitar I had wanted would have only cost a few hundred Deutschmark, somehow, when it came to a much more expensive piano, there were no obstacles, perhaps because of a mixture of sentimentality and social prestige. Neither my father nor my mother knew how to play any instruments. My mother remembered some happy evenings with her piano-playing father and my father immediately had the idea that I could play the beautiful songs of Richard Klayderman, a famous pianist on TV at the time, in front of invited adult guests. A piano was acquired, and almost right from the start, I preferred to play my own compositions, at least among my small circle of acquaintances. But I was reluctant to play Klayderman's "Ballade Pour Adeline", and there was no one who could show me how to play this piece anyhow. Certainly, my piano teacher was more into the discourses of Bach, Beethoven and Mozart and I found the mastering of difficult classical passages quite boring and frustrating. Don't get me wrong, I had great regard for the classical composers, I loved listening to their works, but I could sit for hours each day at the piano and would experiment, which was much more exciting.

Soon enough the instrument became an object of conflict, because Dad was dismissive of my playing; in his opinion the tunes were mere noise. And yet in my afternoons at home after school, it was the piano that grew increasingly to become my confidant, my friend, my emotional lifesaver over the next few years. My music teachers at secondary school even predicted a career in music for me. Music became the only subject in which I consistently achieved the highest mark, a distinction. Everyone could see, hear and feel my talent – the two people who did not, were my parents.

Trapped in their own world of fear and their own imaginary ideas about who I had to be, instead of who I was, they were blind and deaf to what and who was before them. I was the generation after the Shoah, supposed to stand in for all that was lost, achieve great things and above all, make them proud. Despite his personal love of music, my father often told me that being a musician was a beggar's profession. From the perspective of a man who had grown up in a Polish small rural town, it may have appeared like this. The piano was at best, what educated better-off families had in their house, used to show off their status.

14

My Father, the Survivor

Some survivors of the Shoah are said to have burried themselves with work. This would leave little time for too many thoughts about the past to settle. Affection and love were difficult for them. Others claim that such behaviour was simply the way in which past generations expressed themselves overall, whether they had survived the Shoah or not. I wonder about that, regarding my father. After all, my paternal grandfather passed on a lot of his skills and knowledge to my father and his siblings. Hence the fact that my father was largely unavailable to me was a great loss.

When I was still a boy, I had no greater desire than to prove to my father that I was able to master things. Such attempts, be it skiing or football, would often be accompanied by my invitation of "I'll show you how it's done!" They were, however, answered with a faint smile and at best with the comment "very nice!" uttered in a most dismissive tone, that made me even more keen to convince him otherwise. There was certainly more to these interactions and reactions of my father, than those of an annoyed busy father to a little nosey boy.

It is rather odd how some moments imprint themselves onto your memory. I wanted to help with some DIY that my father was busy with. This involved hammering nails into a board or a wall. Carefully, and eager to help my father, I tried my best, but my father laughed in

My Father, the Survivor

utter disdain. What had I done wrong? I should have held the hammer handle further back to give the hammer head more momentum. I hit it a few more times, but my father had passed his judgement. Not a word of encouragement. This was but one example. Nothing was ever good enough.

What was going on here? Maybe it had something to do with the harsh laws of survival in the forced labour camps during the Shoah. People who demonstrated inexperience in manual tasks, whether children or adults, or who did not get it right first time around, would have had little chance of survival in this cruel order. Perhaps this had ingrained itself into my father.[48] Either enslaved forced labourers understood the expected work immediately, even if they had never done such work before, or they were condemned to die. Being at the mercy of my father's ridicule was of course unfair, and as I have already argued, even my father had initially had to learn his skills from his father, but my father lacked empathy, understanding and patience, and perhaps also sufficient comprehension and ability for self-reflection.

What my father did tell me was that apparently, I did not only have "two left hands", but also "two left legs." I have knees that are outwardly fixated. Years later, during my Pilates training, I learnt that humans can have a variety of differently aligned knees and feet, which are all part of the natural human range. But as far as my gait was concerned, it was yet another thing that gave him opportunity to critique, ridicule and mock me. He called "*Schlomo Ko-Koltel*" after me, or something similar, possibly the nickname of some person from his childhood or youth that he and others must have teased, or some figure to laugh at in Yiddish folklore. Whoever it was, my father seemed to think that this mockery would transform the way I walked, that I would change my ways because I did not want to be called that name. Instead, I felt shunned and truly

---

[48] It is important to mention that repeated testimonies also prove that the people imprisoned in the camps tried to protect children collectively within their limited possibilities.

did not know how to deal with such mockery by my own Dad for something I barely was able to change.

You may wonder at this stage whether I am perhaps displaying degrees of oversensitivity; maybe I was the problem? Well, my father was so obsessed ridding me of my apparent imperfections that he and my mother made an appointment for me at some crazy Munich orthopaedic surgeon. I was probably no more than nine or ten years of age. The surgeon explained the procedure in detail. He would be breaking my healthy bones, and I would be about six months in plaster whilst the bones regrew "better" aligned. The outcome would be by no means certain. I am not sure if he was completely serious in his explanation, or if he exaggerated to draw a picture that would certainly be dismissed by any sane person. In any case, he did not discourage my parents, and I do remember that in spite of my young age, I declined to go along with any such plan. It was not to be the last time, that my father tried to dismiss me with his devastating opinions and remarks.

15

"Worse than the Germans"

My father's past experiences during the Shoah left their mark on him, not only physically, but also emotionally. My mum and I were often privy to the outbursts of rage that he would experience. He could even get violent in such moments or at least threaten violence. As a young boy, I was hit a few times with "the spoon", an oversized wooden spoon that was intended to be used as a wall decoration. It was not terribly harsh, but the fear I felt was immense. I was terrified, hiding under tables to save myself. Once, when he was overcome with anger, he had a large, sharp kitchen knife in his hand, as he had been working in the kitchen, and waved it around whilst he was shouting insults. The fear of large knives remains with me to this day, because of this. He also often threatened me with the "Riemen" – a leather strap.

Although what Germans had done to him and his family and others was the cause behind his anger, when he lived it out, it was often directed at us, my mother and myself, the people closest to him. When I was growing up, he could not cope with my natural journey towards increased individuality and independence. It was the final part of chain of events in his life that he was neither able to control nor to influence. I was amazed when, while researching this book, I read about the way the enslaved forced labourers had been treated in the Hasag camps (see

Zol Zayn Shulem II: Faroys

Zol Zayn Shulem I: Zores). The descriptions of the use of truncheons, whips and straps in the 1940s brought back my own memories of my childhood in the 1970s. Here in Munich, more than 25 years after the end of the Shoah, I didn't know that aspects of the horror and fear I felt as a child may have originated in the camps where my father had been imprisoned, enslaved and physically and emotionally abused, and for which he never received therapy.

And my Mum? I don't really know. I am certain there was psychological torment. There may be arguments in all families, but rarely have I experienced such loss of control and frequent and intense outbursts of anger as my father displayed. Even a German school friend of mine remembered it 40 years later.

The fact that his much-hoped-for child developed independently and failed to fulfil his own cherished dreams, and what he had wished for, was too much to bear. Sometimes it was a shirt that I didn't want to wear, sometimes a meal he prepared that I didn't want to eat. The songs I did not play on the piano or indeed the wrong way of walking, Later it was girlfriends, what I studied, and eventually the woman I would marry, all of this upset him again and again, even if he could otherwise pretend to be the calmest, friendliest person. After all, self-control and emotional shutdown, was also a required quality in the camp. When things happened in the camps, you had to keep calm and swallow your emotions, rather than react, if you were to continue to live. So to people on the outside, he would control his emotions, but I was supposed to be controlled. He struggled with fantasies and imaginary nightmare scenarios of what could and would be, and what others might think of him and the family. He would throw all sorts of accusations at me: Frequently he claimed that I was "worse than the Germans," that I should have a "*shwarzen Soff*," a dark ending, the same he wished for many German perpetrators, or that I was "a good-for-nothing with two left hands and two left feet." Decades later, in the last ten years of my father's life, he refused to talk to me. I, who had chosen "a *Shwarze*" (a black woman) as my wife, was now "like the dead to him."

Due to my later training as a school's executive I now know that such behaviour was within the range of emotional child abuse and was behaviour that exposed the mental disarray the Shoah experiences had left my father in. He truly was a victim of one of the greatest crimes to humanity, but his experiences had led to behavioural challenges that were at the very least now directed towards me. I could not rely on outside help and support either. None was forthcoming. Thus, when I was 15 years old, I was very much attracted by the idea of creating distance, and thus decided to flee to Israel, away from this confining, frightening and humiliating world. I would not have called it a flight at the time, and did not understand all the contexts, but I do think subconsciously it was in "flight."

I see all of what happened in those years as unprocessed psychological pressure from the irrational violations of human dignity, day in, day out, screaming camp overseers, Ukrainian guards, German guards, Jewish Kapos, repeated arbitrary or explicit sadism, hate-driven or indifferent murder. The murderers and tormentors knew no bounds in the way they tortured their enslaved workforce. My father, one of their countless victims, and my uncle Abraham (as I learned from observing his behaviour towards his daughter, my cousin Bracha), could not stop their hysterical rage even years later, triggered all too often because of small insignificant things, but which represented a momentary loss of control for our fathers. It made them threaten with violence, they shouted crazy, destructive words, endangering themselves and us, and all of that caused new wounds atop the existing pain of their souls.

More than once, my father threw a tantrum while he was at the wheel of his car, and my Mum and I regularly expected a bad accident. The car in which we were sitting close to each other, in which an argument erupted, would veer towards a tree, ditch or oncoming car, whilst my father shouted enraged insults. In those moments, I was the uncontrollable bad son, who should go to hell, would be condemned to death. It was as if I was resisting a camp commander that my father had temporarily transformed into, where I had to be suitably punished for putting the commander's authority into question.

And what did my Mum say? I shouldn't have provoked my father, I should do what he wanted, because "You know what Dad had experienced, don't you?" So she appears to have grasped why we were going through all of this but allowed his experiences to be his apology. Because of what had happened to him, I was to accept his rages and keep quiet.

I will write later about the time I received therapy from experts in London after I had been diagnosed with PTSD acquired during my childhood and youth. I will also tell you how in the end I confidently walked towards a different script, one of hope and confidence for the future.

16

Dalfsen – Netherlands

When I was at kindergarten and to some extend in primary school, my mother and I used to travel to the Netherlands for long periods, especially during the school vacations. Initially we went by train, later on my mum drove her fully packed red Renault 5 all the way from Munich to Dalfsen. At least once or twice, I think my aunt and uncle also came (by car), though memories are vague. My grandmother owned a cheap, simple bungalow there halfway between Dalfsen and Ommen, with two bedrooms and a large living room that had a huge window. The land on which it was built was part forest, part meadow, and the house stood on a slight elevation, as I was told, to protect it from potential risks of floods from the nearby Vecht-River.

When I was four or five years old, I planted trees around the fence with my parents. Some are still there today, although a later owner to my great frustration, uprooted some. The bungalow increasingly became our other home.

The surrounding forest became a landscape I would become very familiar with. I roamed around in nature and enjoyed a complete degree of untamed freedom. I soon knew every corner of the huge, wooded area, could tell you where rabbits lived and where one could watch the dairy cows and their calves and talk to them, as I did. Whenever my father had one of his anger tantrums when he visited, I was often ordered to my room. But instead of staying there, I escaped through the window and disappeared for hours strolling through nature. By the time I returned, my father had often calmed down, but frequently my parents hadn't even noticed that I had been away for hours. Even today, it is hard for me to believe that I regularly had to escape to the "safety" of the surrounding nature like that. I might have lacked help in other regards, but at least there was the vast forest and Dutch landscape into which I could immerse myself and forget momentarily what had gone on at home.

Due to these frequent stays in Dalfsen, I acquired basic Dutch language skills, because I also played a lot with the children there. They were mainly from families further up West who would come here for weekends and holidays. I loved everything about the Netherlands, the Wednesday markets, the barrel organ orchestras, the Chinese-Indonesian restaurants, croquettes, patat (French fries), the bicycles, and the relatively relaxed nature of the people there, where most shops were usually closed at lunchtime. I loved vla (Dutch vanilla pudding), Hagerslag (Dutch chocolate flakes for toast), Pinderkaas (peanut butter), stroopwafels (maple syrup wavers) Dutch tea, smoked eel and cheese with herbs. The consumption of Double Zout Dropies, the double-salted Dutch liquorice sweets, sealed my affiliation with the Netherlands. Nobody in my family today can stomach these – I think you have to have grown up with them. We not only shopped in Dalfsen but often made excursions to the idyllic town of Ommen (which these days is sadly totally regenerated beyond recognition, with many of the little shops I still knew having disappeared) and to Zwolle, the largest city in the region. Often, we travelled to Zwolle only because my father said he needed to get a German-language newspaper to feed his news habit. Interestingly, neither my mother nor anyone else in the family thought of acquiring bicycles. I didn't get one either, not even a second hand one, despite the many years in which we regularly visited the Netherlands and my consistent requests for one. Maybe that was just as well, for if I had had one, I probably would have travelled even further from home.

My grandmother (she only moved back to Germany permanently in the early 1980s) and my great-aunt Martha (Margje), my grandmother's sister, lived an hour and a half drive by car in the small town of Ugchelen, near the city of Apeldoorn. Martha's motto in life seemed to me to be pragmatically positive, even though she was said to have suffered in her first marriage (I do not know more than that). Once that relationship was behind her, every day was a good day for her. She had this marvellous infectious, very human charisma around her. On my very first visit to the Netherlands, I was even still able to get to know "Grandpa Valk." As my great-grandfather, Arie Valk was the only real personal grandfather figure from my family I ever had the privilege of knowing, as all previous generations on my father's side had been murdered and my maternal grandfather had passed away in 1956. But Grandpa Arie still lived in his home together with my great-aunt Martha in Beekbergen when I met him. The house was located inside a dense wooded area that was also near Apeldoorn. This was where my mother had often lived during the war years in her childhood when she wasn't in Amsterdam.

I can recall that my grandfather was sitting in a large, slightly dark living room, in which also stood an aquarium. I immediately noticed the anchor tattooed on one of his arm, which hinted at his time spent on ships (he managed a team of sailors). He cut off a slice of an apple and asked me in Dutch "wil jij ook een stukje van de appel? – if I would also like a piece.

The next time I saw him about a year later, he was lying in an open coffin in a funeral home behind a large window. I asked my mum what he was doing there and was told that Opa Valk was "sleeping." "But what if he wakes up and he can't get out of there?", I replied concerned.

Not long after that, Jenni and Evert, my great-aunt Martha's eldest son from her first marriage, got married. The professional soldier married in a traditional uniform with a sabre, which was both impressive and disconcerting for the young boy I was.[49] His brother Cor, on the

---

[49] Years later, he would become one of the Dutchmen who served as UN troops in Sarajevo when their forces could not prevent the mass killings there, some claiming

other hand, was, at least back then, somewhat "wilder" in nature. His motorbike, long hair and the symbolic freedom that came with that, made a big impression on me.

Later, when the family had moved to Ugchelen, the two sisters, my Oma and Tante Martha, lived next door to each other. I would occasionally find myself alone in their "salons" (Dutch for living room). They were very tidy living rooms with lots of ticking clocks. Martha, who smoked all her life, always had tobacco or cigarettes on the table. Both sisters owned dogs that I could play with. Martha also owned a little red DAF. Her heavy-handed, abrupt way of driving was famous in the family, but she managed and got about, nevertheless. After the separation from her first husband, Martha met a humorous, fun-loving man called Anton. He owned a chicken farm and was an optimist who was seemingly always in a good mood. All this was a stark contrast to the constant gloom of my own family. By saying grace over meals before eating, she was also expressing a daily degree of gratitude to a power beyond her own, whilst she had a likening to a small glass of Dutch Genever, especially when guests were over for dinner.

My father felt unusually safe among the Dutch family of my mother, and I think everyone there accepted him. Every now and then, however, we were called "*Rotmoffen*" (a derogatory term for Germans that roughly means "rotten lot") by Dutch people in general. This was mainly the case when our German licence plate was spotted. On one such occasion my father was driving over the speed limit on a Dutch motorway and a Dutch Rijks-police car stopped us. They thought we were normal Germans because of the licence plate, but then they learnt from the conversation and going through my father's blue stateless passport that my father was a Jewish Shoah survivor and that my mother was born in Amsterdam. What could have been a tricky situation ended with only

---

they did not try hard enough. See: Guardian 28.6.2017: Srebrenica massacre: Dutch soldiers let 300 Muslims die, court rules. https://www.theguardian.com/world/2017/jun/28/dutch-soldiers-let-300-muslims-die-in-bosnian-war-court-rules retrieved 16.2.2022

a verbal warning to watch the speed and wishes for a pleasant onward journey.

Another time, I was maybe ten or twelve years old by then, an older boy in Dalfsen whose name was Marcel and who lived on one of the nearby farms called me *Rotmoff* and shouted the Nazi greeting "Heil Hitler." I was really upset. After my father spoke to the boy's parents, he never uttered another word and kept an ashamed distance from me.

17

At the School of the Germans

Preparations for secondary schools in Germany begin in year four. After that, children are divided into three categories, those who attend academic secondaries, those who attend a mixture of vocational and academic secondaries and those who attend schools that prepare children for a life of non-academic work. The system is not just criticized for inducing undue stress on mere nine- and ten-year-olds, it can also entail particular disadvantages for migrant families and their children, especially those from non-German-speaking countries and those who for various reasons have no family experience of how the German educational system works.

I understood that when our year four class teacher, a certain Frau Kleinert, taught us suddenly some Latin, that it had something to do with the transition, but what exactly happened from year five onwards, besides a school change, was a vaguer concept. Certainly, neither my mother nor my father had any relevant insights or experience of academic or even grammar school type secondaries. My father had learned the essential basics in school, how to read and write, plus biblical Hebrew from the Jewish classes in the Cheder and conversational and written Yiddish and then continued with acquiring his father's trade through a family-based apprenticeship. My mother likewise attended a primary school in the Netherlands and a secondary middle school, where she would complete her training as a seamstress, probably aided by helpful hints from my grandmother and my grandfather. With regard to the academic *Gymnasien,* the German academic secondaries, most of my classmates aimed for (as if it was the only correct avenue for these children from German middle class families), most parents had attended such schools or were even university graduates. I, on the other hand, was completely clueless and unprepared, at the very least, for what was to be expected. I knew nothing about the selection process, how to choose where to go, or what speciality that school would have, and what it meant, be it science based, language based or centred on classics. There were further distinctions between state-supported schools (solely under the auspices of the Conservative Bavarian government) and municipally run schools, where the social-democratically run city-council of Munich had degrees of influence.

Those of my friends whose parents had studied academically, almost all of those around me, experienced increasing pressure during year four. My friend Dominik H., for example, was no longer allowed to play with his friends until he had finished his daily learning exercises. As I was one of his closest friends, that left me at a disadvantage. Others suddenly also started coming out to play games less often. They all vanished as if by some invisible force. Where were all my playmates?

The teacher said that I had to make a choice. Which stream of secondary school was I going to apply to? I selected a school concentrating on classics, called "humanistic" in Bavaria, though it would centre principally on the humanities in their classic form, Latin, Ancient Greek, ethics or religious education. That school choice was determined by the fact that it had been the choice of my friend Dominik or rather perhaps his mother. I simply followed my friend out of mere camaraderie. I did not understand that this choice meant that I was going to attend an arch-conservative Bavarian state-run school, the Maximiliansgymnasium. My grades were overall high enough to pass the acceptance requirements.

The "Max" boasted of the fact that Franz-Josef Strauss, the Bavarian conservative king surrogate, CSU Prime Minister of Bavaria at the time, had once been a pupil there. When this Bavarian Ersatzkönig came to visit, and he did honour the school frequently with such visits, there would be long preparations to get the school to look at its best; sometimes, usually a day or two before such visits, anti-CSU graffiti would appear on nearby walls.[50] It was a hint to the fact that the school had other alumni that it did not speak about so proudly; Andreas Baader and Ralf Pohle, who would later become members of the brutal far-left RAF terrorist group, also attended "the Max" once. On the other hand, one of the less controversial alumni was the German author Michael Ende.

The architecture of the school stood in stark contrast to the architecture of the modern and visionary postwar primary school I had attended in the Olympic Village. The "Max" was "old Germany," even prewar. It was housed in a neo-classical building erected in 1912, three-storeys high, shaded in pastel brown and decorated with marble. To this day, two large "Bavarian" lions guard the entrance, and the staircase is adorned with columns, the corridors are long and high and there is even a statue of the Roman she-wolf over one of the gates. Intended to inspire young people, the built architecture alone exuded a special kind of child-hostile coldness, at least it did for me. This was a place that taught serious subjects and aimed to transform its young people into mini academics, years before university.

I responded badly to this approach from day one. Having always been considered a good pupil at primary school with a real thirst for learning, within just a few months I sank into the absolute abyss of failure, bringing home fives and even six, the two worst marks in the then German system, equivalent to "unsatisfactory" and "failed." Here almost all parents of the children in my class had academic qualifications or professional careers that required a university education. Some of the parents of the children in my class were lawyers, academic professors, journalists, and qualified medical doctors, a few also leaders in business.

---

[50] Ersatzkönig – German for surrogate king

In contrast to my parents, they were able to prepare their children for the academic environment or even help here and there, if not just set expectations. They were also predominantly German, by which I mean Germans out of Christian German families for generations, again unlike my parents, neither of whom could speak flawless or even academically correct German.

In no other subject was I more lost and left behind than in Latin. I didn't grasp the new learning pace that was now expected, nor was I comfortable with the fact that Latin had so much to do with Christianity and was, in a historical sense, the language of the people responsible for the destruction of the Second Jewish Temple and the expulsion of Jewish people from their land.

Unfittingly for a Jewish child, the school initially taught lessons also on Saturdays, though it would be true to say that because my family did not attend synagogue, it was more a retrospective issue for me. I had fallen into a dry and, above all, decidedly Germanic environment that had me as outsider from the very beginning and on multiple levels.

My first music teacher there, a woman who was about to retire, was old enough to have lived through Third Reich Germany as a young adult. Was that why she had us only sing German folk songs, I remember a "Schön ist die Welt" and old Christmas tunes? I wasn't the only one who loathed this repertoire with the passion of a schoolchild. Back in primary school, the teachers were a product of the late 1960s – only at Christmas time, which still receives far too much attention in multi-cultural, multi-religious and non-religious Germany today, would they revert to religious and traditional songs.

There was a reason why some of the Old Guard were still teaching in German schools. After the fall of the Third Reich, the initially intended denazification of public services, including in schools, came to a rapid end when the state realised that there would not be enough "trained" specialists, or teachers, to do without those who had also been working during the Hitler years. Whether my music teacher was one of these, or whether she simply didn't know a repertoire that went beyond old

Zol Zayn Shulem II: Faroys

German songs remains an open question.

But someone else was there. None of the teachers at this elite yet state-run school was as strikingly memorable as a certain corpulent man with a very strong Bavarian accent. He was our biology teacher. Was his Bavarian joviality deceptive or was it even symptomatic? Were there other teachers like him? This biology teacher felt so comfortable and unconcerned in his own skin that he told all the children in his classes about his "legendary" war adventures again and again, uninhibited, unconcerned, proud and heroic.

Without the slightest degree of regret of his past, without any sign of ever having reflected on what had happened, his "behaviour" was deeply questionable and conveyed social illiteracy, deliberate or intentional and all of this to a high degree.

Even in the early 1980s he remained an enthusiastic aviator. Behind the mask of a kind teacher's face stood the "chubby-cheeked grimace" of an actual former Stuka Luftwaffe flying squadron member: broad-mouthed, stupid, a coward and unrepentant man.[51]

Mister Luftwaffe loved to show us some of his proud collection of "educational films." Modern educational films in colour had long been in use in the 1980s, but what he dug up were black and white film reels. The hairstyles of the children, the short-haired boys, the girls in dresses, together with his own obscure personality on display, made me suspect at the time that some of the films were indeed from the Third Reich era. It was very uncomfortable.

Retrospectively I doubt they were Third Reich films. They were probably from the 1950s and 1960s. However, his overzealousness in describing his infamous everyday life in the German Third Reich air force, coupled with his dubious behaviour and the odour of historicity that surrounded him, made those films no less suspect than him.

I felt more and more exposed and out of place. Sitting opposite

---

[51] Stukas were dive-bombers, usually Junkers Ju 87, amongst others used in the Blitzkrieg Operations

this man was the son of a Holocaust survivor. I was a boy who had been denied the pleasures of a grandma and grandpa and a large family because Germans had murdered or gassed them or maltreated them to the point of death because they were Jewish. My rebellion against school and my aversion to some of the teachers grew more and more. It was defensive instinct and worked on a conscious and a subconscious level.

I just about passed the fifth grade, but things got worse in the next year at the "Max." Because of my low marks, much loved sports activities such as the winter skiing I had engaged in every year since I was six or seven years old, enjoyed immensely, and was reasonably good at, were unceremoniously cancelled by my parents, as if depriving me of such pleasurable activities would guarantee better grades. I was forced to take private tuition in Latin from people who were from a different world to my young understanding instead. One of them, a recommendation from my Latin teacher, was a retired teacher whose flat always smelled of some strong food; quite possibly it was "Sauerkraut", fermented cabbage. I began to ask myself where on earth my playful, good and happy childhood and my freedom had gone? How quickly and suddenly it had all come to an end.

I failed year six and as it is usual practise in Germany had to repeat it and struggled for another three years at Maximilians-Gymnasium, failing year eight again, before I left the school.

18

Adult?

Barely grown out of my childhood in 1982, I became an adult at least according to Jewish tradition. My father seemed to have no idea how to go about this, even though he had a bar mitzvah himself. I was not sent to classes or prepared otherwise for that day in the way tradition had demanded for millennia. What my father did is incomprehensible to me today, because now an adult, I have witnessed many bar mitzvah

Adult?

readings in the many synagogues in London, and of course there was also, much later, my daughter's own bat mitzvah.

According to my father, the ultimate plan had always been for the family to emigrate to Israel, where I would eventually receive an Israeli and thus a Jewish education.[52] The day on which my whole family would leave Germany never arrived. Before my bar mitzvah, other problems arose. My father explained the reason for this years later, and perhaps that was at the root of it all:

> *Halachically you were not Jewish. Your mother was brought up Dutch-Lutheran. Judaism is only passed on from the mother. Before the bar mitzvah, I spoke to the Munich rabbi. Only after that was your mother accepted into the Jewish religion. Normally it's very complicated when a Jewish man marries a non-Jewish woman. But because of her family history, it wasn't that difficult for your mother. We invited someone from her family from Chile, who had remained Jewish, to confirm everything to the authorities. After that, they allowed your mother to adopt the Jewish faith.*[53]

This shows that my parents had been thinking about my bar mitzvah long before I ever knew about it, at least the bureaucratic stuff with the religious authorities. However, it still doesn't explain why I wasn't properly prepared for the bar mitzvah with the help of a trained and capable person. About six months before my twelfth birthday, far too late for any real prospect of achieving a reasonable level of traditional Torah reading during a Bar Mitzvah, the reading being the actual important core part of the ceremony, I was sent to a teacher at the Sinai School, the Munich Jewish primary school, to learn Hebrew letters in a few private lessons. I didn't go there many more times, and I don't think a proper plan for learning was executed, for whatever reason. Next, I knew, a few months

---

[52] Zylbersztajn (1995) p.17
[53] Zylbersztajn (1995) p.17

before the bar mitzvah, we had a conversation with the headmaster of the "Max," to request some leave of absence for the ceremony just before the winter break. That granted, my parents flew with me to Tel Aviv to visit my uncle Abraham and aunt Ruszke. Here the remaining preparations for my bar mitzvah were conducted in no more than a week or ten days.

Uncle Abraham found an orthodox scholar who lived nearby his Tel Aviv home who would teach me the absolute basics in no more than two sessions. My entire bar mitzvah education, a time of dedicated study and an opportunity to strengthen the bonds with tradition with a well-meaning teacher, usually including bonding with a group of teenage peers of similar age, who had the same task before them, was reduced to only two lessons. Only two men, my uncle and my dad, who had given up on G-d and Jewish religious tradition could produce such a thing. The scholar explained to me that I only had to learn the *brachas*, the blessings for bread and wine, and that I had to learn to put on the *tefillin*, the Jewish prayer straps.

Had he asked me for Christmas carols instead, I would have been able to oblige within an instant. German school education had drilled these into me since kindergarten, one even partly in Latin, with the phrase "bededicamus domino." I knew all the verses of these songs by heart. But Hanukkah songs like "Maoz Tsur," "Nerli," "Sevivon," "Oy Hanukkeh," or the well-known Passover song "Ma Nishtana", all songs that I would later have to teach my daughter and some of which, I only learned myself as an adult, and which normally are part and parcel of the repertoire of Jewish children, were unfamiliar to me. I was also ignorant of the words of a prayer like the Amidah or the blessings after a meal, nor was I capable of reading it. Thanks to my father, I became a stranger to the tradition and culture which he himself took so much pride in and which made us apparently different as a family to other Germans. If I am honest, I only knew "Hivenu Shalom Alechem" and "Shalom Chaverim" and the Israeli National Anthem, the former two taught in the German and Christian-dominated schools I attended. The only prayer I knew of was the Shema, and that too came not from a scholar, but from a film about the Israeli Olympic hostages in Munich, in which one of the hostages recites the Shema before the helicopter in which he is trapped is blown up with a grenade. My father was at war with G-d because Elohim had, so he argued, watched the murder of millions of innocent Jewish people in the Shoah. My father's conclusions on faith meant that he failed to teach me, or have others do the job, in any practise of the Jewish religion in a meaningful way, nor did he teach me Hebrew or Yiddish.

I learnt the prescribed blessings by heart and the laying of *tefillin*, in the way the scholar had shown me. My uncle helped me. A party was planned by my father with members of the family. The Dan Hotel, one of the oldest and most prestige hotels in Tel Aviv, was chosen and a meal was ordered for some 50 to 100 guests. All those invited were family members or old friends of my father – some were part of the very few survivors from Szczekociny or people who had been in the camps with my father and now lived in Israel and a few friends of my uncle. I, who was supposed to be the centre of attention, didn't have a single friend of mine with me, nor was I familiar with the great majority of the guests. What's more, at that time, I didn't have a single Jewish friend of the same age, but numerous good non-Jewish German friends. Is that why they weren't even considered to be invited by my parents? If my Israeli relatives and acquaintances thought it was strange, they didn't say anything. Strange? Not really! Years later, I read, that other children of Shoah survivors had experienced the same. The psychoanalyst and child survivor of the Shoah Alfred Garwood wrote that his bar mitzvah in the 1950s had been exactly like mine.[54] So all the fuss about my bar mitzvah, an event at which I saw no synagogue from the inside, wasn't really for me, it was a celebration of the survivors with a reference to the next generation, nothing more. We children just had to play along dutifully. Given what my father spent a small fortune on this, it must have meant the world to him, and given that all his friends and family came, it must have meant the same to them. It probably was something they needed for closure and hope.

Before the rabbinate in Tel Aviv admitted me to the status of "bar mitzvah" all kinds of tests were prescribed. Above all, my mother's

---

[54] Garwood (2021), p. 29

Zol Zayn Shulem II: Faroys

Jewishness was once again scrutinised and certified. My parents hadn't told me about her conversion to Judaism a few years earlier. But as far as I know, it was a sometimes painful procedure. Applicants to the Jewish faith can initially be rejected and repeatedly questioned as to why they wish to convert. Once my mother was certified as a Jewish person, the next question was whether my brit milah had been performed according to halachic requirements, as my mother was then not yet officially Jewish. It was further obvious that my father had done little to raise me in accordance with any Jewish notion of tradition, apart from a few visits to the synagogue on Yom Kippur and celebrating Passover. The rabbis of the rabbinate of Tel Aviv decided that this *yingel* needed to repeat the incision that is normally made when boys are eight days old.[55] I was asked if that was what I wanted. According to the regulations, it was not as bad as it sounded. Given that I was circumcised already, all that was required now was an incision that yielded the flow of a drop of blood.

At the bar mitzvah I was asked to recite the *brachot* that I had learned. Then I had to demonstrate that I could lay *tefillin*. Finally, three orthodox Jewish men whom I didn't know, including a mohel, came and asked me to undress in a small room. Once done, one made a cut in my penis with a strange-looking little knife. It took less than a second. A little blood was visible. In this way, I had been marked as one of G-d's people a second time, and I was given a plaster on the wound as my first reward. The procedure made me feel fainty, though. It wasn't the pain, because there was hardly any, but it was the feeling of being completely at the mercy of men whom I did not know and whom I had to trust blindly. I was totally out of control. But it was all over in a breeze and my duty was done. I was able to leave the room again, where my uncle Abraham and my father waited to welcome me. Then we took a taxi to drive to a *mikve*, a small square tiled traditional religious bath with fresh water.[56] Entering the water naked, I was asked to dunk under

---

[55] *yingel*, Jewish little boy
[56] Mikveh, Jewish ritual bath.

three times. A blessing was recited, which I was asked to repeat. Here I finally became a Jew. And a "man"? Instead of reading a Torah chapter in Hebrew and delivering a Dvar Torah, the personal interpretation of the passage, I found myself in an unfamiliar world without support, no friends, no real community of faith. My Hebrew name was not after my father, but after Abraham, the father of the Jewish faith. Daniel Zwi ben Avraham Avinu. Basically, it wasn't a real actual bar mitzvah but my mere acceptance into Judaism. The synagogue I attend today, a Masorti synagogue, which is an egalitarian modern conservative community, allows my mother's name and my father's name when I am called up to the Bimah. I may very well prepare one day for a symbolic adult bar mitzvah, only to have gone through the learning that I should have been exposed to back then. So far, it has been difficult to fit it into my busy adult life.

From left to right, Uncle Abraham, Uncle Moisze, Aunt Chaftje, my father, my mother, and I. Every single adult in this picture is a survivor, refugee or child of a refugee or survivor.

Zol Zayn Shulem II: Faroys

The day after the procedure, it was Shabbat evening, we went to the hotel at the Tel Aviv's seafront. I think my great-uncle read a passage from the Torah on my behalf. An entertainer booked by my parents played hits and Yiddish melodies on an organ: Am Israel chai - the people of Israel live.

19

My Family in Tel Aviv

My visit to Israel in 1982 for my bar mitzvah was not my first visit to Tel Aviv. In fact, my first visit was around the age of two years. Many other visits followed. My cousin Zwika, the son of Uncle Abraham and my Aunt Ruszke, 20 years my senior, always waited for us outside the Ben Gurion Airport and then drove us to Tel Aviv in his Subaru. In Tel Aviv we stayed with Abraham and Ruszke. Mum and Dad would lodge in their living room, whilst I got a bed in a smaller room. My mother recalled that on her and my father's first visit to Tel Aviv as early as the 1960s, they slept "in a shabby hotel on planks." Back then, they had also travelled to Israel by boat rather than flown. It is evident that Israel had a central place in their lives from early on.

During each visit I also got to know my aunt Ruszke (or Rosza) better, and she is a person I greatly miss today. Tante (aunty) Ruszke was a small, robust woman who attached the utmost importance to chic clothes, fine perfume, soaps and deodorants, and who regularly went to the pedicurist, manicurist and hairdresser. She was a woman who had not been allowed such fine things for many years in the camps she was stationed in, which last included Bergen Belsen, from which she was rescued almost dead.

One of the reasons Ruszke survived Bergen Belsen, she had personally told me, was because she was able to sing beautifully. She told me that she was handed rations of bread by others, in exchange for well-known Yiddish tunes and songs. Although most people were in a starved state, it appears that for some people, food for the soul sung by a young woman was more important than physical food for their own body. My aunt had a tattoo that showed a thinly written number on her left forearm. It was the concentration camp number the German Nazis had given her.

Ruszke was the most educated member of the family. She read a lot, was very intelligent and spoke Polish, Hungarian, German, Yiddish, English and Hebrew; she also learnt French. An image that stayed with me is how she lay on her bed in her house dress in quiet moments, perhaps early afternoon, reading her favourite German magazine, "*Frau im Spiegel*", which she had subscribed to. If it wasn't that, she would study her French lesson book.

That wasn't everything that was great about my *doda* (hebr. aunt). Her soups were unrivalled dishes that you could but dream of, and yet she served them weekly, and her salads had an unusual vinegar and mustard sauce that I still can't quite replicate today. She also baked the best cheesecake and the best *leykach*, a kind of moist honey cake. While my uncle worked in his household and chinaware shop, she did all the shopping, often shlepping the many bags over long distances to the house she lived in on Joshua-bin-Nun Street, part of what is called today Old Tel Aviv, and then carried the load up to her flat onto the third floor, all without a lift. Her flat was kept spotless.

Nevertheless, some people thought Ruszke's life was a waste. I cannot pinpoint where I picked that up today, but it must have been somebody in the family who said it, or one of the family's friends. It was said that she should have gone to university, and she certainly had the intellect for it. I think it was my mother who told me that Uncle Abraham did not wish for that. He probably thought such studying was nonsense. In the camps, there was often a big difference between the academically educated, for example from cities like Warsaw, and those from the rural regions, like the Zylbersztajn brothers. Those who survived in the camps

My Family in Tel Aviv

were usually people who could work with their hands, as my father would put it. In addition, my uncle may have clung on to old patriarchal structures, just like my father, according to which the role of the woman was inside the house.

I was fortunate enough to hear some of Ruszke's songs, the very same that she had once sung in the camps. After she had done so repeatedly, I suggested to her to record them on a tape recorder. She didn't instantly comply, but I asked her again and again. Eventually she did and her children, my cousins Bracha and Zwika, ended up with a recording of her songs because of that. I remember "Tumbalalaika" and songs by Edith Piaf, such as "La Vie en Rose" which she sang in French and in German and "Bei Mir Bist Du Shayn," made famous by the Barry Sisters. Although her songs were highly regarded in the family and she had sung for others in the camp, she did not mention this important fact in her filmed testimony to the Shoah Foundation (spoken in Hebrew). For some reason it did not come up. This shows that this testimony only reflects a fraction of what she experienced, and perhaps that is how it was with many testimonies.

When I spent long mornings and afternoons with my aunt during the bar mitzvahva period, I wrote poems in German and Ruszke always thought they were "sensational" and "marvellous." The opinion of this always positive-thinking wise woman with a heart that by far overreached her short stature was a judgement you had to take seriously. Years later, she judged her grandson Yaron in the same way. He later became a lawyer. I became a journalist. But it was not just that. Ruszke had made loving embraces and kindness towards others the very purpose of her life. Some twenty years older than my mother, Doda Ruszke was almost a surrogate grandmother to me.

She was also proud of a celebrity that lived in her neighbourhood, the Yemeni Israeli singer Shulamit Damari. It was probably the glimmer of a career that also could have been open for her. Ruszke's other often repeated story was that an American who had heard her sing in Sweden, where she was rehabilitated after liberation from Bergen Belsen after the war, had offered to take her to the USA so that she could use her talent and voice to make a career for herself there. She decided otherwise, perhaps lacking in bravery to trust the promises of this stranger.

Uncle Abraham spent his free time studying newspapers, just like my father. Especially on Friday eve (Shabbat) he would spend a few hours combing through the weekend edition of the centre-right newspaper *Yediot Achronot*. In his shop in Allenby Street at the corner of Tchernichovsky Street, he always had visitors, friends and family who would stop by, most of them Yiddish speaking, but also some Jewish people, now Israelis, who had fled Germany. There was the 80-year-old butcher Julius of Shuk-ha-Carmel (the central market of Tel Aviv), a native of Berlin who always maintained a very strong German accent in his Hebrew and who always brought fresh meat over on Fridays, including, would you believe it, on special request, ham for my uncle who didn't keep kosher. Rudi Weissenstein was another person my uncle knew, a photographer who had also had his business on Rechov Allenby for decades.[57] And then there was Joseph Yoshkowitz, also a Jewish refugee from Germany. He came every week to the shop to say hello, and was an incredibly nice, older and quite fit man with frizzy hair, who went swimming at Tel Aviv beach every morning, regardless of the weather, and who had once worked with my uncle. Visitors like us who came from Germany always made Joseph particularly happy. The Jakim, as Israelis nicknamed Jewish people who came from Germany, the word coming from the German word *Jacke*, a jacket, because they would stereotypically continue to pay attention to appearance and wear a jacket even during work or hot days, were a loosely bound community. In Tel Aviv I would find second-hand bookshops on Ben Yehuda Street as well as German and Austrian Jewish cafes, such as Cafe Mersand with aging refugees and survivors enjoying an Appelstrudel or Cheese Cake and

---

[57] Rechov, hebr. Street. When passport photos were needed, we usually went to his shop. It was a dark shop with cameras and photo prints that seemed to be stuck in the 1950s.

My Family in Tel Aviv

Moca there, as well as the sighting of old acquaintances, whose numbers diminished over time.[58]

In my uncle's shop it wasn't only German Jews that stopped by, family members too stopped by the shop, including Ella, my aunt Rosza's sister, and her husband Leon, and Hanka and Cella Schwarzbojm, my father's cousins.[59] They would sit on the small benches in the shop, and everybody would discuss the latest news and chitchat.

Sometimes Zwika and Abraham would take me with them on supply rounds. Zwika would drive his estate car into the back streets towards the south of Tel Aviv, which were narrow and long, where one trader after another run their wholesale stores. Some of them knew Zwika and Abraham well. Zwika would ask for certain items, and following payment, boxes of the items would find their way into the car. The purchases would usually somehow fit in the dusty storage room of the shop that was already filled to the brim with goods.

A lot of the goods also came from Germany, especially high-quality porcelain figurines. These were often stored in Munich and then either brought back personally when travelling to Israel or, well packaged, sent by post. I remember how I was allowed to help with the careful packing of the figurines. Whole stacks of boxes filled with porcelain or Solingen cutlery found their way to Israel alongside items for the family.

When the wholesale exporters began to import Japanese and later Chinese goods, imports from Germany and my father's involvement became less important.

Ruszke and Abraham's flat, a building from the 1950s, was modern and functional, and they were one of the first in the street to have sliding windows installed on their balcony, which enlarged the living room. The windows facing the street let in all kinds of noise, whether it was the birds of the neighbourhood, the rubbish collection at 06.00 in the morning,

---

[58] read Kaufman (2018) concerning the final days of Café Mersand
[59] Orla Schwarzbojm was my grandfather's sister, I don't know much about her, but she was one of the refugees who fled to Russia shortly before the Germans arrived.

the old goods collector with horse and cart, who shouted "Alte Sachen" – old things in Yiddish – but was probably an Israeli Palestinian, or the meowing of squabbling cats. There were two palm trees in front of the house. At the northern end there was a corner shop where an older couple worked. My aunt frequently bought milk and bread here, although they also increasingly used a modern supermarket that had opened a few streets away. Some houses further on, a Jewish East European shoemaker whom my uncle and my father knew ran his small workshop.

As mentioned, Ruszke and Abraham already had two grown-up children at the time I started coming there. Zwika was born in Poland in 1949, while Bracha was born in Tel Aviv. After his military service, which included serving in the harsh Yom Kippur war, Zwika followed his father into the porcelain and household goods business and assisted there until he took over after his father's death. He and his wife Leah, who had immigrated from Russia in the late 1970s, would soon have two children, Yaron and Eli.[60] Through Yaron and his wife Rinat, Leah and Zwika would later become grandparents of a four grandchildren. Eli also had a son.[61]

Bracha followed her mother's example. Body care, make-up and clothes were also her passion. She lived in my aunt's and uncle's old flat. Later, in keeping with the Zylbersztajn tradition, Bracha would be *broiges* with my mother and me because, in her opinion, there was still some "matter" to settle between my late uncle and my father after my father's death.[62] Zwika hesitantly followed suit, although he would still communicate with me, but things would never be the same. Every visit they would bring up the old quarrels. The last time all the Zylbersztajn first degree cousins came together under one roof was to honour my father's death, I think for the stone setting ceremony a year after his death. Again, death contributed to the fracturing of family bonds, in a

---

[60] Leah (née Liberman, 1951)
[61] The children Yaron and Rinat Zylbersztajns (Zlberstein) are Tal (born 2009), Itai and Maya (born 2012) and Ben (born 2020)
[62] *broiges,* jid harbour a grudge

way that was unimaginable, only years before. I think our fathers and mothers would not have allowed it.

These rifts in our family were particularly tragic for we were people who had already lost many due to the Shoah. My father and his brothers Abraham and Moisze had looked after each other after the war, helped each other and built up their respective livelihoods together. My father, who earned more in Germany, was able to assist his brothers, for the terrible price of having to stay behind and having to live in the land of their family's murderers.

The rifts that developed over the years may also have been caused by underlying mutual mistrust, the feeling of being taken advantage of; things that were not said became misunderstandings, the boundaries between friend(family) and foe blurred.

Uncle Moisze, his wife Chavtje and their daughter, my cousin Hannah lived near Abraham. Moisze was the epitome of a Jewish "macher," a go-getter, procuring all sorts of things for business, be it money to exchange, small goods or anything else. Their flat was smaller than Ruszke's and Abraham's, they both slept on a folding sofa in the living room, while their daughter Hannah (born 1955/5715), whose nickname was Hanni, had a tiny room to herself until she married. I found them to be nice and warm people. Moisze always had a friendly pleasant smile when he greeted us: "*Nu, wuz hart zih?*" (yid. now, what's the latest?). One of his favourites were tapes, possibly before that vinyl-records of "Jiddishe Komedianten", Yiddish speaking comedians, such as the Yiddish-Israeli duo Shimon Dzigan and Israel Schumacher.[63] When he gave me a present, he always began the delivery with the Yiddish words: "*Ich hob eppes ganz besonderes, eppes, eppes.*"(I have something special, something, something). Sometimes it would be empty casettes for music recordings, when I was lucky, it was a "zaiger", a watch, as it is called in Yiddish, usually some Japanese models, he got his hands on.

---

[63] Hear for example the programme with the same name of this book series: "The best of Dzigan & Shumacher" Zol Zain Shulem-Yiddish. *https://www.youtube.com/watch?v=OJt_CA857aU* (accessed 21.2.2025)

A visit to Chaftje and Moisze for lunch was obligatory, whenever we visited Israel, although Abraham and my father were a bit closer, possibly because of their shared experiences in the Shoah or due to Abraham's business. We would sit on the balcony at a table set in white. Chaftje served chicken or fish, accompanied by wine or something stronger, to the sound of loud and lively conversations in Yiddish.

After the death of her parents, Moisze died in 2001 (5761) and Chaftje the year before, Hannah said that she had also suffered greatly under her parents. Her father had hundreds of secrets, the kind that only people who had learnt the hard way not to trust anyone could have. She had to live in relative poverty for forty years until, after the death of both of her parents, she realised that the family owned more than she was aware of. Moisze didn't even trust his own daughter when it came to money matters, even when she was an adult and he a frail man. When she and her husband Awi Shushan (Awi is the son of Moroccan-Jewish refugees) were given the opportunity to buy a cheap flat in Jerusalem, Hanni asked no questions. Her twin sons, Idan and Itai, born in 1997 (5757), grew up there.

Due to the age difference of between ten and twenty years, my Israeli cousins and I never grew particularly close. My father also had an uncle and some cousins in Israel, but to me they were even more distant. Ruszke, Abraham, Moisze, Chaftje, Zwika, Bracha and Hanni were Tel Aviv to me.

20

German School

In 1982, the Lebanon War broke out, during which Israeli armed forces crossed into Lebanon to go after militarised Palestinian groups. Some of my German friends and their parents had questions about the conflict after my bar mitzvah trip in Israel or rather were more interested in the former than the celebrations I had just returned from. It put me, a 13-year-old boy, in a strange position where I had to account for what happened in that war and hold an opinion about it. Coming back to Munich was also the return of the problems at the Max.

Having failed year six due to very bad marks in two subjects, one of which was in Latin, I had to repeat that year. My new class not only had children who were one year younger, but where a certain Herr Doctor Ross reigned over the young souls.[64] Ross was a pedantic perfectionist who confused school with university, and even there, his behaviour may have raised eyebrows. Starting in September 1983 I was at Ross's mercy in Latin and in German Medieval History. The realm of Germany during those medieval times stretched far and wide, crusades occurred, and Jews were expelled and slaughtered in many German towns. Ross took pleasure in getting to grips with me and putting me on the spot

---

[64] Name changed.

regarding the legacies of popes and Christian emperors. Was it because I was Jewish? At least that thought crossed my mind, though, to be true, he was nasty to others too. Whilst Latin and History became increasingly abstract and irrelevant to me. Ross wasn't horrible to everyone. Those on his wavelength (in the higher years) were even taken to Latin championships between different schools at some point, which were exactly the kind of achievements the "Max" wished to brag about.

Then there were the "*Judenwitze*", jokes about Jews, that were deliberately being recited in front of me by other pupils. Ha, Ha, it's only a joke, we bet you don't mind, we don't mean it, Daniel. The art teacher, a man with a long beard, enjoyed "washing children's ears." It was a form of punishment. He would rub children's ears so hard with both his strong hands that it hurt. He found the degree of terror that it would cause amongst us children quite amusing. One of the PE-teachers was always in a bad mood, allowing for much speculation amongst us children as to the causes.

For most of my school career at the "Max", despite the way teachers saw me, my school mates had elected me as their class's representative. The reason was that I knew how to speak up against authority without fear, but this meant that I spoiled even more relationships with teachers, for example with our German teacher, who was quite the yelling commander type, after he handed out irrational punishment assignments to my classmates. Less contentious was the ethics teacher Herr Hollunderbäumer, literally Mister Elderberry-Tree, who taught philosophy and ethical virtues in overdramatic theatrical fashion. The much younger maths teacher was nicer. However, even there I was unable to keep up with his pace and demands and very soon lost track of what I was supposed to know. Looking back, it was partly the school itself, but also the fact that I had simply been thrown into this environment with not enough advance preparation and help. I do not think that I was ready for this kind of school.

On the other hand, we were certainly anything but angels. Over time we got used to the hard ways. So, when inexperienced teachers taught us without the firm grip of Germanic discipline, we took full advantage of it. There was a maths teacher who had no talent for leading the class or explaining things. He often carried on talking whilst the class had erupted before him into complete and utter chaos. Those sitting at the back of the classroom, including myself, couldn't hear a thing anymore. Another trainee teacher, who was talented and was even active in a band of the "*Neue Deutsche Welle*" genre at the time, also saw the worst of us. Anti-authoritarian and young as she was, the class in front of her took full advantage of her softness. Soon she was standing in front of this mob crying out of desperation and lacking the tools to get us back to listen. I liked her as a teacher because she had tried to make music with us with methods that were unconventional. It was closer to the way I was taught in primary school. But she didn't stand a chance here.

Alexander Jäger was my friend and classmate at Maximiliansgymnasium. He also lived in the Olympic Village, though in a different street. His parents divorced during that time and Alexander ended up moving and stayed with his mother in a small flat not far from the school. He also failed the hurdle to advance into the next year twice. His problem was not any lack of intellectual capacity, but most certainly the emotional turmoil at home. Another of my best friends in those years was Carl-Friedrich Laue. "Kalle's" mother had been diagnosed with terminal cancer. I got to know her when she drove Kalle to school and offered me lifts. She was lovely, very "motherly." At the time, I didn't understand why she always wore a headscarf. Carl-Friedrich's father, on the other hand, was a more distant figure and was no real comfort to Kalle after his mother had died. He was an ophthalmologist who was quite preoccupied with his work and himself after the death of his wife, at least it was perceived like that by my friend. Kalle and his older sister were often left in the care of their grandparents. In the end, on top of it all, their little dog also died.

The "Max" was not prepared to deal with such "problem children." What more is required than a little empathetic listening, a little bit of affection, advice and interest in a child, a little bit of humanity? But there was none of that at the school. The humanism that was preached there was mere theory from antiquity.

Alexander, Kalle and I were soon taking private lessons at an after-school tuition centre in a different part of Munich, not far from Rotkreuzplatz. Many of the children there came from families where parents either didn't have time for them or had no idea how the local school system worked, or they faced troubles at home, like divorce or other issues. Quite a few children also came from wealthier German families.

Instead of getting to grips with Latin, I started to smoke other people's cigarettes during the breaks. To be "real men", we smoked "extra fine" cigarettes, Dunhill, Benson and Hedges, or on the other end of the spectrum Gaulloise "for strong men," according to the advertisements of the time.

When even after-school tuition failed to make me pass year eight, I was old enough to understand that I needed to leave the "Max." I transferred to another academic school, the Oskar-von-Miller-Gymnasium, which was separated from the "Max" merely by a shared courtyard. This school, which centred on languages, including yet again Latin, was a completely different world. In terms of performance, my marks improved because the teachers were more humane. Nevertheless, there was never any interest or discussion about personal issues, my identity, religion, parents or any difficulties I encountered. I was now two years older than the rest of my class and the difference was particularly noticeable among the boys, most of whom were smaller in size and not yet streetwise. Had it not been for two girls, Katherina and Doris, girls being oftentimes a bit ahead, I would have despaired. The three of us were interested in wider world affairs and politically aware. Ronald Reagan and cruise missiles were amongst the many topics of the time, as was Chernobyl.

My emotional escape throughout these years remained music. Playing the piano and singing increasingly became a hobby at the "Max" and was encouraged by one of the music teachers there, Mr Niedermayer, one of the few people who was truly an inspiring and engaged teacher.

I sang in the school choir and gave it my all – amongst others we sang a scene from Handle's Jephta, "Heil sei Dir Dein Heldentum" – 'Hail Glorious Conqueror' at a university performance. It was at "Max" that I started playing and singing in front of the whole class for the first time, mostly improvised pieces. When I switched school, this continued. Herr Piehler, the music teacher there, an older and experienced man, even thought I was a rarely-seen talent and said so quite openly several times. No wonder I brought home the highest marks in music.

Still at the Max I had started to try to form a band. Latif Hamid, a boy with a background from India, Bangladesh or Pakistan from a single-parent household, and who was another of those who really struggled at the school, was one of those who soon became a member of the band. I think he played the bass guitar and loved The Police. I remember visiting him in his home and him playing "So Lonley" to me, which he wanted to play also in the band.

21

Love and Deaths

At the after-school tuition centre I got to meet "Kitty" – I no longer know her surname and maybe "Kitty" wasn't her real first name – a girl, half goth, half punk, with short leather miniskirts, black fishnet stockings, thick black leather jacket, red, sometimes black lipstick, mascara, and red-coloured hair.[65] Her outwardly self-confident, rebellious and creative demeanour cried out loudly for liberation and independence. I felt like that back then too – f*** the lot of them! Underneath the thick leather jacket, I discovered a loving and kind young woman. Kitty had a warm charisma, was basically completely uncomplicated, and the attraction was mutual. What was outwardly repulsive to some was an appeal to want to be loved. It didn't take long for the first impulsive kisses, one of those very first moments that you take with you on your journey through life. Kitty was even more remarkable than just that, for which I am grateful for the rest of my life.

Kitty came from a middle-class family and lived with her parents on the outskirts of Munich in a terraced house with a garden. However, there was another more troublesome side to this young woman. When I met her, she had started experimenting with drugs encouraged by a few "friends."

---

[65] Her surname could have been Fuchs, but I am no longer sure. It was a very long time ago.

Love and Deaths

On a date at her parents' house, I told her, naive, curious and love-blinded, that I wanted to try whatever she had too. It was LSD or perhaps even cocaine, I don't remember exactly. Kitty refused. "No, Daniel! I'm already addicted to it and it's not good. I don't want to get you involved. You're too good and too important to me." I was offended. Kitty and I saw each other less after that, as she forced herself to keep her distance from me – out of love, aware of her own ever-increasing problems. We lost sight of each other. A few years later somebody asked me if I knew that Kitty was dead. She had died of an overdose in Berlin. If the rumours are to be believed, she was in the end, so addicted and desperate, that she was forced to work as a prostitute to finance her habit. That may or may not be true, it is certainly possible. It's shocking. I had read "Zoo Station: The Story of Christiane F." Now I had a real-life personal connection to this grim world. I owe my health and perhaps my life to my encounter with this young woman. She was, if you like, the first angel who protected me from experiences that could have destroyed, damaged me or have shaped me forever. What's more, she was not the only young person to die early.

Sadly, it was Alexander Jäger who died a few years after that. After a night of heavy drinking, he is said to have swallowed some pills. He allegedly succumbed to a cardiac arrest while lying next to his girlfriend and a friend in his sleep. Up until his death Alex had a very troubled life, experimented with petty theft, got caught and was referred to a youth offender institute, whilst he also dropped out of the Max. He started drinking heavily and to listen to loud punk music like the Dead Kennedys, but also loved Frankie Goes to Hollywood. In the phase that I still knew him, he was always on the search for some excitement beyond the misery surrounding him and to be in control of partially forbidden things, only too loose ever more control, after he got caught and started damaging his health.

Alexander and Kitty remained a personal warning to me. But as always, it didn't have to be that way. Where was counselling, care, help and empathy, especially in wealthy Munich, the capital of Bavaria? With her intelligence and good nature, Kitty could be the missing doctor, social worker or teacher, or Alex the missing manager or business owner.

22

Münchner Freiheiten – Munich Freedoms

Around 1982 a few of us boys bunked some classes, it must have been either a double PE or double Latin-session and we escaped to Café Münchner Freiheit opposite our school across Leopoldstraße, next to the public transport station. "Münchner Freiheit", where we had hot chocolate or maybe a small breakfast is the name of a place in Munich. Translated it literally means "Munich Freedom."

Was it time to rebel? In 1983, I practically moved out of my parents' flat and into a "hobby room" in the Olympic Village. The room, meant as an extension to any of the apartments for hobbies or other pastimes, was self-sufficient and a few blocks away from my parents' home. It had a toilet and shower, but no cooking facilities. There was only a small window to the outside with a frosted glass pane. There was neither a doorbell nor a telephone (both of which I would only organise years later). There were some office rooms next door. One was frequented by a woman who was always in a bad mood and looking to cause trouble. She refused to improve the appearance of the corridor so that she could scuff the concrete surface to her heart's content with her trolley. There was also a room that served as storage for an antiques dealer, where he sometimes spent the night, even though there was no toilet there. Despite these circumstances, and initially piles of boxes of stuff that would be sent on to my uncle and other junk in the room, this hobby room finally gave me much needed distance and reprieve from Mum and Dad. The spirit of freedom was also part of the music culture of the time; "Come on Eileen" by Dexys Midnight Runners, and the songs of the band Culture Club particularly expressed that new looseness, breaking of norms, positivity and longing for freedom, personal or otherwise (we were still in the age of the Iron Curtain).

I was looking for normal freedoms. To name but one oddity, my parents felt for a long time entitled to meticulously search my belongings well into my adulthood. I needed distance for privacy and without it I would have suffocated. In later group therapy with other people from the "Second Generation," the adult children of survivors of the Shoah, I heard that others has experienced similar behaviours. Not all survivors behaved like this, but enough to mark it as a significant phenomenon. It was mostly about the loss of understanding of "normal" boundaries.

What did I do with that freedom in this hobby room? Modest and normal teenage behaviour, such as listening to loud music. Another freedom was going out in the evenings. My parents no longer had any clue what I was up to in the evening. In the beginning it was trendy cafés, like Café Reitschule on the edge of Munich's large city park English Garden, where in the 1980s the chic, well-heeled Munich teens used to sit together and sip drinks. After that, more and more people went to an indie club called Parabel, incidentally not far from Café Reitschule, perhaps a 15-minute walk.[66] The club was situated in the basement of a 19th century building and the DJs played a mishmash of post-punk, New German Wave, New Wave and Goth, Depeche Mode, Frankie Goes to Hollywood, Ideal, Sex Pistols, The Pogues, Yazoo, Soft Cell, Heaven 17, Anne Clark, and Falco. Many of these songs had a melodramatic and dark or nihilistic theme to them. There were also songs with extremely

---

[66] See https://www.muenchenwiki.de/wiki/Parabel, accessed 21.10.2023

strange lyrics. D.A.F.s "Tanz den Mussolini, tanz den Jesus Christ, tanz den Adolf Hitler," I thought was just macabre and had crossed the norms for acceptable lyrics I was prepared to dance to.

Reminders of the Third Reich were omnipresent in Munich in any case, be it in that club when it played that track, or Odeonsplatz, or Königsplatz, where Hitler once had appeared. Once we were chased through the streets of Schwabing near the Parabel Club by a troop of contemporary German neo-Nazis around midnight. While I escaped with others due to better knowledge of the local street corners, my friend Alex got caught up and claimed to have exchanged fists and kicks with them, as he proudly recounted later.

This second life at night also changed my appearance. I had my hair cut short on the sides and wore long, slicked-back top hair. We acted beyond our real age, smoked cigars and consumed certainly too much beer. Alexander and Carl-Friedrich were often with me during these nightly excursions, but I trumped them by going more often and to a greater variety of night clubs. I was only 15 years of age, my only limitation was having enough money, but I would rather drink water, than miss out.

After the Parabel came the Mirage, then the Park-Cafe and, as I will report later, finally the P1, Munich's top night club, frequented by the rich and famous. If I am honest, I am speaking with hindsight, there was always something dark and heavy about Munich nightlife, despite the amazing sounds that were booming out of the speakers, from Prince, Sheila-E, Janet Jackson, to Bronski Beat and sometimes AC/DC.[67]

This nightclubbing society was a gathering of people on the run from daytime society. In this country it was also an escape from being too German, from German history, from German parents or grandparents, from those who had started the Second World War. I once heard

---

[67] I understand others flogged to Punk, Goth and Rock club called the Crash. It did not pull me in. I preferred those venues that decisively followed the club scenes of places like London and New York.

that they have clubs like that in Beirut, a city where people are also on the run from social conformity and the memories of war or the fear of the next.[68] In these Munich clubs I was also searching for the, yet to be discovered, meaning of life, sometimes in the lyrics of one or the other song or in between the cold, drunk or drugged false, proud faces that often hid an only too human fear behind meaningless small talk. The hot love some made in the toilets was as bizarre as the rest. Was I freer as a teenager because I allowed myself to enter this world earlier than it was intended? Munich, that little sometimes a touch provincial alpine metropolis, became part of a bigger world, with sounds and visitors from New York, London, Tokyo, LA – places around the musical corner.

Looking back, it constituted a far too early introduction to that superficial world devoid of meaning, which basically led nowhere, and yet it was of course exciting. The postwar children who had grown up in a now relatively safe and well to do city, without war, afforded the luxury to waste their energy and abilities in clubs like these. I was one of these children, and yet, I think it had to be that way.

Music gigs were another novelty in my life. Queen was one of the bands I saw, alongside my friend Alex. Some guy behind me grabbed my buttocks, another first experience. I turned around and protested loudly and that put an end to it. On the next day we had a Latin test, for which at least I had left the Queen concert "early." I still got an F, despite the "sacrifice." It's an F as in Freddy. My Latin of the day is forgotten now, but the memory of seeing the late Freddy Mercury live has stayed with me. Alexander stayed for the full length of the concert and failed the Latin test in the same way. On another occasion I saw Tina Turner in the Munich Olympic Hall, singing the classics Proud Mary, Private Dancer and It's only Love. Through a telephone campaign I won some free tickets to a music venue (Alabama Hall). Luckily, the youngish

---

[68] See Meret Michel & Traboulsi, Tanya: Partying like there is no tomorrow in Beirut. In NZZ 29.07.2024, *https://www.nzz.ch/english/in-beirut-parties-continue-despite-the-threat-of-war-ld.1841288*, accessed 21.10.2024.

co-ordinator of the venue took a liking to me. Why, I am not quite sure, but she kept treating me to free guest tickets. Was it because of my Jewish name? I did not care, as by virtue of this free access I was able to see a few bands of the day like The Styles Council, the unforgettable Sade Adu, Shakatak, Dead Kennedys, The Pogues, and other bands whose names I have forgotten. There were also concerts in the Olympic Stadium – the Rolling Stones, Bruce Springsteen, Joan Baez, Santana. We were able to gain free entry there too, as we had figured out how to enter through a hole under the fence of the Olympic Stadium hidden by bushes. I also sometimes went on my own to the Munich jazz club "Die Unterfahrt", which had been the home of jazz in Munich since the late 1970s, to learn from and observe the musicians there.

It wasn't all a time of senseless enjoyment. Amid the music and the search for meaning, my identity as a Jewish person kept cropping up, sometimes in a strange disguise. A friend of a friend knew the son of the then head of the German Republican Party, Franz Schönhuber. The Republicans were a far-right party not much dissimilar to the later AFD. Schönhuber was the former head of the Munich daily newspaper *tz* and of the Bavarian Journalists' Association. But as a young man it wasn't positions like that he was after. He had voluntarily joined the notorious German Waffen SS, amongst the worst of the Third Reich Nazis. Now, in retirement, he proudly bragged about this past, finding the courage to say it hadn't been all bad. "I Was There" was the title of his autobiography and in that spirit he founded the Republican Party for like-minded Germans. Anyone who says that Germany now has a problem with the resurgence of the far right and points to areas of East Germany must not forget what had happened in West Germany back then. Schönhuber was just the latest reincarnation of the far right in the 1980s. Back in the 1970s the German far-right NPD had already cropped up in places. But back to Schönhuber. I ended up twice in the Munich apartment of this former and unrepentant member of the vile Nazi murder squad. Why? We were visiting his son Florian! My friends assured me the boy was OK. That may have been quite true, a son doesn't have to be quite like his father. I met once, decades later, when I was already a journalist in the UK, the son and grandson of the British Fascist, Oswald Mosley. His son was a committed anti-fascist, and his grandson was dating a Brazilian Woman of Colour at the time.

Schönhuber's apartment was close to the Bavarian state parliament and not far from a wall where the words "*Nie Wieder Krieg*" (Never Again War) had been written in huge letters for several years during the 1970s. In Florian's room, which had a separate entrance, a Pink Floyd poster hung on the white wall next to an electric guitar, and from there a second door led into the spacious main flat. I had a queasy feeling, as if I was doing something forbidden. It also felt like some kind of triumph that I was in this place, and yet it meant nothing, the words of the graffiti had still been too small to prevent the rise and popularity of the father of this young man I was visiting. Schönhuber made a bit of noise for a few years, but it didn't take long, and he disappeared as quickly as he had risen. May it remain like this.

It was during this time that I also organised a "legendary" party (judged from the fact that people still talk about it today decades later) in my hobby room. My friends and I had advertised it so well amongst the school communities that the flow of teenagers that tried to press themselves into the small room was unending. Alex was DJ, my father even baked pizzas, thinking it would be a different kind of party. But there were lots of teens, there was lots of alcohol, there was vomit and urine in the hallways, and the neighbours were up in arms. Wanting to be the coolest kid in town, we certainly convinced many. However, by ten in the evening the arrival of the police and a slap in my face from my Mum ended the party. Demanding freedom and learning how to deal with it can be a tough business.

23

Mates

At this point I have to mention three special friends. They are Gregor Kollmar, Christian Haverkampf and Kai Kulp. Like me, they all grew up in the Olympic Village in Straßbergerstrasse and they were all extremely important friends to me, although they were hardly friends with each other, but rather each one with me individually.

Kai was was the image of nice boy from the neighbourhood, though always ready to be part of any naughty misadventure. One day, we had plans to take the mickey of students who lived in the Olympic Village's student quarters. The small houses in which they live are right opposite each other. Their front doors open inwards. So the plan was to tie the door handles of two apartments opposite each other tightly together with a rope and then to ring the doorbell on both sides. The students tried to open the doors but couldn't, and somehow it seemed to them like somebody was pulling the other way. Desperately they would emerge on their terraces one level up and seeing what the matter was, asking us to please remove the ropes. It was great fun, and we were probably about ten or eleven years old at the time. Kai and I also modified our bikes with paint and all sorts of bits and bobs, such as extra strong lights and the like, and then we would cruise around the Olympic Park like kings of the road. Kai was also the first to have a home computer amongst my friends. We spent long evenings playing silly games like "Frogger" and "Commodore Olympics." Kai's father was an IT expert at Siemens, his mother a bank clerk. However, she quit her job when Kai was about 13 to open a boutique, first in the Olympic Village and later in Neuperlach, where Kai's father worked. With his parents always busy, Kai was often left at home alone after school and we would frequently spend time together because of that. Kai was my best mate for a long time, someone I could rely on all my life. Kai also was the tallest boy I knew. Growing up, he would measure over two metres. Just as my parents complained about my legs, his parents found the medical equivalent expert concerning growth issues and the question arose whether to give Kai some drug therapy to restrict his growth. Kai also opposed this with vigour. We remained close friends throughout, although Kai didn't go along on most of my nightlife excursions.

Kai's mother was there for me when things didn't work out between my father and me. In the end, my mother no longer trusted her and also Christian Haverkampf's mother, another friend in the Olympic village, because for a while they knew more about me than she and my father did. This went against the unspoken law of not getting too close to non-Jewish Germans, and yet what could I do?

Christian Haverkampf lived in Nadistraße in the Olympic Village. His father Karl was one of the GPs of the Olympic village and our family doctor. Christian's mother, Elisabeth, became a kind of emergency mother figure for me in the 1980s, again when arguments with my parents, above all my father, strangled me. I don't know what Elisabeth knew or suspected, but she was training to be a psychoanalyst at the time and was open-minded in any case. The Haverkampfs were among the few people in the Olympic Village whom I, as a child of Jewish parents, was most likely to trust and by whom I was most likely to be understood. They were also the ones who understood my father best, not only because Karl had an idea of what my father had gone through, but because he had seen his medical records.

Elisabeth herself had a Jewish uncle in Israel. There is a lot I must thank the family for during my younger years, especially the fact that I could always ring their door, whether I came at a good time or at a bad time. Unfortunately, Christian's parents couldn't use their wisdom and knowledge to save their marriage. Elisabeth and Karl separated years later in a protracted and painful divorce. However, there were happy moments too. Elisabeth always organised an "after-party" with friends on the second Christmas Eve and I usually attended and frequently played the piano. My parents were always invited, but never came.

The Haverkampfs were not the only parents of my friends who invited my Mum and Dad to certain family celebrations or other joint activities, but my parents habitually declined.

Years later, Christian converted to liberal Judaism after his marriage to a Jewish-Swiss woman (whose parents were also survivors of the Shoah). As a result, he changed his name to Jonathan. Unfortunately, this marriage did not last. Today he lives with his second wife in Dublin.

Gregor Kollmar I had known since primary school. He was always cheeky and bright and, as his mum assured me, a passionate challenger. Gregor had been diabetic since birth. It wasn't until Gregor was older that I learnt that he had undergone several operations as a child. He wore thick glasses and kept his hair long. I would often visit Kai and Gregor one after the other, as they didn't live far from each other. One of the key things Gregor and I did was further experimenting with music. There are probably recordings on music cassettes lying around somewhere, with Gregor and myself copying some of the performers of Gregor's unusual music tastes, which included Klaus Nomi, a now deceased German New Wave singer who celebrated success as a countertenor, or Nina Hagen, the classically trained singer who fled East Germany and constantly reinvented herself in the freedom of the West. Gregor's parents were another couple who were divorcing at the time of our youth. Eva, Gregor's mother, became the third "emergency mother figure" for me. She was a warm, loving woman from whom Gregor often wanted to free himself in his moments of involuntary dependence due to his condition. But truly, he could not have asked for a more dedicated mother. Gregor's brother Richard, who was a few years older, was soon to live in the USA. There he would marry a Jewish colleague, who had moved to the USA from Azerbaijan. So at least two of my friends or their families came very close to Judaism, while Kai always tried his best to understand things as well as he could.

I was lucky to have these three friends and their families in my life at that time.

24

On the Piano

From the start of my time at Maximiliansgymnasium and then as I progressed through puberty, amid my alleged and certified incompetence at school and additional social and cultural insecurities, it became increasingly important to have a grounding place for my emotions and thoughts. The place for this was not only the aforementioned "hobby room," where I could live out my fantasies and lock the door, but also my parents' living room because it held our piano. Whenever my parents went out and were away, for example on their regular walks through the Olympic Park or while shopping, I would take the opportunity and play and experiment with the piano for hours. Only our budgerigar, whose birdcage stood next to the piano, would listen in, often even sitting on the instrument or my shoulder, fluffing itself up and chattering along to the sounds. At first, I was attracted by Yiddish melodies and old gospel songs such as "Tumbalalaika," "Belz," "Go down Moses" and "Elijah Rock." Gradually it became more freely played meditations. When I was about 15, I started to build up a repertoire. It consisted of basic schemes around which I would improvise. I also began to experiment with my voice and started writing lyrics. In 1985, I made a 40-minute recording of various songs. I duplicated it on tape and gave it to several friends. Some can still remember that today. One recording has survived to this

On the Piano

day – not my best – including the song called "Fotomodel", about a model who always has to smile for her work. Was there a deeper meaning here? Did I always have to put up a smiley face in front of my parents? My problems were never real problems, my father repeatedly claimed dismissively. In his opinion, I had nothing to complain about in life, only reasons to laugh.

Another typical song of this time is "1985", as I call it today. It is a composition that was inspired by listening to Keith Jarrett. It was certainly not on the level of the famous Jazz Pianist, but still an important step in my musical development.[69] "1985" began with a fast chord sequence before drifting into a melodramatic, quieter musical journey and picking up speed at the end. It was pieces of this kind that I soon played frequently in front of spellbound audiences, such as in front of my school classes, at parties, Christmas celebrations or at the Jewish youth club (see later). All I needed now was an experienced and good teacher and creative and supportive environment to help me climb further, push me to learn and improve. I understood that.

It came initially as a surprise that many people told me that they really liked the material I had come up with. Encouraged by this, I decided to revisit the idea of a band. It wasn't difficult to get a rehearsal room at the school in the afternoon. At Maximilliansgymnasium, there were others who played music, one of whom turned into a city legend decades later: Titus Waldenfels.[70] He was two or three years older and at the time he and a few others played the repertoire of rock songs that young people demanded at festivals, such as Deep Purple, Santana and the like. It would not be until 1986 that my band made its debut, and it was the first and last appearance at the Oskar-von-Miller Gymnasium summer festival. Together with a saxophonist, a second keyboarder, a drummer and two backing singers, we bravely presented ourselves to

---

[69] "1985" can be heard here via the Internet https://soundcloud.com/zylbersztajn/1985-1 The more experimental photo model song, still rather undeveloped in this recording, can be found here https://soundcloud.com/zylbersztajn/fotomodel-1985

[70] Titus' current website is https://titus-waldenfels.de/ (retrieved 18/12/2022)

119

the audience. It wasn't ideal, the drummer, just like the two female back vocal singers, could only come to one single rehearsal, but I insisted we push through regardless. We had sought also for a bassist and guitarist, but we couldn't find anyone quickly enough. Except for one song we performed that was by somebody else (Billy Idol's "*Eyes without a Face*"), all had been written by me, although the gig would not have been possible in that form without the help of the others. The highlight was the song "That's Our World", of which a rehearsal recording has survived to this day. I would place it somewhere between two popular bands of the time, "Super Tramp" and "Ultravox", with relatively simple lyrics.[71]

I don't want to claim that these songs or our skills were perfect back then. But I believe they were a solid and sincere attempt on my part to introduce myself as a singer and songwriter, with more to come, given a chance. I was pretty serious about it all and it was a strong part of my identity. So serious that it became a prerequisite for my next step.

That's my life,
that's our world,
these are the people,
can't you tell me,
if you want to live here forever?

Daniel Zylbersztajn-Lewandowski, That's my life (1985)

---

[71] That's our World" 1986 Rehearsal recording https://soundcloud.com/zylbersztajn/thats-our-world

25

Jewish Awakening

1983 was a busy year in many ways for me. One thing I started back then was to attend the meetings of the ZJD (Zionist Youth of Germany) in Munich. Despite its name, the youth club had hardly any political character but was simply the only Jewish youth club that existed in Munich at that time.

After all the missed and failed opportunities due to my father's inaction, here I was in control, and I attended whenever I could. Back then, the meeting point of ZJD-Munich was in the then new Jewish cultural centre off Prinzregentenstraße. Geographically that was a long way from the Olympic Village where we lived, but a new underground line made the trip a little less dramatic. The centre was situated in a secluded building. The entrance was secured by cameras and it was always guarded. A green and white police car was also parked in the courtyard or in front of the entrance. All the windows were shatter-proof and had special security curtains for protection in the event of a bomb attack. This potential vulnerability and need for such protection at gatherings was the norm for Jewish life in Germany, I never knew it any other way, and it is still like that in many countries today. Jewish people, overall, a small minority in most countries except in Israel, are and remain vulnerable.

Zol Zayn Shulem II: Faroys

The centre staged Jewish themed public seminars and concerts. For our small group of Jewish teenagers there were opportunities to discuss topics such as Germany, racism, the Bavarian right-wing Republicans, hatred of Jews and antisemitism, Israel and Jewish people in the Soviet Union, and Israeli politics. Some of us started dating each other. I still remember some of the people I was closer too back then. The older youths also frequented the *Shalom Night Club*, which had been opened by the Israeli folk singer Motke Dagan, though its hey days were in the 1970s when many Israelis such as Dagan were received with cultural benevolence. Kalmon Hener, the Reichert Brothers, Vivian Kanner, Paul Günczler, Deborah Stobnitzer and Avi Blumenfeld – all without exception were children of survivors of the Shoah, or less often, their grandchildren. Rarer in those days were young people whose parents had moved to Germany from Israel and unlike today there were not yet large numbers of Jewish immigrants from (former) Soviet Union states. Only around a third of the Jewish youngsters of the 1980s that I knew continued to live in Germany as adults. They largely moved to Israel, the USA or Great Britain. At the time, many adults, German and Jewish alike, hoped that we would become Germany's new confident Jewish generation. Some did, but not as many as there could have been.

At ZJD I gave more small piano concerts in front of others in my typical improvisation style, often at the request of my new Jewish friends. I was confided many years later that I was the talk of some of the girls back then. I must have had my head somewhere else, or they were too shy, because I didn't notice much of it.

When the ZJD told me that we could travel to Israel for a whole month in the summer together with other German-Jewish young people to explore and familiarise ourselves with the country, I was immediately hooked. Of course, my parents also thought it was a good idea. Whilst I hardly needed an introduction to Israel, a trip together with other teens through the best of Israel, who could say no? The trip delivered nothing less than promised. We travelled through all parts of the country from the upmost South to North and from West to East in an old bus with sliding windows, and had fun together, sang, learnt, visited the old town and Kotel (Holy Wall) in Jerusalem, inspected Haifa, Acre, Tiberias, the Golan, the Dead Sea, climbed to Masada, and admired the stalactite cave of Rosh-ha-Nikra at the border to Lebanon, and watched the Red Sea at Eilat. Towards the end of the trip, when we stayed in a hotel in Eilat, I made the acquaintance of a young Israeli woman of my age, Yamit Zahavi, at the swimming pool.[72] Yamit was of Sephardic-Jewish background. Her parents had emigrated to Israel from Turkey. Yamit had shoulder-length golden-blonde hair in a pageboy cut and an athletic figure. I had my hair short on the sides with highlights and in those days was a slimmer version of my older self. Many people at the time compared me to a singer from the band "Duran Duran."

Yamit and I fell for each other, although nothing much happened apart from the promise to see each other again and we agreed to write to each other. I have to confess in typical teenage fashion, I met another girl, Daphne Klein, who was on a visit from Australia, on the beach in Tel Aviv a few days later.[73] We spent a romantic evening in front of the waves near the marina and watched the sunset. Time was short. Within the blink of an eye, Daphne was back in Sydney, Yamit back in Haifa and I was back in Munich. Letters and photos from both young ladies reached me. In fact, Daphne continued to send me letters long after her teenage years, so many that even my father remarked that she must be a nice Jewish girl that I ought to go after. Almost 15 years later, I met Daphne in London, then travelling through Europe. She had contacted me, met me in a bar near Piccadilly Circus and wanted to know if there was a chance at all to finally try it together. There wasn't – in fact I had married the year or so before.

After receiving letters and photos from Yamit, I begged my parents to allow me to fly to Israel in the winter to visit her. I gambled on the hope of my parents that I would eventually move to Israel. Of course they agreed, but convincing my parents had been the lesser part of my

---

[72] Name changed.
[73] Name changed.

problems because it turned out to be a nightmare trip. Yamit was well informed about me coming, and we also phoned, and I kept my promise, but when I called her from my aunt and uncle's flat in Tel Aviv, she suddenly seemed strangely cold rather than excited. When I arrived in Haifa by train the next day, I soon realised why. She had been just as cheeky as I was, and, in typical modern teenager fashion, had gotten herself a brand-new boyfriend and, important and impressive at that age, a boyfriend "with a car." It may have been the smallest of cars, a tiny Fiat, but I was told in no uncertain words that I was yesterday's news. I spent a painful day in the small flat of Yamit's parents, who felt sorry for me and disapproved of the conduct of their daughter, but likewise knew they couldn't do anything about it. Yamit even went as far as introducing her new flame to me.

In Eilat at the time oft he trip in Israel when I met Yamit.

With a broken heart and humiliated, I left Haifa the next day and surprised my aunt and uncle, who now had no choice but to put up with for the rest of the two weeks I had left in Israel.

I spent my days visiting my uncle's shop and wandering around Dizengoff Street and the old heart of Tel Aviv. The smells, the humid air, the city's cats and the building style, the Yiddish of my family, my aunts and uncles and cousins, all of this would always have something appealing and familiar for me, given my now frequent visits there.

The country and its people gave me a feeling of a second home that I had never been able to find in Munich. In many regards, at my Aunts and Uncles I found a world that was identical to the home my parents had created, with similar food and fashion tastes. The only other place that evokes similar emotions are the Netherlands. However, at the same time, Israel was also a bit foreign, and it was this foreignness that inspired my curiosity and eagerness, wondering whether Israel could perhaps become my actual home after all. During my group trip in the previous summer, we had already been told that it was possible to go to school in Israel in special boarding schools run by the Jewish Agency (Aliyat-Ha-Noar).[74] In Munich, I was two years behind in school and damaged by the Bavarian academic secondary school system, or at least the one of the Maximillians Gymnasium. I started to wonder if a school in Israel would be right up my street.

Upon my return to Munich, I began to research that option more deeply. Amongst others, I hoped to finally acquire all the knowledge I had missed out on regarding Jewish religion and culture. A representative of Aliyat-ha-Noar from Frankfurt visited my parents and met me to discuss the prospects of that education. He showed us a few photos of a school he had in mind and claimed that this particular school, Alonei Yitzhak, which is located between Tel Aviv and Haifa, was the best option for me. I didn't care one way or another but had one solemn condition which I

---

[74] Aliyat ha Noar is the Zionist youth organisation that coordinates the education and training of Jewish children in Israel.

made absolutely clear in unmistakable language. Only a school where I could further build on my music skills and where I could take A-Levels in music would be acceptable. I can't say if there were other discussions between the delegate and my parents, where they agreed on other things.

The "*shaliach*", the German envoy of the Aliyat-ha-Noar recited marvellous things. A music centre had just opened at Alonei Itzhak. It was my only and best choice. The deal was done, not least because it was what my parents had in mind. My father hoped that this step would ensure "that I wouldn't assimilate too much with the non-Jewish Germans."[75] He thought it was a losing game in any case, because of the family name and because antisemitism was deeply embedded in German society, as he saw it.[76] After all, he had history to prove it. Hadn't German Jews once assimilated and adopted the German way of life? And look what came of that! German Jews were murdered just like those from Poland.[77] Now I was to emigrate to Israel, as he himself felt no longer able to. He said he had gotten used too much to the "German way of life." It was an incredible way to look at his family and his son. He, who always felt foreign in Munich, had totally overlooked the fact that this city was almost everything I had ever known, was my birthplace. Not only that, but I was doubly entitled to live there as a German Jew and Munich resident on the account of the family of his wife, the Lewandowski family. I know that my father also believed that I was up to no good in Germany and, as I mentioned already, was totally dismissive of my musical interest, which displeased him. The fact that I wanted to go to Israel was a heaven-sent opportunity as far as he was concerned. I did not see all of that. If you asked me, I was sure that the move to Israel was the completion of my drive to independence, which had started when I stepped out of the window in the Netherlands, later moved into the hobby room, and now I was leaving home altogether at 15.

---

[75] See Zylbersztajn (1995), p. 18
[76] Ibid.
[77] Ibid. p.19

26

Welcome to the Hotel California!

One day in late September 1986 the time had come. My mum stood at Munich Riem Airport with tears in her eyes. "Daniel take care of yourself!" she managed to utter. I probably laughed bravely with a "Yes, yes" and pretended it was all but nothing so as not to upset her or allow my emotions to come to the surface. Later, passing through security and now all by myself, a few tears still came anyway and uninvited. I had left my parents' home and travelled into the relative known unknown, trusting in full the promises of the Aliyat-ha-Noar's representative and my own experiences in previous years.

A long stay for education abroad was rather unusual for most young people in the 1980s, certainly amongst my circle of friends. Most of my friends stayed at home until they were about 19 (after that, they either did military service, social service or went to university). The only exception was my friend Christian Haverkampf, who was now studying at Dartmouth, USA, after he too had been put into the category of the allegedly incompetent by Maximilliansgymanasium (Christian qualified later as a medical doctor and became a lawyer and psychotherapist – so much for being declared incompetent by the teachers at the Max, who were probably incompetent as pedagogical professionals to start with).

Zol Zayn Shulem II: Faroys

It was already dark when I arrived at Israel's Ben Gurion airport. Back then, still in the old airport building, with the reception outside, Alonei Yitzhak's slightly corpulent delivery driver, whom everyone only knew as Moshe, was waiting in the hazy heat of the Israeli September with the school's white Mercedes van. On previous arrivals, Zwika, my cousin, had been there in his place and would drive us to Tel Aviv in his silver Subaru, his pride and joy.

"Daniel?" asked Moshe. "Alonei Yitzhak?" "Yes!" Moshe could barely speak English, let alone German, but he was familiar with a few basic words of Yiddish. I put my suitcase in his van and Moshe started driving through the empty streets leaving behind the Tel Aviv I knew so well. We drove on the motorway northwards for quite a long time.

"Where on earth was this school?" I asked myself, as we moved further and further away from Tel Aviv. From my journey last year, I was familiar with Wingate, the sports academy that was on the way, and which we now also drove past. Eventually he turned off before the town of Hadera, continued along small country roads to a place called Pardes Hanna and drove through its famous tree alleys, and then, at a lonely crossroads surrounded by dark fields, he turned right and drove along a long, straight, unlit road towards the village of Givat Ada, passing through nothing but agricultural fields. Moshe switched on the main beam and accelerated the car. So far, I had only seen the school on a few photos; it was many years before the age of Google, where almost everything geographical can be checked quickly.

It turned out that Alonei Yitzhak was close to Zichron Yakov, where the Jewish-British philanthropist Sir Moses Montefiori had once founded a winery, according to the local tourist guides, and equally close (this we had not been told) to the Palestinian-Israeli village of Kafr Qara, at that time not yet separated from the Jewish areas that encompassed Alonei Yitzhak and the village Givat Ada through the A6 motorway (constructed from the 1990s onwards). Directly in front of the school, on the other side of the access road, there was a small nature reserve. I spotted avocado trees, banana palms and orange plantations. At the end of the road, behind the school, one would reach Kfar Glickson kibbutz within three minutes, from, where you could still hear the clanking noises from the cows' sheds day in, day out. I don't think these poor animals ever had any exercise back then.

Givat Ada, the village on the opposite side, had hardly developed any new infrastructure since the late 1950s. There were no more than a few grocery shops, a terrible barber (he almost shaved me bald once), but extraordinarily there were two banks, a post office, a few street cafés, snack bars and a swimming pool in the village (today nearby Benyamina and Givat Ada form one municipality).

Just before Kibbutz Kfar Glickson we entered the boarding school area. I checked out the surroundings and I mistakenly thought that the many small villas were the young people's accommodation. However, they were only the teachers' and carers' houses. At the very end of the path, there was a two-storey house from the 1960s in shabby unpolished condition – by German standards – because it looked bare and unfinished. Inside, the light bulbs had no lampshades, the orange curtains were relics from the early 1970s. Curious glances fell on me as I entered. I was taken to a room.

Everything I had expected and dreamed of about my Israeli school had fallen into the deepest abyss. I shrank back from the repulsive odour of others' sweat, and the shock that I was about to share my room with three other boys. "Why didn't anyone say anything about this?" I screamed inwardly at myself. Why on earth did we not travel to Israel first to inspect the school? Towels hung over plastic chairs and cheap white trainers could be seen under the beds. The furnishings were spartan and also indicated that they were from the early 1970s, a wardrobe made from pressed wood, a simple bed with a cheap mattress and a blanket. Pictures of topless female singers hung all over the room, Samantha Fox, Madonna, Pamela Anderson. I made my bed, an ugly tubular steel frame, and I suspected that neither the blanket nor the mattress had been freshly washed and cleaned. Next to the bed was a scratched desk, also made of pressed wood, which had to be shared by two teenagers.

Zol Zayn Shulem II: Faroys

The neon lamps in this compact construction were blinding at night if you went to bed before the others. In the centre of the room, a waist-height wall divided the room into two areas. Each one was for two boys. Everything was cramped. The floor was made of stone tiles and there was no heating or air conditioning. Then I went into the bare, relatively dirty and wet communal bathroom, which served over 20 boys. The girls' were upstairs. Here I brushed my teeth and went to the toilet. I came to realise that none of the doors could be locked for privacy, and the toilet paper was cheap and rough.

Soon I was lying in bed in a dark room with my eyes wide open. I can't remember any conversations that evening, I probably arrived after the enforced night's rest had begun, or I was simply completely exhausted. Music was blaring from one of the rooms, a male voice with a strong Israeli accent was singing slightly out of tune "Welcome to the Hotel Californja, la la la la", doors kept slamming open and there were voices I couldn't understand. Where on earth had I ended up? Where was the promise of a modern boarding school? And I was supposed to stay here for at least three years? Something was completely wrong here.

"*Bokertov! Lakum Chevre!*" – Good morning, get up people! – the group housekeeper Alisa woke us up the next morning at around 7.00 am. I soon would welcome her typical morning round with little approval. Months later, when I and my roommate refused to get out of bed straight away, Alisa punished us by pouring a bucket of water over each of our beds.

Alisa was about 40 years old, with thick horn-rimmed glasses and shoulder-length hair. She was a habitual smoker, one cigarette after another, never mind she did so in front of the kids, and she spoke with a predictable deep voice. Each year group was put under the supervision of one of these "em habeit", which translates as house mothers. They were responsible for ensuring that we cleaned the house properly, that the beds were orderly made, and for the collection and distribution of laundry. Each class also had an assigned Madrih, a youth-worker.

Now in the morning the same bad music as last night was remerging, pop songs which were quite uncool in Munich. Samantha Fox seemed to be a favourite: "Touch me, touch me, I wanna feel your body!" Devastated, alone in my misery and confused as to what I was to do, barely aware of the people in my room, I got dressed and left the building, cautiously following wherever the others were heading, hopefully to the dining hall. What would breakfast be like?

Now in full day light I could see all the young people around me. They looked strange, not because they were mostly Israelis, but because they were far removed from any fashionable style that I was familiar with and could understand. Some looked unkempt. "Hey, how arrre youuu do'ing?" some of the boys asked me in broken English, while dozens of eyes scrutinised me. A newcomer! The first judgements soon followed. I was a "homo", they argued. In complete contrast to today's open and LGBTQIA+ communities celebrating the freedoms of Tel Aviv, and figures like Dana International, who rose to fame in the 1990s due to the Eurovision Song Contest, the 1980s in Israel seemed to be still stuck in the Stone Age. Other people began to label my appearance as "punkist." They had no real understanding of what a punk was, it was simply a term to express their inability to place my different appearance. I looked unfamiliar to them with my blond highlights and my gelled short hair and the clothes that in Germany were nothing unusual. In Israel however, such clothing and appearance lay outside the norm, and doubly so in this school far from the metropolitan centres of Haifa, Jerusalem and above all Tel Aviv. That's why I was now "Homo Pankist!" Somebody with a strong accent asked me in English: "From wherrr arrre you frrrom?" I was probably still smiling in a shy and friendly way, unsure who would be friend or foe. "Germany! I answered. "Ichtn-bitn-baten" was the echoed response – imitating German, as it sounds to Israelis. Was I supposed to find that funny or were they laughing at me?

Breakfast consisted of tea served in hard plastic cups, the plates were also plastic, some with cut marks. There was some kind of scrambled egg dish, jam and a fatty chocolate paste they made themselves in the kitchen. In the dining hall, which was in a building with a large kitchen and cold storage rooms in the centre of the boarding school grounds, I met David, a Canadian who was about a head shorter than me but also in my year. This boy from Toronto immediately understood what went on in my head. Quite possibly he had exeprienced the same reception. David told me that there were two beds available in his room and that we could ask if I could move there. I was immediately in favour and approached the group leader, Akiva Yaakov, a dynamic, also frequently cigarettes smoking man, then in his mid-30s, who was of Jewish-Yemeni descent. He agreed and hours later I was allowed to move, and I also received a better blanket and mattress; although neither was new, at least they had been washed.

At dinner, some of the Israeli boys, I would later know them as Menachem and Raffi, sat down next to me. They asked me to go to the dinner ladies to order a portion of "*chara*", which was, they swore, really good. *Chara* is the Hebrew word for faeces. The kitchen staff – most of the women working there were big-hearted Moroccan-Jewish women over 40 – understood immediately what was going on here, it certainly wasn't the first time this old and rather boring joke had been played out on newcomers who did not speak Hebrew yet. One of the ladies asked me who wanted this *chara* and I pointed to the boys in question. They were immediately reprimanded with loud insults, which struck the two boys even harder, because their family background was also Jewish-North African. Beyond getting wise to stuff of this kind, I also had to learn quickly how to get enough to eat in the first place. As soon as the school's leader said "*Boter Avon*" (bon appétit), it was all about being the quickest at the table of eight to secure yourself the best portion. I learned how to become a super-fast eater and started to have my first experience of vegetarian food there, not for higher ulterior reasons, but simply because vegetarians were served their own separate portions

Then, a few days later, some of my clothes and music cassettes began to disappear. Nobody had told me that the cupboards had to be locked with their own lock and that some of the kids stole, or perhaps I was too inexperienced to know better, open to be exploited. It would be a few weeks and some more stolen goods before I could get hold of a lock that put an end to the long-fingered thieves.

Besides David, another boy called Eli Z. lived in the room. He was from Belgium/France. A few months on, Marcello W. joined us as the third room occupant, while David would soon be expelled from boarding school (see later). In his place came Gustavo L.. Both Marcello and Gustavo had come to Israel from Montevideo, Uruguay, together with their parents. The boarding school was intended to help them to acclimatise and integrate into Israeli society.

Eli, on the other hand, had no family. I do not know what the circumstances were, he did have a mother he spoke about, but there were reasons as to why he was not with her. His only relatives, an uncle and an aunt, lived in London. Eli had to cope with this somehow. He sometimes would succumb to anger about his situation but would otherwise be a quite nice and friendly person.

This reveals a particular characteristic of the Israeli organisation Aliyat-ha-Noar and its boarding school network. From the onset its mission was to rescue young people from Nazi Europe and resettle and integrate them into what was then still British-controlled Palestine and later Israel. Overall, there were three groups of young people in Alonei Yitzhak, all between the ages of ten and up to about 18 years. While one group were the children of new immigrants and refugees whose parents had stayed behind, back then in particular from Soviet States and Iran or India, other children and young people came from socially disadvantaged families in Israel and from families who had just immigrated. The third group were young people like myself. Their parents lived in Western Europe, Australia, South Africa, Canada or the USA and they had come to Alonei Yitzhak to gain experience of Israel and Jewish life and then return to their own countries, or with the approval of the Israeli state, they would remain in Israel. For the "privilege" of living in this boarding school, some in the West, my father included, were asked to make monthly contributions, if they were able to.

Zol Zayn Shulem II: Faroys

This mixture of young people from different backgrounds meant that there were fundamental social, linguistic and cultural differences between us. Youth workers like Akiva lacked the expertise to handle these differences constructively and through education, and the school's social worker, I think there was but one, had her hands full with actual hardship cases. Cultural power struggles, integration problems and homesickness were among the smaller problems that could be shoved to the side. As it would turn out later, the school management missed spotting serious, disturbing and literally criminal problems amongst some of the children. The net result of this was that the Israeli kids stayed in their own group and the more recent immigrants grouped themselves into language groups. There was an Iranian-Jewish group, a Spanish-speaking Jewish group, a smaller French-Jewish group and there was the English-speaking Jewish group. There was even a tiny group of German-speaking Jewish kids. I still add the proposition Jewish in here, but in effect, we were all Jewish.

I met Leon B. and Martin (David) P. on my second day in the school. Both came from Germany and were a year above me. Leon was from Dortmund, Martin from Berlin. They suddenly stood in front of me in my room and were grinning. "Wir haben gehört, das Du auch Deutsch sprichst und aus Deutschland kommst", they said – so, we heard you speak German too? We've heard you're from Germany! I smiled and said "Ja!" I didn't need to tell them how I was feeling and the sense of relief that was coming over me, and inevitably we became close friends for some two years, until their own school days ended, Leon serving in the army, Martin returning to Berlin.

Apart from Leon and Martin, there was also Shirly D., from the German Westerwald region near Essen. Later we were joined by Micol Rieger from Munich, both girls, being one year below me. Micol, was the granddaughter of the former Munich fur-trader Hertz Rieger from Rieger Pelze. My dad and her grandfather knew each other. Micol became almost like a sister to me during the boarding school years. Her sister Laura followed Micol a few years later, though after I had left.

Three other children from Germany returned soon after their arrival in Alonei Yitzhak. One of them was Arie M. (who nevertheless, amazingly, volunteered for military service in Israel later). All of us suffered equally from the deprived conditions in the school, which compared poorly with what we had been used to in Germany.

It was always the same pattern. Bullying about the way we looked or the things we liked. Decency, subculture, individuality was perceived as threatening and it led to social exclusion amongst the majority here. Apart from Shirly, who, like Leon, later joined the Israeli military and then married an Israeli. None of us German kids, stayed in Israel after finishing school or for some, after service in the IDF, although almost all of us would continue to have a relationship with Israel and visit Israel regularly. The last I know is that Micol moved to New York, where she married an Israeli jazz musician and works as a social worker. Leon lives in Ohio, Arie in Frankfurt, and Martin moved back to Berlin. Nobody has heard from him since, though one hopes for the best.[78]

It wasn't that I didn't want to go back to Munich straight away, after the first day. But my parents refused. They were supposedly still toying with the idea of moving to Israel themselves and of course nothing came of it, before or after my school years. Frustrated and without support, I resigned myself to be stuck here for now.

After just a couple of weeks, I noticed for what seemed to me a young, attractive Israeli woman – Yael. She had a North African-Jewish and French Swiss background, long brown hair, an athletic figure. I was stunned. She was one year above me. I discovered that she also felt something about me. But, apart from one kiss, nothing came of it. Martin and Leon, who were also in Yael's year group, didn't get on with her at all, nor with any of her friends. I had to choose between Yael and my life insurance in the school, my German friends. I chose the latter but

---

[78] The last time I saw him, on a visit to Berlin in about 1991, he was involved in fights between anti-fascists (his side) and radical right-wing skins.

regretted the loss of my first flame in school as soon as I had made the decision. Nothing I could do, to try to talk to Yael, and I really tried, would help. Soon enough, she dated somebody else from her year group, and the two stayed together until they left school.

Apart from a brief relationship with a Jewish girl from South Africa (she left as quickly as she had arrived because she didn't like it in the school either), I didn't have a girlfriend at school until I graduated, although there were several platonic friendships, first and foremost with Micol, but also Shirly and Hannah M., a girl whose parents had come to Israel from Zambia having fled due to political activities for the ANC. Hannah also suffered from the conditions at school and later moved to New York. Another boy in our group of boys who stuck together was a Jewish-South African boy, who was in Martin's and Leon's year, was Micha Z.. By the time he came to school he already had years of Kung Fu training behind him. This he passed on to us in weekly training sessions, for which he had the agreement of his own Kung Fu master. After years spent in Taiwan later, he became a self-defence expert and instructor with a licence from the Israeli Defence Forces. He also went on to teach Chinese in Israel.

There was also a somewhat aloof boy called Billy, who was the best friend of David, the Canadian in my room. David and Billy tried to bring American street culture into the school. They sprayed graffities, but also sniffed glue to get high, inhaled laughing gas, and engaged in other nonsense. It was through David that I was introduced to Beastie Boys, Run DMC, and The Real Shante and other earlier rappers (our tastes clashed with Marcello, who had a great likening for the Beatles and The Clash). Eventually, David got himself expelled from school because he had somehow obtained marijuana in Jerusalem, where his parents lived and repeatedly brought it into the boarding school and got caught. But the craziest of all was red-haired Martin, that boy from Berlin. He always wore combat boots and an earring in one ear and listened to Indy rock on his loud sound system; his favourite bands were Jesus and the Mary Chain and Depeche Mode. Martin was curious about demonic cult stuff, in part to shock others. He exhibited a cat skull of a dead cat he had found and prepared on one of his shelves and was breaking all the rules in the book. There was an Argentine boy in his year, with whom he shared a room, who would go along with some of that. Martin enjoyed his outsider position which was feared and reviled by the Israeli kids in the school, not the least because he had no hesitation using his fists when someone got in his way. He liked to climb onto the roof of the school's library or sit on the windowsill of his room on the second floor to listen to loud music and have this feeling of being above everybody else.

I was not as much of a hate figure as Martin in school, but it did not mean that I was not also seen as an outsider. One day, when an Israeli boy kept greeting me over several days with the words "Heil Hitler!", I decided to put an abrupt end to it and hit him in the most spectacular fashion. I smashed my fist through the dining room window, right into his face. Everyone in the dining-hall looked up at that moment as the boy fell to the floor in his chair with a loud bang. What's more, I wasn't punished for my deed after the facts had been clarified. According to the school's management, what had happened to the boy served him right. He would never torment me again. I also hit another boy for the same Hitler greeting and was able to utilise my newly acquired Kung Fu skills. Although the boy was taller and stronger than myself, he fell to the ground like a sack, which surprised me in terms of my strength and the potency of Kung Fu. He also never bothered me again. Again, there was no repercussion from the school's management. It was hard justice they seemed to tolerate.

In my own year group, Raffi E. was the slim leader of the Israeli boys of Moroccan family background. He kept trying to have a go at me and bully me. I thought he was a slimy braggart and too mouthy for his weight. One day I seized my opportunity, when I caught him sitting on the toilet. He may have uttered something insulting to me there or just before that. I had just bought some IDF parachute boots and happened to be wearing them. What is there to say? My kick landed with great force on the toilet bowl just in front of the boy's "holy of holies." I asked the baffled young man, who was feeling quite vulnerable caught here with his pants down, if he wanted more and if I should give him a good smack. It worked – for a while. Eventually Raffi, enraged by my sudden advantage over him, challenged me to a fight on the football pitch at the edge of the school. I knew he possessed a knife. Martin, Leon, Micha and I agreed that I should meet the challenge. They would be there with me, hiding in the bushes in case I needed help. And so it was. We went to the agreed place, surrounded by the darkness of the night and the sounds of grasshoppers and frogs. Raffi had seen that I wasn't shirking, nor was I unprotected. He was probably particularly unsettled by Micha being involved, with his knowledge of Kung Fu. And so it was that the challenger did not turn up but ducked out.

Retrospectively, I cannot believe that I was so close to being involved in a fight with a knife. London, the city in which I have lived later for many decades, has seen countless of young boys killed for nothing more, often one stab could be enough. Whilst nothing happened that night in school, if something had occurred, it would have revealed fundamental shortcomings in the way the school was run. The school that my father had hoped would sustain me, had its own risks.

Another boy, Nissim, who was also of North African Jewish descent, received a black eye from me after he had poked fun of an abstract and expressive oil pastel painting that I had created, and had decided deliberately to destroy it. I now believe that the fact that we clashed in this way was not entirely our fault. It was in part also due to those whose job it was to negotiate and break down any perceived differences between us, not doing much to that effect. The work to reduce perceived assumptions about the other could have done much to lessen conflict in my school, perhaps even beyond its boundaries.

While I had managed to be supported by a small group of reliable friends in Alonei Yitzhak, some students lacked any protection. One very corpulent new boy, who was probably suffering from an illness and therefore smelled unpleasantly, was one such person. Unfortunately, I was also amongst a group of his tormentors one night, and I am ashamed of that today. The boy left school at some point, probably because of the bullying.

Some girls had even less protection. There was one boy in our year who was quite small, He had a distinctive slimy voice. "*Ma-injanim?*" "How are you?", he often asked me and others, with some degree of superiority and smiling to himself. It was not uncommon to find him standing naked in the shower when you went to wash. Showering would later become his trademark to cover his tracks, for this young man made a name for himself a few years later as the worst sexual mass-offender in Israel's history at the time. His case became widely known because he later managed to escape from the Israeli prison system, though was caught again later.[79] He is said to have attacked and raped over 20 women. I don't know whether he also molested or raped girls from my school, but it cannot be discounted. The thought of having lived under the same roof as this man, even having showered in the same bathroom is abhorrent. What made it worse is that the boy was known to the school as somebody with complex problems.

Much of what I, in fact, most of us kids from the West had been promised by the representative of Aliyat Ha Noar in Germany about the school did not correspond to the facts on the ground. Shirly told me that the Aliyat-ha-Noar representative had told her in Germany that the school had all brand new and modern accommodation. That was only partially true. New accommodation units did exist, but at the time they were used exclusively for Jewish youth groups who came to visit for a few months from Peru and Colombia and would never stay more than three to six months. I had been assured that I could do music A-levels at the boarding school and that there was a brand-new music centre. That was also a half-truth. The latter existed – but the centre wasn't even finished when I arrived. The centre did have practice rooms, a piano, a mixing desk and a few other instruments, but there was no music teacher

---

[79] He does not deserve to be mentioned by name in this book. But his identity can be found out easily.

for A-levels, and you could not choose music as a subject. The school management had made no efforts whatsoever to integrate this centre into the lessons. Instead, the centre was used to rehearse cheesy performances by various classes for Shabbat evening, or larger performances under the direction of a B-listed musician by the name of Motti Hammer. The songs were mostly uncritical Israeli folk songs, probably to the delight of the school management or Isra-pop and what's more, had little relevance whatsoever in terms of professional music education, certainly not with any academic or professional outcome in mind.

I continued to play piano whenever I had access to the practice room, that becoming a problem in itself. I only had limited access and so I couldn't make any real progress. There was no opportunity to learn from others at concerts to get to grips with music, as the school was in the middle of the countryside. Only one pupil, who had come to the school with advanced classical piano training, managed to persuade the school to give her additional lessons, which took place somewhere far away from the school, in Jerusalem, Haifa or Tel Aviv. She eventually passed high-school exams accordingly. Leon, who also played the keyboard, didn't seem to mind so much and did his best within the constraints of the school. Another boy, Freddy G., a multi-talented musician who had emigrated from Romania to Israel, also pushed hard for the promised music teaching. He got the school to acquire an E-guitar for him, but he too was not able to do any diploma or A-Level in music. This harmed him in his hope to at least make it into one of the official music groups of the Israeli army. Decades later, he was to become a recognised and, as far as I know, globally sought-after studio musician, who also left Israel (after IDF-service) and most recently lived in Scotland. What was sold to us back in Germany or elsewhere and made us leave our homes, parents and friends to be stranded in a rural area of Israel was nothing short of a scandal. It was a misleading betrayal whose victims were underaged young persons. I hope the man was one day found out and sacked, because getting us to go to Israel was not all. He abused our interest in Israel by selling half-truths as truths. I would have never consented to go to Alonei Yitzhak had I known what I found out when it was too late, and my parents turned their backs. What makes it worse is that Israel was not a country that lacked in the ability to provide a stimulating grounding for those interested in music or be it any other interest. It was totally possible to attend a school that offered growth and A-levels in music and had the right teachers for that. The question was where to place such young people who were also interested in coming to Israel.

When I celebrated my first birthday at the boarding school in December 1986, almost six months after my arrival, my parents called me in the early afternoon via the school's office. I had sipped on a bottle of vodka "for my birthday", which I had bought without permission that same morning in the small supermarket of Givat Ada. This act was purely an act of rebellion and frustration, and not because I liked this terribly tasting toxic drink. The challenge before me was to make sure that the school administration didn't notice that I had been drinking. They didn't. By the evening, the little bottle was almost empty. It was a birthday without any of my old friends, without my old life, without my music and almost without hope. Years later, Christian's mum, Elisabeth, the psychoanalyst, felt that there were some cross-generational patterns between my father, my grandfather, my mother, and myself. We all had been uprooted – but mine was unnecessary.

In addition to school, everyday life in Alonei Yitzhak consisted out of one and a half days of labour service, in the same way it was done in kibbutzim. I was assigned to the gardener Shmiel, an older unmarried Hungarian Jew, and Shoah survivor who was rather short of words and seemed to live a solitary life. A day's work under Shmiel consisted of weeding, digging, mowing the lawn, blowing away leaves and the like. The other half of the day consisted either of cleaning tasks such as wiping of the classrooms, or kitchen, or either setting or clearing the more than 50 tables in the dining hall, or of washing up the dishes in the dish-washing room. There were also work shifts in our respective residential buildings, such as cleaning the toilets, taking out the rubbish and yet again mopping the floors. Some of the jobs were divided by gender. As far as I was concerned, I always wanted to help in the kitchen or do the ironing, but these jobs were only to be done by girls, whereas in my three years at boarding school I never once saw a girl working under Shmiel, nor in the tomato and cucumber plantations, or in the workshop.

When I notified the school about a week after my birthday that I couldn't work because I wasn't feeling well, they still forced me to go to work. Two days later, we all left for the Hanukkah break. I went to stay with my aunt Ruszke and my uncle Abraham in Tel Aviv. The lovely dinner that Ruszke had cooked in my honour ended up on the floor just hours after I had eaten it, and I kept throwing up until the early hours of the morning. My whole body began to shake, and I developed a fever of over 40 degrees. Eventually I was taken to Tel Aviv's Ichilov Hospital. X-rays gave a clear diagnosis of advanced pneumonia. I had been already il, requiring rest, when I had informed the school, and by forcing me to work, they had made things worse. I was soon inside an intensive care unit. An elderly patient died next to me on the second or third night. The only good thing was the presence of a younger nurse, some five years older than myself (I remember her well, we even switched roles as I gave her advice concerning her problems with her boyfriend). The care of that wonderful woman, and the soups that my Aunt Rosza brought me every day, helped me recover. After a good week of penicillin by drip-infusion, I finally felt a bit better. But the doctors said there was more to be done. There had been a large build-up of fluid in one of my lungs, and it was best if they removed it. In spite of the local anaesthesia and something they gave me, it was still a rather painful procedure. After they were done I fell into a deep sleep.

To this day, I believe that my condition then was not only physical, but also psychological. Everything in my body was resisting this boarding school, I wanted to go home, I wanted to be able to continue making music, enrol on music A-levels and have competent teachers that work with me. As I already said, nothing here corresponded to the image of the school sold to me or the experiences during the exciting tour of Israel we had had. On the contrary, Israel now seemed like a dead end, a nightmare, a prison in which I was trapped. And, would you believe it, despite the illness, and finding myself in intensive care, my parents, perhaps more my father than my mother, were in denial of the facts before them and did not permit my return.

What should I have done? Maybe I should have been more rebellious? Or go away? But where to? Apart from my family and the boarding school, there was no one in Israel I could hang out with. My Israeli cousins, all over ten years older, were disinterested in me. So, my options in Israel were limited. Perhaps I should have simply gone to stay with a friend in Munich during my next visit, but most of them were still living with their parents. It looked as if I had been left to my fate. I thought the best thing to do was to accept the circumstances and work something out and indeed, by the coming summer I had learned how to navigate in this environment (though the sacrifice was giving up on my music). From time to time, parcels arrived from my parents with chocolate and clothes, sometimes with books, which I had asked for. As if that alone would help.

As I am writing here from the luxury of the future, there is one more thing to add. As already mentioned, my father paid Alonei Yitzhak a monthly maintenance allowance of 300 Deutschmark. My uncle also gave me monthly pocket money, which he wrote down meticulously and which my father paid back to him. Then there were the flights between Munich and Israel, that were still not cheap in those days, probably between 450 and 700 Deutschmark. If you count it all up together, I could have gone to an excellent private school in Germany or anywhere else in the world for that sort of money, if need be, even in Israel. There were better schools, and schools with music emphasis. Instead, I was sent to a school where academic excellence was not exactly what made the school stand out. Many of the Israeli children didn't have to pay a penny to study there, unlike my father and other overseas parents, who paid for a substandard educational facility, not to speak of the rapist they had overlooked.

Another disappointment of Alonei Yitzhak was the complete lack of religious life; there was not even a small group that observed religious traditions, which would at least have given the fact that I was in a Jewish school some meaning. The only reminder of something akin to "Jewish" religious tradition was Friday evening in the dinner hall, when the headmaster Dan Levy gave a long speech and one of the year groups sang pretty Israeli songs. One Saturday, I think it was still in my first year, I decided to go to the village of Givat Ada for nothing less but to attend its only synagogue, a small Sephardic house of prayer, for Shabbat. The next Saturday Michele, a French boy with red frizzy hair, whose father was a Hungarian Jew, would come with me. He felt the same religion and tradition deprived vacuum as I did. There was a certain moral, cultural and religious emptiness at the school.

But the Shabbat services in the village were by no means inspiring. We always remained more like unwanted guests in the community and despite of our expressed interest by coming down to the house of prayer, no one took the time to engage more deeply with us. Here, too, we remained strangers.

Michele was one of my best friends for many months. We sat together in the evenings and Michele played and explained to me some of the songs from the Charles Aznavour and Jacques Brel repertoire. As we listened, our thoughts wandered to the concert halls of Paris and Brussels, whilst I added New York via Aretha Franklin and Patti La Belle to the repertoire. Michele often told me about his father, who had joined the French Foreign Legion to track down former German SS soldiers. I could only imagine what he did to these. Unlike me, Michele couldn't bear Alonei Yitzhak any longer, or rather his parents allowed him to return to France. As far as I remember, this was only for a few years, and he later gave Israel a second chance.

In 2022 I discovered a letter from our headmaster, Dan Levy, in my parents' files in Munich, dated 15 April 1987, eight months after I had arrived in Israel. The letter was written in English, and my parents probably didn't understand a word of it because neither of them spoke English. The headmaster reported in the letter that I was still finding it "very difficult" to get used to the school, that I had not adapted socially" and that I did not accept the "necessary behavioural norms" of the school community. In other words, it was all my fault. The lessons themselves, he argued, also proved difficult for me, although I was beginning to be interested. However, he went on, I had recently made significant improvements in my attitude to lessons, completed my homework well and was making progress.

As he was either not understood, or because he gave some hope in his final sentences, as far as my parents were concerned, his blame shifting and finger pointing, whilst he kept the upper hand of superiority, changed nothing for me.

27

Jude!

During this time, I returned to Munich twice a year. Here I met up with my old friends and sought comfort in the left behind fragments of my former life. It was mainly Gregor and Kai that I saw. To get some much-needed cash, I looked for summer jobs. My friend Kalmon Hener from the ZJD [our fathers knew each other from back in the years of the Jewish Möhlstraße (see Soll sein Schulem Part I) had a temporary job in the Deichmann discount shoe shop in Kaufingerstraße, Munich's main shopping street and put in a word for me there. My main task was to fetch shoes from the warehouse on the upper floor. Here, shoe boxes were stacked up to the ceiling. There was a strong scent of rubber. I could see the busy street beneath through a small window. Occasionally I also had to help in the sales department and quickly learnt that as far as I was concerned the shoes always fitted when customers expected them to fit. I would also work there the next summer. At first, I felt a bit like I was following in the tradition of my paternal grandfather and my father, but a discount shoe shop selling machine-made shoes was a poor comparison. I knew that the Lewandowskis ran their corsetry and lingerie shops not far from here. Their grandson and great-grandson now worked in these streets again, but I was merely a simple temporary employee. Still, it was the thought of a connection that counted.

Jude!

But what really happened during these holidays in Munich was a kind of double life. Firstly, I did not admit to anyone in Munich how miserable I had been in Israel. On the contrary, I bragged about the weather and Tel Aviv. I had my tanned skin to prove it. I was telling white lies, because I did not want non-Jewish Germans to know that it had really been hell. Most of all, I think I was lying to myself.

While I was in Alonei Yitzhak I was relatively outside any cultural zone, which meant that I milked Munich for all it had, thirsty for what I couldn't get in school. Shortly before leaving Munich, I had visited two new key night clubs the Park Café and the Jazz Café. Now I had my eyes on the P1, Munich's top elite night-club. It was part curiosity and part challenge to see if I could get into this club at the age of only 17 (you had to be a minimum of 18 years old). At the time, it was still located in the Eastern part of the "Haus der Kunst" – The House of Art – a building the Nazis had erected (along with Swastikas built into its ornaments, which were now no longer visible), where celebrities such as Prince, Madonna, Mick Jagger, Fabrice "Fab" Morvan and Rob Pilatus of the music duo Milli Vanilli, well known football stars and others would mingle for a night out. My challenge required a strategy of sorts. Although I didn't get past the bouncer the first time I tried, my plan involved to pop by every now and then and dressed a bit eccentrically when I did. At some point, I thought, the man at the door would recognise my face. After about half a year, several attempts, and time in between spent in Israel, the time had come. I could not believe my luck, that it all paid off and I entered this temple of the night, with its terrace and surprisingly small dance hall, where I would never afford more than a single beer or a Coke at best, because the prices were exorbitant, and even a Coke set you back considerably. To feign an older age, I also had got myself an old car key. In truth, I arrived by push-bike. My story was that my car was being repaired following an accident. Another trick I adopted was to refill left behind empty glasses with tap water and pretend that it was an expensive drink I had purchased. After all, I was just a teenager with very limited financial resources. In return I got to experience what the

P1 was all about. Sometimes the club really went wild, and the sound system was incredible. This was amplified by the fact, that the dance hall was not the largest and people literally surrounded it, even the first floor and staircase enabled observation of the dance floor, like a performance stage. But even the achievement of entering this well guarded world became boring after a while. I began to hang out with some of the bouncers, the very people who had not let me in for months before. From them I learnt some of the city's dark secrets. Their stories were tales about broken marriages, debts, scandals, affairs, alcohol and drug addiction, as well as better cities, or places where things were even worse. I heard about London, New York and Los Angeles.

What was it that drew me into this nightclub? On the one hand, it was the quality of the sound. The sound system was top-notch, and the DJs knew how to fire up the club, but on the other hand, it was above all the international flair, which, at least at the time, transcended the provincial Bavarian and Munich borders.

An experience with my then friend Claudius Casagrande, the son of the entertainer Vittorio Casagrande, who popularised Italian hits in Germany, proves just how provincial things sometimes were in Bavaria. Claudius and I also got to know each other through Munich's nightlife, but we already knew each other from the after-school tuition centre before my years in Israel. Later on, we often worked together in temp-jobs, for example in the Munich high-end furniture shop "Vereinigte Werkstätten" or late at night filling envelopes at "Europauhren" a clock-store in Senden, Neu-Ulm.

Munich nightlife gave Claudius something of the otherwise absent worldliness, but in his search for the "ultimate" party he also checked out events in the surrounding Bavarian countryside, as if that party was secretly lurking somewhere there. It wasn't completely wrong. Some very wealthy people lived in some areas around Munich, and sometimes they would indeed organise their own private parties. One weekend we set off together on a two-hour drive from Munich to Passau, where, Claudius assured me, there was supposed to be a promising new club.

Unfortunately, the club was a complete flop and almost empty. Perhaps to compensate for that, the doorman reacted in the most unusual way, when he learned that I was Jewish. He couldn't believe it. I might have just as well have fallen from the skies. "Really?" he remarked incredulously. "*Bist echt a Jud?*" he asked in Bavarian, meaning "you're a real Jew?" I wondered if I had to let my trousers down soon for the ultimate confirmation and recite the Shema. He asked again and again. And so, it went on until we left to make our way back to Munich. What we encountered there wasn't vicious antisemitism. The man had probably only known of Jews from history books, and here I was, a young man interested in dance and club culture who said he was Jewish. I have no idea what was going through his mind. Perhaps he expected me to have a long beard and *payot* (Jewish sidelocks) and wear a kippa. But as far as I was concerned, it was precisely this objectification of my person that drew him away from the actual person standing in front of him and that was problematic. I was Jewish, but I was also interested in music, we wanted to see what was going on here, get to know new cool people. Suddenly, the only thing that became important was the fact that I was Jewish, and that felt extremely limiting and restrictive. I encountered such behaviour on more than just on that occasion in Germany, but this incident is the one I remember best. As for Claudius and my disappointment, we made the best of our drive home, listening to good music tapes on his brilliant car stereo.

Music culture and nightclubs were not the only things I enjoyed during my breaks in Munich. There were also moments of political activity. Every time I came back to the Olympic Village after many months in Israel, I often had the vague feeling that the history of this place and the drama that had once taken place here had almost been forgotten, or at least that no-one was talking about it anymore. I wanted to change that personally, using my own initiative and with simple means. In the summer of 1987, I bought a bucket of black paint and a brush and got busy, writing "Don't forget 5.9.72!" on several walls in the Olympic Village, including on the side of a guardhouse in front of the entrance to the university sports complex, which was located at the end of Conollystrasse, quite near where the tragedy had begun in 1972. I also wrote it on a wall in the shopping street, and on the pedestrian walkway that connected the Olympiazentrum underground station and the Olympic Village. In Connolly Street I wrote "*Shma Israel*" "Hear, oh Israel", in Hebrew, but to my great shame, I have to confess, I misspelled the words in my over-eagerness.

On one occasion, I think it was on the stretch between the underground station and the village, a passer-by caught me in the act, snatched my pot of paint out of my hand and threw it over my head. But the graffiti was already done, and, to my great surprise, it would remain there for a number of years, before it was removed. I see it as my contribution to insist on remembrance – a fact that only became manifest another three decades later, and against the resistance of the alleged majority of Olympic Village residents.

Don't forget 5.9.72. Graffiti in front of the TU training ground in the Olympiadorf circa 1986-1988.

Jude!

As a Jewish teenager who had grown up in the village, I felt the historical amnesia at the time so strongly that it needed to be on the walls.

28

Soweto in Tel Aviv

Me, 1986 or 1987 in Alonei Itzhak.

Although Tel Aviv already had a club scene back then, it remained relatively undiscovered by me, unlike Munich. The reasons were both my aunt's concern and the lack of people I knew who were familiar with it.

In Tel Aviv I lacked the freedom I enjoyed in Munich. I was supposed to be back at my aunt's and uncle's home by eleven in the evening, and one o'clock was late. Nevertheless, I discovered a reggae club in a basement in Frishman Street not far from the hotel mile alongside the beach. The DJs in the Soweto Club played above all booming roots reggae, with various MCs often performing live, such as the Israeli MC Sister Orli, who had released a single called "DJ Queen" in 1984.[80] One of the big hits at the time was also Alpha Blondy's "Jerusalem." The Soweto was not only frequented by Israelis, but also by many black American basketball players, as well as Jewish-Ethiopian Israelis.

However, my aunt, as I mentioned, demanded I did not stay out late into the night (little did she know what I was usually up to in Munich). Once, after she had been waiting for me on the balcony at around two in the morning because I was late, I promised myself that I wasn't going to push boundaries again. I decided instead to spend school holiday weekends and holiday breaks in the almost empty boarding school on the countryside. It may seem strange that after everything, I preferred to stay here in this remote place without any night life or culture. However, the feeling of that relative freedom was more important to me than Tel Aviv with the well-intentioned restrictions imposed on me by my aunt.

Left behind with but a dozen teenagers, mostly those who didn't have families elsewhere, including my room-mate Eli, I could listen to any of my music as loudly as I wanted, and move freely around the grounds without the presence of others and without any supervision whatsoever. For a few days at least, I enjoyed almost complete freedom within the confines of the school and was soon familiar with every corner of the school grounds, which in turn gave me an advantage over all the other students.

From now on it was rare for me to leave the school. There were exceptions. James Brown's Tel Aviv concert in 1988 for example. It was an unforgettable experience full of rhythm, style and power, and I stood

---

[80] See *https://www.youtube.com/watch?v=23lFsPVzjeU* retrieved 22.10.2024

right in the front of the stage to the beat of "Living in America" and "Sex Machine." I saw another one of the greatest musicians of the 20th century in 1989 with special permission from my school's group leader Akiva. I must have given them a lecture on how they had done nothing for my musical development to get permission to attend the gig. Miles Davis made a stop in Israel on his "Tutu" tour at the Roman amphitheatre in Caesarea right in front of the Mediterranean Sea. It was just as magical as it sounds. It suggested a world beyond the confines of the boarding school and Israel, and also that my passion for music, suppressed by the circumstances I found myself in, was still lurking in me.

29

Model Student

The first classes I attended in Alonei Yitzhak were "Ulpan classes", special classes that were adapted for foreign language speakers who had to acquire Hebrew language skills. The Ulpan was located somewhat separately from the rest of the school in a wooden hut, but directly in front of the schoolyard, and that class had all age groups thrown together.

Due to my dislike of the entire boarding school, however, my Hebrew did not improve as quickly as it would otherwise have done. I much preferred to speak English and German with those I considered as my friends. Those who learnt the fastest were of course children who had no other option than Israel, at least not at that time. These were mainly Jewish refugees from Iran, and a few others. However, after eight emotionally charged months of the first year, I began to wonder what was going to happen to me there if things stayed the way they were. Firstly, there was no longer any hope of a meaningful musical education, nor was there any real option of returning to Munich any time soon, as I understood it.

The Ulpan classes were no substitute for the normal school classes. Batyah, the head of the school (she was a Shoah survivor herself who understood and spoke German), refused to speak German with me on principle because of the Nazi past. She made it clear to me that everything was up to me. I could either leave Alonei Yitzhak in two years without anything or I could have the choice of doing a full A-level diploma here. The time to choose was now, as there were two more years of secondary school before me. To be honest, I didn't have to deliberate long to choose the second option. Now the fact that I had come to my own conclusion, and had made my own decision and owned it, changed everything. It shifted my attitude from the disinterested rebel I was (of course it was to some degree justified, but my hands were tied) into a focussed model student within only a few months. In addition, I had made the acquaintance of a literature teacher that accompanied the Jewish Peruvian children that were temporary guests in the school, because he had studied German literature and of several Jewish US-American volunteers who did a student gap year in Israel (one of whom is still in contact with me today, whilst the Peruvian teacher and I exchanged letters for about 18 months after he and the kids had left). These contacts to more mature people helped also to clear up any doubts in my mind.

Soon I had my reward and transferred to the normal school class with all the Israeli students, and the school gave me extra Hebrew tuition on top. Biology, English, incorporating English Literature, Tanakh and Geography became favourite subjects.[81] Economics and Maths, however, were soon dropped. This was mainly because of teachers who certainly failed to inspire me, especially Fruma, the maths teacher, who was the embodiment of a teacher from her native Soviet Russia and who was in her late 50s at the time. It wasn't just how she taught her maths. She went far beyond her brief in classes, making fun of my appearance, both my Western youth-style clothes and my small ponytail. We mutually lost interest in each other, but of course it was only to my detriment; she was a teacher, I was a student. In economics, the teacher, who had come to Israel from Bulgaria, was also schooled in Soviet style methods. These were subtle things you simply felt, a certain coldness and unemotional

---

[81] Tanakh, Hebrew writings of the Old Testament

strictness. Fruma the maths teacher was more calculated in her attacks on me though. I did not fit the expected system of order – remember the letter, the boarding school's head wrote. I would not say that she lacked emotion, for she embraced others in a motherly way. And then there was Awi the sports teacher, an Israeli, and husband to the economics teacher. His mentality and goals for us were also alien to me. I had experienced sports tuition in Germany that was oriented towards team sports and athletic disciplines. Contrary to any sports lessons I had previously had in Germany, and to my time spent in a basketball club in Munich, Awi's classes were basically preparatory training of the young people under his supervision towards the upcoming service in the Israeli Defence Forces. He cannot be blamed for that; it was what the country required and what was relevant there. Different countries, different customs! I liked sports and I would get both vocational and university degrees in sports years later, but I didn't know that at the time.

Despite it all, there were some sparks of brilliance, at least in the way I understood it. Some of the teachers in the school were of the 1960s anti-authoritarian generation and hence similar in their approach to the best German teachers I had experienced, particularly during my primary school years. They regarded young people as their equals and were really interested in what we were doing, and this nurtured our expectations.

They really wanted to teach us something for life and enjoyed being teachers. Above all, the English teacher Talma, who was born in South Africa, the biology teacher Gideon, the history teacher whose name I can't remember, the literature teacher Thelma and the Tanakh/RE teacher (I can't remember her name either) were such extraordinary people. I never forget how my RE teacher, she was a sandal wearing short-haired feminist and progressive Israeli intellectual, said, that the religious conflict could be "easily" solved, if all would agree to share the Temple Mount Haram al-Shariff, as all prayed to the one G-d, and arrangements could certainly be made to serve all needs under that fundamental understanding.

Against the backdrop of an often undisciplined, noisy class, the methods these teachers employed were exploited by some, but also inspired me. I began to acquire extra study material. In literature, I was so moved by "Macbeth" that I bought an expensive MC of the entire opera by Verdi and on a windy grey day listened to it on my stereo on full volume when the school was empty during the holidays, with everybody else gone. It created not just a spooky atmosphere but really helped me to get behind the storyline of that Shakespearean play. For biology, I would elect to undertake my own project and chose to examine the water quality in the surrounding areas (it was awful), and, in geography I learnt above the required load with the help of German textbooks that I had bought. In history, I studied the entire history of the state of Israel. In English, I was inspired by the stories of the teacher Talma, including a wonderful short story by Bernard Malamud.[82]

There were gaps. In history we were not taught much about the Third Reich nor about the Palestinian Israeli conflict in any meaningful way, and it certainly did not compare with how the Third Reich is taught in European countries, especially in Germany. There was also an almost total lack of world and global history. But there were also things that were not in any curriculum in Germany, not just Tanakh and Hebrew. We were taken to army bases to prepare most of us for service in a few years. Once we went to an army base in the Golan Heights and once to the Negev desert in Sde Boker. We were taught how to handle a basic rifle (which came in very handy at the next funfair in Munich). One incident that left a lasting impression was, when, in Sde Boker, it was the middle of winter, I asked one of my classmates to hold up a water hose, meant for washing military vehicles because there were no showers. In that way I washed myself with cold water while everyone else remained dirty and sweaty, complaining about the lack of showers. "*Ata Meshuga* (you're crazy)!" said many of the others. Was this extraordinary need for hygiene a German trait?

---

[82] "Angel Levine" is one of Malamud's short stories "The Magic Barrel" (1958), Farrar, Straus & Giroux. It exists in filmed version with Harry Belafonte in the role of Angel Levine.

During these army experience days, specialist soldiers explained and presented all the military units, discussed the career options and expectations and made it all sound like a piece of cake. For my Israeli classmates, this was deadly serious, as it was about what they had to do in about one year's time. They had to undergo psychological and fitness assessments beside declaring their choices.

I was not against the Israeli army and absolutely understood the need for Israel's defence capabilities, but at the time I opposed the military presence in "ha'shtachim," otherwise known as Yehuda and Shomron or the West Bank and Gaza, which made me a minority in class. It led to frequent comments like, "You don't understand this, because you're not Israeli." But I did understand some things. When I was already in eleventh grade, at the beginning of the first Intifada, a young man from the previous year came to visit the school. He had been serving in the military for about a year and boasted about how he had "beaten the shit out of the f**** Arabs in Gaza." Whether he was just bragging, he wasn't the cleverest of guys or telling the truth, who knows. However, the fact that he found it necessary to brag about his service in this particular way was a symptom of a certain attitude among at least some. It was one of the experiences that made me decide not to stay in Israel after graduating from high school. That said, there were also people who had a much more grown-up attitude. A small group, also of the year above me, reflected more critically on what could happen in war. At one point, this centred on their public screening of the feature film Platoon in the school's cafeteria which depicted the raw violence and desperation of the Vietnam War. There was also a youth worker who worked at the school for a year, Tuli. Tuli was politically left and close to the peace movement *Shalom Achshav* (Peace Now) and to Shulamit Aloni's *Raz* party, the Israeli civil rights party (later *Meretz*). On a few occasions I visited Tuli in her flat on the school grounds and we discussed politics. She showed me that there was a diversity of thought in Israel and that people who thought like me at the time were very much part of Israel. She thought that I should stay in Israel. "We need people like you here", she said

Zol Zayn Shulem II: Faroys

and was more convincing than any of the other nationalist flag-waving youth worker of the Jewish Agency.

My decision to put my dislike of school behind me also meant that I stopped a bad habit – smoking. Instead, I started jogging and soon became the school's long-distance runner. But it wasn't just about the running, it also gave me the opportunity to get out of the school grounds, eventually even with the expressed permission of the school. So I began to run all over the area. The normal route was from the boarding school to the end of the country road near Binyamina and was about ten kilometres long. A few times I even ran as far as Hadera and back, around 25-30 kilometres in total. Occasionally I got lost on the search for short cuts, and a couple of times this meant that I had dogs chasing after me.

Ironically, now being stationed in Israel, my favourite school subject became German. Shirly, Micol and I were, after some strong lobbying on our part, given special German literature tuition in the city of Haifa, together with pupils from another boarding school. Among them was Ruth Brauer-Kvam, who later would become an Austrian actress. We Germans would often be sitting on the balcony of an old house of the city of Haifa, and it was there where we discussed Goethe, Lessing, Heine, Lenz, Kafka and other writers and their works with a teacher who was German-Jewish herself and who lived in Haifa. This meant that we had to travel from the school to Haifa and back, requiring the use of two buses.

Once, when we were on the public bus travelling back from Haifa after a long day we were chatting happily in German, when we heard some of the passengers complaining about us in Hebrew. "Those damn Germans, I wished they weren't in our country", said one, and others agreed with her. I felt that needed to be replied to. In my best and sharpest Hebrew I asked who they thought they were, making such comments. Yes, we spoke German, but we were Jewish, and we were here because we believed in Israel as much as they did, so much so that we elected to go to school here. Micol and Shirly let me know that they fully supported what I said. An awkward silence filled the bus for the rest of the journey.

Model Student

Studying in an empty classroom late at night in 1989.

We ended up taking our German Bagrut exam (A-level) with a senior professor of German literature and German Studies at the Hebrew University in Jerusalem. He was a real "*Jacke.*"[83] When it was my turn, he didn't just ask me about literature, but enquired how I liked Israel. I stuck to the truth and pointed out the good but also at the not so good and the difficult. To my surprise, he agreed with my criticisms, but added that he hoped that I would remain in Israel.

In the last few months of my time at school in Israel, I studied until the early morning hours outside at night under street lanterns in the schoolyard as well as in empty classrooms. The transformation in terms of achievement from the previous year's report was remarkable and emphasised what is possible when young people decide to take responsibility and ownership of their own learning. I got a distinction in German and the rest of my A-levels were also above average, despite coming in from the cold and in a foreign language. During the biology exam, other

---
[83] Jacke, Hebrew word for German Jews,

classmates, who knew I was one of the best in the class, asked me for help. I couldn't say no but should have. Wasting time on those who had not bothered to study as hard as I did, meant that I run out of time to answer all questions, and didn't achieve the mark I deserved. There was a learning point in that too, however. Sometimes you don't have to help others, when doing so means that you harm your own deserved progress. There may be a reason why the name for the Israeli A-levels is Bagrut. It means as much as a Diploma for having grown up, from the Modern Hebrew verb *lebager*, growing up. Growing-up certainly requires more than just having learned how to study.

30

Kafr Qara and Other Forbidden Places

The routines, the fact that you were basically not allowed to leave the school grounds, encouraged young people like me to find ways around it. Martin and I did this primarily through our appearance. As already mentioned, Martin always wore a goth-punk inspired outfit, I stuck to contemporary club-fashion wear, amongst others from Boy George's boutique Boy in Tel Aviv, which was as close anyone could get to these styles in Israel.

Already during my very first year, I defied the school ground's fences and set off into the surrounding "dangerous and forbidden world." I began to explore the entire region. Later I also got to know many of the natural landscapes around the school through my running. I had to be careful though, as there were snakes, if you went into zones where humans were not expected. Passing numerous fields along a small dirt track, I ended up several times in Kafr Qara, the small Palestinian Israeli town at a distance of some three kilometres from the school. It took just under an hour on foot. On the way there was abandoned trash including car wrecks or stinking rotting animal carcasses in the ditches. Some of the farmers there still had donkey carts. Not far from the entrance I discovered a small coffee shop in the north-west of the town. Somewhat cautiously, so as not to reveal my true identity or the fact that I had left school without permission, I introduced myself in English to the Palestinian Israeli café owner as a German visitor from Kibbutz Kfar Glikson. The idea of being but a German who spent some time in the kibbutz, as many did, appeared to me safer than to say that I was from the school nearby. The men in the small café (only men were sitting there) reacted by sharing their enthusiasm about Germany and praised German car brands.

I didn't leave it at that. Once I also took Micol and someone else with me. I don't know whether we were believed to be Germans from the kibbutz, but we clearly all had a strong German accent. On the other hand, our school was not unknown in Kfar Qara. At that time the school even employed a Palestinian-Israeli maths teacher from Kfar Qara. He had curly black hair, a moustache, wore sandals and spoke in a soft voice. His name was Motti and those who had him as a teacher only had very good things to say about him.

As I learnt many years later, Kfar Qara was anything but a "normal" town. Its residents were especially proud of one particular achievement, the level of academic qualifications: in 2007, admittedly after my time in Israel, they were ranked as the community with the highest number of citizens who were qualified doctors in Israel, as well as the highest number of people with academic qualifications in general.[84]

My visits to a Palestinian town should not be underestimated. As far as the school administration was concerned, I had probably breached the absolute fundamentals of their safety policy. Alonei Yitzhak was not only a place with night patrols with an armed guard. My Israeli classmates' general view of Palestinians was often emotionally charged. Attempts to explain the regional state of affairs in more nuanced ways or even just to question it were immediately taken as an attack, weakness, stupidity, or all of the above. News reports about actual terrorist attacks, which happened regularly, reinforced this view.

---

[84] Lori (2007)

But it wasn't just Kafr Qara that we escaped to. When my Canadian first roommate David, myself, and an American boy called Mo were once punished for something we had done and were not allowed to go on a one-day class excursion, we defied this verdict and decided to make our own excursion by simply taking buses to the beach in Caesarea. Given that our class was thought to be on excursion, we figured people would think we had just come along on the trip in the end. Nobody would look for us.

Unfortunately, our plan to be back before our class returned failed miserably as there were only a few buses back to Alonei Yitzhak. This meant that we arrived late. We got caught and a week of washing up dishes as punishment followed, but we felt the trip had still been worth it, and we got more time to spend together and talk about it all whilst we cleared up and washed the school's dishes.

Last but not least, there was a completely different act of rebellion, one that involved the wider world and one that didn't originate from any one of us. It was almost impossible for foreign students to speak to their family back home in those days before internet and mobile apps. You could call home from the school's office, but had to pay for it, or you could use the public payphone at the back of the dining hall. Not surprisingly, some started to experiment if it was possible to cheat the system. It was! First, there was the thread trick: a thread was pulled through the round, hollow telephone coins (*asemonim*), which were then carefully sunk into the coin-slot of the telephone, or superglue was smeared over the coins before insertion. The real experts even did both in order to get the coin into the right position before gluing it. I never mastered this skill, not for want of trying, but I certainly benefitted from the skills of others. In this way, relatives in all corners of the world could be called for free for days on end, and at our boarding school there were relatives and family members all over the world: Germany, France, Spain, Columbia, USA, Canada, Peru, UK, South Africa, Italy, Argentina, Uruguay, Romania, and who knows what other countries, maybe even the Iranian boys called home. It took days until the phone company found out about it.

Zol Zayn Shulem II: Faroys

Our Day Out at the beach in Caesarea 1987, to my left Mo, to my right David.

In the first year of my time at Alonei Yitzhak, due to my gardening work, I also discovered a small former bunker carved into the chalk stone in the middle of the school park. I was asked to deposit leaves there. We, that is David, and a few others, "borrowed" suitable tools from the workshop and began to dig out the bunker – it was to become our own secret little cave in the middle of school. We dug at it for months, until at some point we lost interest. It may have been here that David secretly got high with Billy. But at some point, even they had had enough of the place after allegedly a snake had taken up residence in there.

However, the biggest secret of all was only revealed to me in my final year at school. Boys from the year above us had stolen or copied keys to the kitchen. When their school years were over and they had no longer need for the keys, the question arose as to whom they would pass these on. They chose me. I was able to use the keys to open the door to the kitchen and open a few fridges. For three or four months, I supplied most of my classmates with fruit yoghurt and chocolate cream. Good-natured and trusting as I was, I shared the spoils with the whole class. I felt like Robin Hood. At last, I had a very high status in my year.

Kafr Qara and Other Forbidden Places

My justification was that the school never gave us enough good food, although it is true to say we always had enough food (even though it was often just bread that we stuffed ourselves with). Fancy an unlimited supply of chocolate cream? Ask Daniel!

All "good things" have to come to an end however. The tell-tell-boy who burst the bubble lived in my own room and slept opposite me. My roommate Marcello and I had an argument. He wanted to study in the small room after bed-time at night, I wanted to sleep. When even his judo skills didn't help, Marcello decided to blow the whistle on me in revenge. One night, when we – I had a younger German-Jewish accomplice – had gone back into the kitchen on a chocolate pudding raid, Marcello trumpeted our mission to our group leader. Hence when I came out laden with yoghurts and puddings, I walked straight into the trap Marcello had set for me. I had no choice but to confess to the whole thing and give up the keys. Two weeks of washing up duty were my penalty for this. At some point, it took a long while, Marcello and I spoke to each other again and we are still in contact today.

However, there is something almost uncannily subliminal about this story, for despite all its silliness, this smuggling of chocolate desserts within a boarding school cannot be separated from my father's experiences. Why was I smuggling and distributing food? What significance did it have? What must my father have thought when he heard that his son was secretly stealing and smuggling food from the kitchen of the boarding school, after the secret procurement of food in two of the camps he had once been imprisoned in had contributed to his survival?

This comparison is not entirely accurate. We weren't starving at all in Alonei Itzchak and there was no danger that we would never see or phone our relatives again with the payphone. And yet some things may have been passed on to the next generation. This constant urge for freedom, the collective strive to helping each other out, standing up for each other, secretly doing things that are "forbidden", constantly observing our surroundings with suspicion and keeping a watchful eye on them, has at least some resonance with the past. Would they also be "legacies" or bequests of the survivor generation to us, which we simply lived unconsciously and without giving it much thought, or are we reading too much into it?

31

Shir-Lifnei-Ha-Sehara

When my class put on a graduation show at the end of our time in school, I insisted on writing and performing a farewell song. The song I wrote, "*Schir lifnei ha-Sehara*", the "song before the storm" consisted of tough but true words about the school, a kind of final reckoning. I wanted to also show them that I could write, play and sing songs, and that I should have had access to musical education. Freddy G. played the bass. Mazal, a girl from my year, provided a second voice in the song. The song brought friends like Micol and Hannah to tears and left the school administration uncomfortable, angered and speechless.[85] I basically said thank you for nothing!

---

[85] The song can be heard here in the original recording https://drive.google.com/file/d/1nEO9ZreMswU_gql7HGFD6arsXyL8AT-N/view?usp=sharing retrieved on 17.2.2022

Zol Zayn Shulem II: Faroys

The song before the storm. Me at the piano at the graduation ceremony in Alonei Yitzhak, Israel

Main chords, with thanks to Bob Stuckley, for writing it out.

שיר לפני הסערה

"Shir lifnei ha sehara" - "Das Lied vor dem Sturm"

Daniel Zylbersztajn (1989)

כשבכיתי וחיפשתי אני מצאתי את עצמי לבד כשביקשתי ורציתי אני מצאתי את עצמי לבד	Kesche bachiti we chipasiti Ani mazati et azmi lewad kesche bikaschti, we raziti Ani mazati et azmi lewad	Als ich weinte und suchte fand ich, dass ich alleine war. Als ich verlangte und wollte, fand ich, dass ich alleine war.
והם אמרו שזה בסדר אין לי מה לבכות אם אתה לא חזק תקבל מכות , כשברחתי והתחבאתי. אני מצאתי את עצמי לבד.	We hem amru she se beseder Ein li ma livkod Ha Chaim lo kalim, we ein matanot Im ata lo chasak tekabel Makot Ke she Barachti we hitchabeti Ani Mazati er azmi lewad	Und sie sagten, dass sei in Ordnung Ich hätte keinen Grund zu Weinen Das Leben sei nicht leicht, und es gäbe nichts umsonst. Wenn Du nicht stark bist, kriegst Du Schläge Als ich weglief und mich versteckte fand ich, dass ich alleine war
לא האמנתי מה שהם רצו, לא רציתי מה שהם חשבו	Lo Imanti ma she razu Lo raziti ma shem chaschwu	Ich glaubte nicht, was sie wollten Ich wollte nicht, was sie glaubten
כששנאתי- הקאתי אני מצאתי את עצמי לבד	kesche saniti - heketi, Ani mazati er azmi lewad. She barachti, hitchabeti ani mazati et azmi lewad	Als ich hasste und mich übergab fand ich, dass ich alleine war. Als ich weglief, und mich versteckte fand ich, dass ich alleine war.
והם אמרו שזה כדי להישאר לשתוק ולסגר את הפה עם שיער קצר ובגדים נורמלים	We hem amru kedei lehischaer Lishtok we lisgor et ha pe zaarich lihiot kmo kol achad im sahar kzar we begadim normalim	Und sie behaupteten, es ist sei besser zu bleiben, Die Klappe zu halten und den Mund zu verschliessen Mit kurzen Haaren und normalen Kleidern
לא האמנתי מה שהם רצו, לא רציתי מה שהם חשבו	Lo Imanti ma she razu Lo raziti ma shem chaschwu	Ich glaubte nicht, was sie wollten

Zol Zayn Shulem II: Faroys

			Ich wollte nicht, was sie glaubten
	איזה מוזר, מְטוֹרָף, איך הוא הולך איך הוא יושב הוא מצא את עצמו לבד ואני מצאתי את עצמי לבד	(Kol): Eise muzar, meturaf, Eich hu olech, ech hu joshw Hu maza et atmo lewad - We mazati et azmi lewad	(Stimme:) Wie seltsam und verrückt er ist, Wie er geht und sitzt Er hat sich allein wiedergefundenn - Und ich fand, dass ich alleine war.
	ועכשיו, עכשיו אני אדבר שתקו כולכם למדתי לקלל, למדתי לבגרות	We achschaw, achschaw ani aedaber Schteku kolchem, Lamadeti lekalel, lamadeti le bagrut	Und jetzt, jetzt werde ich das Wort ergreifen, seit alle mal leise. Ich lernte zu fluchen und das Abitur zu machen
	אתם יודעים הרבה, אתם יודעים הכל! אך אני אוהב את העולם הזה חופש ולעשות מה שאני רוצה ועכשיו כשאני יוצא מכאן כמו ציפור אני בטח לא חזור	Atem jodim betach harbe, atem jodim ha kol! Ach ani ohew et ha olam ha se Chofesch we la'asot ma'sche ani roze We achschaw she ani jozeh mi po, Kmo zipor, batuach lo chozer	Ihr wisst sicher viel, Ihr wisst alles! Ich liebe diese Welt Und das zu tun, was ich will Und jetzt wo ich hier heraus komme Werde ich wie in Vogel nicht mehr zurückkommen
	ואתם עוד לא יודעים מה כן הולך ואתם טיפשים כרגיל נישרים	We atem od lo jodim ma ken holech we atem tipschim, ke regil nischarim	Und ihr wisst immer noch nicht, was schon möglich ist, Und ihr bleibt weiterhin wie immer dumm
	אני רוצה פרחים ולצחוק אני רוצה אהבה ולא לשתוק	Ani rozeh prachim we lizchok Ani rozeh ahewa we lo schtok	Ich möchte Blumen und lachen Ich will Liebe und nicht den Mund halten
	כשיו זה הרגע לשינוי למה אתה לא רוצה לשמוע מילים טובות ילדים רוצים להיות שמחים בחיים וזה השיר שלפני הסערה לפני הסערה	Achschaw she ha rega le schinu Lama atem lo rozim lischmoa milim towim Jeladim rozim lihiot smechim ba cha'im We se ha schir lifnei ha sehara Lifnei ha sehara	Jetzt ist die Zeit für eine Veränderung Warum wollt ihr keine guten Worte hören Kinder wollen glücklich im leben sein Und dies ist das Lied vor dem Sturm. - vor dem Sturm
	ואני מצאתי את עצמי לבד	We ani mazati et azmi lewad	Und ich fand, dass ich alleine war..

English translation of *Shir lifnei ha Sehara* –

The song before the storm

*When I cried and searched
I discovered; I was all by myself.
When I demanded and desired,
I discovered; I was all by myself.*

-

*And they said it's all OK,
I didn't have any reason to cry,
Life wasn't easy,
And there is nothing for nothing
If you are not tough enough,
You get beaten up.*

-

*I didn't believe, what they wanted,
I didn't want, what they believed.*

-

*When I hated and when I threw up,
I discovered; I was all by myself.
When I run away and hid,
I discovered; I was all by myself.*

-

*And they said, it would be better to stay,
To keep quiet and my mouth shut,
With short hair and normal clothes.*

-

*I didn't believe, what they wanted,
I didn't want, what they believed.*

-

*(Voice) How strange and crazy he is
How he walks and how he sits.*

Zol Zayn Shulem II: Faroys

He found himself left by himself
(Daniel) I discovered; I was all by myself.

-

And now I will speak,
Be quiet everyone!
I learned to curse and to do high-school-exams
You surely know much,
know everything.
Oh, I love this world,
And to do what I want,
And now, that I am able to escape this place,
Like a bird I surely won't return anymore

-

And you still don't understand what is possible,
And like always you remain stupid,

-

I want flowers and want to laugh,
I want love and not shut my mouth.

-

Now, is the time for a change,
Why do you not want to hear good words?
Children want to be happy in life,
And this is the song before the storm!

32

School in Israel in Retrospect

I lived in Israel for three years. Although the school did its best within the limited resources they had at their disposal, the representatives of Aliyat ha Noar had raised completely false hopes in children and young people who left behind their homes and all they knew based on that promise.

In the school there was a lack of any serious attempt to bring young people of different backgrounds and cultures together and accept each other. Other differences were also not dealt with. For example, at least two boys in my class were gay, a fact that I only learned two decades later.

There were other silent omissions. Some of them led to the failure to notice the development of one of the most dangerous sexual predators in Israeli criminal history. The ordinary needs of other young people, uprooted from their homes, were almost totally ignored. It was to some extent survival of the fittest.

The lack of opportunities for a music degree thwarted my career prospects in music, which had still looked very promising before I left Munich in 1986. The half-truths of the *shaliach*, the envoy of the Israeli Aliyat-ha-Noar, designed to lure us to Israel from the outset on false pretences are totally unforgivable to this day, and they did not produce the result the Israeli state might have had in mind. This is demonstrated by the fact that few of us remained in Israel, as already mentioned.

There was a lack of understanding that promises needed to be kept, and that content and living standards were essential to attract Jewish youth, admittedly from an Israeli perspective, spoilt and free Western states to Israel. In my case, however, the least that could have been done would have been to fulfil the promise of music tuition leading towards music A-levels or at least higher proficiency in music. The second thing would have been the provision of proper Jewish religious education to whatever level young persons wanted to take it. The very thing that was so hard to achieve in some of the places we came from, unless you grew up in a strictly religious family. Life is about options. I was in Israel, that was my choice, but I was not given much option about the school in which I was placed. What was the point of the exercise of dragging me out of my home then, at merely 15 years old?

The good news is, that these were the 1980s. The information-age and the Internet and the age of the smart-phone have made deceptions of the type the representative of Alyat-ha-Noar for Germany indulged in then much more difficult if not impossible today. People can scrutinise much more, what they are signing up to and if things do not add up, they are far easier to report.

With a lot of flexibility and deep thinking on my part, I managed to pass my A-levels in Israel, and in a language that was initially foreign to me. This was not due to the Aliyat-ha-Noar, nor the boarding school management, but due to the talent of some amazing dedicated and kind anti-authoritarian individual Israeli teachers. My successes came from ownership of my own decision rather than through coercion. Those progressive teachers had something in common with the German teachers, my Munich primary school and children's programmes such as the Munich "*Kinderstadt.*"

But how Alonei Yitzhak was perceived and experienced also depended on where the children came from. To give an opposing view here, my school friend Andrea Aderet, who came to Israel from communist Romania, told me, that unlike myself, for her Alonei Yitzhak was liberating. Yet even she no longer lives in Israel, but in the United States.

In the end, the many clashes with Israeli young people and the circumstances I had to deal with on the ground were most certainly also a kind of training in the widest sense. Children from richer Western countries often waste their fortunate position through destructive behaviour. I wrote about some of these experiences in Munich. These children often lack a connection to reality. They are often unable to recognise and appreciate the value of education, development opportunities and chances, whilst they may sit right beside such opportunities without seizing them because they do not represent exactly what they had in mind. There is also often a lack of cultural exchange and opportunities including exposure to other cultures.

Despite the many conflicts, frustrations and disappointments, Alonei Yitzhak taught me to see people as people and to be satisfied with less in life. Some things took a while, but today I appreciate the traditions and cultures that I initially perceived as very foreign. Sephardic, Jewish-North African and Jewish people of Syrian, Egyptian, Iraqi and Iranian descent grew close to my heart (I wouldn't have any significant contact with Palestinians until later, but I did go to Kfar Qara a few times as reported). Through research, I discovered many years later that I am closer to this world, at least genetically, than I had ever thought. The opposites were always more of an imagined construct contrary to the basically obvious common humanity and a shared Jewish and human background.

I also have gained an insight into the political dynamics of Israel. I would soon return to Israel and conduct my first political interviews there. Ultimately, the experience also set the course for my academic career and positions I held later in my life, including my work for the Israeli Palestinian peace village Wahat-Al-Salam-Neve Shalom, my short-term position as managing director of Meretz-UK, and my long-term position as a writer and correspondent in London for the German Jewish *Jüdische Allgemeine* and for *taz* newspaper.

The fact that we had to work at school gave me a pragmatic attitude to work of any kind, and as far as my diet was concerned, I left Israel as a pescetarian, which would soon change into a vegetarian and for a while I was even vegan. And, my farewell piece of music "*Shir-lifnei-ha-Sehara*" left a noticeable impression on everyone, many of whom can remember it to this day.

33

Lehitraot Israel

In winter of 1988, I met Alice Levy, a young Israeli woman in a bar in Tel Aviv.[86] Alice was of Algerian-Jewish background and lived in Kfar Ha Yarok, another Aliyat-ha-Noar boarding school near Tel Aviv.[87] She had long black hair and was about a head shorter than me. I thought she was distinctly beautiful. What's more, she was cool to hang out with. The attraction was mutual, though both of us were also incredibly shy. One evening in the spring of 1989, when it was raining heavily, I sneaked out of the boarding school and hitchhiked to her school to surprise her. It made her day, though I stayed only briefly. The distance between her school and my school made things difficult, not made easier by the fact, that Alice always travelled to the South of Israel during her breaks, as that was where her parents lived. We wrote to each other instead (there were still no mobile phones about). It looked promising without us having had the chance to spend much time with each other. When I finished my Bagrut, the Israeli high school diploma, I decided at first to stay because of her. However, there were a number of problems. Firstly, I lacked any

---

[86] Name changed, Lehitraot, hebr. „See you again! "
[87] Incidentally I would later learn that Kfar Yarok would have been far more suitable for me to study at, it had a part Waldorf-Steiner strain and was far more able to teach arts and had a better name all together than Alonei Yitzhak.

kind of livelihood, so I was at least temporarily dependent on my family. Secondly, where could I stay? I could hardly continue to be a burden on my aunt and uncle. I needed at least a room or a flat somewhere, but I had no idea how to get one without an income. If possible, I knew that I wanted to live near Shenkin Street, which was the centre of Tel Aviv's In-scene at the time. I knew some of the bars and clubs there, like *Ha-Osem-ha-Schlishi* (The Third Ear), there were record and clothes shops there too, as well as the hangout of the Israeli left-leaning liberal intelligentsia and arts-scene inside Sarah Stern's legendary *Café Tamar*.[88] This part of Israel, of Tel Aviv, was more interested in liberal culture, left politics, contemporary music and art. Whilst my cousin and uncle found a room nearby, in a flat that I was to share with an old man, there was only a thin sliding partition wall separating me from the old man, without sufficient degrees of privacy. Toilets and bathroom were to be shared. I declined. Meanwhile, that was the third problem, my visa was due to expire within a few days or weeks and an extension would mean that I would have to become an Israeli citizen, because I had stayed the maximum period that was possible on a student visa. If I became Israeli, it would automatically mean that I would have to sign up to three years of IDF army service. It was all a bit much. I decided to leave Israel for the time being. I would be able to work and study in Munich straight away, or so I hoped, and, after all, I had my own "studio flat" in the form of the "hobby room" there. I thought that once I was secure in Munich, Alice and I could easily visit each other. It was only after I had been back to Munich that I learnt that Alice was not allowed to travel abroad during her military years, which had just begun. I continued to receive letters and photos from her, but attention evaporated in Munich, where life had its own rhythm.

---

[88] An obituary to the famous Café Tamar can be found here, in Kessler (2015)

34

Back in Deutschland

I was in high spirits about my return. I had completed my A-levels and that would give me access to study. At the beginning I was, however, sad that Alice and I somehow could not stay together. I really liked her. What I did not expect, but should have known better, was, that Bavaria was Bavaria, at core a conservative Christian state, that had a history of behaving cruelly towards Jews and had the possibility to continue to behave strangely in the present.

As everything in Israel was focused on the army as the next step, I was left fully unprepared to apply in time to study in Germany. The application deadlines had already passed and they were not taking second servings. To my great disappointment this meant that I would have to wait at least another year to study. I had several ideas about potential career paths, none of which any longer included music. That was, because I felt that I could not catch up on three years lost on that account and was better advised to check what I could do with those A-levels and other interests that I had. I considered studying biology or veterinary medicine, because I was considered to be good with animals and had enjoyed biology at school, the alternative was journalism. As it stood, I now had a few months to look more closely at these options. Firstly, I met with a vet to ask her about her work, then I completed a one-week internship at the Max Planck Institute to see what being a scientist entailed. The vet explained that I would have to be prepared to possibly work in a slaughterhouse if I studied veterinary medicine and that if I ever became a vet for pets, I should know that most problems of pets were at least in part caused by their human keepers. The scientists at the Max Planck Institute were, as you would expect, completely dedicated to research and had hardly any other interests. They made a rather strange impression on me, because I also had a strong interest in politics and the world. Nevertheless, I signed up for the medicine psychometric test, which you had to pass if you wanted to study veterinary medicine, without realising that one ought to prepare for it properly.

In the mean time there was time to make some money. I started various jobs in the household goods and decoration department of the Munich Oberpollinger Department Stores, in the Vereinigte Werkstätten furniture store, based at Munich's Odeonsplatz, as a sales assistant in fashion boutiques such as Marc O'Polo and as a seasonal assistant – I was particularly proud of this at the time, because it was very cool, – at the Avantgarde Fashion Show, which was held in the Congress Hall of the Deutsche Museum, a building with a Nazi past. There I helped in all areas. Including the set-up of the venue, backstage assistance where the models were. As a reward I was able to hang out with Munich's most fashionable, beautiful in-crowd. It all had a very international flair and was related to the world I had left behind three years before.[89]

At that time, I had a few fleeting relationships with young women. I also became friends with Kirsten Wiseman, a friendship that continues to this day. Like myself, Kirsten also enjoyed hanging out in Munich's nightlife. I still knew her from Oskar-von-Miller-Gymnasium. Kirsten had an English father who worked as a doctor in Munich and a Jamaican-born mother who had worked partly as a model and later trained as a psychologist. The two of them had raised their children,

---

[89] I had already worked at Avantgarde Modewoche during the holidays in Munich when I was still at school in Israel.

Kirsten and her brother Stephen, to be highly disciplined and successful. Both Kirsten and her brother became medical doctors, sang and acted as children and teenagers in the Munich Opera at Gärtnerplatz and defied all supposed barriers and stereotypes.

After passing my driving test, I got another "dream job" for some three months. I was hired as a driver at the BMW customer collection centre, which at that time was still in Munich-Freimann. People who had purchased a BMW, and who had opted to self-collect, would pick up their car there. My job was to drive the cars between different preparation and examination points and to and from the car park. The cars were all brand new and there was the full range of models, including the most expensive luxury and sports cars that BMW produced. When I didn't want to extend my contract, my immediate boss was quite disappointed, because he told me that people with A-levels had real career opportunities at BMW and because he was seriously very happy with me.

One job I was not suitable for was my attempt to be a waiter in a fashionable new nightclub. The club had a rule of not charging people until they left. On opening night people drank the most expensive drinks and the club was bursting. In fact, it was so crowded that you did not notice when people disappeared without paying. I made a loss of several hundred Deutschmark. The club's manager wanted to make me liable for the losses. After this shift I had learned my lesson and did not try again.

There are also few words to be said about the job I had at Karstadt Oberpollinger mentioned earlier. Having previously worked for the decoration team of a furniture store, the job as an assistant in the decoration department of one of Munich largest department stores appeared suitable to me. Whilst I still had to carry and shift things about, the job could be quite creative and less tied to the daily sales routines or annoying customers. Nevertheless, there was something about the job that chipped at my conscience. The problem was mine alone and was related to my family history and religious background. You see, the Karstadt-Oberpollinger decoration department was located adjacent to the underground car park that belonged to or was used by the department store. There was direct access between the two buildings. This meant there was always only artificial light there. But it wasn't because the place was gloomy or scary but because of another fact of history that I felt uncomfortable there. The underground car park had been erected exactly below the spot where once Munich's main synagogue had proudly stood until November 1938, when it was destroyed by order of the Third Reich. That location was the edge of Herzog-Max-Strasse. I was never happy about the fact that I was working right on this very spot, out of all places, and for that reason alone, I decided not to extend this contract, even though I got on extremely well with my colleagues. I can still remember the feeling of going down that basement. It carried the taste of the forbidden and immoral, before the silence whilst walking down would be interrupted by the two Bavarian-speaking employees who would never have suspected what was going through my mind. Today, years later, I would not accept the same job, on principle. I would even go as far as calling it a disgrace, that on the site of the synagogue a car park had been erected. It's important to clarify here that the staff I worked with were not antisemitic, as far as I could tell. It was simply the place where their decoration department was housed, probably because it allowed them to park the van there and have some storage ability nearby. Those who had planned to build a car park here, and the others who allowed it, were however liable.

Incidentally, I always had similar emotions whenever I visited the town of Dachau, which, after all, was the place where my grandfather Gerhard Lewandowski had been incarcerated and mistreated back in 1933 and 1934. In fact, there are buildings and places of this kind strewn everywhere across Munich, be it the Führerbau on Königsplatz, the Haus der Kunst or the concert hall of the Deutsche Museum.

Besides the buildings, there were also situations that reminded me of darker historical events, and often quite unexpectedly. In 1990, I took part in a march against the occupation of Kuwait by Sadam Hussein. I participated out of a desire for world peace, and I came openly with placards that read "Jew for Kuwait" and "For Kuwait, Israel and Palestine."

Before I attended, I had been in contact with a pro-Kuwaiti organisation, which sent me some material about the invasion. They knew that I was Jewish with links to Israel and did not make it an issue whatsoever. By chance, I met a young Kuwaiti woman in a café at about the same time. She was wearing a hijab and was dressed otherwise in a very modern way. We exchanged phone numbers without any expectation. I was not prepared for the fact that she would promptly contact me secretly a few days later. She soon learnt that I was Jewish. She asked to meet me in an expensive hotel where she stayed. Nobody knows what would have come of it. A young Kuwaiti woman from an upper-class, wealthy family on holiday in Germany secretly meeting a young Jewish man with links to Israel, against all traditions and religious rules? Young people often have the greatest potential to overcome supposed barriers. But even though she called one more time, I did not take her up on the offer, not the least because she was only temporary here.

What went on in the heads of two curious young people was one thing. On the streets of Germany, however, self-important activists with big mouths were deciding how world politics should be assessed. When I went to the peace march against the Kuwait occupation, I unexpectedly met many demonstrators who declared the invasion of Kuwait to be a Zionist plot. I suddenly felt completely out of place. It wasn't to be the last time in my life.

There was other politics too. I joined the local branch of the Social Democratic Party (SPD) and attended the meetings of the local association of the Munich district of Milbertshofen. It was the promise of an orientation towards social justice, environmental concerns and an international outlook that attracted me to the party, besides the fact that the Conservative Party of Germany, in Bavaria represented by the CSU, firstly, had Christian in its name and secondly, I saw the CSU more as a homogenous right-wing nationalist, Catholic and German-Bavarian party. There was also a historical link with the right-wing parties of the past. They were later proud CSU members who had once been rather enthusiastic about other political ideals between 1933 and 1945: Alfons

Goppels, Georg Graf Henckel von Donnersmarck, Volkmar Hopf, Fritz Kempfler, Gisbert Kiey, Theodor Maunz, Hans Schütz, Alfred Seidl, Richard Stücklen, Hans Troßmann, and also Oberleutnant (senior lieutenant officer) and former Nazi supporter, Franz Josef Strauß – yes that patron of my former school, the Ersatzkönig (compensatory king) and perhaps also an ex-buddy of my former biology teacher? I don't want to deny that the party did stand up for Jewish people or the Jewish community after the war, and yet, the fact that such links existed gave one pause for thought. In the CSU's sister's party, the CDU, there was an even more well-known case, in Federal Chancellor Kurt Kiesinger.

At some point in the late autumn or winter of 1989, I had left my details at the Bavarian SPD HQ, stating I was looking for work as an office assistant, or really anything that would be useful. Patrizia Althoff, the personal secretary of the then head of the Bavarian SPD and later vice-president of the German Bundestag, Renate Schmidt, took my contact details and surprisingly soon enough got back to me. A young assistant happened to be exactly what she had been looking for. I started with office jobs, but soon after that supported SPD candidates in the October 1990 state elections. A colleague and I were handed over a VW Bus in Bonn, which was loaded up with party materials. With it, the two of us travelled for months to various local party associations across Bavaria, setting up information stands, distributing materials for the many candidates and delivering leaflets.

After the elections, Patrizia asked me to continue to help her in the Bavarian SPD office at Oberanger (Central Munich). I ended up processing Renate Schmidt's mail, looking over the weekly news on Bavarian SPD matters, making coffee and helping with the distribution of the monthly magazines, not the least filling envelopes. Patriza Althoff was a woman who lived life to the fullest and was a chain smoker. At work, she talked about friends in her age group and the intrigues of the party. I somehow became her protégé, and I was also a useful assistant to Renate Schmidt for all the things she didn't have time for.

35

The German Test

There was a reason why I was still working instead of studying in September 1990. An official from the Bavarian Ministry of Culture (responsible for Education) did not recognise my Israeli A-levels and refused my admission to German universities. I required a certificate from his office, that would allow me to apply with Israeli A-levels. It wasn't the quality of the foreign award he questioned. He argued that I had to prove to him that I had command of the German language through an official test, in spite of the fact that I was born in Munich and had attended German schools and kindergarten up until 1986 and carried a German passport.

I began to explore alternative routes to university. One way was via university registration in Bremen through the help of a friend who lived there, and where I could apply for the same document. Unbelievably it was granted after just a few weeks without any problems, but it was only valid for the State of Bremen, and for the university there. An acquaintance of my friend's parents, Christian Haverkampf, who happened to be a high-ranking Bavarian ministerial officer, heard about my plight at the Bavarian Ministry of Culture, and smelled a rat. He was horrified and immediately initiated a review of the decision of the officer who had refused my acceptance to university in Bavaria. In his opinion, this decision was not entirely correct, as I was a German citizen of the

Jewish faith who had only spent a few years in Israel to try to receive some Jewish education, which was not available in that way in Bavaria. Believe it or not, the review by a higher officer was all it took. A few months later, I unexpectedly received the Bavarian recognition of equal status in the post, which, however, was of no use to me for the coming academic year (1990/91). I would only be able to enrol in 1991/2, and thus had effectively lost two years since finishing my A-levels. The official who stood in my way was peanlised, I was told. Was the official just being fussy and not pragmatic or was it a case of antisemitism? We will never know for sure.

In the meantime, I had started to take my first steps in journalism. I had used the money I had earned in various jobs to acquire professional equipment and had also applied for membership of the German Journalists' Association. My first plan was to travel to Egypt on my own, to explore how Israel is viewed there. I had already applied for a visa and had an international press card. But when I started looking for a place to stay in Cairo, I started having second thoughts. Any doubts as to whether I should go or not were resolved after the 1991 war with Iraq had began.

Nevertheless, I now owned a laptop (back then, some three kilogram in weight) and a printer and that triggered a real writing frenzy. I had previously typed everything on a semi-automatic typewriter, and before that on a mechanical typewriter. It was a transition, because I liked the rhythmic pressing down of the keys on the old equipment. One of the first texts I wrote on my laptop was an article dated February 1991 and entitled "Arabia, between religion and revolution." It is a kind of philosophical treatise that deals specifically with the subject of "holy war," Iraq and Saddam Hussein, but poses fundamentally philosophical questions.

I then distributed my writing among friends, acquaintances and work colleagues and tried to send it to SPD magazines. Initially I did not have any success, but it would not be long before I would achieve my first publication.

Since a trip to Egypt in the middle of the Gulf War was no longer a good or safe idea, I travelled instead to Tel Aviv to do interviews there.

After all, I was able to stay with my aunt and uncle for free, was familiar with the place, and there was far less risk. It was all about gathering information and impressions and then seeing what I could do with the material. I had also sincerely hoped to see Alice, whom I was still in contact with. It was unbelievable, but precisely in the week I was there she was stuck in her military base. We did not get to see each other. When I arrived in Israel, the first thing I did was interview tourists near the beach about whether they feared that rockets from Iraq could hit Israel. I then interviewed two political senior figures, Esther Korn, the foreign spokesperson for the *Raz* party, and Elieser Garnot, the spokesperson for the Israeli socialist party *Mapam*, and took part in several press conferences, including one on security. The interview with Raz's foreign affairs spokesperson was published in *Schlaglichter*, the magazine of the Socialist Youth Germany (SJD), a sub-group of the Jusos (Young Socialists) of the SPD.[90] I was a little apprehensive about my very first publication and used a pseudonym, Max von Sylvenstein. I first wanted to see what happens when you publish something. What did I expect, phone calls, antisemitic attacks? Only decades later, when I started to write for *taz*, was there behaviour of that sort, but after the German police got involved, that ended quickly.

I offered the tape with the reactions regarding the war to the Bavarian main station Bayerischer Rundfunk, but they had no use for it; not only was I a greenhorn without any established name, but I didn't quite appreciate at the time that they were obligated to use their own correspondents anyway. I should have offered it to independent radio stations elsewhere, but I was only starting and learning on the way. Another of my own projects resulting from my visit consisted of the translations and descriptions of 30 modern Israeli songs, including from artists such as Chava Alberstein, Yehuda Ravitz, Ofra Haza, Rita Farouz, Maschina, Chaverim shel Natascha, Schalom Chanuch, Yehuda Poliker and others.

---

[90] Schlaglichter Issue 3-4-90 Peace should have nothing to do with religion, under the pseudonym Max vom Sylvenstein

I researched these performers and translated their songs lyrics as best I could, along with a master tape of these songs. I then sent a bound folder and cassette, all in all the work of two to three months, to a relevant music and culture editor of Bayerischer Rundfunk, the Bavarian State Radio Station. He actually took the time write back to me, in words something along these lines: "*Thank you very much for your suggestion and work. Unfortunately, we can't do a series like this because you haven't done any research on the Palestinian music scene.*" What a dose of hypocritical neutrality, although I may include an artist like Amal Murkus today, who is Palestinian with Israeli citizenship.

Not being admitted to uni, I made the best of my time to learn and research with the resources and facilities open to me. Only 21, I gave a lecture in March 1991 at the *Frankenwarte*, an academy for political education in Würzburg, as part of their series on "Right-wing extremism: tendencies and threats in Germany and Europe." Alongside three academics and international guests, I spoke on the topic of "Meir Kahane, the Jewish ultra-right." This talk was followed by a second presentation in Munich for the Jusos (SPD's youth movement). I used mainly public libraries in Munich for my research. What's more, both the project on Israeli music and Meir Kahane were prior to the establishment of the world wide-web, and hence required looking up of sources in book form, wherever they could be found.

After the seminar in Würzburg, the editor of the magazine *Rechter Rand* asked me to write about the issue. I had happened to see Kahane in person once when he was lecturing passengers in Haifa from the roof of the bus centre. I was struck by this ultra-right-wing figure in Israel, as I knew little about the Jewish ultra-right and had always heard that they were connected to the Jewish settlements in Yehuda and Shomron (the West Bank), which were seen as a problem for the peace process. Just a few years later, in 1995, Israeli Prime Minister Yitzhak Rabin was assassinated at an event in Tel Aviv by a radicalised religious far-right supporter.

My reports also landed on the desk of Professor Michael Wolffsohn, who at the time often shared his opinion on the Middle East conflict on television and whose latest book I had just read. I asked him what he would suggest to me, to prepare for a career in journalism. He replied, without going into much detail, that I should study history and politics at university. What else would an academic say? It was also common practice in Germany, in contrast to the UK, where many journalists traditionally write their way to the top starting at a local paper, although this tradition has increasingly given way to the study of journalism. Either way, after receiving permission to study from Bavaria, I applied to study politics, history and Islamic studies at the universities in Munich, Mainz and Bremen.

However, I had also sent an application to the School of Oriental and African Studies (SOAS) in London as a third option. Since 1987, it had been possible to study in other European Community member states under the Erasmus programme and the same conditions as in one's home country. SOAS, a specialist school which had once developed as a place to train colonial envoys and administrators and is part of the federal University of London, was and still is regarded as one of the world's leading universities for the study of various aspects of African and Asian, Indian and Middle Eastern Studies. To my surprise and joy in July 1991, I was offered a place to study there. Everyone whose opinion I asked advised me to accept it. The thought of soon living in London, even though rather abstract, had a certain appeal. Young people like me "knew" London mainly through the broadcasts of the music channel MTV and its dominance at the time in music culture, street fashion and the diversity of people, which by far exceeded the diversity of German society. Who could say no to that? Not me!

36

Fears, Hiding, Running Away

Before I left Munich, I had my two first rather serious relationships. The assurance a relationship provided came a bit as a surprise to me, as my life had so far been marked by running from one place to another. There was one shorter relationship with a young Irish woman, Caragh.[91] I had met her, (no surprise!) in an Irish pub in Munich, and we hit it off immediately. She came from a small town in the North-East of Ireland and was in Munich for work. Whilst we must have been together for a month or two, the relationship made me ran from it out of fear. I will say more about that in a moment.

I also had a longer relationship with Dalia, a Romanian-German young woman who had been a school-friend of mine at the age of seven.[92] That relationship too broke down. I eventually imagined that Dalia's family, which was of German descent, was incompatible with mine. One moment where this revealed itself was regarding the meaning of 1989, a big year for Germany and Europe, with the fall of the Berlin wall and the eventual reunification of Germany. For many of us Jewish people in Germany it was a matter we observed with some degree of

---

[91] Name changed.
[92] Name changed.

concern. I found a diary entry from that time, where I left some thoughts concerning the first anniversary of the German reunification (see the original in the next chapter). Dalia and I assessed the events totally differently, and we strongly disagreed with each other. Too self-absorbed in my own fears, I failed to understand that perestroika meant the end of the tyranny of Soviet communist dictatorship for many. But that was only one issue that put some strain on our relationship.

Any relationships with my girlfriends, but if I am honest, even with my male friends, caused my parents anxiety. My mum had and still has a great concern and irrational fear of "strangers coming into her flat." It was the projection of a hostile outside world that was to be kept out. She and my father were unable to embrace my girlfriends and often also saw my male friends as a threat. This is also why they turned down all invitations from my friends' parents, whether it was for coffee and cake, swimming or going to the theatre. Basically, my mum and dad lived withdrawn from everyone. Neighbours and people in our social circle were all judged according to the criteria of the Second World War. It was about how these people positioned themselves in relation to Germany, Jewish people or Israel. In the end, the only safe place that remained was home. It was a space of absolutisms rather than a negotiated space. They were barely able to build relationships with, as they saw it, unsafe people in general and non-Jewish people in particular, and with increasing age and lacking the daily contact with others in my father's restaurant, my father, and my mother also, became increasingly isolated. "You can never trust anyone," they preached without end: "Your friends are worth nothing, only your parents give you assurances you can rely upon", they justified themselves to me. They claimed they were interested in me and yet they destroyed so many things that were important to me by completely ignoring my deepest wishes, desires and talents.

The only people they described as trustworthy, indeed invited into their homes, were other Jewish people of their generation, mostly men and their wives. After the passing of both Edith and Henrik Goldfarb, two other Jewish families of similar background, the Kucharskis and the

Groß-Family replaced the space the Goldfarbs had left behind. After they too grew frailer or died, my mother was left alone, especially after my father's death. Her anxiety is so much that I am unable to tell her about any problem, not even that I have a cold, without her "not being able to sleep for nights on end" from worry.

Whatever natural predisposition my parents may have had, I believe that the Shoah drew out vehement psychological obstacles for them and left them with deep inner wounds and blockages to the soul, not that they would admit to such a thing or that they might need to seek some help. Even if they had wished for it, for decades there was a complete lack of any psychological help for survivor families in Munich, or people near us, that would normalise the fact that psychological scars were to be expected after the traumatic events of that time. Being aware of the pitfalls of those scars would have eased the burden and possibly shown them strategies to deal with it. Fear of others did not have to be a normal state of affairs, however understandable, not even for Jews after the Shoah in Munich.

In the end, my parents even fell out with the very last members of the family with whom they still had any contact. They were Uncle Marcello and Aunt Gerda, because Gerda, rather thoughtlessly, repeated local provincial opinions about Germany. My parents also broke off contact with Evert, Mum's cousin, and his wife Jenni in Holland, "because Jenni had once said something about Israel and Palestinians", and according to my parents, it was meant in bad faith. They felt that Jenni and Evert were on the side of people hostile to Jews and Israel. I heard similar condemnation by my father of his German accountant. The lady in question was a little too interested in Israel and had managed to compare the actions of the Germans in the Third Reich with those of the Israeli armed forces in front of my father during the 1967 and 1973 wars. In fact, this is an act of Holocaust relativism and trivialisation and is categorised as a form of antisemitism. I believe that living in Germany made this much worse for both my parents, and had they lived in Israel, the USA, Canada or the United Kingdom or any other country, it would have been a little less personal for them in this respect, although within certain limitations. From my cousin Hanni, who lived in Israel, I learned that her parents saw her future husband as a threat because he came from a Moroccan-Jewish family and not from an Eastern European one.

In 1991, I realised that leaving the confines of the closed world of my parents would be essential for me to move on and beyond this type of mental imprisonment.

To get back to the issue of Caragh and Dalia, with which I started this chapter. It wasn't Dalia's family background that became a "problem" for me at all. Dalia loved me unconditionally and was somebody who would have gone through fire for me. Caragh, whom I was with before Dalia, also loved me, there was no doubt about it. My relationships with both these young women could have been long lasting. Given my age and experience I was not in the position to have the necessary insight and introspection concerning my own psyche, but I think I can say with some confidence today that the problem in those relationships was totally of my own making.

My parents, who had never sought psychological counselling or pastoral care, had installed a psychological construct of constant threat in me, in a way that had now begun to destroy my relationships with people close to me, indeed with people who deeply loved me. I literally hid from my relationships when they became too serious, when they got too close, when women knew me as a whole and I could no longer run away from them. Love was dangerous, for my parents loved me, yet suffocated me and trampled upon the person I was. The strategy that sustained me was to run. Perhaps that was also already a problem in Israel, when I listened more to my German friends than to Yael.

In short, I chose to avoid Caragh and I told Dalia that it would be better if we split up because I was going to London.

A relationship is always about giving up some freedom and security. Together, people gain a new stability and experience love. I thought running away made me free. I didn't realise that the love of these women was different from that of my parents, that it could have liberated me, that it could have grown and even protected me instead of tying me down. In the years between 1991 and 1994, I would still have to face a lot of emotional upheavals. A solid relationship with someone who loved me could have spared me some of these experiences or could have made them easier.

I owe Caragh and Dalia a sincere apology and must thank them for their unconditional love at the time. For at least another seven years I was unaware of, or did not connect with, insights into the psychological and emotional turmoil of some, although not all, children of Shoah survivors.

37

Concerning the First Anniversary of the German Unity

"I wasn't happy. I didn't want a big Germany. I was happy with a small one. I didn't want them to become strong."

Wolf Zylbersztajn 1995[93]

I have translated the following extracts loosely into English, to carry forward the strength of their conviction. They reveal strong emotions, and I apologise for their original tone. It would however be wrong to withhold these lines, expressed in that way at the time.

DIARY ENTRY, HANDWRITTEN *(orig. in German)*

Munich 2 October 1990

Tomorrow is now being turned into an artificial public holiday by the Germans. They have recently started calling 3 October 1990 the Day of German Unity. From tomorrow, West and East Germany will be reunited. Oh Gloria! I am sorry, I am unable

---

[93] Zylbersztajn (1995) p.10

share this euphoria with the people of racial and cultural superiority. The creators of the greatest slaughter, the people with the dirtiest conscience – and I mean above all that large proportion of murderers who bear innocent and defenceless people on their conscience and who are still alive today, with secure pensions – they all stand to attention today while Catholic church bells proclaim unity at the turn of the day.

What have all those who would have received the death penalty for their crimes in so many other countries around the world lost? A woman, a man, a leg or an arm?

Oh, how I pity them, those with their mendacious laughter and beer mugs in their hands.

For their non-punishment, for their repression, their lack of awareness of guilt, for their national reunification (they were gifted this). May they die the dirtiest, most miserable, slowest death on this earth, for the fact that they are doing so well now!

They are to be chased into the night by visions of sweat-filled horror, that are not visions, but repressed memory.

Why do the victims of that time still suffer today, and why do the former murderers and butchers still laugh?

Justice is probably one of those words, whose definition is still to be explored, because justice doesn't seem to exist.

This reunification represents yet another stab into the heart of every former victim of the Nazis, because there was no extensive punishment of the Germans after the war.

40 years of separation cannot be a punishment (which is what they like it to be seen as).

Germans of today must live but for peace, indeed exclusively for peace in the entire world.

Their aim in life (should be) to save human lives. But instead of doing this, today they shout louder. Alas, when Kurds, for example, seek their salvation here in Germany, everything appears forgotten, the past, just like the world around Germany.[94]

Once again, a process of centralisation has arisen in their minds. Germany is seen as the centre of the world. Yes, Deutschland, Germany über alles.

No, I don't see the world as grey. I just see and hear, and perceive reality without forgetting the past.

And people like me, who are German, are very, very rare, not even the SPD provides assurances, because the party serves as a possible shield for some NS members, suggesting that they are certainly guiltless because of that party's membership.

No, no German unity will never make me forget what happened! No German unity will conceal who you Germans are, as long as you Germans do not acknowledge your shame by doing justice and finally let murderers, murderers, be murderers who – this is an unrealistic consideration – have to face up to the truth themselves.

It's just a pity that I have a somewhat weak faith in G-d, otherwise the thought of a divine judgement would certainly be of great comfort to me.

May the Day of German Unity be for me a day of remembrance of the shameful deeds of Germans, in G-d's name!"

---

[94] A reference to hostility towards Kurdish refugees shown at the time.

38

My Father, Not a German!

For decades, Dad dragged himself around the world with his blue stateless passport. In the early 1990s, it were probably pension issues and the burden of having to apply for a visa every time he travelled abroad, even if he wanted to travel to Israel, that made him apply for official citizenship of the Federal Republic of Germany, so he could have a German passport. Without a clear nationality to his name, my father had different ID numbers over the decades. They all had the same basic data, but because they were not official German passports it caused a bureaucratic nightmare. Things were registered with him showing a particular ID card in the 1960s whilst by the 1970s the number was different. I found in total four different numbers over five decades. Should there even be four Wolf Zylbersztajns, all with the same first name, birthday and place of birth? In the minds of some officials, yes. Lawyers had to be paid to prove the opposite. That was the trade-off of that blue passport.

The reason for all this trouble was that my father did not want to be a German citizen or German under any circumstances. He saw himself firstly as a Jew, and secondly as a Polish Jew, or so he told me.

I never saw myself as German, the (German passport) has no meaning. You know, I refused to have a German passport all those years. Only now have I had enough of all the difficulties of being a stateless person. The German passport doesn't change the fact that I only see myself as a Jew. The Jews who survived the concentration camps can't be German Jews. According to the papers I'm a German Jew, I have a German passport, so I must be a German Jew, but in reality, it's different. When I meet someone, I always say, I'm a foreigner, I'm a Jew.[95]

My father emphasised this point together with an anecdote that he liked to retell. He mentioned it in 1995 and repeated it again during the Shoah Foundation interview in 2001. He described a scene from his pizzeria, where he had just revealed to someone that he was Jewish. The customer at the counter reacted with the following words, as recited by my father: "Oh, you're Jewish, but that doesn't matter to me."[96]

My father said he didn't understand why the person had said, that it didn't matter. For him, it was as if this remark made him into an example of a good, exceptional Jew. They didn't like Jews, but because they knew my father, at least he was OK, he was a "good Jew."

"I'm not fully accepted. You (the person who addressed him) only said it to make a complement of sorts. Such talk means nothing else than that Jews are not properly accepted in Germany. But I remain a Jew."[97]

I asked my father what one should make out of the fact that he was watching German television and reading a German newspaper every day? His answer was that he had no choice. There was no Yiddish cinema or television programme here, he replied. Actually, there wasn't anywhere, not even in Israel or New York, at best a Yiddish theatre group or a

---

[95] Zylbersztajn (1995), p.14
[96] Ibid.
[97] ibid

Zol Zayn Shulem II: Faroys

singing group. The Yiddish American paper Forward also eventually stopped its Yiddish output, although I did buy him a subscription for a year, when it still was publishing in Yiddish.[98]

Of course there were contradictions in my father's views. He had every right to be German and Jewish. However, his experiences made these two identities irreconcilable, at least in his eyes, due to the hatred projected towards him during the Shoah and the unending crimes that this hatred had brought to light, even when the issue of Jews not belonging to Germany had originally been constructed and spread by Third Reich Germans.

---

[98] This is the real tragedy, and Yiddish is a victim of the Shoah as well as of the decision of Israel and the Zionist movement to accept only Hebrew as the official Jewish language. This has also contributed to the further demise of Ladino and Judeo-Arabic.

39

London

In September 1991 I packed my bags yet again. My initial plan had been to travel to London with my car and bring my cockatiel pet bird, who was exceptionally attached to me.[99] My parents advised against it. Besides, what did I want with my left-hand drive car in London? It wasn't the only thing I left behind in Munich. As already mentioned, I told my girlfriend Dalia that I thought it would be rather unrealistic to try to maintain the relationship at this distance. She wasn't very happy about not having a say in the matter and refused to accept it for at least six months.

Whilst I had been offered a place to study in London, there was another reason for my departure from Munich and Germany, which only appears evident retrospectively. Many of the young Jewish people around me who had grown up in Germany had left the country for good. The ones I know of are Kalmon, Vicky, Pninia, Micol, Laura, Shirly, Deborah, Awi, Yehudis, Leon, Silke – they all left Germany. Some of

---

[99] My car was a red Peugot that I had been gifted over the radio by a listener, when I asked on a listners' exchange show if anyone had an old banger to gift to a young adult. Somebody who permanently left Germany then gave that totally intact car to me, which would become an extension of me, with a sticker in Hebrew of the Israeli *Raz* Party on its boot.

them entered great careers abroad. They became lawyers, business-people, therapists, social workers and artists.

Subconsciously, as far as I was concerned, there was something else that made me leave, and not take up the opportunity to study at the German universities that had offered me a place in Mainz amongst others, even after all those significant years I had lived there. No, it was not just a subconscious thing. It was the combination of the man in the disco in Passau, the people at the peace demo who had a problem with Israel, it was Franz Schönhuber, the "Tanz den Mussolini, tanz den Adolf Hitler" track in the club, it was the long-standing refusal to look the Olympic 1972 terror in the eye, the refusal of an official to recognise my Israeli A-levels, it was the genuinely good friends who insisted that their parents and grandparents had not been involved in National Socialism, and most certainly that biology teacher, bragging about his past in a fighter plane over Berlin – all that history kept constantly flaring up. I needed a break from that too.

There were notable exceptions to this among those of my generation of German-born Jews, and Germany should consider itself lucky to have them. What I write here, I promise, is not my last word on Germany, but only an explanation of what played a role back then in my decision to leave.

And so it was that in the end I travelled to London by plane and from there to Hendon, an area of London with a relatively high Jewish population. There I met Gideon, a former schoolmate from Alonei Yitzhak. He promised to help me find a room in London and I soon found one in the neighbouring area of Golders Green. A man in his 40s, his name was Mr Rogers, offered the bedroom that used to be his parents. But by December he had raised the rent almost monthly. Because I knew absolutely no one in Golders Green, and even though the few Jewish shops, like the bakery Happening Bagels, and the opportunity to eat falafel in kosher restaurants, was a bonus, it took about an hour to reach uni. I decided to move closer and found a room in Kings Cross in the London ads paper called *Loot*. My room was to be a sublet in a council flat with a biker, who was himself a sublet tenant. But now I was only a 15-minute walk away from SOAS. So much for where I first stayed.

The shabbiness of London surprised me from the start. This former heart of the British Empire was truly a run-down, broken, dirty, noisy city and years behind developments in German cities like Munich. The city demanded distance, detachment and alertness, if you didn't want to be taken advantage of.

SOAS, my university, was located near Russell Square, in the centre of the city, and housed in an old brick building from the 1920s. When I arrived for enrolment, the first thing I had to do was to queue in front of the registry office. I was wearing a black jacket and a shirt, quite possibly even a tie. Being finally able to study, after two years of unnecessary delay, meant the world to me.

Well, who doesn't know that common wisdom that one can't run away from oneself or who you are? There in the queue in front of me stood a young, slim, blond man with a long page-cut. A non-Jewish German student! Erik Dege had come from northern Germany to study economics and Korean at SOAS. His father was professor of Korean geography in Germany, his mother a US-American translator. And so it was that this coincidence led to Erik and myself becoming relatively good friends for the next few years. We both soon met another German – Klaus-Peter Kozott – and his girlfriend Doo-Ri Lichtenberger. Klaus was the son of Germans who had migrated from Silesia to West Germany, Doo-Ri was also German, but born in Korea and had lived for a good while in Brussels. Both had lived in Bonn before coming to London. Doo-Ri studied sociology at the London School of Economics (LSE), Klaus had followed his girlfriend and wanted to do a year abroad in politics at SOAS. However, he was a hopeless case academically. It wasn't due to a lack of intelligence, but because he enjoyed hanging out in London's pubs, bars and clubs too much. Doo-Ri, on the other hand, fluent in four languages, would not only finish her degree, but later work for the UN in Bonn. If it wasn't for that job, she would have had plans for a PhD. Stefan Ploch from Augsburg, who eventually became a recognised linguist, was another German in our small group. In addition to these Germans, Ruhma, a young British woman whose parents had immigrated from Pakistan, and her future husband, Nicola, who was Italian, both studied at SOAS and became my companions during these years. A not insignificant fact in addition to this was that Micol Rieger from Munich, who also had gone to school with me in Alonei Yitzhak, would soon follow me to London to start a degree in International Relations at the LSE. For as long as she studied in London, Micol and I remained close friends.

My move also came with some disappointment. The promise of a possible scholarship that Renate Schmidt from the Bavarian SPD had proposed to me could unfortunately not be fulfilled, because the fund did not allow for the study of complete degrees abroad.

It was difficult to combine the desire to study with the excitement of being a young person in London. Klaus-Peter, who had already decided that he preferred the nightlife, constantly invited us to night-time tours of various pubs and clubs, but there was a limit as to how much I was prepared to go along with this. Studying was immensely important to me.

And my music continued to be shelved. I never got round to playing the piano again, as I lacked both an instrument and the time. However, I played a few more times in front of friends and later, between 1994 and 1996, I even took singing lessons which had the advantage of not needing an additional instrument. I sang with a London Community Gospel Choir and took lessons with a jazz singer.

In December I met Afiya in the SOAS university student bar.[100] She wasn't studying at SOAS but was friends with a Lebanese colleague of mine. Afiya was originally from Uganda. Her father had once been politically active and was either forced to flee to London after the political takeover of the new leader Museveni, or he had been working in the Ugandan embassy during this change of power, and made an asylum

---

[100] Name changed

claim after that, I can't remember the exact details. Afiya told me that her family had once led a very comfortable life in Uganda, and that she had even gone to a very good private school in England for several years, a fact that her distinctive Queen's English supported.

With the political situation in Uganda, the circumstances for the family had changed dramatically and Afiya's world had become unstable and troubled. There were odd things about her. Whilst I thought we were dating, I would repeatedly not hear from her for weeks before she showed up again.

Photos Afiya had given me of a model shoot she had done, like the ones many young women did of themselves at the time, looking quite like a stunning model, ended up accompanying me to Munich when I visited my parents. At an opportune moment my mother rummaged through my belongings without me knowing and discovered Afyia's photos between the pages of some book. My mother and my father would often carry out such searches throughout my younger life, looking for evidence of wrongdoing contrary to their world view. In this respect, expert studies have revealed that violations of privacy are one of the more common possible behaviours that showed themselves in significant numbers of families of Shoah survivors.[101] The find of Afiya's photos was what my parents had been looking for – proof that I wasn't living the way they wished me to live.

I only knew of it, after my mum burst into hysterical shouting, the first of many rants on this subject, which was immediately followed by my father in full tantrum. I was given a lecture about Africa and AIDS and then the words "*Oy Gewalt*, you will not bring a *Schwarze* into my house!"[102]

When he added that it would be better if I chose a German girlfriend, I learnt that black people were behind the ranking of the supposed evil

---

[101] This is what I learnt years later from the holocaust survivor and second generation expert Gaby Glassman
[102] Oy Gevalt, (expression of desperation in Yiddish, Schwarze, yid. a black person).

Zol Zayn Shulem II: Faroys

(non-Jewish) Germans within my father's' universe. It was an unpleasant and completely unexpected confrontation. I no longer understood the world. Firstly, my father was by no means a religious man, and secondly, he was a person who had experienced racism at first hand and seen with his own eyes what it does.

What was going on here? The Hungarian psychoanalysts and trauma experts Tihamer Bako and Katalin Zana may give a possible explanation. Bako and Zana wrote this about the behaviour of traumatised people:

> *Victims of severe trauma who are unable to categorise it have the experience that fantasies – fears and nightmares – come true, that the ghostly becomes reality. The boundaries between the "what-if"-reality and reality become blurred, giving free reign to imaginary visions. The victim's past experiences are thus teleported into the present and become permanently real. The experiences of the past represent a constant danger. It is no longer the trauma itself that maintains the traumatised state, but the distorted imaginary concept that is projected (here) into reality.*[103]

Bako's and Zana's more recent studies refer to long-known observations already made in the 1950s and 1960s by William Niederland and others.[104]

And so back to my parents and their fears: In the case of my parents, a person of darker skin colour symbolised the possibility of being singled out as an object of hatred by others (Germans or Nazis) and therefore also triggered huge anxiety and fear. They had been able to more or less hide their Jewishness in German society for decades, only revealing it when they chose to, or so they thought. Certainly, my father's speech was clearly infused with Yiddish, and in his restaurant, many knew he

---

[103] Bako & Zana (2020). S. 28 (retranslated into English by me)
[104] Niederland (1961), see also Steinberg, Arlene: Holocaust Survivors and their Children, in Marcus & Rosenberg (1989), p. 25

was Jewish, to the extent that his restaurant had been targeted a few times by racists. According to that concept, anyone who stood out as looking "different" could become a victim again. It is a philosophy that allows racists to dominate rather than fighting for the right to be equal.

This was also mixed up with the question of survival and the death of so many others. As my father's son, I represented his guarantee that all the murdered people in his family would be followed by a new next generation. There was a future to the family. His son's own wishes for his life did not fit into this fantasy.

As my mother had also decided to reclaim the faith of her grandfather David, I too had to ensure that our family was to remain Jewish. Such demands weighed heavily on my shoulders. Fundamentally, it didn't even matter if I had a Ugandan girlfriend from East Africa or anyone else as a girlfriend or boyfriend, it would never have satisfied them, not even the imaginary German woman my father mentioned. Possibly not even a Jewish girlfriend would have done, because she may not have been the "real Jewess", as my cousin Hanni experienced after she had met her husband Awi, who came from a Moroccan-Jewish family and is the most kind-hearted person. I could never fulfil the role assigned to me as a substitute for all those murdered in my family, or the destroyed trading empire of the Lewandowskis, even if I had tried.

There was certainly also underlying racism in that mixture, based on what one picked up in the German press about people who came from the African continent or had a dark skin colour. Anyone who had a son with a Black East African girlfriend was no longer part of German society, or not German at all, or that's how it must have looked to my father. Adding Jewishness to that made one even more of an outcast. In their fear, my parents didn't realise that this was literally bowing down to racism, views that should no longer have had a place in Germany.

What happened in the winter of 1991 in my parents' apartment was the start of a confrontation between my parents and myself that would last nearly until my father's death 20 years later. For now, I was to promise to end my relationship with Afiya. I remember traveling back to London at the time. I felt abandoned and I realised that I couldn't live according to my parents' fears and rules. The pain of not being understood, which started years before that, the always missing father who never helped me or passed on what he knew, the parents who didn't understand me when I came home with bad grades, the parents who dismissed the musical talent everyone could see but them, the parents who refused to allow me to return to Germany, when I wanted to leave after a short time at the Israeli school for a variety of reasons and after I had been terribly ill. At that time, it was not yet possible for me to discuss these things with friends. The only consolation was that I was now living in London, far away from my parents' world full of anxieties. In that sense the flight back to London was as easy as it was hard. It felt like a departure to which there was no return. I remember that I went to a Central London night-club where the singer Rozalla was performing her dance hit "Everybody is Free!" I was right in front of the stage singing and dancing the words loudly, whilst the eyes of the singer appeared to meet mine and I felt she was giving me an acknowledging nod. "Everybody is free, to feel good!"

A poem in English, which I wrote in 1993, reflects something of this moment:

> *"Africa so deep inside me, forgot the colours, found a woman, so close we brought these continents, I am a man, she is a woman, that's bloody all I can see, what must be and what must not be, invented identities,"* I wrote there.

I would not put it like that today, as I see the person more than the person's background. I am not saying this out of hypocritical ignorance of people's backgrounds or colour, but "Africa" is such a broad term that the poem also reveals limitations of my own understanding at the time. Afiya was neither "Africa", nor was I "Europe" or anything else. However, the poem goes back to this one moment in my life.

London

Man and Wo-Man Africa in me so deep,

forgot the colours – found a woman
So close we moved these continents

What has to be and shouldn't be, identities made up.

A man, I am, A wo – man, she, that's bloody all, that I can see

But woman, she – she is not mine, for better people are they there, controlling dirty colours.

I love her, woman – without rules Us – we turn this world,

with colourless boys and girls,

no more cultures and no more passports, identities made up.

A man, I am – A woman, she, that's bloody all, that I can see

40

Crooks and Racists

Kings Cross was not a place I could stay for long, at least back in 1992. This area of London was at the time well known for its junkies, prostitutes and their clients. Some of the working women carried out their trade in the basement of the house where I stayed. The flat was kept dirty by the biker and the balcony of the top-floor flat was populated by noisy pigeons.

I started to look again, and initially had the idea of squatting in a place that seemed to have been empty for weeks. I told my friend Erik about it, and he agreed. The day after our inspection, we found the place boarded up, as if someone had spotted us. I discovered an advert from a family in North Kensington between Notting Hill and Ladbroke Grove in the office of the University of London's Housing Exchange. It contained an offer of living with the family on very low rent. In return, I would have to look after a twelve-year-old boy for three days a week in the evenings, as his parents were often not around. The attractive thing about it was that I could live close to one of the trendiest areas of London for very little money, and the bonus was that the family's house was located not far from my new London friends Doo-Ri and Klaus-Peter. Portobello Road and Ladbroke Grove were still a recognisably anarchic area at the time, although it was already in the early stages of gentrification.

In the early 1990s, there were a good number of people hanging out in the streets who were the forgotten and left-behind remnants from the 1960s. They strolled around here and there with spliffs in their mouths, and a general atmosphere of hedonism lurked behind many of the window shutters, in the pubs, streets and shops. Londoners of Caribbean family backgrounds who also called this area a home moved about, whose annual public cultural highlight was the Notting Hill Carnival. They had experienced racism in this neighbourhood for a long time and fought against it. The carnival symbolised resistance, cultural pride and belonging to London. In the 1960s, another group of young people proclaimed several houses they occupied as the Independent Republic of Frestonia. All of that was the area legacy, together with a left over of an area reserved for Irish Travellers, a remnant of a larger presence that went back to the 19th century.

Our weekend routine here looked something like this. We got vegetarian food from a little shop called Grainshop, and Cava from the Spanish supermarket Gracia & Sons. Armed with that we would sit in the sunshine in Tavistock Square, one of the central spots of Portobello Road where sometimes musicians, sometimes crazy people, played any type of music and often danced around stoned. We also often strolled to the Portuguese Café 'O'Porto and to Lisboa patisserie on Goldborne Road or decided to visit the street's second-hand market. Every Friday, musicians played the finest blues from Otis Rush and John Lee Hooker at Bob's Good Time Blues Bar on Latimer Road. We would also often hang out at a bar on the corner of Latimer Road that was at the time called the Market Bar, where DJs would play the latest Dance Beats.

We were part and yet not part of this community. With mainly German friends, who in turn had Australian friends (there was a regular Ozzie night in yet another bar in the area), we lacked a real connection to the actual local community at the time. We lived here because of the supposedly cool reputation, but we were too preoccupied with ourselves to look beyond our horizons. We failed to understand the significance of the Mangrove restaurant, for example, the centre of black consciousness in this area and the scene of constant racist police violence, especially in the period between the the 1960s and 1980s.[105] As far as we were concerned, all of us coming from less diverse corners of Europe or Australia, the sheer diversity of people in this area and the freedoms they seemingly had, was "liberating" in itself. The Reggae record shops like People's Records or the fact that you could buy Caribbean food here, or the reasons as to why there stood an aray of steel drums under the arches of the raised 1960s Westway motorway that cross-cut through the area failed to trouble our conscience as to their deeper layers of historical significance. We thought we engaged with the area, but were merely surfing on its reputation.

Had I had another chance today, I would do things differently. Today I am much more interested in local people, and their life stories. I say that as a journalist of a certain age. That said, the curtains of racism were soon to open themselves, showcasing the other side of Britain and providing me with concrete knowledge about this country I didn't yet possess. It arrived on its own and without any warning or invitation, or an introduction from those who might have known better.

The family whose three-storey house I moved into was that of Caroline Smith, a local conservative politician.[106] Her Conservativism was an ode of "feminist" admiration to Margaret Thatcher. They had bought the elegantly furnished house relatively cheaply, or so they said, in the late 1970s, when the neighbourhood was not yet as desirable as it was later on. In fact, estate agents had converted these houses, which were often divided into numerous flats, into three-storey single-family mansions. They boasted private gardens that were totally closed off, and soon enough became much sought-after properties worth millions.

I would describe the street in North Kensington where the family lived as a wealthy island in the middle of a still in parts mainly impoverished area. The family also owned property somewhere in the country,

---

[105] Taylor, Diane (2018)
[106] Name changed

and they travelled there regularly in typical English aristocratic fashion. Both Caroline and her husband came originally from Southern Africa. They were both of English background and their ancestors had moved to Southern Africa at the start the British colonial Empire. She and her husband had left Southern Africa in the late 1970s

I have never heard anything derogatory about Black or African people from Caroline or her husband. But in their large kitchen, a family friend who once came for a visit mocked at the breakfast table what he saw as the apparent inability of black South Africans to ever govern themselves, or so he claimed. "Only Europeans are capable of making such countries prosper", he argued. I listened in disbelief, unable to take in that this man, who was clearly a racist, was so sure of himself.

Afiya didn't want to come to visit me in my new place after hearing about the background of the family. She was there once anyway, and after the dog barked, she joked that the dog probably had a problem with Black people too. Finding all of this still too restrictive, not the least because of Afyia, I decided to move out by Easter, my third move within a year, into a flat I had found via *Loot*. It was relatively cheap and located in a social housing estate in the North of North Kensington. It consisted of two rooms, kitchen and bathroom on the third floor of a brick building block from the 1930s. Again, it was not far from Ladbroke Grove, Latimer Road and Portobello Road, and from Doo-Ri and Klaus-Peter.

The man who was subletting the flat assured me I could live there at least for a few years. On that note, he asked for a three-months deposit. We came to an agreement, and I paid in cash, naive and inexperienced as I was at the time. To reduce the costs, I invited a young fellow student from SOAS to live in my flat with me. He was of French-Belgian-Algerian background and preferred playing guitar and smoking dope to studying. In return for part of the rent, I gave him the small bedroom while I moved into the living room.

We decorated the flat as well as we could with lots of colour. For my room, I bought a fancy, huge new mirror and we added whatever furniture we could find. I used wooden pallets as the foundation of my bed with a mattress over it. A blue velvet fabric adorned the wall, along with chic black blinds, I had bought.

With this roof over our heads, it was time for a housewarming party. We prewarned the neighbours and bought them all a bottle of beer and earplugs. About 30 people came to the party, which had the theme of world music. I hired some DJ equipment, speakers and disco lights, and played songs by Fela Kuti, Cheb Khaled, Ofra Haza, Mzwakhe Mbuli, Reggae and Salsa and much more. The neighbours in the house itself had left us alone, but we had not taken account of the neighbours in other blocks of flats, our music echoing between the walls. Youths from the neighbourhood began to threaten our guests, letting us know that we had not yet earned the right to cause such a disturbance in this area; besides, nobody had invited them. They forced their way into our flat for a moment but soon left again, with some loot, as it turned out, taking amongst others my flatmate's leather-jacket. If that was bad, we had it coming properly soon.

Two weeks later, on a Saturday, Afiya finally visited me for the first time in a long while. I wasn't quite clear anymore, whether we were still together at all, but then she did come.

I wanted her to have a good time and had it all prepared. In the morning on Sunday we were having a champagne breakfast when suddenly, at around 11am, there was a loud knock at the door. Who was going to visit us on a Sunday morning? I suspected something unusual. The answer came promptly. "Police, open the door!" Three police officers stood in front of us. One immediately ran into our flat without a search warrant, then another followed, and both examined the flat. We were all shocked. I could not help but wonder if they had gotten the address wrong. "My flatmate and I are university students at SOAS, Afiya, is my girlfriend, I informed them.

They explained that they had been sent here because we allegedly squatted the flat. I explained that everything was kosher, and that I paid rent. Not satisfied with my answer, they decided to make sure their visit wasn't in vain. They asked us to identify ourselves. My Belgian flatmate and I had our passports, but Afiya had no ID. Even though there is no compulsory ID that must be carried in the UK, they decided to arrest Afiya for this reason alone. They said they were taking her on suspicion of being an illegal immigrant. They had not come for that, they had said they thought that we were squatters, and they had no credible reason or evidence to suspect Afiya to be illegal. Had they asked any person on the street to identify themselves, the vast majority may not have held an identity card on them. Hence they had no right to arrest her. To them she was suspect merely on grounds of her colour. Racism by white English male police officers in this area was rampant and well known, I later found out. Afiya was arrested and carried away before our eyes.

It turned out that I had fallen prey to a rental scam and a fake landlord. We learned that the whole block in which we stayed was about to be emptied to be completely renovated. The alleged landlord had had no authorisation to rent out the flat.

Without knowing how I could help Afiya, without any contacts or friends familiar with something of this kind, and without knowing where to find her, I knew one person I could ask: Caroline Smith. As a local Councillor, surely she could help? I had written down the numbers on the police officers' badges and gave them to Smith. Smith knew me well enough to understand that I was not a criminal and that the arrest of Afiya was suspect. She promised to contact the local Police Superintendent, whom she said, she knew well. When I asked her if I should come with her, she replied that I couldn't help, but that I could rely on her word. Due to Smith's intervention Afiya was released within a few hours. It was not until the evening that I was able to reach Afiya on the phone in her flat (the phone was used by several people, and on previous calls they informed me, that she was not there). Afiya lived so secretly that I had never been given her address. It was therefore not possible for me to visit her and support her otherwise. She told me that the officers had even gone as far as to take her fingerprints. What was going to be a romantic weekend, shattered due to police racism and abuse of power.

Zol Zayn Shulem II: Faroys

Having lost my flat and money and having been ordered by the police to vacate the flat immediately, I packed my belongings. With the very little money I had left, given the fact that I had paid a rental deposit and for some furnishing, I booked a bed in a room with six people in a cheap guesthouse. My roommate found a place with another friend. But as soon as I saw the bed with its worn-out mattress in a room in which also others would sleep and the unhygienic conditions in the toilet, I fled the guesthouse just 15 minutes later, having lost even more money. Instead, I spent the night behind some bushes near the Italian Water Garden in the middle of London's Hyde Park. The night was surprisingly cold. I couldn't sleep properly, too nervous that someone might steal my few but important possessions. In the morning, I made my way to SOAS at 7.00 am and learned that they only opened later at 8.30 am. Once there, I was able to take a long hot shower, shaved and brushed my teeth, as the uni had a shower room near its sports-facilities. Later, I didn't want to admit what happened to my friends. I was embarrassed and ashamed that I had been tricked. But in the afternoon, facing the question as to where I would sleep this night without any money on me, I finally informed Doo-Ri and Klaus-Peter. They were angry with me, but only because I hadn't said anything the night before and, without thinking twice, they offered me the only space they could offer, behind the sofa on which they slept themselves inside their tiny flat in Cambridge Gardens.

But in spite of all, I was not out of luck. After some research, I found out that Sutton Housing, the owners of the council house I had been living in, had rented the flats to the housing co-operative Infil (later Westminister Housing Co-op). The man who had tricked me was one of their tenant-members.

Founded in the 1980s, this accommodation initiative specialised in short-term rental contracts for flats that had been selected to be renovated soon. Until these works would begin, the flat being vacated and empty, the members could stay there. Their presence would mean that nobody could squat in the flats, and instead there were known and registered people in them, who explicitly promised to leave on request. Members could live in them for very little rent, compared to the normal rates in London. Unsurprisingly, many of its members were single people, including many LGBTQIA+ Londoners and people who had immigrated from abroad, all of whom could find it more difficult to find affordable accommodation in London. Infil had some 200 to 400 such members, sometimes more, sometimes less, and they would be scattered in housing units over different areas of London. The members managed the association co-operatively from an office in Camden.

Infil contacted me soon and their staff told me that they had decided to expel the man who had sublet the flat to me and in return offer me a membership, especially since I had become homeless with little money left. They planned also to take legal action against the fraudster, but he soon disappeared and could not be found. After about two weeks in which I stayed with Doo-Ri and Klaus-Peter, I was given the keys to a flat in Great Titchfield Street in the heart of the West End of London. There were lots of tiny fashion wholesale shops there and it was less than 20 minutes on foot to SOAS.

But my housing situation was only one of my problems. What about Afiya? For Afiya, the racist arrest was another traumatic event in a chain of dramatic life events. Smith told me that she gave the police-chief a warning. A few years later, the London Metropolitan Police would be brought to justice for their shabby investigations of the murder of Stephen Lawrence by a group of white young men. The police made several unforgivable mistakes during their response to the murder and during the investigation. The McPherson Inquiry into the circumstances of his murder and the Met's handling of the case concluded that the police was institutionally racist, a charge that was confirmed again in 2023 in another Police Inquiry, unrelated to Lawrence.[107]

After she was taken away that fateful Sunday morning, I didn't see Afiya again for many years. It was only much later, perhaps over a decade,

---

[107] see McPherson (1999), The Baroness Casey Review (2023)

when we met again. I learnt that Afiya had joined a Christian Evangelical sect and had been observing religious celibacy for several years by then. I don't know how this came to be. Perhaps membership of this sect gave her a sense of security.

The young woman I knew at the time was a woman whose existing potential could not be realised, but who was young enough to try again. Uprootedness, conflict in her parents' country, trauma, rejection, insecurity and fear in a new racist society are not easy barriers to overcome. I also know that she later worked as a receptionist for a large company in London, using the one thing she had taken with her from her years in an exclusive English private school, namely, that distinct very upper-class English accent, to her best advantage.

One of the new things I had to do was to attend the monthly housing management meetings at Infil's central office at Chalcot Road. The members employed three staff members.[108] Members were encouraged, but not forced, to take part in the meetings. Their participation was rewarded with pizzas, travel expenses and, most importantly, points! Points were also being awarded for each move. Once a year, the person with the highest number of acquired points was given the keys of a permanent home, so they no longer had to move. I worked in the Co-operative for over seven years, and later my wife Claudia also joined in the effort. I even became elected Vice-Chair and Claudia even rose to become Chair, and so we accrued many points on our account, rising closer and closer to the top.

Although there existed a great diversity of people amongst the members and many, sometimes heated, arguments erupted between us, and although the employees grabbed themselves the best from the organisation, especially good wages, somehow the system still worked, and we always had a roof over our heads. At least that was the case for as long as we were with them. Every time members like us had to move, we received

---

[108] The office was located at 51 Chalcot Road, on the corner of Manley Street, an upmarket neighbourhood near Primrose Hill.

a small decoration allowance and the guarantee of a functioning kitchen, bathroom and toilet. The flats had to be in an acceptable condition at a minimum standard. It turned out, that we had to move on average about once a year; a few times we could stay longer, sometimes it was shorter.

41

The World is Bigger!

**British Library Reading Room, photo Wikipedia,
Diliff, Attribution 2.5 Generic (CC BY 2.5).**

I have not yet said enough about the very thing I had moved to London for. Since summer 1989, I had been waiting for my opportunity to study. Here I was in SOAS, one of the best-known universities in the United Kingdom. At the heart of SOAS stood its library, which to this day has one of the most important collections of documents, writings and books from Asia, India and Africa. During my time there most of the lecturers and professors were still Europeans, a fact that would slowly change over the following ten years. SOAS soon had the first ever Black female director of any British university in Baroness Valerie Amos.

I was enrolled in introductory classes in history and politics. There was the history of the Middle East up to 1800, a comparative politics course and a course entitled "Development and Underdevelopment in the Third World." The assessment was based on coursework and an end of year exam. There were weekly tutorials in addition to the lectures. Apart from the general introductory politics course, the classes were relatively small. In Middle Eastern history, there was even a small group of four with Professor David Morgan (1945-2019), an expert in Mongolian history. Morgan saw students as young academics to be taken seriously. He served tea and coffee in his small office, and at the end of the year he treated everyone to a meal at a neighbourhood Bengali restaurant.

Soon enough it became apparent that although I understood and spoke English well, my ability to write English on an academic level was not quite where it should have been. I was recommended an additional course in academic English in the evenings, which rapidly improved matters.

Just a few months after starting my studies, I obtained a readers' pass for the British Library on the basis of my membership in the International Federation of Journalism. Undergraduate students on their own were usually not allowed this privilege at that time. I will never forget the days I spent in the British Library's original 1857 reading room, placed in the heart of the British Museum.[109] Here, on the old green upholstered benches and tables under the large dome, once sat Karl Marx, Marcus Garvey, Mahatma Gandhi, George Orwell, Vladimir Lenin and Virginia Woolf too. You only had to look up into the dome and the high bookshelves to be immediately inspired to study, even if it sometimes took a few days for an ordered book to be ready.[110] I seemed to have come to the right place. Another library I used frequently was

---

[109] It closed in its function as the centre of the British Library in 1997.
[110] I think it was a huge mistake to close this legendary reading room, which has always been the heart of the British Library. That said, the new British Library is now a well-established feature of London, but it doesn't quite have historic quality of the old hall.

that of Senate House, the central library of the University of London. Here, in the 19-storey Art Deco building from 1937, the neoclassical Periodicals Room became my most loved and adored place of study.

About three or four months into my studies, I realised that the topics many people were studying here in London were hardly comparable to what was offered and taught in Germany. This didn't just apply to the course content at SOAS, but also at other universities such as LSE, UCL or Goldsmiths College, to name a few. This gave me the idea of founding a German-language intellectual magazine for all German-speaking students at London universities, not only for the local but also the German market. I called the project German Writing Society. However, I made a big mistake and relied on the SOAS student union to at least provide me with a space and some financial support, such as free access to photocopiers, essential for the distribution of papers, prior to the onset of the Internet Revolution.

There were all kinds of student groups at SOAS. There were Islamic, Jewish, African-Caribbean, Asian, Palestinian, and Korean groups to name a few. However, nothing could prepare me for the self-righteous way in which the application of a German Writing Society would be perceived and immediately rejected by the leadership of the SOAS Student Union.

I had already been labelled as an enemy of sorts by the very pro-Palestinian Student Union. Most of their then leaders were often male and English and hard-left activists. They defined their political identity through engagement for South African and Palestinian liberation. As radical socialists, the SOAS Student Union leadership claimed the right to pass judgement on everyone. The fact that I was ideologically close to the Israeli peace camp at the time was irrelevant to them. In their eyes, Israel was a European colonial state to be completely rejected and had no right to exist. These English men, helped by a few others even asked the few Palestinians at our university not to talk to Jewish Israelis and Jews. Most of us ignored it and used the rare opportunity to meet and exchange ideas. It was a time of hope, the time of Camp David under the leadership of Yitzhak Rabin,

Yasser Arafat and King Hussein, but it was also 1992, decades before huge crowds would march through the streets of London and label Israel a terror state.[111] SOAS was a place of encounters and crossing boundaries. I had Kurdish friends, Lebanese Shia friends, Israeli friends, friends from Black-Caribbean, Turkish and British Muslim-Pakistani families but also from different African and South-East Asian countries and there were students from numerous European countries and so on. A young Muslim Egyptian woman stopped me once in the stairway, and confessed to me that she really liked me, and that she was confused because I was the last person her family would wish her to date. In the end she was safe, as we didn't end up going out. A young German woman who had been studying at SOAS for an MA, and was a friend of mine, ended up secretly dating a Jewish orthodox colleague of mine. A Muslim Pakistani friend married a Christian Italian – they are still together. There was lots of stuff like that going on.

But when I arrived with my plans for the German Writing Society, I was judged with the SOAS Student Union's skewed and already biased worldview. Because what I wanted to do was to create a German-writing group of sorts, it was automatically labelled a fascist undertaking. I was told, I remember to this day, that I could expect neither funds nor any support, because "why should the Student Union support German Nazis?" Although my family had been victims of the Third Reich Germans, I too was labelled a Nazi without distinction, by these self-righteous apostles of an apparent "better" world.

In the end I managed to book a room and advertised it with flyers I had paid for myself. A few German students from other universities came to the meeting, including Claudia Schmid, who was studying at UCL and who became a long-time friend during my studies. Those who came all liked the idea, but we lacked the necessary resources. Only 15

---

[111] Well almost and more from my perspective, some London friends told me that all of this had suffocating antes in the late 1970s and 1980s. They were in women movements as Jews and suddenly discovered that they were not wanted.

years later, we could have easily produced an e-magazine, but this was 1992 and the Internet was yet evolving. If you wanted a magazine you needed to be able to print or at least to photocopy.

In 1995, in my last year at SOAS, the actions of the SOAS Student Union led to controversy. They invited representatives of Hezbollah to an event, just at the time when Arafat and Rabin were close to sealing the peace plan they had negotiated. In protest at what this militant Islamist movement represented, Jewish and Hindu students and members of the LGBTQIA+ community lined up in the auditorium to demonstrate against them with placards. We were generally against the event, but it was not about cancellation, we did listen to what the Hezbollah representative had to say in the name of freedom of expression and some of us even asked questions including one Jewish young female student for whom it was visibly emotional. So far so good. Problems arose, however, when members of the Islamist Salafist youth movement Hizb-ut-Tahrir began blocking the entrance to the university and began an angry and aggressive confrontation when students objected to them. The police had to be called, and we all had to be escorted out of the university via a back exit for security reasons. Hezbollah was proscribed by the state six years later. Hizb-ut-Tahrir in 2024.

42

Trip to West Africa

When I realised from what was taught at SOAS that I might understand a thing or two about Israel, I also learned how little I knew about other regions of the world, especially the history of African countries. Realising huge knowledge gaps, I asked my university personal tutor Kathryn if I could broaden my studies beyond the Middle East. I wanted to learn more about other places, not excluding African countries. She had no problem with this but said she needed a little convincing and proof that I was indeed capable of understanding and studying African histories and politics. We agreed that I should write a long academic essay of sorts. To make the point, I decided that there was no better way to demonstrate the sincerity of my intentions than to travel to an African country and write about it. In late spring or early summer 1992, I thus travelled on my own to The Gambia, West Africa. Due to package tourism, it was the cheapest place on the continent you could travel to at that time, and I could just about afford the flight and a cheap accommodation. There I spent a few weeks researching the working methods of development organisations. I didn't tell my parents until shortly before I left and stated it as something that was routine at my university -just a study trip.

The Gambia, an English-speaking, once British-ruled West African country, is one of the places in the world with the highest number of

NGOs. The reason for this is the small population and small size of the country. This enables aid organisations to quickly claim positive outcomes for their work, which does not necessarily reflect a true picture of the effectiveness of what they do in general.

I searched the SOAS library for any information I could find on The Gambia, but even in this specialised university there was actually very little. Then I started planning my trip, contacted the German embassy in the capital Banjul and was soon sitting on a charter flight to West Africa. The gigantic size of the Sahara Desert surprised me. After about six hours, we landed in the sweltering heat of Banjul's small airport. A taxi driver took care of my luggage and off we went to the capital. Palm trees, West African scenes with people walking alongside the road, some with goods on their head, and then an increasing number of concrete buildings appeared. It reminded me a little of some of the dusty less glamorous cities in the South of Israel.

Despite a lack of contacts, I made my way around and got to know various people with whom I also engaged in political discussions and who wanted me to understand The Gambia from their point of view. Every day I tried to visit another aid organisation, including Action Aid, Save the Children, Medical Research Council, Islamic Relief and a German forest rescue project of the Gesellschaft für technische Zusammenarbeit (GTZ). Many only gave me copies of their glossy brochures, but the GTZ in particular, whose people I got to know through the German embassy in Banjul, made a real effort to give me more detailed information. When I flew back, most of the tourists who had spent their holidays in hotels at the beach here were suffering from diarrhoea. I ate in the villages where the local people bought their food and remained in excellent health.

Back in London, it was time to put my brief experiences onto paper. I had discovered that many projects in The Gambia could not necessarily be seen in a positive light and that the best projects were those that fostered people's complete self-management. I had also realised that there were many people who were not at all in need of help and had jobs like anyone you would meet in a Western country.

The trip had awakened my curiosity. I wanted to understand more about the history of slavery, colonialism, the development of independent African states, West African ethnic groups and their old, proud cultures, which I was not yet familiar with.

After submitting my long essay, SOAS granted the requested change of degree programme, and I immediately asked for permission to also take a course in History of the Caribbean at University College London (UCL). I wanted to understand the entire history of West Africa in modern times, including the transatlantic slave trade and its consequences. I had come to the realization that I still knew very little, but wanted to change this.

After completing my first year at SOAS, I spent the summer back in Munich, visiting friends and going back to earning money through holiday jobs. Munich seemed quite provincial and quiet compared to London, but I enjoyed the familiar, although I missed my car.

43

What the Others Might Think

It was late July or early August 1992 when I was looking for books from the Sahel region in the SOAS library. I had signed up to a volunteer placement with the development organisation SOS-Sahel. They needed some samples of patterns to add to books to be published for their oral history series. When I had finished finding the correct material, I was sitting in the huge room of the Student Union sipping some tea when suddenly I noticed a young woman with long black hair sitting diagonally opposite me, also drinking tea. She noticed me too. We smiled shyly at each other and soon struck up a conversation. As the university and library closed at 5.00 pm, we moved our conversation to a nearby Italian restaurant. To cut a long story short, it was love at first sight for both of us.

Nura was an art expert with a completed doctorate specialising in Islamic Art and came from an Arabic-speaking country.[112] She was from a Muslim family. Whilst she was doing her doctorate, she had struck gold discovering a yet unknown site of an ancient pre-Islamic civilisation. I could be more precise here, but for her anonymity, I will keep it at this

---

[112] Nura – Name changed for anonymity.

rough outline. She was also a published author a I thought I had struck gold. I thought she was beautiful and the conversations we had were on another level. We wanted to meet again soon, and I kept my calm, not to overdo it. But just a week later, she invited me to her home. She had prepared a romantic dinner.

She explained that she had left her country to escape, as she put it, the patriarchal structures there that kept women in their place. She had taken all the freedoms in London that she claimed were not open to her in the society she had grown up in.

We had a lot to talk about and started going out together. I remember evenings when we laughed about words that were the same in Hebrew and Arabic. Nura and I met as often as our schedules permitted. We were both fond of each other.

One day she suddenly let me know over the phone that we couldn't see each other anymore, that she had to call the whole thing off. The reason for this was a fight between "rational conformity" and the "will of her heart", is roughly how she put it.

What on earth had happened? I was distraught and shaken to the core. It was like this: Nura had confessed our relationship to an old male friend of hers because she wanted to tell him how happy she was. She had wanted to take me to a meeting or a party, maybe something this friend had invited her to, and must have said that she intents to bring her new boyfriend along and telling him more about myself. Without knowing me, this "friend" categorically condemned our relationship. Apparently, the trouble was that Nura was ten years older than me. The woman who had escaped the shackles of the patriarchy of her country of birth (not my words, but hers) was now caught up in the patriarchal manifestations of another type of conformity, here in the British Eldorado of Western freedom. A man was allowed to love and marry a woman many years younger than him, but if it was the other way around, she had to put up with hearing from others that she was a cougar with a toy boy. To be fair, nobody could suspect that Nura was older than me by her looks.

The relationship we had was a completely serious adult, intellectual relationship, and full of mutual admiration and attraction with plenty to explore and purpose. There were no barriers between us. I pleaded with Nura, I spoke over the phone, left messages, wrote letters. But no objections on my part helped. This friend had put a spell on her, whoever he was. Once again, perceptions and existing pre-judgements of "other people" had destroyed something beautiful and potentially powerful. Social anxieties around what could be, rather than acknowledgement of what was, won the day.

Nura had forced herself to this step and she also suffered from it, even if she kept it to herself, until a few years later she published a novel in which she tried to categorise the drama of those days and her feelings in a few passages. It was heartbreaking and left me devastated.

44

A Dead End – London East End

It was a great and happy year in Great Titchfield Street. The location was not just close to SOAS but I was also in the midst of where many of the London clubs were based. One night it was UK Garage, another one Uplifting House and yet another one classic Funk. But just as I began to really set roots, the time had come for my first move as part of the arrangement with the housing co-op. It occurred in the depths of autumn and added to my misery after the breakdown of my relationship with Nura. So far, I had only been living here in the West End. in the Kings Cross and North Kensington neighbourhoods, with a brief period also in Golders Green. Infil now sent me to a neighbourhood I was completely unfamiliar with.

My new home was to be in the East London neighbourhood of Shadwell. It was a two-bedroom flat on the ground floor of an over 100-year-old social housing estate owned by the Peabody Trust. This estate was mainly inhabited by white working-class families and immmigrant-families of British-Bangladeshi background. Some of the houses were completely run-down and neglected. On the edge of the area, Margaret Thatcher had the old, dilapidated Docklands rebuilt as a new financial district with tall steel and glass tower blocks. The old warehouses of the Wapping harbour area had become neighbourhoods for wealthy yuppies.

The difference between rich and poor could not have been more sharply expressed. Watney Market, where the nearest supermarket was located, was basically a market like you might find in a suburb of Bangladesh. Most of the population had fled Bangladesh after the genocidal civil war in 1971 and emigrated here, though some had come far earlier through service on British ships. They were partly deeply religious and partly made up of socialists and communists, the latter of whom had been targeted during the genocide. Many lived in this run-down area surrounded by the wealth of others.

The area had a social history characterised by waves of immigration of different people and cultures over the centuries. It used to be the main area for Jewish immigrants around 1900. I lived not far from Cable Street, where I learnt about the Battle of Cable Street through a large mural. In 1938 the Jewish population of London's East End, together with communists, trade unions and other democratic and anti-fascist alliances, had opposed and blocked a fascist march through the East End. Oswald Mosley and 3,000 supporters of his British Fascist Union were defeated in a violent demonstration which ended the prospects of fascism in England. In 1978 and 1993 there were other such clashes.

One remnant of the Jewish past was the East London Central Synagogue in Nelson Street. When I visited the shul on different Shabbats, fewer than twenty people were still praying there. Once I forgot to take off my kippah after the Shabbat services, and I was attacked not by ageing Mosley supporters, but by Bangladeshi young men shouting "Heil Hitler!" at me. Instead of showing solidarity with the history of the area and the previous population, some of these young men had chosen Jews to become their scapegoat for anything. This was in part driven by the activities of Salafist and "Islamic" militant groups, such as the Hiz-but-Tahrir movement. This mood still prevailed in the area most recently. In 2015, three schoolgirls were recruited for Isis there, while in 2022 posters of Hiz-Bu-Tahrir calling for a caliphate or the fight for Jerusalem could be found in the Watney market area. After

A Dead End - London East End

the 7th of October 2023, pro-Palestinian flags appeared everywhere in Tower Hamlets. Incidentally, those who butchered Bangladeshi people in 1971 were mostly other Muslims, predominantly from Pakistan. One of the allegations and accusations justifying those mass-murders were that the victims had not been "proper Muslims." Whilst there were some prosecutions, overall Bangladesh has only seen a limited process of restorative justice without far-reaching holding to account of the thousands of perpetrators and helpers. Do I hear echoes of postwar Germany?

Shadwell was a place that had very clear Jewish traces of a Jewish past, like that synagogue, but this was 1992 and I felt abandoned and distanced far away from my university and the open-minded society of central London.

During this difficult time, I also ended up entangled in a short, quite devastating and disrupting relationship with a woman, that put me under a lot of pressure and outside my comfort zone. Friends tried to help, but it seems I had to walk through it to know better. Over time I gained enough strength to get myself out again and luckily that chapter was over after about a year. It was one of those experiences with people who take advantage of you, but from which you learn, and in the end become stronger. The grim and isolating surroundings of the housing estate in Shadwell very much epitomised that episode. The only thing that gave me some solace during this time were my studies. For one of my major assignments, I utilised my knowledge of Dutch by writing about the history of the Dutch Caribbean: Suriname, Aruba, Bonaire and Curaçao.

The difficult relationship behind me, eventually a far more positive romance developed between myself and a young technical student from Imperial College called Farah.[113] We met working in our spare time for a market research company, she in English and I in German and Dutch. Farah came from a family that for many centuries had been the religious leaders and rulers of a very tradition-conscious, extremely conservative region of an African country I won't name here. The current ruler and

---

[113] Name changed.

spiritual leader happened to be her grandfather. In other words, Farah was really big royalty and, if you like, a princess. After a few weeks, during which it became increasingly clear that we liked each other, she invited me to spend an evening with her. We got on extremely well. We could spend hours together. We were happy and it was a natural seemingly uncomplicated relationship, with lots of laughter and fun. But unfortunately, there was a catch, as I found out when I wanted to take her to the theatre, cinema or a club-night.

I happened to be Farah's big secret, and she wanted to keep it that way. She told me that "when the time came" she could only marry a person of her own ethnicity and Muslim religion, chosen and approved by her family. That was honest and open with me, but it was a heavy burden, and I very much hoped that Farah might change her mind. It was bizarre sometimes. I realised over time that there was really nothing I could do. As a member of the royal family, she was bound by tradition and prescribed norms and expectations, not that you would notice that by her way of life in London, living in a flat share, where incidentally everybody (they were all English) knew what was going on between myself and her and tacitly encouraged it. This time I decided, with a heavy heart, to be brave and end the relationship, to save myself from a more painful and possibly more complicated separation in the future. Farah wasn't going to have it. She called me again and again, begged and wanted to spend another weekend with me, wanted to prolong our relationship. It must have been just as difficult for her, and it certainly was painful for me.

Farah left London a few years later and returned to the region where she would be treated with great respect and honour. In a report of the regional newspaper that I once saw, she appeared tired on a photo. The days of her carefree little freedom here in London with her Jewish-German boyfriend were over. I hope from the bottom of my heart that she nevertheless found happiness.

45

Hitchhiking to Wales

In September 1994 it was time to move again. Infil found me a ground-floor flat in a dreary old social housing block in the immediate vicinity of the Old Street underground station. This flat was so old that it didn't have its own bathroom, only a bathtub integrated into the kitchen, but at least it wasn't that far away from my university.

Being in my last year at uni it was now time to carry out my own major project. I happened also to take a course in Modern African politics and a course at Goldsmiths College on racism and society in the UK. The reason for this was that I had read a book by the sociologist Paul Gilroy a few months earlier. He was just establishing himself as a young British academic and former student of the Jamaican-British sociologist Stuart Hall. Gilroy's book, "The Black Atlantic: Modernity and Double Consciousness", was an inspiring revelation to me.[114] In it, Gilroy not only wrote about Eurocentric culture, but also Black diaspora subcultures, as he called them. He made an important link to the Jewish diaspora because, he argued, the African diaspora, just as the Jewish diaspora was a transnational culture that transcends borders.

---

[114] Gilroy (1993)

With his long dreadlocks, he was one of the few academics at British universities in the early 1990s whose family history was itself partly Caribbean. The breakthrough came with his first book "There Ain't No Black in the Union Jack", in which he exposed the latent racism of the UK in the 1970s and early 1980s.[115]

Gilroy's clarity on race and racism(s) and his brave stance against all forms of racism, even when it was perpetrated by minorities, counts probably amongst the most important influences of my academic studies. With all the critique he had of Black performers in the US, he had some favourites and introduced me amongst others to Curtis Mayfield, whilst Les Back, who taught with him at Goldsmiths introduced me to Mez Mezrow, a Jewish Jazz musician who transgressed Colour boundaries and identified as much with Black Americans as he did with his Jewish background. 1994 was also the year I would meet my future partner and wife to be Claudia, with whom I have been living now for three decades at the time of writing.

We found each other in an unconventional way, namely through a newspaper advert and almost by chance. An initial phone call was followed by letters and photos and a few details. She told me that her mother, a scientist from Sierra Leone, had been fatally injured in a car accident not so long ago. Her mother's former partner, Michael Abberton, was an Englishman from Yorkshire, who was also a geneticist. Following the death of Claudia's mother, Michael brought Claudia, her brothers and her cousin to Aberystwyth, Wales, where he had obtained a scientific position at a research institute.

When I heard Claudia's story for the first time, I felt as if I had met someone who belonged to a group of people whose history was quite similar to that of the Jews and Zionism. Claudia is from a Krio family in Sierra Leone. Some of her probable ancestors were former American enslaved people, many from the US. Most of them would have been Black Loyalists from Virginia, who had committed themselves to the

---

[115] Gilroy (1987)

British side in the American Revolution, for a promise of a guarantee of freedom and land. After the war, it turned out that land would be in cold and barely fertile Nova Scotia, in what is today Canada. Whilst they were free with land, great poverty spread amongst them.[116]

In Nova Scotia lived another group of people of African background, Jamaican maroons. The Maroons established themselves from escaped enslaved people who found refuge and protection in the difficult to access hill terrains of Jamaica. One of the consequences of the Second Maroon War, a war between the Maroons and the African-enslaving British, was the forced deportation of 581 maroons from Trelawny, Jamaica, to Nova Scotia, which was also held by Britain.[117] Their arrival in Nova Scotia increased the hardship of everyone there.

Thomas Peters, one of the representatives of the Black Loyalists, negotiated with London with the help of British politicians, including the anti-slavery advocate William Wilberforce, to find a solution for all the people stranded in Nova Scotia. It was the birth of the plan for a settlement in Sierra Leone, through a "return" of the Nova Scotia community to the African continent from which they or their ancestors had been torn due to the transatlantic slave trade. This led to the foundation of Freetown, as a free city, in 1792.[118] Freetown was particularly suitable for this because of a natural deep bay, allowing larger ships to dock easily. Prior to this, the British had enslaved people from here especially on Bunce Island.[119]

The British did not enter into this settlement without intending to try to further exploit and lucratively profit from it, planning to bond the resettled people into unpaid labour in return.[120] However, it never came

---

[116] Bonikowsky (2013)
[117] Grant (2019), on the Second Maroon War, see Campbell (1990)
[118] From Nova Scotia to Sierra Leone, Black Loyalists, archived former website, in Pybus (2009)
[119] See Olusoga (2016)
[120] To what extent the relocation of the impoverished Black population of Nova Scotia (and even of London in England) was well-intentioned, or was a way to get rid of

to that, due to a lack of co-operation on the part of the population of Freetown, soon to be known as the Krios (from creole). Unfortunately, the first big group of resettled people fell ill from malaria soon after their arrival or succumbed to attacks by the local ethnic groups living in this region of West Africa. Nevertheless, the population of the "City of Freedom" grew rapidly after the abolition of the British slave trade in 1807. As a result, some of the human transports of enslaved people still captured by other European nations and intercepted by the British navy were brought to the province of Freetown.[121] Freetown thus developed into the "Zion of West Africa."

The Krios of West Africa grew into an independent ethnic and cultural community in Sierra Leone, which introduced architecturally colonial styles from the Americas into the area. The community was largely Christian, although there was a minority of Muslims too. It modelled itself in part on American-European traditions, be it in dress and lifestyle or in their education styles, but also retained traces of primarily West African cultures (especially Yoruba), which were reinforced by their new homeland. The Krios also had their own language, which was related to the Patois and Creole of the Caribbean and America's Deep South that enabled people who had been thrown together from different communities in Africa to communicate adopting common words from various European and African languages. Their food also bears a strong resemblance to American soul food and Caribbean cuisine, itself a mixture of European, African and some Native American traditions. In 1827, the Krios established the first West African university based on the Western model.

With their overall Christian faith, acquired in the Americas and England, the Krios led some missionary work in this part of the world, but at the same time had an ambivalent relationship with Britain. Due to

---

these is one of the points of contention in this story.

[121] Some, because a good number ended up on St. Helena, from where they often would still be transported to the Americas where they would have to labour to pay for their voyage. (Source, personal conversations with Peggy King.

their experience with European education and culture, they understood the British and other Europeans all too well. Increasingly, the British therefore attempted to undermine them and control the region through the policy of indirect rule, where arbitrarily appointed prefects would be given some powers, weakening the balance of power on the ground as well as the power structures within certain ethnic groups within the region, now referred to as Sierra Leone.

This policy of divide and rule was also to drive a wedge between different ethnic groups of Sierra Leone and the Krios. Independence in 1961 did not change that. The urban flight of other ethnic groups that settled in Freetown led to Freetown's cultural and ethnic distinctiveness as the place of formerly enslaved Africans being further marginalised, exacerbated also by increased emigration of Krios to Europe, the USA and the Caribbean. As in many other countries that became independent, conflicts between ethnic groups were exacerbated when they were crammed together for colonial administrative purposes. The borders of independent Sierra Leone were left unchanged from the colonial division. The once independent free province of Freetown was now just a part of Sierra Leone.

In 1991 Sierra Leone ignited into a civil war. A brutal army of rogue soldiers under the command of Foday Sankoh (Revolutionary United Front) attempted to take over the country. The conflict intensified in 1999 when Sankoh invaded Freetown. This was the final blow for the Krios. In 2002 military intervention by armed forces of the West African Economic Community, supported by British and UN troops put an end to the civil war and Sankoh's aspirations. According to an UN report, the war had claimed 70,000 lives and had displaced 2.6 million people. A total of 50,000 women and girls were thought to have become victims of sexual violence.[122]

---

[122] Kaldor & Vincent (2006) and UN Women. Rape as a Tactic of War. https://www.unwomen.org/sites/default/files/Headquarters/Media/Publications/UNIFEM/EVAWkit_06_Factsheet_ConflictAndPostConflict_en.pdf, accessed 22 January 202

The aspiration and dream of a town, even a province, of Freedom had become patchy. While many Krios continue to live in Freetown and Sierra Leone, others are now back in Europe and America, the very places some of their ancestors were glad to leave.

Claudia's family belonged to the educated and wealthy upper class of the Krios. Claudia's grandfather, Aloysius George, is said to have been one of the first judges of independent Sierra Leone, with an education from an English university. Her grandmother Sissi came from a family that could almost be described as Freetown's old aristocracy, especially due to their high level of education. In the 19th century, ancestors of the family are said to have traded goods between the Caribbean islands of Jamaica and Barbados and the West African country of Togo. Although little of the former wealth of both families remains today, it is said that Claudia's great-grandfather was the first person in Freetown to own an automobile.

Some of Claudia's other relatives are thought to be descendants from the Seychelles, others are thought to have come from Ogun-State Nigeria and Congo.[123] Claudia also has probably Ethiopian and British European ancestors.

I learned that Claudia's aunt Anjabi was already married to a German, Joost Gwinner from Hamburg, when I met Claudia. The family was therefore familiar with Germany, although I made it clear to Claudia from the beginning that there was a significant historical difference in the identity and history of Joost's family and mine.

When we first exchanged letters, Claudia wrote that she wanted to become a nurse. This linked her to family tradition. Claudia's second-degree uncle was Dr Davidson Nicol (1924-1994), a recognised pioneer in the study of insulin.

After the first letter exchanges, Claudia and I decided to meet. Only then did I realise how far away she lived from London. Whilst she was not living in Freetown, she was based in Aberystwyth, a coastal town in

---

[123] For the history of Yoruba wars see: Ajayi, J. F. Ade and Smith, R. *Yoruba Warfare in the Nineteenth Century:* Cambridge, 1964, 1971.

Hitchhiking to Wales

Mid-Wales all the way behind the Welsh Cambrian Mountain range. The train ticket to Aberystwyth was so expensive that I would have had to spend almost everything I needed to live on for the week on it. I decided to save the money, so I would have a bit to spend, when I was visiting and not look like a complete pauper. As the cheaper bus journey would take a full seven hours, my only true budget option left, I thought, was to try to hitchhike.

At around nine in the morning, I took the Underground to get me near the start of the M1 motorway and there I waited, armed with a pen and an A3 drawing pad. After a while, a lorry pulled up and took me all the way to the central English town of Shrewsbury. However, the onward journey proved to be more difficult. After two more lifts, I found myself in quickly disappearing daylight on the side of a Welsh country road in the middle of the Cambrian mountains, still about an hour away from Aberystwyth. It wasn't until around ten o'clock in the evening that I finally reached Aberystwyth, completely exhausted and surprised as to how long the journey had taken.

Claudia had a slim model figure with long braided hair and was about a head shorter than me. She lived in an old two-storey house. It was here that I met Michael, Claudia's mother's former partner, Claudia's brothers, Ishmael and Jahsyl, who were still teenagers at the time and messing about in their room, as well as Claudia's cousin Christiana and Christiana's then boyfriend and husband to be Mark Meredith. Claudia received me shyly and we started talking. I remember that she smiled, evidently my hitchhike did not leave an all bad impression. The next day we went to the town's beach and to visit the ruins of the castle. Apart from the university and the national library, the small old Welsh harbour town didn't have much else to offer.

After a two-day stay, during which we began to learn more of each other, I hitchhiked back to London. My biggest question was whether I should get involved in a relationship at this distance. I wasn't sure, but Claudia put my doubts to rest. As far as she was concerned, she would come to London.

As I found out, she had an aunt in South London who lived in

Peckham and had three cousins living there. In London we were soon walking the streets hand in hand, romantically in love; what a contrast to my former hidden relationship with Farah. I often picked Claudia up from her first job and I too finally got myself a rather well-paid student job at the small ARD studio in London, where I worked as a receptionist once a week. Rolf Seelmann-Eggebert was the London correspondent at the time. He could be both friendly and distant. The fact that I was interested in learning more about the production side of radio and TV rather than just working as a reception assistant was of no interest to anyone. That said, the radio studio later gave a German LSE student some access to learn about production, already an exception. I certainly couldn't be the second exception now. The studio was hierarchical and whoever worked there had progressed through the German system – all except for a few technical members and an English journalist who did all the research. In the end, I messed up the whole job through my carelessness: I had repeatedly forgotten to switch the phone calls from the setting that made them go through the reception to the night setting, that went through to all phones in the building. Desperate producers in Berlin called for the evening news with no one answering as a consequence.

And so it was, that Claudia and I started a life together, went out and met friends. I also got to know her surprising side. At the time, she was still making sandwiches to hand out to the homeless in our neighbourhood and couldn't believe it when someone turned them down and wanted money instead. There was something different with this relationship to all my previous ones. It was more grounded, and in that sense more serious.

46

White Man

Through Jackie Hamilton, who was a good friend, I became familiar with the club scene of "Jungle", a style of music that came out of a mix of drum & base, trance and reggae. It were Goldie, M-Beat, and other artists whose fame flickered up momentarily and are long forgotten since. Jackie was born in London and knew her way around in town. We often went out with her friends, many of them artists, ending up in obscure clubs that were sometimes packed, sometimes totally deserted but right at the cutting edge of production.

One November evening in 1994, a huge club night was to be held at Tottenham Court with many of the well-known DJs of the Jungle scene. Claudia didn't want to go, and Jackie and her people couldn't come either. I decided to venture out alone. A long queue had formed outside the club by 10.00 pm and I got in line. I was the only "white person" among the 30-40 or so people. Suddenly, six young men from the queue surrounded me and pushed me against the wall. They told me to hand over my money or else they would stab me with a knife. I had but £30, enough for the entrance fee and a few drinks, which I gave them, my options being limited. But I wasn't going to let them have it without a comment. I told them, that it was obvious that they robbed the only light skinned person in the queue, one of the few who liked the same music they did. "Doesn't that mean, that I have no issue with Black persons, culture and music?" I added that they had picked someone who didn't even earn much, as I was a student, and "do you know what I'm studying? Racism in the UK and Caribbean and African history!" I gave my little speech so eloquently that the young men ended up apologising and even gave me back my wallet, without the banknotes of course, almost apologising that they needed the money. One of them looked as if he suddenly felt deeply sorry for me. But in a group, what could he do? Now that I had no more money, I went home saddened but also somehow satisfied that I had raised points that appeared to trouble the conscience of at least some of them.

Another time, with Claudia at Euston Station, I was shouted down and pushed by a group of young black men. What was I doing with "their sister", they demanded to know. They were probably having a bad day and were obviously looking for a fight. Here, too, I preached, and they soon let it go.

The "my sister" argument came up again at a party organised by Claudia's cousin, where a slightly stoned friend of her cousin took me aside and decided to lecture me. It was something like a manual for Black women, "his sisters," he claimed. I was the only "white guy" at the party. I told him off, and he got enraged. When Claudia heard about the situation, she got so angry that the man and her cousin meekly retreated.

In the winter of 1994, Claudia told me that her residence permit for the UK would expire the following September. There was an "easy" way to prevent her having to leave the county: Take our relationship to the next level through marriage! I spoke to my friend Jackie Hamilton about it, and she was delighted about the prospects of Claudia and I marrying. She though that Claudia was a wonderful person.

With such a big decision I felt duty bound to make some basic checks with my parents. During the winter holidays, I had briefly brought up the subject of an African girlfriend, pretending that I was still talking about my relationship with Afiya in 1991. As expected, my parents reacted hysterically once again. I remember a book about

London that I had given them at the time. My father and mother had found pictures of Londoners with Caribbean family backgrounds in it and pointed to them.

"Everyone is equal, but everyone stays with their own," my mother explained. It was the philosophy of "separate but equal" and clear racial thinking that they were presenting to me. It was pointless to argue.

I tried to explain to myself again what was before me. Perhaps my father, traumatised by the Shoah, could only see the world through the lens of supposedly different races. I understood his hope for a Jewish family that would be a substitute for all that had been lost. He was caught in a difficult emotional construct. What he failed to realise above all, and not just now, was, I had a right to determine the direction of my own life. My parents spoke with me in German borrowing from a contentious vocabulary that was full of references to "race", my father a Jewish holocaust survivor, my mum scarred by the Third Reich and her father a victim of the Nazis.

If I went on to go out with a "Black woman", it was allegedly the end of the dream of Jewish survival. The two of them thought wrongly. Many years later, my father's granddaughter would proudly become a Bat Mitzvah.

Racist ideology is often based on irrational and unjustified fears or fantasies that have more to do with the subjective experiences of the person holding the views. These in turn are the starting point for fuelling hatred and internalised phobia against people they perceive and view as a threat, although this is not in fact the case.

Having gone through all of this already back in 1991, I quickly realised that there was no point in arguing with my parents and decided there and then to no longer let them be privy to this important part of my life. It would be possible to live together occasionally, whenever I visited, but I had no appetite for any more hysterical tantrums from my father.

47

Freetown and Fights for Freedom

It was time to think about my BA thesis at SOAS. In the 1990s this type of final thesis for the Bachelor of Arts was not yet compulsory but an elective long study project. Students had to elect to do it. It was by coincidence that I came across research that mentioned that young people in Sierra Leone identified strongly with reggae culture and Bob Marley. Concurrently a unit I studied at Goldsmiths College, taught by Paul Gilroy, Les Back and others discussed the symbolism of Caribbean music culture.

I asked Claudia for an opinion, and she agreed that reggae had a deeper meaning in Freetown. Caribbean music, created by descendants of enslaved African people, had crossed the Atlantic yet again and become popular in West Africa, where reggae music and lyrics and Rastafarianism took on their own symbolism and meaning, double-linking West Africa with the Caribbean and the rest of the diaspora. It was obvious that I should have a better look by travelling to Freetown and researching the matter. Claudia and her family agreed to help, making some of the initial contacts.

As I was planning, early in 1995, Claudia received terrible news. One of her aunts, who was like a mother to her, suddenly and unexpectedly died of septicaemia. An initial tiny, small wound had become so infected that it killed her. Claudia was forced to travel to Freetown for the unplanned funeral. In addition to the elaborate preparations for this sad event, she explained my project to some family members, already knowing we could not afford to travel there together.

Thus, I arrived in Freetown in April 1995 without Claudia. At the airport I was met not only by Claudia's aunt Bola and her cousin Abdul, but also by her grandmother Sissi, the eldest living member of the family and therefore the most important person. Tall and well over 70 years old at that time, she was friendly but firm at the same time, and everyone spoke to her most respectfully.

We boarded a bus and then a ferry and set off from the airport for Freetown. From there we travelled through dense, old, small cottages, some over 150 years old, to the area of Freetown where the family lived. The family house was large and modern with a wide veranda. Three generations of the family lived here. From the veranda on the first floor, you could watch the hustle and bustle on the main street, on which vendors had their stalls. Diagonally opposite was a small soft drink bottling factory, which made loud rattling noises when in operation.

Grandmother Sissi was fortunately favourably inclined towards me, and was also pleasantly surprised that I was Jewish, although it meant that I didn't believe in Jesus (she was a devout Anglican Church Mother). Nevertheless, being Jewish was something that had a place in her own deep Christian faith.

Ulrika, Claudia's cousin, had slaughtered a chicken especially for the occasion of my visit, and only found out later that I was a vegetarian. The chicken was eaten by others instead and I was always given egg dishes or dishes without fish or meat afterwards. I'm sure I was not able to fully savour the extraordinary Krio cuisine, due to my vegetarianism. However, I was not the first at least in this family to be vegetarian.

As far as my study project was concerned. I met dozens of people and conducted lots of interviews. I even made the acquaintance of Hindule Traore, who was Sierra Leone's Minister for Transport at the time, a contact for which I had to thank another of Claudia's aunts, Bola. Traore took the time to talk to me about the importance of reggae for himself. I bet he was delighted, for once, not to have to answer deep political questions on policy. I also got to know Freetown's Rastafari community, the "Twelve Tribes of Israel." Initial mistrust was followed by co-operation and help. During a visit to a traditional "Hunting Society" I was even initiated into it and given a new name. They called me Samba Bangura. I met artists and actors, interviewed people on the street and met the academic Dr Jo Opala, whose own published research had given me the idea for this project in the first place.

My research was only "almost" a ground-breaking success, as it triggered a dispute at SOAS. The senior SOAS professor for African politics, Prof. Cruise O'Brian was disinclined to accept the argument. Rastafarianism had a whiff of rebellion among conservatives in Britain, although Bob Marley had intervened in the politics of African countries, for example in support of the liberation struggles against apartheid in South Africa and against white supremacy in Rhodesia, now Zimbabwe. In London, Rastafarianism was part of the culture of self-assertive black youths. A younger slightly more junior SOAS academic, Dr Richard Jeffries, who was a Ghana expert, had, however, observed similar enthusiasm for reggae in Accra. He was therefore eventually given responsibility to mark my work. Paul Gilroy was also satisfied with my research.

It wasn't just my BA thesis that opened up the big topic of West Africa for me. West African history was multi-layered and rich. Usman Dan Fodio's religious procession, the migration routes of the Fulani, the Sokoto Empire, the Akan of Ghana, the Wolof of Senegal, the Yoruba, Ibo, Hausa and Mandinka, the civilisations of the Sahel zone, with their own cultural heydays and resistance to Europeans, the enslavement and the contemporary engagement in global politics, the brutal civil wars, or the architecture and music of Mali, all this, rich in history, art, mysticism, traditional genius, was what had moved me, perhaps more because it had not been part of anything I had been taught previously. I felt the same thirst for knowledge about other parts of the world, my knowledge still has many gaps, even today. I have the one-sided and limited horizons to thank for this, which overemphasise one's own areas and, above all, the European and Western world to the exclusion of the rest of humanity or only some mentioning in passing. My high school years in Israel were extremely limited in this respect. Even though it expanded my knowledge of Judaism somewhat, I would not say it was significant. In Munich, there wasn't necessarily what you could call a global education either. Education was too much focused on the Romans, Greeks and medieval Germany. That, for example, the Mongols and the Islamic civilisation, yes, even Jews, had made huge contributions to the development of Europe, or that it owed its riches in part to looting from other regions and in part from the proceeds of cruel forced labour of enslaved persons, was not exactly acknowledged.

What's more, I always had the feeling that there were local traditions even within Europe, for example, in Bavaria or in northern Europe, Dutch and Low German, that contained something moving and important and that this had a right to be recognised and understood. These cultures were also victims of the urge to standardise culture towards a Western norm. When, years later, I travelled through Great Britain as a journalist, I experienced something similar in the peripheral regions, which were also losing their race against the Western economic model driven by large-scale corporate interests.

The example of West Africa opened a cosmos for me that was more differentiated and richer than anything I had known and understood before. Of course, there is a cosmos like this everywhere when you care to look, but perhaps I also saw something tangible here because the traditions of my father's family had been broken and largely disrupted by the catastrophe of the Shoah. And of course, there was Claudia, soon to be my wife, and her background.

When it came to planning my next step, it was now logical to apply to the University of Birmingham for their Master's degree in West African Studies. After good recommendations and a personal interview, I was offered a place on the programme, which I was truly delighted with.

The University of Birmingham is still one of the most recognised universities in England today, and it certainly was then. The faculty of

West African Studies was the only one in the United Kingdom of its kind and one of the few in the world to specialise in West Africa. I thought of learning French and perhaps Portuguese as well, the two other European languages, besides dozens of local languages, that are spoken in West Africa. Claudia and I also agreed that my future career plans could well be in the foreign service of the Federal Republic of Germany, working for UN aid organisations or pursuing an academic career.

Telling my parents about me being accepted at Birmingham was a huge mistake. What on earth was I thinking, they complained. What was it with me and Africans all the time, my father accused me.

I should have told them whatever lovely fairytale they desired instead of the respectful truth. What happened here was, I later learned, a typical scene for some people of the Holocaust generation and their children, though with its own details. The boundless and intrusive interference in the lives of even grown-up adult children was a frequently observed symptom among these families, as independent studies have repeatedly been able to confirm.[124] It was about loss of control and loss of the familiar, the perception of an existential threat, as I have already mentioned.

My parents resorted to blackmail. If I chose a different subject, they would pay for all the expenses. It was a difficult decision and to some it would be clear that the choice would be, I should do what I wanted! But unfortunately, I must admit, that I wasn't yet strong and confident enough, and I would only be able to study in Birmingham straight away, if I had enough funds to support myself and pay for my tuition fees, possibly working part-time somewhere. I should have done this. Given the option however, I looked for alternatives instead, thinking I could still find something I might enjoy and benefitting from costs being covered.

In Brighton, I found and applied for a postgraduate conversion degree in law. It was an idea forged only within a couple of days, not on the basis of long studies or investigations. Brighton accepted my application. However, it seemed as if they accepted me only because they

---

[124] For example, Rose & Garske (1987).

wrongly assumed that I was an overseas student, a lucrative business for universities where they get paid far more in tuition fees than for a home student. When I told them that I was a student who had been in the UK since 1991 and was an EU citizen the enrolment office was confused, only telling me two days later that yes, I could get onto the course for the far lower EU rate.

Why all of a sudden law? I convinced myself that I could work on international human rights cases and that it fitted in with my SOAS degree. The cheque from my parents, along with some extra pocket money, arrived promptly. I truly hadn't explored the options enough and it would have been better if I had resisted my parents at the time and done what I had intended to do. But fate has its own ways of correcting mistakes. With the help of experts, I first had to learn a lot about the psychological trauma that the Shoah had caused in some survivors, and the dynamics families like my own, in order to understand how to recognise the behaviour and to make the necessary conscious changes in my life. Subconsciously, I had already resisted a lot since the age of 13, perhaps as early as when I climbed out of the windows in Holland. However, for real change I needed to be equipped with knowledge. That struggle was to last at least another 15 years. Over all those years since I was 13 years of age, the inability to stand up to pressure created by my parents ruined my musical potential, my relationships and now also my chosen study route, something I enjoyed was again trampled upon, and disregarded . One of my later psychotherapists put it this way: "The second generation (children of survivors) are equal to other people in everything, but they need longer for some processes, such as being able to separate from their parents." Everything at its own pace.[125]

The course change wasn't the only terrible thing that occurred that year. There was a double life developing. On the one hand, Claudia and

---

[125] These observations can also be extended to other traumatised people. However, the Shoah and the age-old hatred of Jews would repeatedly destroy and traumatise communities and human lives over generations.

Zol Zayn Shulem II: Faroys

I attended lectures by the elite of British American, Black, anti-racist, cutting age thought. Unforgettable is a weekend at the London Cultural Institute (ICA); "Mirage, in recognition of Frantz Fanon's *Black Skin, White Masks*", with Stuart Hall, bell hooks, Homi Bhabba, Paul Gilroy, Lola Young, Isaak Julien, and others, or the lecture with Jacob Howard, the artist of the Harlem Renaissance, and another with Maya Angelou.

The confidence and strength that these lectures engendered contrasted with the seemingly racist views my parents confronted me with.

But that wasn't all – I now knew that they preferred it when I told them white lies. I slowly transformed into an actor. For my graduation, my parents were supposed to come to London to attend the graduation ceremony. They would stay for five days in a hotel near Hyde Park.

Having learned the hard way, I decided to give my parents what they expected, expected and hide any signs of my true life. I hoped that this deception would make my relationship with them easier. In retrospect, the whole thing turned out to be a fragile peace for a few more years, which ultimately came mostly at my expense, especially mentally. The biggest imposition of all, and I am still ashamed of it today, was that Claudia had to temporarily move in with a friend for a week whilst my parents visited London, to perfect the illusion of me being a single young man.

I knew that they would also come to my flat during their visit and I expected them to search for any clues that might point to a possible girlfriend. In fact, that's exactly what happened. I remember how my parents rummaged around the whole flat and couldn't find anything that gave them the opportunity to complain about me. At the time, I thought I was in control of my parents, but it was only in therapy with experts who had seen many children of survivors that I realised that it meant my parents were still in control of my life.

My father arrived at the graduation ceremony at SOAS in his best suit and my mother was also elegantly dressed. We took a traditional photo on the steps of the university with me being dressed in the academic gown. It was truly sad that Claudia was missing here, firstly because she was my girlfriend and secondly because my successful thesis was also thanks to the support of her family. While I was thinking about it, I overheard my father complaining that things were "too international" at SOAS. I prayed that nobody had heard him. For my father who had grown up in a provincial part of Poland and who lived in Munich after the war, this diversity of people was probably not in line with his image of university life in England.

Apart from the fact that I had acquired a university degree, I don't think my parents grasped what I had studied. I remember conversation with my father about African countries and how he looked at everything from the point of view of the clichés he had picked up thanks to German media. It was about Idi Amin and Bokassa or conjuring up images of starving and suffering people and of course the AIDS crisis. Nevertheless, my mother and father were proud. Like my Bar Mitzvah, my graduation became a symbolic celebration of and for my parents, rather than a celebration of *my* graduation and what I had achieved and learned. The people closest to me were missing. I was the very first of the Zylbersztajn family to graduate from university, after generations of ordinary labourers and craftsmen. There were no academics among the last two German-born generations of Lewandowskis either, except for the Berlin legal scholar Eugen Lewandowski, a cousin of my grandfather. Shortly after me, one of the sons of my second cousin Zwika, who studied law on the Zylbersztajn side, and my cousin Claudia, who studied biology and genetics, and also Sonia, the daughter of my mother's brother, graduated. My parents' pride contained the hope that I would have it easier than my father, perhaps earn more. I was the son of a man who had only attended primary school, and I was now a university graduate.

After my parents had inspected my flat, I showed them around London. It was their only ever visit of me together. The diversity of the city, the haste, and the noise seemed to overwhelm them.

At that time, I also met my cousin Claudia in London, going clubbing with her one night. For now, I kept quiet about my other life.

48

The Tube Strike Wedding

A month before our scheduled wedding in August, Infil, the co-operative Housing Group that provided us with our housing, informed us that it was time to vacate Old Street and move again, and that we ought to do so less than a week before our "Big Deal," as we described it in our invitations. We asked for an extension. We had never before breached the conditions of our stay or asked for an extension, something many others did. But they were relentless, and no extension was granted. Given that we were high up the waiting list for a permanent flat, and had accrued many points, we could not risk over-staying either. The inflexible heartlessness of the housing group became clear when we realised after we had done the impossible and move out amidst the stress of preparing the wedding, that others were still living on in the old house for up to three months longer. Our new residence was yet again dreaded Shadwell, East London, particularly bad this time as it had been the smallest flat we had ever been given – was that a cynical wedding present, perhaps?

Coordinating our wedding at the end of August 1995 became a huge challenge under such circumstances. We not only had to transport our belongings to Shadwell, but also had to buy, store and then deliver the wedding catering to a venue that was now far away, but close to our old

The Tube Strike Wedding

flat. It was all done by us; we had no money to hire big companies that do all that kind of stuff. To make matters worse, London Underground staff gifted us with further blessings – a strike action on our wedding day. Our registry office, the only one in the whole wider area in and around London that still had an available slot for our wedding that Friday in August 1995, was in Epping, a location on the Eastern edge of London, where the county of Essex begins. Simply put, you couldn't get there without the tube or a car.

This meant that I had to hire a car for the day, and that Claudia, who would arrive separately from her cousins, based in the South of London had to be driven by them to Epping. Friends could only join, if they had access to cars too.

Among our guests were many friends and acquaintances from Germany and Wales. They included Gregor, Doo-Ri, Kirsten, Claudia's aunt and uncle from Hamburg, and Claudia's family from Wales. My parents, of course, were not there. Our party in the evening was held near Old Street, booked at a time when we had no idea we were going to have to move. Between our mutual "yes" declarations and that party, we had to rush to Shadwell, load the car and drive several times to the party hall to bring all the stuff. A friend of ours acted as DJ, Claudia's family dished up the best of Krio cuisine, and we had beer sent to us by Claudia's aunt Anijabi and uncle Joost from Hamburg. As things often are in the UK, at 11 pm on the dot, the caretaker came and told us to start putting the lights on. Well, perhaps it was just as well, because Claudia and I still have the lights switched on after 30 years. There are some studies following thousands of couples that suggest that those who have less to spend on their weddings, as opposed to those who can afford lavish events, last longer.[126]

If surviving the move and the wedding was already a task, two weeks later, Claudia and I had to travel to Brighton to look for a flat, where we would live during my studies there. Our flat in London we would rent to an acquaintance during that time. This was not allowed according to Infil's rules, but after Infil had made our marriage so unnecessarily difficult, at the time, we honestly didn't care.

---

[126] See Francis-Tan & Mialon (2014)

49

Brighton's Shadows

Claudia and I identified a small flat in a terraced housing estate ten minutes from Preston Park station. We really thought we would be OK and comfortable in this southern English seaside town. Brighton had a reputation as a left-wing tolerant and green bastion, with an active and very visible LGBTQIA+ community, and an elaborate music culture, due to the presence of two large universities and the many English schools. Claudia soon found some care work as there was an unusual abundance of retirement homes here near the sea, and a course that would prepare her for her own future study plans. Meanwhile, I was gearing myself up to the law conversion.

In the 1960s and 1970s, the University of Sussex was one of the key institutions where the student revolt and demands for social action played out. It was precisely for this reason that my first few days there came as a massive shock. Most faculties still had some of the spirit of the rebellious past except for one, and I seem to have hit the jack pot. That one exception was the Faculty of Law. Almost the entire class of around 50 students consisted of people who merely saw the legal profession as an avenue for making good money and for status. There was a flair of English provincial small-town conservativism in the department coming both from students and staff, quite possibly because the towns surrounding Brighton were, and in some cases still are, small rural regions, which provided country based estates and villas for the overspills of wealthy London. Two people were exceptions amongst my co-students. One was Warren, at the time a vegan animal rights activist and Vinay, whose parents were immigrants from India. Vinay and I were the only two interested in human rights, but I soon learned that this course didn't cover any study of human rights, instead teaching the fundamentals of tort or property law, contract and commercial law, public law and criminal law.

Anyone interested in human rights had to complete these units first, then train as a lawyer, and only then could they specialise in human rights, in other words in three to five years from me starting this degree. This long-winded avenue has now been abolished and students now entering legal studies are able to specialise directly, be it human rights or another area, if they so wish. There was another thing that made me stand out. Among all the students, I was actually the only one who didn't come from an English-speaking country. There was a group of foreign students, including some Israelis, but they were part of a different group of already qualified lawyers who needed to gain only some knowledge of the English system and were tested under different criteria. And whilst they were there, in my own group of some 50 UK-based students, there was also no other Jewish student. In short, culturally and according to my future aims and my previous basic academic education, it turned out I was utterly out of place here. But here I was. My father had already paid the tuition fee and Claudia and I had moved to Brighton. It was with envy that I now walked past the Faculty of Development Studies (IDS) at the University of Sussex, which was located on the way to the Faculty of Law, because it had something of the feel of SOAS, the university I had just left, and because it reminded me of the degree I could have studied at Birmingham. I felt similarly sentimental when I read what courses were offered at the Faculty of Social Studies. My prior knowledge would have been an excellent fit here.

And then Claudia and I discovered that Brighton did not only have good music clubs and a culture of left-wing politics, but also an active neo-Nazi scene. Groups of right-wing skinheads would regularly frequent the seaside town. It wasn't long until Claudia reported that she had been harassed with racial abuse on her way home from work. Another time, beer cans were thrown after her from inside a passing car. The N-word came up a lot. In the evenings, when we sat alone in our flat on the outskirts of Brighton, we wanted to console ourselves with our friends from London and therefore invited them to come and visit. But we didn't get any visitors from London because for many it was too inconvenient and somehow too far. So, we were left to our own devises in a city that wasn't ours, with people who didn't seem to welcome us, indeed some of them seemed to hate us, especially Claudia, who couldn't hide the colour of her skin. Our stay in Brighton was in no way her fault. Every week we asked ourselves whether all this was perhaps a big mistake, a punishment perhaps for not standing up to my parents. It would have been easy to call it a day. But I wasn't going to give up without trying as hard as I could, that was the resolve. Perhaps things would be worthwhile one day.

To fuel some hope, I applied for work experience, they call it mini-pupillages in England, in two of London's most reputable human rights law chambers, Tooks Court and Doughty Street, for the recommended short traineeships and was accepted by both. I soon joined Michael Mansfield and Helena Kennedy, both well-known human rights lawyers. After my first exams, however, it was clear that understanding the abstract concepts did not come naturally. It would take time, and I would have to be prepared to no longer be amongst the best students. I passed everything but with lower marks.

One rainy, dark December evening, Claudia and I attended a concert by the then British R&B group Eusebe, whose revived version of Marvin Gaye's hit "Summertime Healing" temporarily went up in the charts in 1995. It was good to be surrounded by a greater diversity of people who reminded us of London. We made our way home in good spirits after the concert and we were still in the city centre near the junction with the Brighton clock tower when someone suddenly shouted something racist towards us. When Claudia replied, two young men suddenly began to physically attack us. We defended ourselves as best we could but ended up on the street with wounds and bruises until the police arrived, far too late. In keeping with the notoriously racist behaviour of the English police at the time, they initially believed the two men, who had claimed that Claudia was a "savage" who had attacked them, innocent white men, without restraint. The two were, as it later turned out, of English-Greek descent. Although the police took notes, they did not carry out any further forensic investigations or assessments of our injuries. When we got home, Claudia and I took our own photos of our wounds, just in case (then still on a normal film camera. This was just before the mobile phone camera age) and we then went to our GP that morning. The police recorded and assessed our wounds only a day or two later, after we had insisted on it. Later in court, the defence lawyer alleged in cross-examination that Claudia and I had inflicted the wounds onto each other after the incident to incriminate these two men. I had never heard anything more absurd. Again and again, the lawyer used the argument of the young men, that indeed Claudia was "a savage", in line with the racist image of the "angry black woman." Incidentally, the public prosecutor who was supposed to handle our case only arrived shortly before the trial began, not leaving any time for any material discussion between us. Unlike the men's defence lawyer, he was quite unprepared. After two days of the hearing, the judge decided to throw the case out, due to, as was stated, insufficient evidence as to who was to be blamed for the incident. In other words, there was a chance that Claudia was perhaps indeed a "wild African" after all – whatever that meant in racist imagination – and that we, the young couple, were perhaps playing a sinister game with these poor young white men. That's how the English prosecution, defence and judiciary still operated in England in 1996. It was obvious that this attack was symbolic of the racist and right-wing hard wired and small-town-conservative climate we had experienced in Brighton.

Three years before this incident, Stephen Lawrence had been stabbed to death in Elton, South-East London. I already mentioned the case earlier in connection of the arrest of Afiya in Kensington. It is now well-known and an established fact, that the police had worked sloppily, and with racial prejudice in this case. Among other things, when the police arrived at the scene, suspicion was initially placed on the Black victim rather than the white racist perpetrators or keeping an open mind. Anyone who was Black or a Person of Colour was always a suspect in the eyes of British police officers, while people of lighter skin shades tended to be held as naturally innocent, sound-minded and peace-loving. In 1999, a full six years after the crime, it was concluded, that the London Metropolitan Police was institutionally racist. Even by 2023 this had, according to the later Casey Inquiry, not changed.[127]

My experiences with law ended with my entrance exam for the bar law school. A hesitation in my speech was judged negatively. Perhaps the dismissal was also down to the fact that I spoke with an unfamiliar accent. I cannot prove it, but at the time, I thought anything was possible. Whatever it was, my performance was deemed to be inadequate. And then, in spite of what we had experienced on the streets of Brighton and the miscarriage of justice afterwards, the law department of University of Sussex was quite unsupportive and almost cold shouldered me. Nobody came forward with a warm helping hand and kind supporting words or advice. I think I was told by the head of the course that I could request an extension if I needed it, and that was all. None of the other lecturers said anything. I decided that this was it for me with law, in a direct and in an indirect sense. For the first time in my life, I threw in the towel.

---

[127] McPherson (1999), The Baroness Casey Review (2023)

50

Postgrad Avenue

As a result of our experiences in Brighton, Claudia and I returned to London several months earlier than we had planned. I considered returning to the course at University of Birmingham, but I wasn't going to drag Claudia yet again to another city, just so I could do my post-graduate degree. Looking at all available options, I found out that Paul Gilroy and Michael Keith (a sociologist who was also head of the London Borough of Tower Hamlets at the time) had launched a new Masters course. In addition to urban planning, geographical, social and historical aspects, the MA programme 'Contemporary Urban Studies', included two course-units, one that took a close look at the role of race and racisms in European philosophy and another on the "Discontinuity of Modernity and its Others", by which Gilroy meant above all the intertwining of the progress of modernity with racism, othering, the Maafa (the transatlantic slave trade) and the Shoah.

To learn more from Paul Gilroy, especially after the dreadful year that was behind us, was a very attractive option. The urban studies that came with it were of secondary importance. What mattered was that it connected to my BA and who I was intellectually. I applied and was accepted immediately. Interestingly, my friend Ben Gidley, who would later become an academic and with whom I had already taken a class at

Goldsmiths two years earlier, had also applied for the same course, for exactly the same reasons.

Claudia also invested in her career and was doing a diploma course in Film Studies at Birkbeck College, the evening college of the University of London. We both had the idea that she might like it as a degree course, as she enjoyed dramatic TV and radio programmes. After successfully completing the course, she applied to Middlesex University for their undergraduate programme in Film Studies and English Culture whilst she continued taking shifts in care to finance her studies.

With that, everything was more or less back to normal and the grim experiences from Brighton slowly faded. The fact that it was a new chapter in Claudia's and my life was also symbolised by the allocation of a new flat by our housing co-operative. I had to change my home eleven times since 1991, a fact that a psychologist would soon identify as a contributory factor of instability for us. But what were we to do? We didn't have enough resources to buy our own flat or rent a more expensive one in a better neighbourhood.

Our new lodging was going to be the top floor apartment of a house opposite the beautiful Clissold Park in Stoke Newington Church Street. The flat was small, but the view into the park was priceless. However, there was a downside: a man with severe mental health challenges lived in the basement. He suffered frequent outbursts of rage, throwing objects around, shouting and standing behind drawn curtains. Not knowing whether this unpredictable man could also be violent frightened us. But for as long as we had lived there nothing happened to us.

At Goldsmiths College I quickly achieved very good grades again. The course dealt with topics such as the Shoah, trauma research, racism, marginalisation in cities and African American history. We read the most diverse types of texts by the most popular and extraordinary authors. One of my papers explored whether Hegel and Kant, in terms of their racist thinking regarding African people, were just "victims of the thinking of their time." They were not. I came across German texts by a ship captain, a well published contemporary of Hegel, who had written down and published his travel memoirs at the same time as Hegel. Unlike Hegel, he did not describe the people he had encountered in African regions as bestial or people of inferior intellect but attributed these qualities to Europeans for their treatment of Africans instead.

How Slavery and the Shoah intersected was the topic of another paper, but it triggered something unexpected in me. Zygmund Bauman's "The Dialectic of Order: Modernity and the Holocaust," Daniel Goldhagen's "Hitler's Willing Executioners," and Primo Levy's "Drowned and Saved," brought about an end of my willingness to continue to speak German. Through these works, I finally understood something fundamental about the extent of German crimes between 1933 and 1945. At the same time, German senior citizens took to the streets to protest against the Wehrmacht exhibition. As it happened, my father confronted them at Marienplatz, Munich's central square. These former Wehrmacht soldiers claimed that they had not taken part in the murder of Jews, and that it had only been the SS who committed genocide. My father confronted them: "I was there, you were all involved in the killing, I saw it", he bravely told them face to face.

Whilst a few years earlier, I had still been trying to set up the German Writing Society, I now felt deeply that I was not part of Germany. I felt betrayed. I wanted to erase everything that was remotely German in me, and I asked myself why my father had assumed that it would be okay for me to grow up in the country? It was difficult. German was the language I knew best but also the language and culture of those who had murdered and tortured my family members. There was such positivity attached to everything German. German ideas, German music, German culture, German philosophy, perhaps even German cars and German football. But where did this "good", the high culture of German ideas, German precision and technology, end in the 1930s? Added to the fact that my father had not given me access to a proper Jewish education as a child, I saw all of that before me and the extent of what Germans did in all its meticulous detail. So now that I had a choice, why should I not refuse to accept it all? I decided not to speak German and tried to improve my

Hebrew here in the middle of England. This inner rebellion and refusal lasted a good part of a decade and only ended in 2008 for very specific reasons that I will come to later.[128]

After reading Baumann's analysis of industrial killing processes, I was so disgusted by the human potential for violence and mass-produced death that I also chose to become vegan. I stayed vegan for 15 years, long before it became a trend. During that time, I met quite a few militant vegans. I did not share that stance. Although I spoke openly about my dietary choices, I rejected the moralising, preaching and marking of territory. My parents initially welcomed this lifestyle cynically, but many years later, my father told me, that I had been right all along, because people really do treat animals terribly.

When the time to prepare my Master's thesis approached, I remembered my plans in 1991 to study history and politics for the sake of journalism. I felt I hadn't done enough to link up my studies to something that would be part of a linear pathway and felt that perhaps the degree needed a directive tweak. This is how I made the decision to write my thesis about something relating to journalism and towards radio at that. Here is how it came about. I briefly drove an Austin Mini during this time and often listened to the radio while driving, in particular London pirate stations that would broadcast via FM frequencies. In East London there was the reggae-infused *Station-FM* and in South London the Black Power oriented *Genesis FM*. Both presented themselves as radio stations for "London's Black community." At the same time, the first programmes specifically targeted for the alleged interests of British Black people and People of Colour were being broadcasted on the BBC. I wanted to know and understand more about these attempts to represent the Black community and what was meant by the very term in the first place. To this end, I analysed self-portrayals by broadcasters, DJs radio stations, and programmes that purported to serve the Black or African community. I interviewed a total of 23 protagonists in depth and created

---

[128] Baumann (1991, Goldhagen (1996), Levi (1988)

a questionnaire. Whilst crowds danced to the rhythms of Lady Saw, Shaggy or Iwer George, I handed out the questionnaires to visitors of the London Carnival in 1997. In the end, I had so much material that I could hardly keep up with the analysis.

The essence of my conclusions was that the communities according to Benedict Anderson's theories were all ultimately constructed. They revealed a variety of different forms of community, which sometimes also set clear boundaries. For example, there was a presenter from the Black Power radio station Genesis FM who spoke a lot about politics and aired recordings of El Hajj Malik El-Shabazz and Marcus Garvey, but did not consider black people from the LGBTQIA+ community to be worth mentioning.[129] Sometimes the boundaries were blurred. In the case of Kiss FM and Jazz FM, the terms "Black community" or "urban music" were merely commercially exploitable values whose content, dumbed down rather than expanded any kind of community. A large part of the work also dealt with the issue of measuring minorities and black people, with insights into the work of the sociologist W.E.B. Du Bois and others.

Two months after submitting my thesis, I received the official notification that I had passed. It was a very good feeling to have accomplished that and having my Masters degree in my pocket (at the time I was so short of money I could not even afford the graduation ceremony, for which the university demanded a fee and a gown, that needed to be hired).

Even during my Master's degree, I had the desire to give something back to those who had not achieved so much. In 1997, I came across a project that felt right. The Dalston Youth Project offered mentoring opportunities for adults to help teenagers who had been caught up in the justice system. I signed up, underwent some selection procedures and checks and received training. Soon enough I was introduced to Jamie M, a 14-year-old boy whose parents were from Montserrat and St Lucia and who lived in the Clapton area of East London. We met weekly and

---

[129] El Hajj Malik El-Shabazz is the name under which Malcolm X died.

I would usually listen to him and gave him advice. Jamie's dream was to become a musician.

He came from a religious Christian family where almost everyone played music for the church. I looked for things that would support and encourage his dream, ordered him a book from the USA that some described as the bible of the music business and showed him the music faculty at Goldsmiths College, where I introduced him to the music professor. He was not aware of this dimension of music at the time. A year later, I persuaded his mum to allow him the experience of the London Carnival for the first time. Jamie had never experienced it so far and he was thrilled.

He and I and a few other mentoring teams ended up meeting the new British Prime Minister Tony Blair and his Home Secretary Jack Straw. The project became a showcase for the New Labour government, which, after decades of Conservative domination, finally wanted to pursue a more socially open policy and demonstrate how young people at risk could get back could get back on the right track. Jamie and I lost touch with each other after that, as the guidelines of the youth project demanded; after all, Jamie was a minor and after 18 months of mentoring, he was supposed to make it without his "big brother."

Years later I discovered a report about Jamie from 2014. He was then 31 years old and, according to the report, he was now a producer who had worked for Amy Winehouse, Ed Sheeran, Wretch 32 and Justin Timberlake and was trying to make a name for himself.[130]

During that time, I also found my way back to Judaism. There was a Liberal synagogue in Stoke Newington, 20 minute's walk from our flat. I started attending on Shabbat to make up for the lack of Jewish religious education, even though I struggled with the concept of G-d, especially when I read the prayers in English. The choice of a Liberal synagogue seemed natural. Firstly, the gender segregation in traditional synagogues did not appeal to me at all, and secondly, it was important

---

[130] Shekha Vyas (2014)

to me that I was in a Jewish community where Jewish people who had not married a Jewish partner were fully recognised and accepted. I felt that "Conservative" Judaism was at that time still not ready for that and feared that they would treat me as a second-class citizen or speak dismissively about Claudia or our marriage. Many years later, I would, however, end up in a modern and emancipated egalitarian Jewish Masorti community, but more about that in its right place.

I should add at this point, that being a member of a synagogue for me is a restorative act, rather than one of deep faith. Given my father's position and him being done with G-d for allowing the Shoah to happen, I figured out that aiming to upkeep a tradition was essential so that the links to the past would not get totally severed. It contains very useful life rhythms and wisdoms and moments of reflection. Over the years, I haven't yet been able to answer the question if my father, or the people of deep faith in the synagogues I attended, were right. But, not being able to solve this, does not mean, that I will give the heritage, tradition and even the religious practices and wisdoms up. One can stay and continue to argue with oneself and others and, indeed G-d. The two words *isra and "el" that later became "Israel"* mean exactly that.[131]

One of the factors that were a plus in Stoke Newington was their then Rabbi Shulamit Ambalu. She was liberal but also firm in terms of a basic foundational requirement she expected, such as knowledge of Hebrew. I liked her as a person, and she would become a family friend over the years. Claudia and I were proud to attend her wedding to her long-term partner Rebecca. Shulamit was the first female Rabbi in Britain who was married to a woman.

---

[131] In Vaishlah, Breshit (Genesis) 32:4-36:43 Jacob wrestles with an angel representing G-d and receives the name Israel as a result

51

No Work

Achieving an MA in Contemporary Urban Studies, in addition to my Bachelor at SOAS, both University of London colleges, also meant that it was now time to look for a permanent job in the UK that corresponded somehow to my training.

With my work experience, which included working for the German Bundestag's Vice-President and a few other jobs during my studies, my role at Infil housing, as well as my involvement with the youth project, I thought I should have a good chance.

The first thing learnt was that I couldn't apply for government jobs, as only British and Commonwealth citizens were eligible at the time in the UK (this was changed years later). I therefore tried to get research assistant posts in local authorities, urban planning research posts, equality posts, applied for training programmes at the BBC and jobs at international organisations.

The closest I got with any of my applications was for a representative and communication role of an international animal welfare organisation, where I was one of the last three candidates. But after more than four months without further success, I registered with the Government Job Centre.

Claudia was now often away for longer periods. It was her turn to study while I kept looking for work. Due to my frustration at the lack of success in my job search, gradually my confidence sank, and depression began to creep in. It manifested itself by losing the strength and impetus to get up in the morning. I felt numbed. When I told Claudia about this a few days later, she insisted that I see my GP. He prescribed what doctors do: Prozac! The feeling after the first few pills was so strange and made me so drowsy that I didn't touch the packet again. Of course, I was aware that things were not quite OK with me, and something needed to be done. I read somewhere that regular exercise could help with depression and so I decided to replace the prospects of pills with an exercise and a gym membership. That helped a little.

After 120 unsuccessful applications, I decided to report my experiences to the then British Labour Minister Alistair Darling. The new Labour government under Tony Blair appeared to want to take care of such things. He thanked me for my honest account, but he couldn't do much for me personally. Nobody could explain to me why I was having such difficulty finding a job.

Was it possibly even something as obvious as my name? There are studies that show that applicants with a foreign or unfamiliar sounding name can experience discrimination when applying for a job. A study at Oxford University in 2019 found that such people had to submit up to 80 per cent more applications to be successful.[132] Should I change my name to Smith? I also lacked connections. Claudia and I were both immigrants without wide networks, often already established on parental level or during childhood years. A guy from SOAS who was permanently drunk and stoned in the student bar during his years there and who, everybody knew, had copied his essays from friends, landed a job with one of the best BBC programmes. We heard later that his dad was also in the BBC. I would see similar things happening over my lifetime, where name or status and connections opened doors in Britain, it was undeniably a factor.

Whatever the cause, not the least a non-conventional degree, with the lowest point of my depression behind me, it was time for self-help

---

[132] Siddique (2019), DeCelles (2016)

and a positive rethink. I am by nature somebody who gets up and does things. After I visited the office for volunteering in Hackney to see if I could get a placement with someone, the director drew me in and said she could do with a study on volunteering among Turkish speakers in this part of London, because she had difficulties reaching this community. She asked me if I would be willing to research something like that, though without pay? I agreed.

In the meantime, I continued to concern myself with politics and writing. An article in the 1998 winter issue of the magazine *Jewish Socialist* bears witness to my work and my thinking at the time. I took issue with the categorisation of people by race in the UK:

> *In the UK, as in many other contemporary societies, there is an unquestioned adherence to concepts of racial purity and cultural essence based on the colour of a person's skin, or their surname. The United Kingdom likes to present itself as harbouring Europe's most progressive system regarding ethnic minorities, even attempting to influence EU policy. But is it possible that what they offer is nothing more than a reproduction of racial theories that are now banned in Germany? It is impossible to imagine, for example, that a German questionnaire would ask applicants for a job to tick categories such as German, Turkish, Jewish, African, Gay/Lesbian, Disabled, Gypsy, or another minority.*[133]

I concluded this critique with a call to reappraise rigid definitions of supposedly pure forms and essences of cultures and nations.

Despite these serious attempts to showcase my abilities, which could be added to my CV, I still didn't have a paid job yet.

At this time we also had to move again, this time we were given a flat in Stamford Hill amidst the ultra-orthodox community, but it was only for a year or so, before we were moved again, this time to the edge of Bloomsbury into a tiny garden flat.

---

[133] Zylbersztajn (1997), freely retranslated into English.

52

PTSD – Decades After the Shoah

At the lowest point of my depression, after the doctor prescribed Prozac, and I felt it wasn't for me, I also contacted Shalvata, a centre that offers psychological counselling for mostly Jewish people who had directly experienced the horrors of the Shoah, i.e. survivors, but it was also open to their children and grandchildren, the so-called "Second Generation." It wasn't just about unemployment. It was also about trying to make sense of the strange dynamics between my parents and myself. Was it possible that there was a connection between my family's history and my situation I found myself in?

I got an interview with a psychotherapist who put me on a waiting list. Six months later or so, I began my first series of psychotherapeutic counselling sessions. I cycled to North London once a week for my therapy. I told the therapist that I didn't just want to avoid falling into another bout of depression, I also wanted to begin to understand the dynamics between my parents and myself. I had been married for three years now without my parents knowing.

The atmosphere in the practice seemed always a bit overwhelming, if not actually depressing in its own way. It started with the security system through which patients had to be channelled, and the windows of the building had dark tinted glass. But it was most likely also due to the heaviness of my own thoughts and what we were talking about there.

With the encouragement of the therapist, I tried to look into the mirror and be honest about myself to myself. I was encouraged to discuss fantasies and fears and my outlook on life. It didn't take the psychotherapist long to identify behavioural markers in me and in my family, with which he was all too familiar. It wasn't just about my father but also about my mother's behaviour. The distance from her own father, my grandfather's trauma as a victim of the Third Reich and as a refugee, and my mother's early attachment and marriage to my father, had also influenced her and thus had a further impact on the way I had been brought up.

It had never been easy for my father to show feelings of love and trust. An easier way out from getting entangled in emotional baggage was "financial support." For people like him, true emotional closeness was too risky based on his life experiences. Love made him vulnerable, because those he had loved in the past were torn from him violently and unjustly during the Shoah. By that logic, it was better not to love on a deeper emotional level, but to protect yourself from pain through distance. It had an advantage, because the financial support of a child could make the child dependent and subject to control by the parent. As far as my father was concerned, my life was to replace all those who were murdered. That was implicit also in my second name, Zwi, the name of my grandfather in Hebrew. Of course, it is a role that no one can fulfil and that is already enough to damage or even destroy the individuality of any person, in this specific case the children of survivors.

My psychotherapist had simple and good advice for me. He made it clear to me that it was essential to free myself from the ability of my parents to control me. This liberation should at the same time not aim to devalue my parents but I had every right to make my own decisions about my life. The basic and fundamental prerequisite for this was to no longer accept any offers or gifts, financial or otherwise.

It was the beginning of a long, deep journey through my psyche. It was to take me another ten years or so to tackle the personal after effects of the trauma of the Shoah on a deeper level.

53

Power Years!

The pit I had fallen into at the beginning of 1998 because of my unemployment, and my resolve to get up and work myself out of it by any means necessary, initiated the process of understanding myself better. Having had little success on the British labour market, I now began, possibly overzealously, to take several paths at once to escape further unemployment. Essentially, I had two plans: (1) I would prepare myself for a doctoral programme in preparation for a potential academic career, and (2) I would try to do practical journalism training.

And so it was. Between 1998 and 2000 I established myself as a freelance radio journalist for Deutsche Welle (DW), and during the winter of 1997 and spring of 1998, I started looking for a university for my doctoral studies. Paul Gilroy was unfortunately unavailable because he had just accepted a position at Yale. Eventually I was accepted at the University of Leeds. I officially started my doctoral studies in 1999. But there was more. I received a one-week scholarship from the organisation Rene Cassin to travel with other young Jewish people to Geneva for the Human Rights Council meeting.

There was a third opportunity that arose through the offer of a study scholarship for people who were unemployed. The basis was my nearly daily sports habit, that I had adopted to distance myself from depression.

It entailed cycling, gym based work-outs and runs. This is why between 1998 and 1999, I also studied Sports Science on postgraduate level at the University of Bedfordshire with a scholarship from the European Social Fund, and was awarded a Postgraduate Diploma in 1999 (degree without thesis). One part of the Sport Science programme was the enrollment onto a fitness trainer course, which I then developed into becoming a personal trainer. In December 1999 I started working with two different people as a personal trainer, while at the same time I got a temporary job at Goldsmiths College as a research assistant.

At the beginning of 2000, I founded a nationwide British group for postgraduate and doctoral students whose research focus included Black Cultural Studies. The reason was that there was hardly any support for this topic at British universities. So, being a "*macher*," I decided to set up a network through which students could support each other.[134] I met some really interesting people through that, and we organised a group trip to the then still new slavery exhibition in Liverpool.

Somehow, I balanced all of that- I also continued my psychotherapy.

Claudia and I had to again move flats twice during this time, but finally moved into a permanent residence in South Camden in 1999, after we had accumulated more points than anyone else in the co-operative housing group.

I will explain some of these steps in more detail in the following chapters.

---

[134] *Macher*, yid. somebody who does things

54

Radio

During one of those days, that I went to the local library to check the newspapers for jobs, I came across a poster that advertised for a diploma in radio journalism via a local radio station in Hackney. The station and the training programme were run by some radio journalists with BBC-experience. You had to be unemployed to benefit from the training, which was free of charge and supplied by an educational foundation and charity called Sound Radio.

I applied and soon enough learnt how to cut ¾ inch tape, how to make good sound recordings and how microphones had to be held. We were also introduced to digital editing, a technology, which at that time had only just begun and required expensive computer systems. Within a week of training, I produced my own first works. I created a series about hairdressers who can sing, presented an accordion business and its history, and visited the Algerian community in London's Finsbury Park district, armed with my microphone. As I had been planning to visit my parents, I bought four bottles of English beer from a brewery in Hackney and brought it to regulars in Munich's world-famous Hofbräuhaus to have the beer tested live on mic.

They all reacted with a decisive "Igitt!" – yikes. Then I took beer from the Hofbräuhaus with me to London and we did a drinking test on that side during a live-show.

The radio training was followed by a volunteer position at Talking Africa, a radio programme for Londoners from various African countries. Although nobody said anything, I slowly began to realise that because of my accent, I shouldn't be looking for a job as a journalist in the UK, but that this option would only be open to me in Germany (I was still not speaking German in the UK, at the time).

After asking a friend in Berlin, who was a self-taught computer and music expert, to set up my PC so that I could mix and edit sound on it, I introduced myself to Deutsche Welle (DW) a few months later and got lucky, because they were looking for freelancers for their English programmes who could send features from London for young listeners. It was as if it had been made for people like me. At DW you were allowed to speak English with a German accent. I was soon producing four to eight-minute programmes. I can remember a ghost story set to music and a horror tour through London, contributions about the British-Indian music scene, about the Mobo awards, and a feature on Jewish-Black relations for their religion programme.

The pay, however, was on the lower side, and that was why I started looking for other job opportunities. I asked my friend Ben Gidley, who worked at Goldsmiths College, to send an internal email that I was looking for research assistant jobs. Again, I got lucky. A professor in the Faculty of Education needed someone to transcribe her research interviews. Finally, things began to look much brighter.

During that time, my friend Gregor came to live in London for a year, renting a flat not far from us. We enjoyed many happy hours together and became big fans of the apple cake from a certain bakery, which we would consume when we met. Enjoying the London art scene, Gregor felt, in the end, that London had not enough light, and was too grey. He ventured on to Barcelona next.

55

Sport as a Way Out

There was no other way. I had to earn money to be able to study for the doctorate I had in mind. If possible, I no longer wanted to have my academic studies supported by my parents. During a good workout in a London fitness studio, I had the idea that I could become a fitness instructor, since I enjoyed sports. Beyond that, I knew that personal training was becoming more and more popular, and it was quite well paid. A search on the internet led me to an advert for an MA in Sports Science at what is now the University of Bedfordshire, which was then called the University of Luton and had previously been a vocational college. I wrote to the university and got an interview within a week. I was accepted, fees paid by the European Social Fund, also because I had been unemployed and low-waged for quite a while. Thank you, European Union!

Sports science at university was on a completely different level to the biology A-levels I had completed many years ago in Israel. Basically, it meant that I had to learn a lot of new things. Physiology, muscles, the nutritional cycle, adaptations under performance stress, sports training theory, sports medicine, age, sex, illnesses, diseases and their relationship to performance. Some of it was as abstract as the law course I had tried years ago, other stuff was more applied. Understanding and memorising it all was hard, so I wasn't the best of class, but it was actually fun. I enjoyed it.

The course required a vocational component, which my tutor said could be a course where I qualified as a coach or trainer. In this way, I became a fitness instructor, trained by Central YMCA, one of the most recognised English training-centres for fitness at the time.

But there was also a more curious side to the sports course. A young lecturer from Malaysia at the university took offence when I highlighted that her unquestioned citing of racial theories in some of the studies that came out of predominantly US-research and repeatedly quoted in her lectures, concerning apparent racial differences between whites and blacks, were problematic.

I pointed out to her that what she described as genetic differences were more likely differences that related to social contexts. I said that people in the USA, regardless of their skin colour, often had a diverse pool of genetic ancestry, some of which may have come from different regions of Africa, others from different regions in Europe, the Americas and other regions.

There was a further context to this. At that time, I was also already studying on a course at the University of Leeds to prepare me for my PhD studies. I had written a thesis on race, sport and the human body from a Jewish perspective. In the process I dealt with topics such as degeneration theories concerning the "Jewish body" and the thinking of Max Nordau (1849-1923) on muscular Jewry.[135] Through Paul Gilroy's other works such as "Between Camps" or the more explicit American title "Against Race", I came across the book by sports historian and sociologist John Hoberman "Darwin's Athletes"", which dealt in detail with the issue of alleged racial dominance in sport and also critically scrutinised it.[136]

---

[135] Max Nordau in his speech to the second Zionist congress in Basel, 1898 Muskeljudentum: Jüdische Turnzeitung, 1903, in Nordau (1909). See also Gilman (1991

[136] Hoberman (1997), see also my interview with Hoberman on the Olympic and Paralympic Games 2012

At the University of Bedfordshire, the lecturer understood my comment as a threat. I believe that the university environment in the town of Luton made my statement even more striking. Never before had I experienced a city in England where students were so completely segregated from each other.

The people who lived there were very different to those at almost every university I had been to before. Students largely organised themselves according to identity patterns or skin colour or religion, with no major points of contact between each group. I was hardly surprised when I heard that one of the London-bound suicide bombers of 7 July 2005 came from Luton, and that also a key figure of the British far right, Tommy Robinson (whose birth name is Stephen Yaxley-Lennon) had started his activities as a Luton Town Football thug.

Because I had the temerity to speak up, the lecturer made sure I had my punishment at the next opportunity of her being able to mark one of my papers. I guess she didn't think I had the right to object nor that I may have spoken the truth.

56

Doctoral Student

My previous studies and insights had led to many questions. In addition, in terms of political events, the assassination of Yitzhak Rabin had been a key moment for me. Even before that, I had observed and studied radical fringe figures such as the right-wing rabbi Meir Kahane. I knew that resistance was important, there had not only been uprisings in the Warsaw ghetto, but also in other camps. Jewish militias were active in Palestine during the British Mandate. Uprisings, small and large, successful and unsuccessful, were fundamental to the abolition of slavery in the Americas. Self-defence and resistance were deliberately talked down by those who controlled the historiography at the time and are still trivialised today, compared to the over-emphasized up-talking of the role of European aristocratic and clerical men who campaigned for the abolition of slavery.

Self-defence and resistance were therefore important and must be understood in the context of violent input through oppression and discrimination. However, there was, and is, a point where these ideologies, if given free reign, could and can become problematic and even turn against one's own side. Rabin's assassination in Israel and the brutal regime of Robert Mugabe were basic examples of this, alongside movements such as the Stern Gang and Itzl in Mandate Palestine, In the USA, the Nation of Islam under Malcolm X, the Black Panther movement and insurgent leaders such as Nat Turner and Toussaint Louverture were all examples of complex figures and movements in that regard. In London, there was a group of Jews who made life difficult for British fascists with their bare fists after the Second World War.[137]

I asked what role militancy and armed resistance, the fantasy of liberation through violence, and the symbolism of militant strength could play among groups of people who for centuries were seen as the alleged antithesis of Christian "civilised" Europe. Where were the limits of liberation ideologies that favoured or dreamt of violence?

My first task was to identify a supervisor. Paul Gilroy not being around, I turned to Zygmund Bauman, who taught at the University of Leeds. In his work, he had written a lot about the use of violence during the Third Reich. But Baumann was already retired. When he answered my email he hinted at Griselda Pollock, a feminist Jewish art historian and lecturer in Cultural Studies (after Stuart Hall), who was intensively questioning colonial structures after a British-Indian student of hers, Sutapa Biswas, today a famous artist in her own right, had challenged her. I was again in luck. Pollock was interested in my doctoral thesis.

As a prerequisite to study on the PhD programme, Leeds asked me to participate on their Jewish Studies Masters Program for one year (part-time) and register for the doctoral programme whilst doing so. This further preliminary study would strengthen my position, Pollock argued, and there would be sufficient time to apply for a scholarship from the Arts and Humanities Research Board (AHRB) (now AHRC), one of the most recognised university scholarship available in the UK. The Jewish art historian Eva Frojmovic was chosen to become my direct supervisor. For these part-time studies, held once a week, I was awarded a scholarship from the Burton Trust.

I was in the strange and unforeseen position of studying at two universities at the same time. It wasn't intentional, but I couldn't just

---

[137] Zylbersztajn (2021)

say no to either now. Both had their place. Whilst I was awarded scholarships, neither paid for my living expenses. So, in addition to all the academic work, I had to continue making radio programmes and complete transcribing tasks for the professor at Goldsmiths College and, on top, because of the high rate of pay, from November 1999, work a few times a week as a personal trainer.

As if it wasn't enough, during this time, I also received a scholarship from the British human rights organisation Rene Cassin to attend a one-week training and observation course at the Human Rights Council in Geneva. It was an interesting endeavour and a good introduction into the operations there.

57

"Migrants Excluded!"

In the spring of 1999, I applied for the long prepared for doctoral programme. I received a scholarship from the AHRB and was overjoyed for a few hours, as this was a highly competitive award. At last, everything was as it should be! But then I read the letter more carefully. The AHRB had cancelled out all my maintenance payments. The award terms stated that people whose residence in the United Kingdom in previous years was not mainly for gainful purposes would not be entitled to maintenance payments for their scholarship, not even if the scholarship award meant that the applicant's project had been chosen by the elite of British academics as one of the most promising in any given year. After almost ten years in England, and having been deemed equivalent via Erasmus+, this was a damning judgement. I would be paid three years of university fees but not a penny more.

Again, just as in 1989 when I first spoke to the officer of the Bavarian Ministry for Education in Munich there was a hurdle in my way because of where I had come from, even though I had been in Britain for a long time and had worked part-time whilst completing two degrees, I was not treated like a home-student in the way Erasmus+ had been negotiated. I was in almost every way no different to any other UK-student. My parents and I had lived and worked in the EU prior to beginning my studies, and I came to England under the promise of being treated like a home student. I turned to the British Equality and Human Rights Commission suspecting discrimination. They agreed to look at the case but couldn't do anything within their remit. Instead, they advised me to turn to the European Court of Justice suggesting that the UK could be breaking EU law. Others, British born, who had never left the country, were able to study without these discriminatory barriers and received scholarships to cover their tuition fees and living costs. The Erasmus+ programme intended that foreign students should be treated as if they were studying in their own country and, that a European member state would not be seen as a foreign country.

I may have had a case, but I decided not to embark on longwinded legal proceedings. I might have succeeded or not, but I felt it was not constructive in helping to advance my studying if I started to refer the case to the ECJ. It would delay things and take time. Better, I thought, to give in to the circumstances and try to complete my doctoral studies whilst working. However, with three jobs to make ends meet on top of my studies, it was simply too much and still never enough money to live on.

That's why my PhD studies were initially delayed and why I then was changing the degree from full-time studies to part-time. My supervisor constantly complained that I wasn't giving my studies enough attention. She was right, but there was no alternative. Finally, she made it clear it was time to write my upgrade, the first big paper. I sat up all night for many hours, often after my remunerated work was done, to push the project forward.

In the midst of that, my work for the professor at Goldsmiths College (which in the end was based at South Bank University, because she had moved institution) came to an end, and I had to find a replacement. There was interest from colleagues of the professor I worked for, but I settled for a job with YMCA England, where I took on a newly created role as a research assistant to research equality and diversity issues within the organisation. Despite of the *Village People* music hit, that suggested that YMCA was a diverse place, YMCA England was having problems with the representation and treatment of staff and users of different sexualities, People of Colour, and of Black and non-Christian staff. I was to reach out to staff and lay-people to conduct in-depth qualitative interviews. I had been working on the study for about six months, maybe three quarters of a year, and had interviewed over 20 contacts across the country, when, quite unexpectedly, during an interview with an arch-conservative Christian former CEO, I was severely attacked for my Jewish background. I was not prepared to have to deal with the stress of such an attitude on top of all the other workload I had, and the relatively low pay. Whilst my line managers had offered some assistance, I felt it was better to end my involvement and find a job that would not stress me out alongside the studies and two other jobs.

The day came that I finally submitted the first major piece of work, a comparison between Meir Kahane and his Jewish-ethnocentric extreme Kach movement, and Robert F. Jackson, who had armed himself against white racists in North Carolina and wrote a work that attracted a lot of attention at the time, "Negroes with Guns."[138] To visually illustrate the very real point that these people were making, I brought along a tiny toy gun, I had bought in a toy shop. Meant as a visual aid during the presentation, it shook some student's sensibilities. Despite that, I received the "upgrade" status for the work, which meant that I had passed and was fully admitted to the programme. The paper was now the first chapter of my thesis.

Griselda Pollock, who in the meantime had taken over the role of my supervisor, suggested that it would be really good if I could study for a year or at least a few months at Howard University, Washington's proud African-American university. The reason was that there were hardly any academics in the UK who were familiar with the topic of black militant nationalism as a political ideology. I had wanted to travel to the USA anyway to do more in-depth research and conduct interviews. Griselda

---

[138] Williams (1962)

wrote to various funding organisations and to the university fund. None of them was prepared to support me. I can still remember a job interview with a Jewish support organisation in Covent Garden. Although they did not say it, I felt that they were simply afraid to support my topic or didn't understand its relevance. I had also planned to do research in Israel, in South Africa or Zimbabwe and in Guinea Bissau. But if there wasn't even funding for a few months in the USA, what prospects were there for any of that? I truly couldn't afford it on my own.[139] Of course one could modify the research, but that wasn't the point. I had unique points to make and the bare minimum was to research in Israel and the USA.

Towards the end of 1999 Claudia and I faced additional pressures. The situation concerning the civil war in Sierra Leone had worsened and a bloodthirsty armed rebel group run by a man called Foday Sankoh had managed to invade Freetown. Sankoh's fighters, many of whom were drugged, set fire to houses and used terrorisation of the civilian population as their preferred fighting method, infamously chopping off the limbs of those they did not manage to kill. They gave their actions a macabre title: "Operation No Living Thing."

Claudia's family members in Freetown were in direct and immediate danger. Some of the girls and young women went into hiding. One acquaintance, Alex, who had helped me back in 1995 with my BA project, was shot dead by Nigerian troops when rebels forced him to drive them in his car. After almost a year of fighting, Nigerian-led Ecomog troops finally recaptured Freetown with the help of British forces and Claudia's family could finally breathe again, but many had not been so fortunate.[140]

---

[139] A Washington Post report from 2022 stated that the doctorate is increasingly the privilege of people who come from well-heeled elites. See Van Dam (2022)

[140] Ecomog. Economic Community of West African States Monitoring Group. What people in Freetown experienced at the time was reported by the Sierra Leonean journalist Sorious Samura in his documentary film "Cry Freetown" in Samura (2000), among others.

58

Old Hatred in London

Claudia completed her BA in September 2001. One of her last course units was "Melodrama and Women", in which she examined the marginalisation of women, and in which she was very interested. But towards the end of her studies, she realised that there were too few Black people in the film industry at that time. In addition, her course had been completely theoretical. She had gained more practical experience in her preliminary studies at Birkbeck College than in the entire three years at Middlesex University. Training to become a film producer would entail high course fees with an uncertain outcome. In a conversation with her course tutor, a criminologist by the name of Tony Goodman, she came up with the idea of studying something entirely different that was more applicable, which also happened to be on offer at the same university and was led by Goodman: an MA in Youth Justice and Applied Criminology. Once she had made up her mind, she was immediately offered a study place.

Meanwhile I came across a man by the name of Michael King at a trade conference of the fitness and health sector in Blackpool, where he was presenting the Reformer Pilates machine. At the time, King was one of the major commercial training providers for Pilates in the UK. He invited me to lie down on the Reformer, a kind of bed with a carriage attached to large metal springs for resistance and guided me through some of the excises. I had never experienced this kind of precise exercise school before. I was sweating almost more than during an endurance run. A few weeks later, I signed up for one of his London teacher training courses, "mat-based Pilates", for fitness and sports teachers, which incidentally was taught 15 minutes from where we lived. The training modules ran over a few long weekends.

It was on a Sunday around 2.30 in the afternoon, a sunny day. I had been studying exercises within a small group in Michael King's studio since the morning when suddenly, I think we were on a break, my mobile phone rang. It was Claudia. In a panicked voice, she told me, that she had just been attacked by two men and was alone at home in the hallway on the stairs. Shocked, I left the class instantly and cycled home from King's studio as fast as I could, full of fear and worry. I opened the house entrance and there I found Claudia crawling up the stairs on the second floor in her tracksuit. She had a very swollen face and was covered in blood. Claudia had already called the police and emergency services, but they weren't there yet, though they arrived within ten minutes of my own arrival and put Claudia on a stretcher so that she wouldn't move in case she had suffered a spinal neck-fracture. Soon the police were there too. One officer accompanied Claudia to the hospital and asked Claudia more details as to what had happened. Other officers remained in the street where we lived to try to find out more from neighbours.

What on earth had happened?

On her way home from a sports lesson, two white English men, aged between 20 and 30, called her racist and misogynistic names and harassed her when they saw her walking down the road. They said she was a N****-whore and should f*** off. When Claudia replied defensively, the two men became enraged and violent. Soon they both began to hit Claudia. At one stage one was holding her down while the other tried, or so it seemed, to break her neck with repeated and targeted blows. A woman across the street opened the window and cheered from the second floor to "finish off that black f**** whore." One of the two men was known to live in the street.

Claudia reported that she saw other neighbours watching from behind the curtains of their flats' windows. When the police tried to find witnesses in the weeks that followed, none of these neighbours, many of whom were of Bangladeshi migrant families of the first or second generation, claimed to not have seen anything.

South Camden had experienced clashes between marginalised white English and Bangladeshi youths back in the mid-1990s. In 1994, they reached a climax with the murder of Richard Everitt, a 15-year-old schoolboy.[141] Some in the area had been recruited or were attracted by far-right radical groups, others by Islamist movements. We had now learnt that one of the white racist men had lived opposite us.

Claudia was thoroughly examined in hospital. She had received severe blows, many of them to the head and neck, but it seemed as if she had escaped extremely serious injuries, though she suffered pain for weeks.

In the end it was a neighbour, a Black British woman, of Caribbean family background, who was prepared to make clear statements. She had witnessed part of the attack and knew the family. As a single Black woman with several children, she had no scruples about getting involved, unlike the other rather wary neighbours.

The police caught one of the perpetrators. He indeed had lived opposite us. The police ordered him to stay away. The rest of the family escaped any consequences, as it was not possible to prove their complicity due to the lack of witnesses. Moreover, the perpetrator who was captured did not reveal the identity of the other man

The public prosecution brought charges against the perpetrator and the trial took place over six months later. A few days before the trial, our doorbell rang at five in the morning and a male English voice warned: "Drop the charges!"

---

[141] See: The Independent, 7.19.1995. 'School boy stabbed to death in brutal attack'. https://www.independent.co.uk/news/schoolboy-stabbed-to-death-in-brutal-attack-1576315.htm (retrieved on 20 February 2022)

The man's guilt was established in the criminal court. When Claudia was asked by the judge, in accordance with English customs whether she had anything else to add to the case, she asked the judge to not only sentence the man to a prison sentence, but also to order training and programmes in which he could learn to reduce his hatred, ideally within a black community project. The perpetrator received an 18-months prison sentence and hours of community work.

Many years later, Claudia spotted the perpetrator on the street one day by coincidence, but he failed to recognise her. He now had a long scar over one side of his face. The woman who lived opposite us (presumably the perpetrator was her brother) still lives in our street today. We never exchanged a word with these people, because there was never a word of remorse. There are people who can't be forgiven until they admit to themselves what they've done wrong or aim at best to apologise. Claudia always argues that she only learnt about racism in the UK. Our life here in England gave us both quick and bitter lessons about British realities.

It took a while for all the wounds to heal. One of the consequences of the attack was that Claudia still goes to self-defence training courses and practise in Israeli Krav Maga.

The time of upset ended with Claudia completing her master's degree with a *summa cum laude*. After that, she began to work as a youth worker, where she met young people in Islington whose families had been living on the edge of criminality for generations. Somehow, however, her commitment to the young people seemed futile. She believed that she did not have enough resources and support to really help them. During her studies, she had already heard about an opportunity to switch to social work. She applied and was offered a place on a conversion course.

59

Pilates School

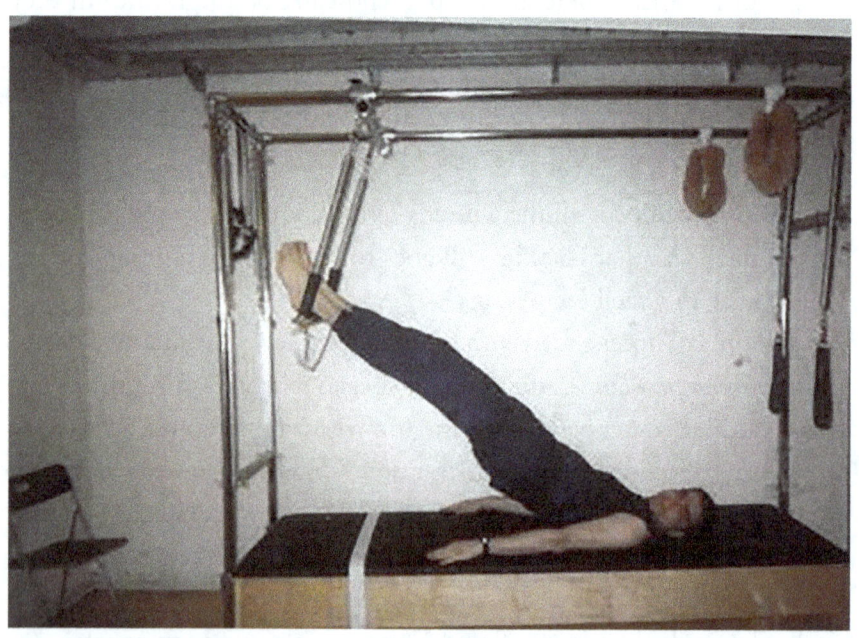

At a Polestar Pilates training course in Cologne around 2002.

Life turns in surprising and unexpected ways. Nobody can predict where you end up and what turns and twists life may take. Nothing, had you asked me in 1989, would have had me predict this. But after several months of training, and despite the terrible assault on Claudia, I successfully completed my introductory Pilates mat work diploma. As a result, I got more and more private exercise clients, and they paid good money. Advertisements about my services appeared in the British *Cosmopolitan* and in *Vogue*. Because everything seemed to be going in the right direction, I decided to invest more into my training to teach exercise. The first thing I did was to get a motorbike licence so that I could reach more customers all over London. My friend Erik sold me his old Yamaha 600 XT for just £1000 with a heavy heart, but conceded that the truth was, that he didn't use the bike much anymore. I also wanted to transform my postgraduate diploma in sports science into a full Masters of Science. At Brunel University in West London, I was allowed to do this, as long as I completed four foundation courses in addition to my master's thesis. I was also allowed to do the whole thing on a super slow part-time basis so that I could work at the same time.

Now it was also time to be honest with myself. I realised that I couldn't continue with my doctoral studies despite my great enthusiasm for them. Even with what I was earning from teaching Pilates, I couldn't finance it, let alone the time required to study alongside my work or the required travel. On the other hand, every course I took in sports and Pilates would justify my high hourly lesson rates in the eyes of my clients. Increasingly, I had clients from London's rich and famous list, producers and famous BBC-journalists, lawyers, bankers or their wives, models, sports people, a famous author, high government officials, wealthy businesspeople. This truly looked like the best option at the time.

And so it was that I also invested in additional Pilates training to obtain a teaching licence for all available Pilates equipment and for all physical problems. For practical and cost reasons, I took many of these courses with Polestar, an international Pilates training provider, that also had branches in Germany, saving me about a third in costs compared with taking the units in the UK, flight to Germany and hotel costs included.

But by 2003, I realised that I needed a home studio as a base to deepen my studies. Almost all the established Pilates instructors had learnt their craft through apprenticeship-based teaching under an experienced Pilates teacher, preferably former students of Joseph Pilates himself. Individual course modules, which are common in the modern fitness industry, did not have a very high status in the Pilates world. Eventually I came across Alan Herdman, a big name in the Pilates world, who had even trained Michael King.

Herdman, who was over 60 when I met him first, had brought Pilates from America to Europe in the 1970s. He himself had learnt it from students of Joseph Pilates, Carola Trier and Bob Fitzgerald. His motto was that one was to correctly understand and pass on the fundamentals of Pilates, which meant quality before quantity, caution instead of acrobatics. "Only those who get the basics right can do more difficult exercises later on without harming themselves", he used to preach and "it's not about copying a series of exercises, but learning how to do them correctly, because many exercises are not at all good for people with specific problems!" The aim was "to correct posture and movement." These words convinced me. After a few trial lessons I was soon one of his students. During the year I attended the apprenticeship course, I was the only student without any previous dance training. That made me the unorthodox exception.

My daily life routine between September 1993 and July 1994 consisted of long Pilates classes taken at Alan's studio in Marylebone and studying at Brunel University, where I extended my education with units in sports psychology and a course on diseases and sports. On top of that I gave private Pilates classes early in the morning and late at night, sometimes during the day. Soon enough I would write my second MA thesis. This one was on the use of image facilitated instructions for Pilates exercises. Family members and acquaintances were used as test subjects.

My acceptance into the small world of Pilates grew because of my training with Herdman and I got more and more work. It went on like that for a few years. In 2004 I received my Pilates diploma from Alan Herdman and my MA in Sports Coaching and to crown it completed a course in holistic massage in the following summer.

For a moment I even toyed with the idea of expanding the knowledge I had built up in sports science and Pilates and carry on with further training in physiotherapy and even medicine were options, but in the end it didn't come to it, not the least due to the training providers being too expensive or requiring me to take further courses before they would accept me.

Claudia's life was also changed beyond anything she could have predicted. After successfully completing her social work conversion, she began working as a social worker in a London local authority. The two of us were quite busy.

60

PhD 2.0

Despite my success in Pilates, after a few years break, I couldn't let it go! I was still annoyed that my doctoral thesis had been left undone. After discussing it with Claudia, I applied to the Jewish faculty at University College London (UCL), then and now one of the UK's leading universities. The reply to my first email should have served as a warning. My doctoral supervisor to be had initially refused to work with me, saying "he had too much to do." But after I wrote to him personally and asked again, he accepted me after all. I enrolled and took part in the university's exceptional PhD management programme. I had to pay for the fees myself this time, even on a part time basis this amounted to around 2000 Pounds a year. Also, unlike at Leeds, UCL required me to provide a written declaration that my studies would not aim to glorify violence, but to advance peace. In return, I would be given free access to censored and even disturbing material at the university, such as videos that attempted to persuade people to commit acts of violence, many using horrific and brutal footage to shock and convince people to act. I certainly watched my fair share of such stuff – it was horrific – and I knew I had to be careful, this stuff could traumatise, and I had no support for it.

To my great disappointment, the same problems I had known in Leeds soon emerged at UCL too. For one, the supervisor there helped even less than those in Leeds and seemed very distant. Further applications for travel grants were again unsuccessful.

However, even though this time I was paying my own fees, I stuck with it at first. Anchored in research into violence, I looked for a counterbalance to violence for my own sanity and to ensure I kept my eyes on violence prevention. Initially, I attended a series of seminars at a church dedicated to peace in the world, St Ethelburga's in the City of London.[142] They offered an introductory course in non-violent protest modelled on Martin Luther King Jr. At the same time, I applied for a job with an organisation run by the parents of a boy who had been stabbed to death in London. They were looking for someone to teach against the use of violence and offer concepts how to address conflict without resorting to violence. After interviewing me, they gave me the job, but the salary they paid was so low that I was better off staying with my current Pilates work. I declined to start, unless they could up the salary a little. They could not.

After a few more months, I came across the British Friends of the Israeli-Palestinian Peace Village Wahat Al-Salam – Neve Shalom, renamed today as Oasis of Peace UK. This village is a place where Jewish and Palestinian Israelis live together, with a centre for conflict transformation and a primary school, amongst others. The UK support group engaged in fund raising and public relations work for the village and also organised courses on the methodology of encounter and conflict transformation. To say a few things, about the methods of the village. They work over longer periods and use both Arabic and Hebrew. Language is a tool, as the leaders use it in order to redress power imbalances. Conflict

---

[142] St Ethelburga's invited all kinds of peacemakers and organisations to their seminars. The background was that the church had been damaged in the Bishopsgate IRA bombing in 1993 and had decided to do everything possible for peace since then. I can still remember the attack of the IRA. I was living in Shadwell, East London at the time. I remember a dull bang and a vibration and buses stopping and broken glass everywhere. Twelve years later in 2005, I would be passing a bus at Tavistock Square on my motorbike that was blown up by a terrorist ten minutes later.

work within each group is crucial to provide for more equal balance of voices, not just the usually male confident know-it-all. The centre also believed that one must not shy away from addressing difference, rather than just celebrating what is in common. However, what was most astonishing was how little each side understood and comprehended about the associations and experiences on either side. In the village where Arabs, Jews, Druze, Muslims, Christians, and Palestinian people live together, all are Israeli residents, there is no absence of conflict, but they try to work such situations through without violence, for example with another meeting, if things cannot be resolved. The primary school educates children in both languages and with both narratives, particularly tricky when the Israel Independence Day is close to the Palestinian Nakba Day.

Initially, I wrote a few press reports as a volunteer for the organisation. This soon grew into a paid position. It was not great money, but it was flexible and regular work, allowing me to continue to work as Pilates teacher and study and, after some years, I was given another role as education officer. I also produced an audio feature about the village and did a diploma in conflict transformation with a London provider.[143]

Then came the 2007 financial storms. Due to the international bank crash I lost six of my regular Pilates customers within several months. Some of these took up to two sessions a week. I lost nearly 60 percent of my income and it was very hard to replace it. Those clients who came through now, only wanted brief sessions to help them with a particular problem. It was the beginning of the gradual decline of Pilates teaching for me.

---

[143] Zylbersztajn (2008)

61

I Die with the Truth

There is a time and a place for everything, and the time had come for that crucial long overdue confrontation between myself and my parents, perhaps a token of my increased understanding of the circumstances that surround me and dictated my life.

It started with my father suggesting he would like to contribute something towards me buying a flat in London. Years earlier at the end of my BA-Studies there had been an opportunity, and I discussed it with my parents. My mother and father, seeing the dilapidated flat I lived in, refused the idea of buying a flat in London when prices were still low. Had they agreed, it would have increased in value four-fold. But they honestly thought, or at least hoped, that I would return to Munich. Now, all of a sudden, my father suggested I should look for a flat somewhere. I didn't realise at the time that my parents had secretly decided to sell the small bungalow in Dalfsen in the Netherlands without telling me, which is probably why the offer was made.

Given all the advice I had been given and my sense of dignity and new-found self-agency as well as a low but stable income, I could no longer accept such an offer without further thought. The time had come to put the truth on the table and end the long period of living a double life. A decade had passed since my marriage to Claudia.

Zol Zayn Shulem II: Faroys

I explained to my father that I couldn't accept this offer without him knowing that I had been married to a West African woman for years. Sensing lack of control and feeling threatened, my father's first reaction was to demand that I end the relationship immediately. He honestly must have thought he still had that power.

I received multiple aggressive phone calls in succession in which my father shouted down the line, with my mother crying in the background. "*Tomma* (yid. if) you don't do this, you are dead to me!" They invited me to Munich for a chat. I had no problems with a direct talk. My hopes that they would let me talk to them ended however as soon as I walked through their front door. It was, of course, just another attempt to put me under pressure on their own turf. There was a lot of shouting from my father. My Mum stood behind him and agreed with him: "How can you do this to your Mother, that she has to walk around with a *Shwarze*?" Then my father repeated his threat and promise that I would be dead to him if things stayed that way. One day before I was due to leave, during another hysterical fit from my father, I had enough. I quietly packed my things and left their flat.

Fortunately, Kirsten Wiseman, a friend of mine for now 20 years or so lived with her then husband just a 20 minute foot-walk away. They took me in for my last night in Munich. I had come to live with the daughter of a Jamaican and an Englishman, of all people, because my own father, a survivor of the greatest racist crime of the 20th century, had thrown vehemently racist views at me. What I was even more ashamed of, was the fact that her then husband's family were Bavarian Germans with a possible Nazi past. They had, as far as I knew, no problems with Kirsten or her family. I returned to London distraught.

I don't know whether it was a coincidence that my father loved the story of Tevye the Milkman by Sholem Aleichem above all others. After Tevye's third eldest daughter, Chava, falls in love with a young Russian and marries him secretly and against her father's wishes, she too was dead, as far as Tevye was concerned, as if she had never existed. The film series *Unorthodox*, based on the book of the same name by Deborah

Feldman (*The Scandalous Rejection of My Hasidic Roots*), deals with the same topic.[144] The expulsion of people from Jewish communities, especially from Orthodox or Ultra-orthodox Jewish communities, of people who have either married non-Jewish partners or who have opened up on their sexual identity, is no secret. It prompted the British Chief Rabbi Ephraim Mirvis some years ago to issue guidelines for schools, that the obligation of godly humanity and approaching all humans with dignity had to come first.[145] The way my parents reacted may have been consistent with ways of behaviour in strict orthodox Jewish communities, but my father was no member of an ultra-religious community, nor was he religious. Yet he took claim to "tradition," as Tevje called it.[146]

---

[144] Unorthodox, Netflix film series (2020), Feldman (2012)

[145] See Mirvis E. with LGBT+ Jews (2018) The Wellbeing of LGBT+ Pupils A Guide for Orthodox Jewish Schools Chief Rabbi Ephraim Mirvis with LGBT+ Jews *https://chiefrabbi.org/wp-content/uploads/2018/09/The-Wellbeing-of-LGBT-Pupils-A-Guide-for-Orthodox-Jewish-Schools.pdf* (accessed 1. Nov. 2024)

[146] Of course, there are also similar problems in other communities, as any search on the topic of "Marrying Out" can quickly make clear

62

The Therapy Continues

Again, the questions arose; what all this was about and how one was to deal with it? In London, I tried to understand what had been going on in my life for over ten years. My first therapist at Shalvata, the London centre for psychological care for Holocaust survivors and their families, had underlined that help was available when needed, and that I was not alone. But Shalvata wasn't able to give me more hours of therapy this time, so I had a conversation with my GP and he agreed to support a referral for sessions through the British National Health System. It would take time, though, before I would get access to sessions, he said.

I came across a therapy group for (adult) children of Holocaust survivors led by the psychotherapist and psychologist Gaby Glassman, who had specialised and worked for years in this field who could bridge that period. I was in luck, and she could offer me immediate sessions and a space in group therapy, where I would meet other children of Shoah survivors. The costs would have to be carried privately, although she considered each person's abilities.

I visited her group once a week in Belsize Square Synagogue, one of the London synagogues that had long served the German-Jewish refugee community in London. All the others in the group suffered from various anxieties and behavioural disorders, either themselves or with their parents. They were all between the ages of 30 and 70, and all were exhibiting symptoms of PTSD in relation to complex family dynamics. Glassman repeated frequently that we were by no means the only ones experiencing this. This was a message of relief for everyone. What I learned in this group from the participants was unbelievable. Some in the group were trapped in their own homes, others in their thoughts, and some could hardly move freely, while still others tried to understand their parents and antisemitism. One patient had even been sexually abused by her father, a man who had survived the Shoah. We listened to each other and deliberated on what Glassman told us. Her specific advice was to live our lives and, where possible, to keep the door open to our distraught and tormented parents despite of everything, although not to the extent of denying who we were or allowing them to control us.

Perhaps half a year after the last session with Glassman had ended, I finally was offered an appointment at the world-famous Tavistock Clinic, the place once founded by Sigmund Freud, thanks to the earlier referral from my GP. During my first assessment interview, I almost got into an argument with one of the psychotherapists, who had probably deliberately provoked me, at least I hope it was deliberate: "I think you have too much to do with the Holocaust and are also the victim of a hysterically anxious mother", she judged. I felt this judgement may have held some truth, but was also unjust, because of the circumstances that were at least in part out of my control, namely who my parents were and what emotional baggage they themselves had carried.

The actual therapy sessions began almost a year after that and under the guidance of a young psychotherapist with a doctorate. Everyone in the group suffered from PTSD, but the triggers varied widely: There was a former traffic warden from an Indian family background who had been attacked and beaten by an angry driver after she had issued him with a parking ticket; there was an Englishman whose father had been a prisoner of war in Japan; there was a man who had been bullied throughout his school years; and there was an Indian-British woman who had survived a serious car crash. There were also two I have forgotten about, because they came to one or two sessions, only to never return. Unlike the other therapists I had experienced, the Tavistock expert hardly spoke in the sessions. It was obviously an attempt to encourage us to heal ourselves as a group.

In the middle of this time, in January 2007, my friend Gregor, who by now was living in Berlin, called me and told me that "time was coming to an end." Gregor was always a bit dramatic and sometimes depressed, hence I didn't think too much of it at first and tried to cheer him up. Nevertheless, I was resolved to look out for him during my next holiday in Germany, if possible. When I received another call the following March, he said he was dying because his kidneys were no longer working. He argued that he didn't want to undergo dialysis or accept organ transplants. Gregor had been through a lot in his childhood with lots of medical procedures and operations and he didn't want to be exposed and dependent on the control of doctors and continuously feeling weak. He wanted to look back on a life where he was strong and could do anything he wanted. A death by toxic levels of sugar in his blood and kidney failure, he claimed, was not so bad. He would only become mentally confused and then fall into an unconscious state and die, he claimed. Finally, he asked me for my opinion. It was an impossibly difficult question. After thinking about it for a moment, I answered that I would stand by his decision because he was my friend, but that I would like to have him as a friend for longer. If he chose to live on, I would be there for him, whenever I could.

Contrary to my hopes, Gregor still chose to die. Even his brother, who had rushed over from the USA, and his closest friends at the time couldn't talk him out of it. And that is what happened. Gregor died in April 2007 in the presence of some of his Munich friends after an emergency transfer in an ambulance from Berlin. Unfortunately, his death was not as pain-free and smooth as Gregor had imagined it. In some way, having control and the power to make his own decisions about his body and his fate was the most important thing to him and neither doctors nor his caring friends or family could make him change his mind. It was a type of freedom he chose, though it was fatal. Others may have judged that life-extending treatment could also be seen as a freedom and conquest over his destiny.

Somewhere there were parallels between Gregor's deadly fight for autonomy and my fight to be freed from the emotional and psychological aftermaths of the trauma of the Shoah.

A few weeks after Gregor's death, his family and friends gathered at his funeral in Munich. I was sorry that I hadn't managed to see Gregor again in person before he passed away. It all happened so fast.

One of the strange stories that came out after he had died was that Gregor, who had always stood up for me, liked to tell old German jokes about Jews every now and then in circles of other friends. If I had known that, I would have had a word with him about it. But it is also true that Gregor was deeply sarcastic, and a master provocateur who wanted to push and experience the boundaries of what was allowed and possible. Gregor even lived in an open three-way relationship before his death, probably so that he could try that out too.

His decision not to take life-saving treatment meant also that he deliberately ignored the love of a woman he had met in Spain years before, prior to his three-way relationship. From what I was told, she really was in love with him and wanted to marry him, perhaps even start a family. But Gregor was usually on the run from such love. "I'm going to die anyway", he joked. He didn't see, didn't want to see or couldn't see, that such love might have saved him, might have kept him alive, and may even have given him a reason to try to stay alive.

My therapy group helped me to come to terms with the death of my friend. I sometimes had the feeling that this kind of therapy might have helped Gregor too.

The therapy gave me further important insights, as did the love and dedication of my wife Claudia. It was Claudia who kept me going, and it was only through her strength that I overcame some of the problems in our marriage. One such problem that plagued us as a couple was my vehement fear and reluctance to become a father. Claudia's position on this was made clear before my therapy at the Tavistock had begun. With all love and patience in the world, she would leave me, if I continued to refuse to start a family. It was an ultimatum and her legitimate right to determine her own dreams.

But why was I afraid of becoming a father? It is difficult to explain this today, but of course it related to the constellation within my family and my experiences.

On the one hand, I was afraid that I would become a father like my own father; on the other hand, I believed that my parents' constant interference entitled me to live my life to the fullest. A child, I thought at the time, would restrict hard-won freedoms due to its natural and unavoidable needs, that would require love, dedication and looking after. Whilst that was understandable logic that I had constructed for myself at the time, upon closer inspection, it was nonsense. Being a father only brought one thing for me: getting to know new aspects of life and emotional growth. Today, on the other side and as a father, I can swear testimony to that.

I carried the ultimatum given to me to my therapy group, where it was discussed. The most impressive thing was that all the group members judged respectfully that I was wrong. It was only my therapist, who had insisted that I had a perfect right to decide not to become a father, and to determine my own destiny and express my own choice on that. What he recognised here was the risk of conformity to the wishes of others to the detriment of one's own wishes. Wasn't that what I had experienced from my parents for so many years?

In an ironic twist, it was his interjection that gave me the courage to do the opposite. The realisation that it was my own decision that I had to carry, not influenced by anyone, and that someone was even defending it, was probably the most decisive moment during the sessions, and it showed me that a healing process was in progress that had probably started years before, though it wasn't yet complete.

During almost daily two-hour walks through Hampstead Heath, including after therapy sessions, I reconsidered many of the past aspects of my life and decided to be braver and to jump over my and others' shadows and explore the unknown. There was also a longer trip I did on my motorbike from London to Granada in Spain. Plenty of time to think, whilst seeing places I had not been to before, including the Alhambra and Cordoba, where I visited the old Jewish quarter.

All this meant that soon I felt that unlike the others in the group, I was getting better. Eight months before the official end of therapy, I decided to drop the sessions. At the same time, I was offered a new job and Claudia and I had found a good rhythm in life. Just before that, the penultimate symbol of change was the fact that Claudia one day emerged from the bathroom and stated that she was pregnant. New life had been created – a triumph!

63

„Shifrah"

It was a new, strange, but also a good feeling to expect to become a father, a sign of my own victory over myself and over the fate of the family, which also saved my relationship with Claudia.

My role as a father began with a research assignment. I studied the ratings of maternity and childbirth care in the UK. The first scan of Claudia showed a clearly recognisable unborn baby, with arms, legs and face inside the womb.

A few months later, I would attend a training course especially targeted at fathers. It was similar to sessions for new expectant parents that Claudia and I attended together. Only a few fathers-to-be thought it was important to sign up and attend either session, in particular the sessions for to-be dads. We were shown how to put on nappies and were told about the importance of being there for children. Only two other dads showed up to the second part of the dads only course. For years I had been running away from becoming a father, and now I was downright enthusiastic about it!

I spent the time of Claudia's pregnancy talking to our child through her growing bump. I spoke exclusively in Hebrew. The last thing I wanted was having to speak German to the next generation. I had still banned German out of my life. I felt it was as a mistake on the part of my parents to bring me up in Germany and speaking German. In any case, there was no contact with my parents, so what was the point in speaking German? To reinforce my decision, I listened almost exclusively to Israeli radio over the internet at the time. But all of that was to come to an end.

Months passed and Claudia became increasingly round. As a Pilates teacher I had accompanied several clients through pregnancy. Now I would show Claudia some of what I had learned. All that time we didn't know if our child was going to be a girl or a boy. Claudia didn't want to be told during the ultrasound scans. Thus, we agreed on two names, one for a boy and one for a girl. In addition, we identified a potential mohel, in the case it would be a boy, we involved Laura Miller, a Jewish Humanist "madriha", to prepare a naming ceremony for us.

Claudia was due for a routine check-up some three weeks before the predicted date of birth, but during the examination, the midwife suddenly discovered irregularities. She decided that Claudia was to remain in the clinic for further observation. I rushed home to bring Claudia something for the unplanned overnight stay. When I returned, they had concluded that the best step would be an immediate induction. This plan turned into a caesarean birth within half an hour, with Claudia being rushed into the delivery room and met by a surgeon and the anaesthetic nurse.

"It's a girl", someone said, and I immediately welcomed our daughter with a loud "Shifrah!."[147] Then this young bundle of joy disappeared for a check-up and soon we heard a soft whine. Shifrah, slightly dried off, was briefly allowed to rest on her mum's chest.

There she lay, tiny, with a full head of black hair and no recognisable eyebrows – our daughter! I thought I could recognise my father's features from the shape of her head. It was all an overwhelming feeling. We were told that the problems had arisen because the umbilical cord had wrapped itself around Shifrah's neck. This meant that Shifrah's middle name was decided; She was given an additional Yoruba name that in

---

[147] Shifrah, in accordance to her great-grand mother is one of her aliases.

Krio culture is only given to babies born with the umbilical cord around their neck, the issue that had caused all the complications.

The first few days passed in a daze. Shifrah had to be breastfed every few hours, her nappies had to be changed, and we watched our mostly sleeping daughter with fascination. I found it difficult to leave our flat to go to work.

I also thought it would be right to tell my parents that they had a granddaughter, and that the girl's name was Shifrah. My father kept himself brief and dismissive on the phone. "Very nice," he answered coldly, as if he wasn't interested, and broke off the conversation. The prediction of some of my acquaintances that a granddaughter would change the relationship between me and my parents turned out to be a misjudged.

About two weeks after the birth, the naming ceremony we had prepared took place. We had rented a large event room at the London Welsh Centre for this, not because it was Welsh, but because it was the only available and affordable place in Central London. We appointed two "honorary parents", Joelle Ferly, an artist from Guadeloupe who was living in London at the time and who had been a member of the Black Cultural Studies Group I had founded a few years earlier, and Ben Gidley and his wife Vanessa, with whom we had always celebrated Passover for many years. Ben and Vanessa were the only ones who later remembered their duty, which led to Claudia making her Jewish friend Vicky Hart another "honorary mum." Claudia's cousin Christiana came with her family from Aberystwyth in Wales for the naming, and helped Claudia cook all sorts of Krio specialities for the party.

Oh, I almost forgot to mention it: Nothing much came of my decision not to speak German to my daughter. One of the first things I realised immediately after Shifrah was born was my lack of any childhood centred Hebrew vocabulary. Given that I had not grown up in Israel as a child, I didn't know a single Hebrew children's song by heart, and I also lacked the knowledge of certain basic words. It was clear that I was not in a position to speak acceptable and adequate Hebrew to my daughter, doubly so outside of Israel, where I might have been able to copy and learn from others. I had to take a final deep look into the unrelenting mirror of truth. In Israel, I had met people who, like me, had refused to speak German and spoke only Hebrew with their children, but they all lived in Israel, where the whole social environment was Hebrew speaking, including the kindergarten and the children's friends and parents. What was I to do? How about English? I didn't know any English nursery rhymes either, at least not yet. My mother had spoken Dutch to me and sung some Dutch nursery rhymes, but my Dutch had been long out of practice and was not good enough, there were no Dutch speakers around us. My Yiddish consisted more of my ability to understand Yiddish than to speaking it.

With a heavy heart, I was forced to admit to myself that the only language other than English that was available to me was German. Was it fair to deprive my daughter of the potential to grow up bilingually because of her family's experiences and her father's dogmatic decisions?

The first sign of a change was my order of a few German children's books. Many more German children's books and DVDs would follow, and it was soon important for me to pass on some of the best of anti-authoritarian children's programmes of the 1970s to Shifrah. If German and Deutschland, then it ought to be the material created by those who had thought a lot about the meaning of parenting in late 1960s and early 1970s in Germany, and who wanted to distance themselves from the historical shackles of the Third Reich that was their parents' and their grandparents' world. Although Great Britain went also through a brief wave of progressive educational experiments in the 1960s and 1970s, it quickly died down there. The result of all the books, radio plays and videos and the German I eventually spoke to Shifrah, is that she speaks and reads respectable German and finished very good GCSE exams in German. The other result was that it opened me up to have a second look at German and Germany.

For the first six months of her life, I walked almost every day all along the Greater Regent's Canal, carrying her inside a sling,. We became such

Zol Zayn Shulem II: Faroys

a regular feature that many of the dog owners who walked their four-legged friends beside the water started to greet us. At the water's edge, Shifrah and I watched the houseboats, ducks, geese, pigeons, swans and of course the many dogs that passed us. I explained everything we saw to her and finally Shifrah uttered her very first ever word. It was "Hund!" Yes, dog in German!

The next question we had to solve was the connection to Judaism. Claudia and I had decided that Shifrah should learn to speak Krio and learn everything that was important on mum's side of the family, but that she should grow up Jewish as far as her religious affiliation was concerned. This gave her access to both sides.

Whilst I had tried to establish a Jewish Humanist Society in the UK together with Laura Miller, after Claudia and I had left Hackney and through that the Liberal Synagogue there, it failed to take off in the UK and was never more than a few meetings with half a dozen of supporters. Being a father now, a loose affiliation without meaningful Jewish events was no longer good enough. It wasn't long before we had a meeting with Janet Burden, the rabbi of our now nearest liberal Jewish community, London West Central Synagogue, right next to the BT Tower, London's television tower.[148] We liked Rabbi Janet, who had a motherly feel and became members. By Hanukkah 5769 (2008 CE) we sat in the toddler group of the synagogue. Rabbi Janet accepted my struggle with the metaphysics. She explained that even in Orthodox communities, some people didn't believe everything. Judaism was also about upholding traditions, recognising Hebrew poetry and philosophical wisdom and songs and sages. What Rabbi Janet told me was crucial at that time. Over the years I switched to the position of Jewish agnosticism, rather than outright and absolute denial, and cherished the maintenance of a millennia-old tradition with its stories, rules and wisdom, though with insistence on equal rights and equality. I can feel our attachment to a tradition of thousands

---

[148] London West Central Synagogue at Maple Street existed up until 2023, when it was given up.

of years, a connection to many previous generations in the past and to the future in the prayers, such as the Kaddish, the Amidah, the Shema. On the other hand, if there is a metaphysical dimension it is abstract and at a distance from the idea of a personal or caring G-d, but more in line with concepts of interconnectedness of life, which gives it a sanctity and a sense of astonishment concerning the fact of life and the universe.

My daughter also had an impact on my still ongoing doctoral studies. When she was born, I was still registered at UCL. I remember the week when I decided to drop the project for good, just before the start of the new academic year of 2008/2009, for which I would be asked to pay fees again. I was lying on our bed while Shifrah slept peacefully on my chest. I could hear her breathing. In one of my hands I held a book about the civil war in Zimbabwe with detailed brutal and gruesome eyewitness accounts. With the child on my chest, I was overcome by a feeling of incredible fortune to live in a time and place where such brutality and violence between people was currently not part of my everyday life. I asked myself why I should have to deal with these dark shadows of humanity day in and day out? It was my first psychotherapist at Shalvata who understood this. People like me tried to understand how violence came to be, especially between 1933 and 1945, to prevent a repetition in their own lives and to hope to be able to recognise the signs of danger in good time, in order to fight them off or to flee. He suggested that I could organise my life without this constant in depth examination, in fact I had a right to do so.

My father, on the other hand, was a captive of television programmes about the Third Reich during his entire life time. He was always keen to find out something he hadn't previously known about the Third Reich and how it all had come about and what atrocities had been committed. I was also interested in such things. But Gaby Glassman, the expert on survivors of the Shoah and their children, and my second therapist, once rightly asked: "What is the point of the survival from the Third Reich, if it is not a permission to a good life?" She was right, surviving also stood for the right to a good and unburdened life, at least as much as that was possible.

Zol Zayn Shulem II: Faroys

I decided that studying murder and violence was no longer going to be my central purpose in life. Instead, there was a child to bring up to my best abilities. It could give me a true purpose in life, at least for as long as she needed me.

64

To Live Life!

Amid all these decisions and experiences, there was also a surprise. In late August 2008, my aunt Gerda and uncle Marcello visited us from Germany to welcome our daughter Shifrah. Gerda, my mum's oldest sister, didn't understand the whole "*Zores* thing."[149] Her philosophy, as a woman who had married an Italian in Munich, was simple: "*All you need is to love each other.*"

The fact that she and Marcello had decided to travel to London to welcome Shifrah was something we had not expected. Claudia and I hired a rental car and took my aunt and uncle on a sightseeing tour of the city. My cousin Claudia and her husband Marcel had also had a child. They called their daughter Johanna and were soon to have a second child, Christopher – another descendant of the Jacob and Minna Lewandowski family.

During a visit to London, Evert, my Mum's Dutch cousin, and his wife Jenny, who both live in Apeldoorn in the Netherlands, also came to meet us and welcome Shifrah.

Most significant perhaps, at some point, a parcel arrived from Munich. It contained a toy that I had myself as a baby, a small silver

---

[149] Zores, yid. trouble, sorrow.

dachshund with a bell and a hand ring. My Mum had sent this and a Steif teddy bear to us, most likely secretly. My daughter still has the bear today. It was a true sign of hope and a surprisingly almost rebellious and independent decision of my mother, that totally changed the script. My Mum had shown she had an independent mind.

This had a little prelude. A few years earlier, I had travelled by motorbike to Beekbergen in the Netherlands to attend the funeral of my Aunt Martha (Margje). I was always incredibly fond of this great-aunt of mine. When my aunt had passed away, my father had already written me off as "dead." My Mum, who had always said that Martha had been her favourite aunt, naturally came to the funeral. She didn't realise that I would be there too. This is how Mum, and I met at the funeral for the first time in a long time. We spoke briefly before my mum tried to escape the family gathering because she did not feel comfortable, as, amongst others, she no longer socialised with Gerda.

This funeral made it clear once more that in my father's destroyed world, life and survival was only possible among other Shoah survivors. They were the only ones with whom human contact was "safe." Son, granddaughter, sister-in-law, daughter-in-law, wife's family, they were all part of a hostile environment, as far as my father was concerned. A lonely and sad life, without forgiveness, and quite harsh on my mother too. It is a terrible price to pay for having had terrible pain inflicted on him earlier on.

In London we started family life. The very thing I had been afraid of before starting a family was now my day to day reality. Above all, it was my own imaginary need to be free from supposed shackles that delayed that for so long. That is why I climbed out of the window at the age of nine, practically moved out at 14, ran around the nightclubs in Munich at 15, travelled to Israel for three years to go to school there and studied in London. The women I fell in love with after I was 20 were neither German nor Jewish, as if I avoided these backgrounds, too close to that world I hoped to escape from. Did that make me freer? I had been seeking illusionary freedom, for true liberation could only be gained from within oneself. Until I was able to work on that, look into the mirror and learn to confront my fears, I would continue to be stuck, not truly being able to live a more complete and truly happier life.

I was not totally wrong back then, when I was still reluctant to become a father. The needs and demands of children are certainly limitless. They really restrict personal freedom and determine each day, especially when the children are still small, tiring parents out. For Claudia and me, there were hardly any breaks or any help from others, no grandma, no grandad or other family to assist us, certainly not from my side of the family and Claudia's closest family was in Wales and Freetown. Being there for someone completely, making a child happy, caring for your sick child and all the hours that didn't allow for much sleep, were the experiences that transformed me and that I wouldn't have missed for the world, actually.

Shifrah is not only my daughter, but also Claudia's daughter, and she has the right to go her own way. Part of her family's history has now been written down. History is a reminder, the dead demand to be remembered, and within that lie many blessings. But the lives of the descendants do not have to be arranged in line with past trauma.

> *Go Shifrah and live your life. This is what those in the past were unable to do, when they were disturbed in the midst of the fullness of their lives. Go without obstacles and enjoy life. According to Jewish wisdom and tradition, this life is the one given to us as a gift and we do not await the transition or ascendance to a more purposeful afterlife, so make use of it.*

What was this new role for me like? Parents can pass on many things onto children. As my father had been a rather distant figure, I also had to re-explore the father-child relationship and found my role model in the ideas of modern emancipated fathers. However, equality does not mean a mere change of roles, where the father is then mainly responsible for the children and the mother works. The roles had to be redefined in the first place so that no-one had to give up either their access and quality time with the children or their career. I learnt this during the production of a radio programme I made on this topic of fatherhood, when I interviewed Adrienne Burgess from the British organisation "Fatherhood Institute."[150]

Virtues I had never imagined grew in me: tolerance, patience, seeing things from a child's perspective, new creativity and, above all, unconditional love! I began to learn to switch off and concentrate despite noise in the house and to appreciate small things. All of this no longer really existed in my father. It had been erased in him, or he was unable to access it properly.

I hope that at least my mother sometimes felt my father's closeness and love, probably less than she deserved, because she suffered from the same problem herself, had her own trauma – a bleak world! I learned that these traumata can be passed down unintentionally to the next generations. This is no longer just a theory in the field of human psychology, but has even been observed in the animal kingdom, as suggested by a study of mice that passed on negative experiences to the next generation.[151]

---

[150] Zylbersztajn (2012d)
[151] Curry (2019)

65

Nothing to Save

After working for Wahat-Al-Salam-Neve Shalom for a few years, the chairman of the Meretz-UK group contacted me out of the blue.

Allow me to explain. When I was still living in Israel, I was very fond of Meretz, the party that evolved out of the Israeli civil rights party Raz through a 1992 merger with the socialist left Mapam and the liberal Shinui Party (Meretz merged with the Israeli Labour Party in 2024). Through my research during my doctoral studies, I came across the civil rights expert Shulamit Aloni, who was an Israeli parliamentarian from the Raz and later Meretz party. Yossi Sarid belonged to the same party. I always enjoyed reading Sarid's critical commentaries in Israel's left-wing newspaper *Haaretz*. What I liked about him was his direct, courageous way of criticising Israeli governments, but without giving up his faith in Israel.

The British group Meretz-UK was part of the worldwide Meretz movement. Its position was progressive-left Zionist and it was strongly in favour of the peace process. Yossi Beilin, who took part in the Oslo peace process as Foreign Minister under Shimon Peres, was also a member of Meretz (Israel) from 2003 onwards. Remembering this, I agreed to consider the request from the Meretz-UK chair and his board. On closer inspection the British group was hardly comparable to the Israeli Meretz party. It was more a group of ageing Jewish idealists in their mid-50s and upwards. Its chairman had been in office for decades and there were no longer any real meaningful elections because the organisation had become so small. The chairman took advantage of this, or so it seemed. He had the expenses for regular trips to Israel to the Zionist World Congress covered for himself and the group's secretary, whilst the minute size of the group did not justify such an expense. Whenever a major event occurred in Israel, political or otherwise, about which the Israeli Meretz party was vocal, the British group never reacted. Every now and then there would be an event when these *vatikim*, who had known each other since their youth days, would get together.[152] I felt that was a sad fact, given the unique position of Meretz in Israel, and it bothered me so much that I had written an email to the UK chapter a few years earlier pointing out their irrelevance to the cause.

That's how the chair came to consider me as somebody who might be interested in attempting to renew the movement in Britain, to bring in younger people, and for that he was going to offer me the position of CEO. In other words, you want it to change, go and do it.

It was a tough call. I would be limited to two days a week pay on minimum wage. Despite huge efforts on my side to structurally and culturally renew the group, I must admit that I failed miserably. Even seminars about the issue of refugees and concerning sexual violence failed to persuade outside people to consider Meretz-UK, though it was early days. I would have continued to build and try to turn the fortunes around, had it not been for the unwillingness of the board to implement a number of crucial reforms I suggested. They defended numerous problems I had highlighted. At a crucial executive meeting they told me in no uncertain terms, that they would rather leave things the way they were. It looked hopeless and I decided there and then to walk out on them, rather than to spend more time hoping for the best.

An acquaintance who is an experienced businessman later explained to me that new managing directors can often encounter such problems

---

[152] Vatikim, hebr. veterans, older members

and resistance. I was just unlucky. The board understood that the organisation needed change, and they wanted it, but as my friend said, such organisations often fail to think through what change really means and are then unwilling to sanction the necessary reform steps. My idea was to organise lots of interesting talks, keep advertising, build the social media and internet presence and start reporting to some degree on what happens in Israel and elsewhere. The fact that the rooms were hired to a kindergarten most of the time also meant that whilst they had an income coming in, there would often not be space for bigger events.

Almost at the same time I left Meretz-UK, Claudia's maternity leave ended, and she returned to work. She found that the department she worked in had failed to keep her position open and had transferred her to another work group in her absence. This was a clear breach of her rights.

Claudia lodged a complaint, and only after considerable effort the case was resolved out of court. From this time onwards, Claudia only worked as a temporary worker for various London authorities until, a few years later, she had enough of that too and decided to build her own business in the wider social care sector. Beside her clear vision it required self-belief and patience on her part, with a steep learning curve, but in the end, she managed to build a respectable company where she now was her own boss. For many immigrants this is the sole guarantor against being pushed and shoved around and to oversee your own destiny without discrimination, though at times she would experience curious attitudes by some, who did not expect a Black West African woman behind her Jewish surname.

66

Children Days

After the end of my time at Meretz-UK and laying my doctorate to rest, I first returned to do more press and media work for "Oasis of Peace-UK."

My options were limited. The arrival of my daughter Shifrah had changed my life quite a bit. I spent the daytime hours with Shifrah, while Claudia did the evening routine after her work, which is when I started to work from my home desk or teach some Pilates, though as already said, after the bank crashes of 2007, I now had far fewer clients.

One of the biggest changes was selling my motorbike and getting back into the world of cycling. I didn't want to jeopardise my life as a father of a young child by riding a motorbike. I invested what I got from the sale into a children's transport bike, one of those bikes where children can sit in a box at the front. Bikes like these, which are widely available today, were still so rare in London back then, that Shifrah and I were frequently photographed and asked questions about the bike. I had ordered the bike in Berlin for cost reasons, when there was still a Nihola-Bike manufacturing work-shop there, which was run by Carlos Labraña Alarcón, a Chilean who had moved to Germany. Carlos and I got on well, and before I knew it, he was ordering English and German translations for his brochures from me. This relationship lasted for several years, even after Carlos had moved on to do other things in Berlin.

Interestingly enough, Carlos' jobs meant that for the first time in many years I worked again with the German language I had banned for so many years, even though I translated German into English.

This time was also a period of contemplating what my next steps would be. I decided, for better or worse, to continue teaching Pilates, but also to try to get back into broadcast journalism, because the truth was that I had always enjoyed it.

Due to the excursions with our Nihola bike, Shifrah soon became known everywhere as "that little princess." Our days together were long and full. We visited almost every park and playground that we could reach, sometimes taking little guests with us, and soon attended many playgroups, among which I was often the only man. Luckily there existed also a new special drop-in play group for fathers and their children, part of Labour's new children services in our area, where it was all about dads.

Given our mobility due to the Nihiola bike, we travelled beyond our own area for the most exciting London playgrounds, One of the key places was Coram's Fields Children Park in Bloomsbury. The playground was the left over forecourt of a former children's hospital, which was saved by the initiative of mostly upper-class ladies, from becoming the site of a lucrative housing project in the 1930s. Here, in a perhaps unusual twist of common wisdom, that says much about the place, adults had to be accompanied by children. We celebrated several birthdays here, including Shifrah's first birthday on one of the grass patches, which were always free from dog poo, as dogs were not allowed in. Years later, I would spark the idea of a user group of the park and playground, which I set up with the support of like-minded parents. We had been alarmed by what we felt was mismanagement of the park by the charity that was charged with looking after the place. Their strategy included renting the place out to adults and sacrificing one of the last spaces for kids. They also hosted large winter adult-entertainment tents, at the time fed by Diesel generators in the midst where children played. We challenged that and a number of other things. High turnover of parents, who are only really interested in a playground when their children are of pre-school age, meant it was hard to keep up the momentum. Some of the aims I had in mind, challenge the very high salaries staff paid themselves (encouraged by a board of trustees who were mainly upper class residents and city and law people who had only limited understanding of the local area), and transforming the park into a true children's oasis in every single corner of the place, as well as opening a street facing café, so the playground could earn more revenue through that, we did not achieve, but one of my former colleagues thinks we set a precedent, that led to a more cautionary approach eventually.

68

Locked Doors

During the autumn holidays of 2008, Claudia and I planned to fly to Munich to give my parents the opportunity to welcome their granddaughter. We planned this with the help of my school friend Kai Kress and his wife Nickie. As parents of two children who were about the same age, they kindly welcomed and accommodated us in their flat near Munich's Rotkreuzplatz. This meant we had a place to stay just in case my parents closed the door on us. I drove to my parents' house and rang the doorbell unannounced, but they weren't in at the time, so I left a note. When we came back the next day, nobody was there again, but the note had disappeared. In addition, my parents' car was no longer parked inside the garage. I had still seen it there the day before. Unusually the car was still missing in the evening. Years later, I learnt that when my parents found the note that stated that I was in Munich with their granddaughter, my father decided to pack the essentials, take the car and book a holiday for my mother and himself in the Bavarian Alps for a few days to avoid having to meet us. I write my father had decided, because I am pretty sure it was my father rather than my mother who was behind this plot. Mum had already sent a secret welcome pack to her granddaughter. I was, or rather we were left standing in the cold, including my parents' granddaughter.

None of my other contacts had a problem with us. We repeated these attempts to make contact with my parents over the next three years and my parents refused to meet us on every single of these occasions. We visited Eva, the mother of my deceased friend Gregor, who lived just a few blocks away from my parents, several times. It was a deeply painful process for me.[153]

We consoled ourselves with the fact that the visits were also about opportunities to introduce Shifrah to German-speaking environments. For this reason alone, I always attended all the children's theatre performances I could get my hands onto with Shifrah. What I didn't expect was, that these early theatre performances were to trigger her later love for the stage and acting.

We never shied away from giving Shifrah everything we could. Shifrah's lavish birthday-parties were part of that. For example on her sixth birthday we arranged to meet Shifrah's friends and their parents at the Charing Cross boat stop, travelled as a group on one of the river boats to Greenwich where we walked through the foot-tunnel under the Thames and stopped at Mudchute Animal Farm for the actual party, with food prepared for over 20 children and a tour of the farm.

---

[153] Kai, Nicki, Kirsten, Eva Kollmar, Aunt Gerda and Uncle Marcello and my cousin Claudia all helped us.

68

The End

My father was always someone who took his survival and life into his own hands, and who acted when something was wrong with his health. For as long as I knew him, he did his morning exercise routine to cure his back that had been damaged by the hard labour in the camps.

When my father was slightly off the scale with his bodyweight, he would fast until his weight was reduced again. Nobody could match his discipline, which probably had something to do with the familiarity of starvation experienced in the most brutal circumstances. When he came down with shingles a few years before our big falling out, one side of his face became paralysed, I showed him some facial exercises that strengthened the relevant muscles and informed him that the body and brain were capable of creating new neural connections to move muscles after injuries. After that he would stand in front of a mirror daily to perform facial gymnastics for ten minutes or longer, sometimes even several times a day. As hoped, the paralysis disappeared. When his femoral head once slipped out of the hip socket, he casually said that it had happened before and pushed it back by himself!

When a cancerous tumour was discovered in 2009, he bravely went through all the stages of cancer therapy, surgery, chemotherapy and radiotherapy. However, in the end, the tumour returned. For my 92-year-old father, it wasn't the cancer that was to blame, but "the damned surgeon" who had, he said, missed parts of the tumour when he operated my father. Being upset was all he could do. He, who had survived the Shoah, was given the clear indication that he was going to die from the cancer as it continued to spread and weaken him.

But of all this I knew nothing. The separation from me was rigorously enforced and maintained. When I called my father in January 2011 to wish him a happy birthday, I was informed that "his time was running out."

Gaby Glassman, my former psychologist and psychoanalyst, had, as I reported earlier, once advised me that it was important to "keep the door slightly open" in spite of all. It was because of that advice that I asked my mother if my father wanted to see me before it was too late. They told me to come, but without my family. Records show that I booked the flight in early April, I presume this was the time they told me to come. When I came ten days later, they asked me to stay in a hotel nearby I didn't quite understand the latter, but I soon learned that it was because my father's care was already extensive and they were, or my father was not, comfortable with me witnessing the extent of his illness and there was also less space for me to stay in their apartment.

I don't know why he didn't want to see his granddaughter. I sent him a picture. He remained stubborn and ignorant about that and yet the reunion was a degree of reconciliation.

It was the first time that I had come to Munich to visit my parents in many years. When I entered the flat, my father was sitting in the living room fully dressed. I could tell that he was ill by the way he looked, and through the fact, that he no longer had the stamina to even watch the football on Saturday evening.

In spite of the little time left, we spoke surprisingly little. On one occasion, with his bed now standing in the spare room, he looked at me for a long time with a questioning look. It was an unpleasantly sad and penetrating stare, which I broke off in the end because it had become too intense, and I was almost in tears. I did not want to make it harder for him or myself. It was the parting look of a father who realised that he would probably never see his son again, who probably wanted to say a thousand words and yet couldn't get a single word out.

When I said goodbye after a few days later and promised to come back in a month, my father informed me, that he would not be able to stay alive that long. I do not know what he knew or felt. It was my Mum and I who didn't want to accept or hear this answer.

I should have listened to him. Back in London, I kept checking with my Mum on the phone to see how my father was doing. I kept hearing about the doctors' positive reports, but which were probably meant for my Mum's ears only, to give her some comfort. I probably should have called the medical team myself to find out whether it was a good idea to come to Munich earlier

After three weeks, my father's condition worsened. His GP insisted that he had to be transferred to hospital for acute care. Could the GP or the hospital admitting him have known that he was near death? It became clear that the hospital knew he was terminally ill because they wanted to admit him to their palliative care unit, advice my father refused. What's more, my mother claimed that my father expressly wanted to die in his own home. He apparently told everyone about this wish time and time again while he was still fully conscious. I don't know whether he had signed the necessary paper work and why his care team thought he would be better off in hospital.

Without clear information, I also lacked clarity about what little time was left. My second visit was scheduled for the 4th of May 2011. Normally, I never came to Munich after just barley one month break, so as far as I was concerned, I returned unusually early. And yet it was all too late, just a few hours too late to be precise. Our house phone rang at two o'clock in the morning on the morning of my scheduled departure. I heard my Mum's tearful voice, and she needn't say any more. The date, Nissan 30, 5771 (4th of May 2011) was my father's last morning. Mum reported she had just received a call from the hospital and was on her way there.

On the eve of his death, my father's last words were that my Mum could go home now. "I'll sleep well tonight because I've had a good injection," he told her. He slept so well that he would not see the sun of the next morning.

I tore my shirt according to Jewish tradition, then immediately contacted Lufthansa and booked an early flight. On my way to the airport I contacted Rabbi Janet. I can't remember if we spoke, but if we did, she didn't give me much to go by. It still took me until 11.30 a.m. to reach the Barmherzige Brüder Hospital in Munich's Nymphenburg district. According to my mother, the staff had taken my father's body away half an hour before I arrived, even though they knew I was coming. If I wanted, they offered, I could still see my father in the freezer. I was upset about this, and declined, simply because he would lie there without dignity. Nevertheless, I still saw the room where he had been lying. I saw that the hospital had failed to remove the cross above the door, usually one of my father's first requests. They put a Jewish holocaust survivor in a room in which he was going to die, and he had no choice but to look at a cross with Jesus. I thought it was scandalous and lacked the bare minimum of care and attention. But who knows if my parents disclosed the relevant information? Had I been there this would not have happened.

Mum and I returned home. Mum covered all the mirrors according to Jewish tradition. My parents had been living in self-imposed social isolation for decades and many of their friends had also passed away. This meant that nobody came to the shiva.[154] My mother wanted to go to the Jewish rabbinical authority of Munich so we could arrange the funeral, and that is what we did.

An acquaintance of my mother and my father's best friend, Mendel Gross, who was very old himself, came to the funeral at the new Jewish cemetery in Munich accompanied by his wife. Louis Lewitan, whose father had once shared my father's restaurant and later took over the

---

[154] Shiva, trad. Jewish period grieving for the loss of a close loved one at home for seven days.

business from my father after his retirement, also came. A few of my friends and a few people the cemetery had hired so that there would be enough people for the prayers also came. My father was placed into the ground in a simple coffin. The rabbi and I recited the prayers for the dead helped by a small minyan of guests and cemetery staff. Soon earth and stones covered the coffin. All of this was more honour than most of my father's family had received after they were murdered in the Shoah, people who lie or are scattered about in unknown locations in or near extermination camps or labour camps of the Shoah, sometimes only their ashes. Only Dawid had a grave, because he died after liberation and his surviving brothers buried him. My uncle Abraham, who died of Alzheimer's in Tel Aviv a year before my father, and my uncle Moisze, who also died of cancer in Tel Aviv in 2000, as well as their wives Rosza and Chavtje, have resting places in Tel Aviv. My cousin Hanni rests in Jerusalem.[155] The graves of those on my father's side who died before the Shoah have been viciously destroyed both by Germans and Poles and are no more.

Whilst my mother and I had no shiva to speak of, we spent a week together in her apartment, the first time in many years. In that sense the time was useful to slowly and carefully learn how to get along with each other.

A month later, Yossi Bornstein and his soon-to-be second wife Agnieszka Piśkiewicz ("Agi") contacted me. I had already met them a few years earlier in London. Yossi Bornstein and his father had been coordinating an organisation of Szczekociny's survivors and family members for several years. Yossi and Aga explained that Szczekoziny was organising a Jewish festival that had been celebrated there for years in honour of the former Jewish population and that it was customary to honour the most recently deceased Jewish citizen with the festival.

---

[155] Chavtje, died 2001 in Tel Aviv c.e. 5760 Jewish calendar, Rosza died 2016

69

Broken Gravestones

I apologise for repeating the point, but for those who have not read Zol Zayn Shulem I: *Zores*, it is worth reminding, that following his survival my father returned to his birth town Szczekociny only once and that was immediately after the end of the war, in order to collect a few of his father's belongings, which had been entrusted to a Polish neighbour. When my father arrived together with his brother Abraham in the small town, they were not welcomed with joy concerning the miracle of their survival. Instead, they were told by the son of that Polish neighbour that his father had passed away and everything they had left in trust had allegedly been taken by the partisans. This was the last time my father walked in the streets of his birthplace. He would never return or even have the desire to return.[156]

My uncle Abraham made however a second visit decades later in the late 1970s or early 1980s together with his family. As he would discover, he was still not welcomed there. He also had to correct some of his childhood memories, as the town looked different from the way he remembered it, with the local river smaller than he once remembered.

Yossi Bornstein and his father, the late Rabbi Itzhak ("Izyk") Mendel

---

[156] Leon Zelman also went back briefly after the war, see Zelman (1995)

Bornstein also visited Szczekociny several times – in the early 2000s. Yossi's father Izyk had been incarcerated in various terrible camps of the Third Reich including in Plaszow and Auschwitz. After the Shoah had ended, he found himself to be the only one in his family to have survived. The Bornsteins were not welcomed either, and Yossi, even had to hire an Israeli bodyguard for his follow-up visits.

Yossi very much desired to reestablish the memory of the former Jewish community, most of whom had been murdered in the Shoah. But one man in particular wanted to make sure that the Bornsteins, or in fact the former Jewish residents of the town, would not have it their way.[157] On the other hand, there were also increasing numbers of citizens who would speak up for Bornstein and who openly objected to the hostilities shown to him, which led to relationships that, in the end, brought about a regular annual Jewish festival in the town. Due to the Bornsteins presence broken Jewish gravestones began to emerge from all corners of the town, with a whole load of them situated in one backyard alone. But I am jumping ahead of myself. Let me explain some of this in a bit more detail:

The story of those grave-stones are immensely symbolic for what happened to the Jewish community of Szczekociny, and in certain ways it goes beyond the murder and expulsion of Jewish citizens of the town, as in this case we are talking about the removal of any sign of the centuries-long existence of Jewish people, and in particular those who had already been dead and buried.

The two Jewish cemeteries of Szczekociny, like anywhere else, were intended as places of eternal rest, which according to Jewish custom should be inviolable. Instead, the graves had been deliberately destroyed and were soon empty grounds without a single gravestone left on them. Initially, the removed gravestones were used to build roads on the orders of the German Third Reich commanders. Later, broken into smaller pieces, they were also set into walls and houses of the non-Jewish

---

[157] Personal account made to me.

residents of the town, all of this, after their Jewish neighbours had been deported and murdered and were thought never to return.

Many years later, just before the total collapse of the Communist regime, I am told, one of the cemetery plots had been "sold" to a high-ranking local communist. Declared as the "owner" of the grounds, he quickly had all mortal remains of people on this ground removed and, according to some of the citizens of Szczekociny, fed these to pigs.[158] Then he had a villa built in the middle of the former cemetery. When Yossi and his father started coming to Szczekociny, this man in particular behaved extreme hostilely towards them.

That wasn't all. The synagogue building had also been repurposed to become a restaurant and a drugstore. In addition, the Bornsteins found public toilets erected on the edge of the former cemetery. Less honour and dignity towards the former mostly murdered fellow citizens of the town can perhaps not be imagined.

When Yossi's father saw the former cemetery and, above all, the synagogue and how the place where his father had been shot had been repurposed, he noted in his memoirs: *"It feels like they're murdering us again."*[159]

Yossi Bornstein was outraged and began to contact some media-outlets but he also arranged for an Israeli group of teenagers to visit the town in order to begin the task of restoring the stones.[160]

After direct and open discussions with the mayor, Yossi addressed the Polish Chief Rabbi, Michael Schudrich as well as the then Polish President Aleksander Kwaśniewski. Finally international media started to pay attention, and his campaign gained momentum. The outrage was so great that the public toilets were soon dismantled and removed.[161]

---

[158] Yossi Bornstein in statements to me and my mother during a visit in 2011
[159] Bookbinder (2013), for the life story of Izyk Bornstein see Borstein (2013), B-94, The Spirit of the Survivor.
[160] Baraka (2004)
[161] Barakat (2004) see also Yoman: Szczekociny – Jewish Cemetery & Gravestones, YouTube 2007

Broken Gravestones

Poster of the Szczekociny Jewish Festival 2011 in honour of my father.

Yossi thought the best thing that could happen was to make use of the left-over, mostly broken, gravestones for a memorial between the cemetery and the neighbouring synagogue to commemorate the town's former Jewish residents. In the immediate vicinity of the synagogue he also suggested a plaque commemorating the famous Rabbi Dov Bar Meisel could be erected.

To begin the process, Yossi invited the then still living first generation of survivors to a meeting in Israel, where most of them lived, to outline his plans. They were all in favour. My father was also invited, but living in Germany, he only met Yossi once as far as I know, and an invitation to a meeting in Szczekociny was left in vain.

As already mentioned, as far as my father was concerned, he no longer wanted to visit this town nor have anything to do with it. He

Zol Zayn Shulem II: Faroys

ignored invitations of the community to visit the town during newly organised Jewish festivals in presence of the Bornsteins. I was told that my father's distant cousins from the Schwarzbojm family saw things differently and came for a visit.[162] Over the years it became a tradition to honour and remember survivors who had died in the previous year. This is why my mother and I were invited for the Jewish Festival of 2011 with the theme "*Razem*", Polish for "Together." The festival was to take place just a few weeks after my father's death. During our visit, a brand-new plaque commemorating Rabbi Bar Dov Meisel (Bornstein had it made and covered the expenses.) was also to be unveiled. My mother and I decided to accept the invitation because at that time we hoped it would bring us closer to my father. The visit of his birth town seemed to be a suitable opportunity.

A few weeks later we both flew to Krakow. The town revealed itself as an imposing medieval city. Our accommodation was close to the main market square, Rynek Główny. Jews had lived in this city with royal protection of their fundamental rights since the 1334. This protection came to an end in 1939 with the invasion of German troops. Polish resistance was futile and as far as the faith of the Jewish residents was concerned, some non-Jewish Poles tolerated and even welcomed the exploitation and mistreatment. Others, perhaps not enough, would help or hide Jewish people during the German occupation. In fact, it is said, that no other European nation had seen as many Jewish fellow citizens saved as in Poland. This is why many Polish non-Jewish citizens are rightly remembered as *Righteous Among the Nations* in Yad Vashem.[163]

Whilst coming to Poland felt like a connection to my father and his family, Szczekociny was also the place from which he and his family was once chased. It is a place where the houses and grounds of my family and relatives and of most of the community are no longer in our possession, because non-Jewish Poles occupy them. Poland was a country where

---

[162] Personal conversation
[163] see Yad Vashem Names of Righteous by Country

we knew that there were still many people holding antisemitic beliefs within a society with almost no Jews left. Coming to Poland also felt like a betrayal of my father. We had come to visit this country and the town of my father's childhood and youth without his personal approval or guidance, or his memories and reflections.

After our arrival in Krakow, we stayed for the night and planned to drive to Szczekociny the following morning. We had breakfast and I left my mother at the apartment whilst I fetched the car. But the car was nowhere to be found. It had disappeared. My initial fears of a possible vehicle theft soon subsided when locals confirmed that I had parked where it was prohibited. They suggested that the car had probably been towed away. We paid a penalty and collected the car from the police. I would be lying, if I would not write that it felt a bit like sinister ghosts of the past were chasing us, because we felt alone in a strange country facing the local bureaucracy. The complication also meant that our departure from Krakow was delayed by some three hours and we would not be able to attend the unveiling of the plaque, for which we were down as special guests. The journey from Krakow to Szczekociny (my father had told me that he sometimes travelled the 75 kilometres to Krakow by horse and cart) took me 90 minutes with our rental car. On the way we passed through a relatively flat landscape with large fields. Again and again, we had to cross through villages. Here and there we spotted farms, elsewhere large forests. The sight made my mum and I understand what had drawn my father so much to the rural, flat and wooded areas of the Dutch Overijssel region, with its many rivers. There was a certain similarity between the two.

Entering Szczekociny, a place so central in my father's and many survivors' memories turned out to be a rather small and simple town without any tall buildings. Most of the houses were at best two-storey detached houses with red tiled roofs. Compared to the market square in Krakow, Szczekociny's market square, where my father's family had lived, was also tiny. We caught sight of the old synagogue with the aforementioned drugstore. During the Communist era the house had also been reproposed, as a grain store.

Zol Zayn Shulem II: Faroys

Agnieszka asked us to come straight to the local school, where we met numerous representatives and dignitaries of the town, including the town's mayor. After various lectures on Jewish history, I was asked to make an address. I thanked everyone for the invitation and spoke about my work with Wahat-Al-Salam-Neve Shalom and the issue of the treatment of people who are seen as "the others." I asked whether there are still people in Szczekociny today who are regarded as others, and was told that there were Ukrainian immigrants and Roma and Sinti in the area. I argued, that taking the correct lessons from the past, was not only to be measured by the reappraisal of history and dignity shown towards the descendants of its former Jewish citizens, but also by behaviour towards their contemporary others. I also raised the issue of reconciliation with Germans, because I understood that whilst some work had begun to heal the relationship with Jewish people, the relationship with Germans could often still be difficult. We shook hands and it was made clear to us again and again that we were guests of honour. There was no doubt in my mind as to whether the people who had come to greet us were really serious about it.

After the official part, Agnieszka even invited us to her parents' house for lunch – an additional personal and heartfelt gesture of honour. We then visited the plaque in front of the synagogue that had been unveiled in the morning. Yossi also showed us the house where my grandparents had lived and where my father and his brothers had grown up. Like everything here, it was smaller and more modest than I had ever imagined, as was the synagogue.

Inhabitants of the town had been worried about the houses and properties that had once belonged to the Jewish people of the town. What if survivors and descendants wanted them back? But the few survivors that still lived made a joint decision. Their decision was that they did not wish to reclaim these properties. Instead, they were very much concerned about the memory of their destroyed Jewish kehilah (community). The houses were by no means high valuable assets, many had been rebuilt, as the Germans had torched them in 1939, and yet I believe that survivors had made this decision from a position of weakness. On the other hand, what had been destroyed, especially the murder of beloved family members and friends, in fact the loss of a whole community, could not be replaced by any token gesture or financial sum in the world.

In the evening the locals organised a heart-moving show. There were Jewish songs and dances, klezmer and other entertainment. Truly, it was a bit inappropriate for us to partake. According to religious tradition, we were not allowed to participate in any festive events so soon after my father's death. Had we had the choice, we would not have attended a cheerful musical show. But in the end, it was the right thing for us in the name of my father and in gratitude for the real attempt of this community, nearly all of them younger generations, to try to do good. We spent the night in the guest rooms of the school's sports centre, all this at the city's expense.

The next morning, I jogged into the nearby forest, at the end of which I spotted a lake. It was quite a dense forest, and I remembered my father's stories and how my grandmother and her youngest son Fiszl tried to hide in that forest the evening before the selection of September 1942.

While we met Yossi and Agnieszka for breakfast, Yossi suddenly received a phone call. He looked disturbed and upset. Someone had damaged the brand-new memorial plaque to the ground overnight. We drove to the old synagogue, and sure enough, the sign was no longer there. Later, someone found it lying in a puddle of mud and dirt. It was a new antisemitic incident on the very day of our visit.

Before we set off again, Yossi hurried to go to the town hall and came back with copies of two birth certificates, that of my uncle Moisze and that of my father. Yossi and Agnieszka also introduced us to a Polish woman who kept gravestones from the Jewish cemetery at her father's house and had made it her personal mission to protect and preserve them for later use.

It was lunch time and time to say goodbye, although Yossi and Aga would meet up with us again in Krakow. However, initially I travelled on with my mother in the other direction. I had heard about the pogrom

Zol Zayn Shulem II: Faroys

in Kielce after the end of the Second World War the previous evening and it had made me curious.

On 4 July 1946, 42 Jewish survivors of the Shoah who had been staying in a house of the Jewish Committee at 7 Planty Street in Kielce had been murdered in a pogrom-like attack under the pretext of an alleged child abduction of the Polish-Catholic boy Henryk Blaszczyk. The boy in question was found healthy and unharmed after the violent pogrom.[164] This brutal bloodbath of hatred was one of the reasons why Polish-Jewish survivors of the Shoah left Poland after the war. I had read on the Internet that a memorial had been erected in Kielce to commemorate this massacre.

At the talk on the previous day Polish attendees had had an argument about this massacre. The question was whether Poles or the Soviet Union had been responsible for the murders on that fateful day. If indeed the Soviets had organised the murders, they were certainly exploiting a pre-existing antisemitic atmosphere. The fact, that considerable numbers of Polish-Catholic citizens of Szczekociny had plundered and then taken over the homes of their Jewish fellow citizens, and that they then had been unwilling to return them to the few survivors that came back after the war, and the fact that Catholic antisemitism, indeed antisemitism in general, continued to exist in Poland after 1945, was enough to answer the question of Polish complicity at the very least.

When we arrived in Kielce, I stopped the car to ask for directions. Nobody could or would tell us exactly where the monument we were looking for was, except for a younger couple. As we got out of the car, a torrential rainfall started. Did it mean something?

We learned that finding the monument, which was in the end not far from the central car park, was but one achievement, because the house where the crimes had taken place was somewhere else. Again, no-one we asked could point us in the right direction, even the staff from the

---

[164] See Engel, David (1998) and Yad Vashem: Anti-Jewish Violence in Poland After Liberation.

ice-cream shop directly opposite the house said nothing, until I was walking past the building by accident, and suddenly spotted a plaque on its wall. After a moment of contemplation and having read the plaque, my Mum and I made our way back to Krakow. We wondered what it meant that people couldn't or wouldn't show us where the memorial and the house were. Was it disinterest, ignorance, repression or just our own emotionally charged attitude on that day?

In the evening, I discovered what seemed to be a very popular pizzeria in the vicinity of University of Krakow. There we discovered a vibrant, worldly and young Poland. It was a glimmer of light after the gloomy clouds of the afternoon. The same hope awaited us when we met Agnieszka and Yossi in the old Jewish quarter of Krakow, where the annual Jewish festival and cultural week was taking place. We walked through the small Jewish cemetery and marvelled at the crowded restaurants and cafés and the number of Jewish books on display.

On the day of our departure, I drove my mum to the airport. I told her that it was just like when we travelled together to the Netherlands years ago, only I was driving now and back then I was still a little boy. The atmosphere between us had changed for the better. Nevertheless, my mother still didn't meet an important part of my life: Claudia and Shifrah. We promised each other that my mum would meet them both very soon.

70

The Key to Tolerance

When in 2022 I visited Lelow, the town of my paternal grandmother, neighbouring Szczekociny, I happened to arrive just before their annual Jewish festival, which was similar to the one in Szczekociny. I was shown how the Hasidic community had built a synagogue and mikveh in this small town in honour of their founding rabbi, Rabbi Moshe Biderman (1776-1851). In fact, a lot seemed to have happened there. Showing me around were Beata and Mirek Skrzypczyk, a wonderful and dedicated couple who have given their all to ensure the memory of the Jewish populations in the region continues to live on and even grow. There is no doubt, that they are amongst the righteous citizens of Leluw. What they do is largely down to their personal initiative and conviction. I was even allowed to spend a night in their living room. In Leluw they showed me a memorial plaque listing who in this small community had lost their lives during the German onslaught and occupation. Amongst the many names are Jewish and non-Jewish Poles, although only men, I noticed. I was also shown an art installation and a photo exhibition about the Hasidic community that visited Lelow regularly now. Likewise, I was also given a warm reception in Szczekociny. I was able to visit the new memorial site, a huge gravestone constructed out of the remaining gravestones from the Jewish cemetery for the first time, but

I also witnessed that there was still a restaurant and a drugstore inside the synagogue building.

The gravestone memorial related to Yossi Bornstein's initiative and persistence and was erected in front of the synagogue in 2013 constructed out of more than 200 broken gravestone pieces.[165] There is, however, no doubt that the realisation of his vision was also attributable to political changes in the municipal council. The new mayor at the time, a man by the name of Stanislaw Wojcik, had campaigned to buy back part of the Jewish cemetery, on which the memorial site was to be erected.[166] On the large, oversized, broken gravestone, the words of Habakkuk 2:11 read:

For even the stones in the wall will cry out.

Yossi and other daughters and sons of survivors expressed the wish that they wanted the synagogue to be turned into a museum. To date, nothing had come of that plan. Requests that the *Aron Kodesh* (Torah scroll cabinet), one of the few remnants in the otherwise destroyed interior of the former house of prayer, should be protected, have also so far fallen on deaf ears.[167]

During that, my second visit, I also learned that a colourful book had been published in 2017 by Yossi Bornstein and the initiative of the *Yachad-Razem* festival, which documented the newly established relationships between the citizens of the city of today and the Jewish survivors and their descendants.[168] Among them was Yossi Bornstein and his wife Agnieszka, who did a lot of the basic work tirelessly on their own.

During my personal visits, the issue of the houses that belonged to murdered Jews did not arise. I will leave it with an anecdote. My dear Aunt Ruszke, may her memory be a blessing, used to tell me the story of how, after the war, she went to the house of her parents in Auschwitz,

---

[165] Bookbinder 2017
[166] Ibid.
[167] Ibid.
[168] Bornstein et al (2017)

where a non-Jewish neighbour had moved in. She reported that she was asked into the house by this woman. The woman claimed that there was nothing left behind of my aunt's family. My aunt said that whilst she said that, she only needed to briefly gaze at the cabinets and shelves, where she clearly recognised her parents' porcelain and crockery. Needless to say, my aunt got nothing back from the woman.

This is not just the story of one woman. The Polish government actually passed a law that judicial claims on properties that go back longer than 30 years should be invalid. That is very convenient when it comes to properties that were once owned by Jewish Poles. I have a quote from the Bible for this still arch-Catholic country and its population:

You shall not wrong or rob your neighbour. Lev. 13:13

But in Poland people like Beata and Mirek also live or the historian and artist Krzysztof Gibaszewski in Skarżysko-Kamienna, who guided me through whatever is left of the former labour camp of his town in August 2022. Gibaszewski told me how he has been almost single-handedly campaigning year on year to create a memorial-site to the many Jews who suffered and were murdered in the Hasag labour camp. When he walked me through the town and forests of the area, I saw that there is a clear preference by the public and state to remember the victims who were Polish, non-Jewish victims and heroes. Whilst the official monument to the victims of the Nazi occupation mentions Jewish victims, visually visitors see only a cross and no equivalent Star of David. Krzysztof is still continuing his hard work. He organises events and talks every year and is in regular contact with me.

I had to make the long and difficult trip, during which I followed the many stations of the Shoah relevant to my family on my father's side, on my own. My wife had no appetite to accompany me through Polish and East German provinces, fearing that, as a woman with dark skin there could be areas where she might not be welcome. Apart from a brief stop in Warsaw, as it happened in an area with many Black African shops, a brief stay in Krakow and a neighbourhood with a high proportion of Roma and Sinti in the Czech Republic, I saw no-one with a darker skin colour during the three-week trip. According to the Polish Statistical Office, that may not have been a surprise. Though the number may have changed slightly since, in 2012, 99.8 percent of all Poles were "Polish white."[169] Margaret Amaka Ohia wrote in 2020 that Black people in Poland are often subject of negative stereotypical portrayals, especially in the media.[170] According to her research, they are perceived as carriers of diseases, as a general danger, as starving people, and as cultural or exotic curiosities. These prejudices exist in Poland for most without any direct or meaningful experience of Black people. Jewish people also can be portrayed negatively in the media. One example of the later occurred, when in 2020. during the elections at that time, Warsaw's mayor Rafal Trzaskowski was accused on public television of pursuing "Jewish interests."[171] According to research conducted by the Anti-Defamation League in 2019, a comparative study covering a total of 18 countries, 75 percent of all Poles believed that Jewish people talked too much about the Shoah, and 40 percent thought that Jews had too much control of "global business." A total of 48 percent of all Poles had antisemitic prejudices, and that was the highest percentage amongst the 18 countries the study had examined.[172]

Black football players can be frequently insulted with racist abuse in Poland, so much so that there have been well publicized complaints, most famously when the Dutch national team was greeted with monkey noises from sections of Polish fans in 2012.[173] Furthermore, players and

---

[169] Departament Badań Demograficznych (2012)
[170] Ohio (2016)
[171] ADL, Antisemtism in European Politics. https://www.adl.org/antisemitism-in-contemporary-european-politics (accessed 2 September 2020)
[172] ADL (2019)
[173] See for example, Peter, Erik (2012). White Pride Worldwide im Stadion, taz 31.5.2012, https://taz.de/Rechtsextreme-in-Polen-und-der-Ukraine/!5092756/ (accessed 2.9.2022) , France 24 (2012). Dutch team complain of racist abuse in Poland, 8 June 2012. *https://www.france24.com/en/20120608-racist-chanting-krakow-euro-2012-problems-football-netherlands-poland-ukraine* (accessed 2.9.2022)

supporters of football teams are often labelled as "Jews", meant as an "insult."¹⁷⁴ Black people and People of Colour fleeing the Ukraine at the onset of Russia's strikes against the country, were attacked by Polish neo-Nazis after crossing into Poland in 2022.¹⁷⁵ The former Polish Prime Minister Mateusz Morawiecki repeatedly attempted to reinterpret history to show that Poland was a victim of German National Socialism, shifting the blame for the fate of Poland's Jews and their property solely onto Germany.¹⁷⁶ In December 2023 the far right politician Grzegorz Braun used a fire extinguisher on a Jewish Hanukkah Light display in the Polish parliament, referring to the candle lightening as "satanic worship."¹⁷⁷

When the war in Ukraine broke out, Poland took a stand against Russia as a member of the EU and part of the Western powers. However, with this position also comes responsibility, which must also be binding in terms of the fight against racism and antisemitism.

Poland can only grow as a democracy if it is prepared to overcome its own denial of racism and its own role in antisemitism. Small initiatives, such as Jewish festivals and attempts of reconciliation, are doing important work in this regard. Donald Tusk is quoted to have said once "There is no Polish culture without Jewish culture."¹⁷⁸

---

¹⁷⁴ Cole (2020)
¹⁷⁵ Tondo, Lorenzo & Akinwotu, Emmanuel (2022). People of Colour fleeing Ukraine attacked by Polish nationalists, Guardian 2.3.2022 https://www.theguardian.com/global-development/2022/mar/02/people-of-colour-fleeing-ukraine-attacked-by-polish-nationalists (accessed on 2 September 2022)
¹⁷⁶ See Marsden, Ariella (2022). Poland tries to rewrite country's role in Holocaust – PM email leak Jerusalem Post 15.8.2022 https://www.jpost.com/diaspora/antisemitism/article-714747 (accessed 2.9.2022)
¹⁷⁷ Walker, Shaun: Far-right Polish MP uses fire extinguisher to put out Hanukah candles. In: 21.12.2023, The Guardian. *https://www.theguardian.com/world/2023/dec/12/far-right-polish-mp-uses-fire-extinguisher-to-put-out-hanukah-candles* (accessed 6.11.2024)
¹⁷⁸ Yossi Melman and Haaretz Correspondent: There is no Polish culture without Jewish culture, Haaretz, 7.4.2008. *https://www.haaretz.com/2008-04-07/ty-article/polish-pm-there-is-no-polish-culture-without-jewish-culture/0000017f-dc4c-d3a5-af7f-feee63470000* (accessed 6.11.2024)

The Key to Tolerance

The new memorial on the day of its unveiling, 2013. In the background, the outer façade of the Szczekociny synagogue. Photo: Yossi Bornstein.

My friend Imran summed his experiences up in a single sentence: "The worst time I was attacked in Poland because of the colour of my skin was at the end of a guided tour of Auschwitz that I led." Imran, who also experienced racism in England, continues to live in Poland. People like him and Yossi Bornstein are a blessing for Poland. They seem to have hope that antisemitism and racism can be conquered through persistent work and dedication. Or perhaps they believe they have less choice because they share their lives with Polish spouses. Poles like Krzysztof Gibaszewski, Angnieszka Piskiewicz, Beata and Mirek Skrzypczyk are, however, growing in their self-confidence. They are the key to an environment of credible and profound tolerance, of selfless exchange and deep understanding of one's own mistakes in history and the attempt, where possible, to begin a process of restitution and reconciliation. Those who profited directly from the invasion and occupation of Poland and the expulsion and murder of Jewish Poles, whether out of "need" or motivated by hate or greed, and still do not realise that this was wrong, and that Jews are owed something, even if it is permanent treatment with dignity and the remembrance of those lost, remain on the side of the perpetrators.

71

Screaming Stones: Auschwitz and Auschwitz-Birkenau

It was eight o'clock in the morning and I had just seen my mum disappear through airport security. I now had a whole day to spend alone in Poland until I was due to fly back myself late in the evening. I could have sat in a café in Krakow, visiting sights there, but, as I still had use of the rental car until the evening, I decided to do something completely different.

Auschwitz-Birkenau, Photo: Daniel Zylbersztajn-Lewandowski.

Zol Zayn Shulem II: Faroys

I did not want to waste the remaining time but rather put it to good use, to try to understand more about the process of German mass murder. Already here, with time available and access to a car, it seemed right to me that I should go and see the Auschwitz and Auschwitz-Birkenau memorial sites. If I had known then what I know now, I would probably also have travelled to Sosnowitz to look for my uncle's grave or even to Skarżysko-Kamienna, where my father and his brothers were enslaved by the Germans and where my grandfather's life ended, or maybe even Treblinka, where my grandmother, her son, my father's youngest brother and his great-aunt had been murdered along with many others from Szczekociny, though this would have required me staying at least for an additional day. As far as I knew at the time, my family had not lost anyone in the death-camps of Auschwitz. At the time, I had no idea that those from my family who met their premature deaths in the Auschwitz camps were actually on my mother's side.

After an hour's journey, I reached the so-called "Judenrampe," where a stand-alone wooden cattle wagon from the 1940s, once belonging to the German Reichsbahn is stationed as a permanent museum exhibit. Because of my father's story, I examined the wagon more closely, especially its floor. How long would it take to chop a hole in the floor with a chisel and a knife? What was it like to be trapped inside one? I wanted to feel it, to think about it, but the waggon was closed up. When I came back in 2022, it was open, due to it being restored. Floorboards were missing in various places. I crawled under the waggon and was able to peek inside through the gaps. What did I expect? I was simply standing under a dark old wooden railway carriage. Light shone through the cracks into the dark brown interior and that was all. Going back in thoughts, visiting sites and trying to feel what it may have been like, trying to connect with the past and those we lost, does have its limits. Was I shocked? Did I feel something? In everything I did for this book-series, it was the research and details I came across, the written down accounts, especially the unexpected passages, that shocked me the most. But the buildings and places themselves that bore witness to all this? If there was one feeling that came up repeatedly, it was the sensation of emptiness and a disappointed inability to access those I could never get to know and of whom I didn't even have photos of, pictures or descriptions. They could not be reached.

In Treblinka, after saying the Kaddish (I was following at the time the Liberal Jewish tradition, which allows for recitation on your own), I tried to appeal to my grandmother's spirit in Yiddish. Here too, I soon realised that there was nothing but emptiness. The murders had occurred eight decades in the past. My best hope was that maybe there was still a connection of sorts, and that if there exists something like a spiritual dimension, my appeal and call was heard and witnessed by my ancestors.

After my stop at the "Judenrampe" in 2011, I travelled on to the Auschwitz-Birkenau camp. I had been to the memorial site of Dachau before and obviously there are many well-known images of Auschwitz in circulation, but I was still taken aback by the sheer sense and feeling of the dimensions of the place, the fact that the 175-hectare camp stretched almost along the entire horizon – not so long ago, death and suffering had been everywhere you looked. I visited one of the still existing barracks and imagined my father lying in one of them. Then I walked towards the destroyed gas chambers and incinerators on the other side. Again, I felt that overwhelming sensation of emptiness and sadness for lack of ability to access more, perhaps to feel the pain more acutely. One of the few images I took in Auschwitz-Birkenau was of a piece of electric barbed wire, in the background the freedom of the sky, but also other parts of the site, trenches and on the left edge a watchtower. That was as close as I could get.

Among the many memorial plaques in front of the destroyed gas chambers and crematoria, I found not only German, English and Hebrew language plaques but also one in Yiddish, which particularly spoke to me because it was the language of my father's family. Every plaque read the same. The plaque in English begins with the words:

Forever let this place be a cry of despair and a warning to humanity where the Nazis murdered about one and a half million men, women and children, mainly Jews, from various countries of Europe.

Zol Zayn Shulem II: Faroys

**Memorial plaque in Yiddish in Auschwitz-Birkenau,
photo: Daniel Zylbersztajn-Lewandowski.**

On these vast grounds in some of the houses human beings had been tortured, and "medical" experiments had been carried out on victims in another. I got lost in the Roma and Sinti exhibition of the Auschwitz Museum and I studied the faces on the many photos of the victims, until I finally discovered one of the still existing gas chambers and the crematorium of Auschwitz. In a brief moment when I thought I was alone, I recited the Kaddish there in the dark; it had probably already been prayed by many here.[179] And so I stood alone in the room that

---

[179] The Kaddish, a prayer to the glory of G-d usually recited in honour of the dead, often in their place for them, who can no longer recite it, is usually read out loud collectively, but at the time I was a member of British Liberal Judaism, which permits reciting the prayer by yourself.

bore witness to the darkest site and side of humanity, where (along with the gas chambers in Birkenau) people were forced to meet their end without hope, in panic, fear and ever increasing choking shortness of breath, grasping in the end in despair for air. Amongst them were people of all ages, highly educated people, craftsmen, strong and weak people, housewives, girls and schoolchildren, old people, fathers, mothers, grandmothers, religious and secular Jews, communists, socialists, Zionists, rich and poor people, Gays and Lesbians, Roma and Sinti, and many others who spoke dozens of different languages. They all died here.

I looked up to the sky and into the distance. The Museum was closing and for me it was time to go back and drive to the airport. Claudia later reproached me for having made this visit on my own and without any emotional support. She was right. I thought I was strong enough because, after all, my father was once more or less alone in the hell of the Shoah too. However, he was not entirely alone; there were always fellow women and men about who suffered alongside him, except at the very end, when he had made his final escape and almost, alone by himself in an unfamiliar place facing an uncertain future, gave up as a result. Some may argue that Elohim was always there with him, though, of course, he himself, when asked, would dispute that, for the fact, that he witnessed so many terrible things. "How could a G-d allow that?", my father begged to know and he loathed the answer some Orthodox gave, of sin and irreligious lives. "What crimes then, had little children committed?", he wanted to know, before providing his own answer: "They were innocent, they had done nothing!"

Back in London, I soon wrote a text that explored the question of humanity amongst neighbours. I had experienced how Bangladeshi Muslims and white British people lived side by side in their neighbourhoods without meaningful contact. I wondered what this meant in view of the expulsion and extermination of the Polish Jews, who also had been neighbours once, friends, acquaintances and colleagues of Christian Poles. I also contemplated on my experiences with the Jewish-Palestinian peace village Wahat-Al-Salam-Neve Shalom. People on different sides of

Zol Zayn Shulem II: Faroys

a conflict zone living near each other. My conclusion at the time was that people had to work harder to overcome the barriers between them.[180] I had offered the text to British newspapers at the time, they did not even write back. It ended up on Open Democracy, where an editor thought it was amazing and actually invested some time to polish it up before publishing it.

During my visit in 2022 I was able to say Kaddish also for the members of the Lewandowski-family who had been murdered there. It seemed that Auschwitz had grown as a tourist destination since my last visit. For some, it seemed to be just a detour when travelling through Poland, people walking through the former death camp in any shape or form. Selfies were taken and I sensed a lack of concern and a lack of respectful and dignifying devotion towards what this place once had been. I found this disturbing. When I saw fridge magnets with a picture of Auschwitz-Birkenau in the shops outside the memorial site, I realised that this place was not just about education or representing a warning from history. How many of these hordes swarming daily through the former extermination camp, this place where over a million people had been murdered, are able to learn anything from their visit? Is it truly more than just visiting another sight? I decided to be guided by research and statistical evaluations of those who scrutinise such things. You see, I don't want to tell people what they should or should not do, because it is difficult for me to determine what does and does not work with different individuals. I can only say that I personally felt hindered in my ability to mourn the dead and to meditate on what this place meant. There was a lack of calmness and a feeling of trepidation. I quietly recited Kaddish anyway. I was determined not to be hindered in what I had planned.

Truly, Auschwitz and Auschwitz-Birkenau today are cemeteries, memorials, memorial centres, and educational institutes. I know from some of the educational directors of the various memorial sites that I visited that they often experience worse behaviour. What I saw was

---

[180] Zylbersztajn (2011)

typical of tourists visiting sights and spectacles of any type, it was no different and also remaining indifferent to the significance of this place.

The Israeli artist Shahak Shapira dealt with the same topic in his photo documentation Yolocaust, for which he photographed visitors whilst they took selfies at Auschwitz and Auschwitz-Birkenau.

But as I say, I pass no judgement on the matter. How much even a casual visit might mean to any one individual is not a matter of my personal perception. If people take selfies on the memorial sites or walk through it with less gravity than people like myself would wish for, maybe we should accept degrees of that response, in the hope that actually there is some impact, while trying to prevent obscene or racist behaviour.

It remains to be seen whether a proposal I have suggested to set up certain time slots reserved for the contemplation of direct family members and descendants of the murdered could give us a bit more comfort during our visits. On the other hand, some may find comfort and assurance to see crowds still coming to visit the grounds.

In 2023 I had the opportunity to visit a site of horror of a different kind. It were two former Caribbean plantations in Grenada on which enslaved African people had once been brutally exploited. I have to say, that the emptiness replicated itself there. Not only that, but some areas had also been built over and repurposed. Lacking funds, the former areas had fallen victims to new developments and owners, and very little was done to uphold the memory. In fact, it is possible that the graves of former enslaved people were being disturbed, whilst elsewhere a cricket ground and new plantations had emerged. One of the researchers of the museum of Grenada told me how difficult his task was to research the past and make it relevant to people in a concrete way. Memory is, I think, a very fragile thing, and yet we all need these warnings and sites in front of which we can contemplate on the destructive and murderous potential of being human beings and reflect on how to avoid it.

72

The Dream

In autumn 2020 towards the end of researching this book, I woke up one early morning from a dream in which my father had appeared. I usually never dream about my father, nor do I often remember what I have dreamt.

My dream transported me to the scene of one of the many visits, that I had made over the years to my parents. I had just arrived. After my arrival, my father sat in the living room in his usual armchair. He was wearing an elegant striped shirt, slightly open at the top, under which he had a white T-shirt. He was wearing braces over his shirt, something he often did in his older years. He also wore his toupee and his glasses.

I was taken aback and asked: "Papa, Papa? What are you doing here? I thought…" I was astonished. Feeling uncomfortable about my next words, I continued: "Everyone thinks you're dead – that you'v died?!"

Contentedly, my father smiles, answering he isn't surprised, this meeting had been planned. He wanted me to see him. "Yes, I faked it. I had the tumour in my face!"

"In the face?" I ask.

"Yes, they wouldn't have treated me, if I hadn't faked it." I study his face and examine it. His face looks good, slightly reddish and with rosy cheeks. He had often come out of the bathroom like this after shaving. In other words, he looks really well!

The Dream

There are no hugs, we keep our distance from each other. I continue to look at him and feel quite puzzled.

Eventually, and with a lot of courage, I decide to ask him about the Shoah and his experiences; even though it feel like this is invasive, it is the right moment for such questions.

"You know, I've been trying to find out more about Skarżysko."

"Skarżysko-Kamienna, yes!" he finishes my sentence loudly, gazing into the distance.

"You were at Factory C! But where exactly?"

"I used to work for a Frederinsky!"

"How did you survive that?"

"I was quick, that's all."

An image appears before my eyes, like something from an old film. I see young men quickly loading grenades that are ready to be pressed somewhere. My father is barely recognisable, but everything is done at lightning speed, and my father is taking receivership of the grenades with pinpoint accuracy.

"And where did you live in the camp?"

He does not answer this question at first. Then he says,

"I'll tell you everything in the morning."

I continue, regardless.

"And the train journey from Flößberg, it took a long time. Historians are trying to put together the exact details and where exactly you escaped. We may have found the place where you hid in the water. If we go to the place, they will make you an honorary citizen. I have a contact there."

My father refuses to answer directly but then he says:

"They have all been *yene falshe*!"[181]

Then I come back to talk about his return, it all seeming real to me.

"Tante Ruszke, she also thought you had died. Now she's dead herself."

My father answers it was meant to be like that.

---

[181] yene falshe, yid. people with quite a false face.

Now I see images, of where he was hiding with my mum when I first came to visit with Shifrah and Claudia. Is it a guesthouse?

I suddenly wake up. I am surprised that I had dreamt about my father, and that it felt like I had him right in front of me, over ten years had passed since he had died.

73

Grandma!

My mum and her granddaughter. On Shifrah's tenth birthday in 2018.

Zol Zayn Shulem II: Faroys

It must have been July 2011 when we went to visit my mum for the first time as a family. My mum seemed happy to finally have contact with her granddaughter, although she found it difficult to allow herself to open up completely. As far as the relationship between her and her daughter-in-law Claudia was concerned, there was for a long time a degree of unspoken tension. But hearing how many discuss their parents-in-law, perhaps that is not the most unusual thing.

My mother's life experiences had led to a life in which all outsiders were seen as a danger, a long-term legacy of having experienced the German occupation of the Netherlands with her father, who had tried to flee from Third Reich Germany to save his life.

Nevertheless, she tried her best and we tried to give her more beautiful moments, with trips to Israel and the Netherlands. I always realised, for example when playing Dutch hits from the 1950s and 1960s to her, that the memories of the Netherlands had never really left her, though she would not talk about it. I had often thought that growing old in the Netherlands would have been nicer and better for her. In Munich, whilst there was nothing she lacked, she continued my father's isolated life and remained in relative hiding. Most of the Jewish community she had known gradually disappeared as most of my father's generation passed away. Even the invitation of the Jewish community's drop-in sessions for senior citizens failed to attract her. Her memories of Israel also remained, but there was nobody really left to visit in Israel. Here too, almost all she knew and loved had died and my cousins, with the exception of Hanni, had not treated her with the respect she deserved as an elder.

But I was particularly happy that Shifrah and her grandmother finally met. My mother came to London for the first time in 2013 for a few cautious days and then again in 2018 in honour of Shifrah's tenth birthday. It was one of our typical, completely out of the ordinary birthdays that we organised for Shifrah. The programme included baking pizza for all the children in Shifrah's school class (a special programme of a pizza-restaurant chain) followed by an evening of entertainment.

Shifrah and her entire school class, and of course my mother Claudia and I travelled to the West End by double-decker bus, where we watched the musical "Thriller" (Michael Jackson).

We were also usually present for my mother's birthday, or invited her to Israel or Holland, including her 80th birthday, which we celebrated in Amsterdam, the city of her birth.

When my aunt Gerda died in 2020, my mother confessed that she felt sorry for the rift between her sister and herself. She now viewed breaking off contact with her sister as a mistake. There was regret in her words and hidden love for a lost sister. My mother put aside the shadows of the past and attended my aunt's funeral. Markus, my Aunt Louise's son, also came, but not Aunt Louise or Uncle Eddie, her other siblings. It was quite a reunion. I had not met Markus since he was a young boy. Another forbidden barrier broken.

My mum with my daughter c.a. 2012.

74

Return to Journalism

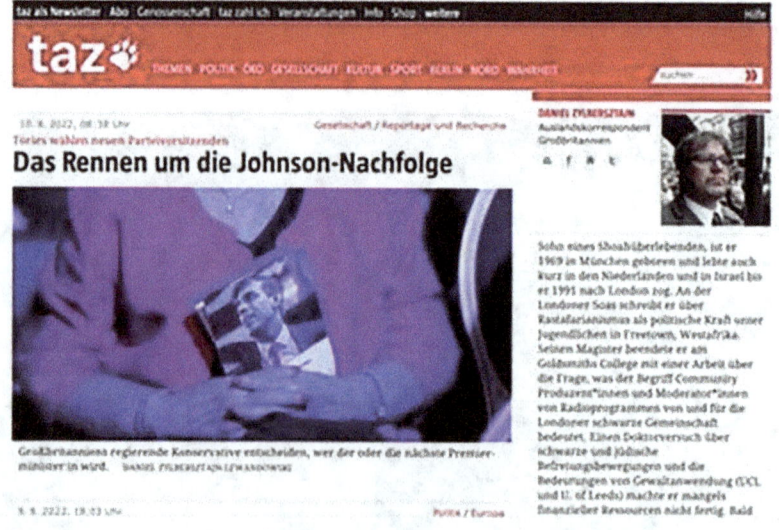

Taz Online, August 2022.

After a couple of years of looking after our daughter Shifrah and continuing to teach Pilates on the side plus some desk-based work in the evenings, I came to the conclusion that I should return to journalism in 2010. Paradoxically, one of the driving factors was my Pilates work, as every so often I had clients who were BBC presenters or editors. While I was giving Pilates classes, I missed my years as a radio journalist. I wanted to swap places, because a big difference between Pilates and journalism is simply the lack of intellectual challenge. Although all clients are different and teachers have to cater to their very individual needs, the classes generally are very repetitive in their fundamental schema, which, to be very honest, bored me in the long run. The last time I worked for DW was in 2001. This was followed by press work for the Jewish-Palestinian Peace Village, for which I also created an audio feature.

My return to work began in earnest in 2010, I acquired the then latest digital equipment for sound recordings, including a new expensive microphone. I soon found radio work again, this time with the BBC, where I now had regular assignments as a mobile recording engineer for the prestige Radio Four Station but also BBC Radio Five and BBC Radio Essex. My job was to record people on location while they were being interviewed by studio-based BBC journalists – not quite yet intellectual, but rather technical and based on reliability. My recordings were then sent to the editors, who mixed them together with the original sound of the editor in the studio. BBC Radio Four "Last Word", which produces weekly obituaries, regularly used my services. But I was employed as an external freelancer and thus did not really have a way into the institution (which advertises internally).

To showcase my return and get to do real work, rather than just holding a microphone, I decided to produce two long English-language radio features, one about modern fathers as primary carers for children, and one about sustainable food co-operatives.[182] They were both broadcasted on "Resonance FM", a London-based radio station for alternative and artistic programmes. However, when a German radio station wanted to have a short excerpt of the co-op programme things went completely wrong. The broadcaster wanted the programme, but they only gave me a one-day deadline for completion and to turn the 30-minute programme in English into a five-minute edit in German. I delivered a finished

---

[182] The radio features in English can still be listened to today, see Zylbersztajn (2012c) and Zylbersztajn (2012d)

product, but there was a technical error that was inaudible on my side, but very audible on theirs for some reason. The team was upset and gave me no second chance. But I wasn't going to give up and registered as an independent producer with the BBC.

Then, after my father's death, came the publication of the text on Open Democracy about Poland, Israel and London. There was no pay for my big features nor for the article on Poland and London, but it was good enough to get my name out there again.

I then started working with an experienced film production team. One of the members was Karen Merkel who had been my radio trainer many years ago at Sound Radio. Together we offered to produce a BBC TV-documentary about German-Jewish refugees and their lives in various places across the world. We wanted to film in Brazil, Chile, Argentina, the USA, Great Britain and Israel and show how their lives varied depending on the locations the refugees ended up in. It was a no. The BBC argued that they had already promised another team a "Jewish programme", a series about the Holocaust (with Simon Schama). The broadcaster did not want to finance another programme with a "Jewish theme" in the same year, even though we had emphasised that it was a now-or-never situation due to the age of the survivors and refugees. It was no use and with Schama we were up against a well-known and established TV-Historian, even though the team I worked with had a former BBC executive in Karen.

The British willingness to deal with the Second World War and its excesses was mainly limited to repeating that they had won the war and were on the winning side. The topic of the Holocaust was mainly dealt with by presenting the history of the Kindertransport, the one story of refugee acceptance they got right. Less is said about the shameful story of the MS St Louis, whose Third Reich Jewish refugees were refused entry and ended up back in Germany. This was already evident in 1945, when the British government refused to support a film by Alfred Hitchcock about the concentration camps. After viewing this film material in 2015, the film director André Singer assumed that this was done for political reasons in order to eliminate sympathy for Jews with regard to their hopes for a state in Palestine, and to not interfere with Germany during its Wiederaufbau.[183]

I also tried to offer a feature to DW, my former station. I soon discovered that since my last assignments, everything had been reorganised and there was only a small remnant left of the once large radio station. However, my idea for a feature about the difference between the German Kasperle Theatre and the British Punch and Judy puppet show aroused the interest of an American editor and I got commissioned. I conducted interviews with puppeteers in Germany and England, visited the Munich City Museum, which had exhibits on the subject, and a British professor of pedagogy. A text version of the audio feature was still available on DW whilst writing this book.[184] Soon I had my first considerable shock. Despite all the effort undertaken, the pay that DW dished out was hardly any better than it had been ten years earlier. But I wasn't going to stop. I thought, I somehow would manage. From then on, I continued to make occasional features for DW, most recently in August 2023 with a report from Grenada, but I also appeared as an expert on the TV news. Sadly, I was devastated when DW ended most of its former radio output in 2024. Other stations suffered the same slow deaths due to changing outputs, and the popularity of platforms like TikTok, YouTube and Instagram. Remember that old 1979 hit by the Buggles? It said: "Video killed the Radio Star, pictures came and broke your heart!" They were right then, and now it was the 2020s!

Rather unexpected was my slide into the newspaper world. It occurred when I wrote a long piece of research on the 2012 Olympic and Paralympic Games in London with dozens of interviews and research concerning all kinds of lobby groups and statements from various companies. I tried to show that the official claim that the Olympic and Paralympic Games were all sustainable were mostly an attempt at greenwashing.

---

[183] King (2015), Wiederaufbau, german for reconstruction, especially after the Second World War.
[184] Zylbersztajn, Daniel (2012a): That's the Way to Do it.

I sent the results of my research to the *Süddeutsche Zeitung*, the *Frankfurter Allgemeine*, *Frankfurter Rundschau*, *Die Zeit* and *Die Welt*, all without positive results. Finally, the lengthy report landed on the desk of Dominic Johnson, a foreign editor at the *taz*, responsible for African countries and the United Kingdom. This, and the fact that the *taz*, as a left-wing socio-critical newspaper, was interested in sustainability and because the paper does not depend on sponsors, led to Dominic instantly agreeing to have a version of the report in *taz* in its special Olympic Games opening edition.[185] Not only that, the *taz* was on the lookout for someone who could write a daily column about London during the Olympic Games. I was given my own daily column entitled "London Eye." These were texts that gave readers a sense of the atmosphere from within London in a way that no other German newspaper covered London day by day.[186] After the end of the Olympic Games *taz*'s sports editor Andreas Rüttenauer asked me, if I could also cover the Paralympic Games in their entirety. I had previously told him that during my MSc in Sports Coaching I had been in touch with senior athletes and coaches and was taught by people connected with the British Olympic Team. I wasn't an expert on athletics, but I certainly had familiarity. I stuck my nose into all sorts of corners and came across many truly original stories beside the reporting on of some of the events.[187]

Simultaneously, I also started working for the *Jüdische Allgemeine*, the German Jewish weekly. In total, I wrote around 50 reports in just two months. Having worked so hard for a re-entry into radio journalism, suddenly I was a newspaper writer, as both newspapers wanted to continue working with me.[188]

Of course, as somebody whose story connected so closely to the games of Munich 1972, I visited the Israeli Team and reported about

---

[185] Zylbersztajn-Lewandowski Daniel (2012b): 29.7.2012 taz.de
[186] London Eye column https://taz.de/!s=Column+London+Eye/ (accessed 24 February 2020)
[187] See https://taz.de/!s=Paralympics+Zylbersztajn/ (accessed 24 February 2020)
[188] See also https://dzx2.net/cv/london-2012/ (accessed on 24 February 2021)

some of their athletes. There was lots of security, but in the end I met ordinary sports people, with whom I sat on their balcony. There was an unsuccessful attempt to have a public silent minute for the Israeli victims of 1972 at 2012, refused by the then Olympic Committee.

There were many other highlights, visually impaired runners, runners with blades, a cyclists with only one working leg from Ghana, tennis champions in a wheel-chair and other truly inspiring people, who pushed the boundaries of what anyone would imagine was possible. It ended with a big finishing event, in which Rhianna and Coldplay appeared on gigantic steel vehicles with fireworks, sealing my comeback.

Back with a stronger footing in journalism, there was, however, a lingering challenge. For over 20 years, I had been working almost exclusively in English. In addition, I had deliberately forced myself away from all German for some ten years. Unsurprisingly, my feel for precise and fault-free German had become quite rusty. I made small language mistakes, sometimes using the wrong word, or an English word instead of a German one, or English sentence structures. Both newspapers insisted that I should stay regardless. I would like to thank all the editors for always prioritising getting an authentic story over a text in perfect and fault-free German. This is not a virtue that was applies everywhere, as you will learn in a separate chapter.

I initially worked as a freelance journalist from London. At first, *taz* wanted me to cover only London and the South of England. When Ralf Sotscheck, who used to be the Ireland and UK correspondent and lives in Dublin, travelled less often to England, *taz* decided in 2018 that I should become their Great Britain correspondent, whilst Sotscheck would continue to cover Ireland and Northern Ireland, which was easier for him to reach.

My reports documented Brexit, the Boris Johnson government, antisemitism in the Labour Party and the Grenfell Tower fire. I learnt a lot about the country and its people and was always more interested in human stories than politicians. Are there any memorable moments worth mentioning? In the beginning, it were the Paralympic athletes who showed everyone that there is no limit to human willpower. Besides that,

Zol Zayn Shulem II: Faroys

I will never forget the Grenfell Tower fire and the surviving traumatised community lobbying for justice, including especially some survivors like the late Clarrie Mandy, Professor Chris Imafidon and Eddie Daffarn. Among the politicians, it was Nigel Farage's triumphant speech after winning the Brexit referendum, which I watched standing five metres away from him, that I remember until today like it was only yesterday. I conducted an interview with him some years later, he kept himself very gallantly and diplomatically, somewhat different to the personality he puts on at political events. I also interviewed Marina Litvinenko, the widow of Putin's long term opponent, Alexander Litvinenko. As he had been murdered by a potion of radioactive poison, administered by Russian agents, she did not drink anything during the entire two-hour interview.

Other "highlights" were my interview with the controversial narcissistic socialist and Israel-hater George Galloway, in that it was an achievement that he would speak to me, I found myself later banned from his account on Twitter. There were also unforgettable visits to Wales where sheep farmers told me they were in favour of Brexit while admitting it could cost them their livelihoods. I covered huge demonstrations against Brexit, smaller ones, that supported it, besides Black Lives Matter and Extinction Rebellion actions. More shocking was meeting a former worker of the former nuclear waste reprocessing and storage site Sellafield. The man claimed to have been a victim of work-induced radioactivity. He said that neither the state nor the unions supporting the industry wanted to know about his case, each, he continued, out of economic and labour interests being held above health concerns. I also met the parents of a boy who had Leukaemia, one of many people who all of a sudden got ill on the West Coast of England in the area where radioactive material leaked into the sea. In addition, there were hundreds of one-to-one conversations with ordinary people who told me about their lives and views in the remotest corners of the country and I wrote a key report on some refugees from Third Reich Germany who were not able to acquire German citizenship, because it had been their mothers or grandmother who fled, the law discriminating against women, as citizenship was once transferred through men. I also met various survivors of the Shoah, as well as immigrants from different countries with stories of hope and racism. The trip in 2023 to the Caribbean Island of Grenada was also special. Here I was on the trail of the "Maafa," the transatlantic slave-trade for *taz* and investigated the question of reparations and reappraisal against the descendants of the Trevelyans, a once aristocratic English family, that once had enslaved people, had apologised for the actions of their ancestors. I saw parallels here with the reappraisal of the Shoah, as well as the traces of my wife's family history. I stood near the place where enslaved African people were once mistreated, but also inside the English manor house that had belonged to those who had profited from the trade and the sugar it produced.

Other moments were a conference on the prevention of violence against women-in-conflict in London, where I met survivors, aid organisations and politicians resolved to stop this terrible feature of war, and a story I researched on corrupt planning in housing.[189] I remember an interview in the midst of nowhere in an English mountainous region, where people who live without much contact with any neighbours expressed unimaginable fear from migrants, or a Muslim woman, who wore a Union Jack as Hijab to make a point after the Manchester Arena bombing (after an Ariana Grande concert). I reported on the Labour years under Jeremy Corbyn and interviewed antisemites and witnessed large Jewish demonstrations against antisemitism or hurried to places that had just witnessed terrible crimes and terrorist attacks, amongst them Islamist terrorism and far right extremist acts such as the one in Manchester, or the brutal slaying of the Labour politician Jo Cox in Batley.

My work principle was and remains first and foremost that I engage

---

[189] Sexual Violence: Zylbersztajn D.: Sexuelle Belästigung: 80 Prozent der Männer sahen zu. Taz, 14.6.2014, https://taz.de/!339176/ and Mediziner und Juristen an einem Strang, 14.6. 2014, https://taz.de/!339181/ Housing: 14 Millionen für ein Zimmer. Taz, 5.6.2015 https://taz.de/Gentrifizierung-in-London/!5009670/?goMobile2=1578441600052 (all accessed on 9.11.2014)

with the fellow human being in front of me, no matter who she or he is. I may not always have shared people's viewpoints or opinions, but I was and am always interested in trying to understand the basis of their outlook, and I have always tried to pass that on as unfiltered as possible.

I always went one step further, sometimes researching until I literally dropped. I always desired to know more, so I turned that extra seemingly unecessary corner, to find out more and going beyond what I was paid for, sparing no extra mile for the benefit of a story. This led me to fishing villages hidden behind mountains like Eyemouth in Scotland, a decommissioned power station in Trawsfynydd in Eryri (Snowdonia), or at 4 am on the Cliffs of Dover to find anti-immigration activists, to give an example.

Journalism nevertheless, and especially with *taz*, remained a very low paid profession and I had to continue supplementing it with Pilates teaching.

What kept me with the profession was and is the ability to witness and pass on people's stories, to try to explain what I find, even help some people. To have seen more parts of the Great Britain and having met a greater diversity of British people than most, and trying to understand different often conflicting issues, all that kept me going.

I always realised that, especially among German correspondents, that I was one of the very few, perhaps often the only one, who was Jewish or from a minority background (though that is slowly improving).

75

Not Quite German?

Nevertheless, I hinted to this, I have to write something about the issues that can arise when perfect German is more of a priority than delivery of original content. In 2020 some incidents at work urged me to write the following essay:[190] I apologise that this chapter repeats some points made earlier. I nevertheless made the decision to include it, because it can stand as a summary of many issues.

An essay on writing in German and belonging to the sphere of authors writing in German. By Daniel Zylbersztajn-Lewandowski (March 2020)

> *Dad and Mum were at home in Munich, but never felt "at home." I would describe their life as living in an ocean with many islands. Most of the seas were considered hostile and dangerous. That meant navigating from Jewish Island to Jewish Island. There were many small such islands, be they in Munich or in Straubing, for example, where a distant relative lived. The largest island was Tel Aviv, the Israeli city which two of my father's brothers and their families and many relatives and friends had made their home. Another rather non-Jewish island was a forested area in Dalfsen, Overijssel,*

---

[190] Adapted fort the English edition of the book.

in the Netherlands, where my Dutch grandmother had a holiday bungalow, that over the years became a kind of temporary refuge for my parents. For my mother it meant she could stay in her birth country, for my father (I only discovered this after his death, when I travelled to the town where he was born) it was a memory of his childhood in a small town surrounded by woods and fields.

In Germany, I grew up speaking principally German. The German education authorities had discouraged parents of migratory backgrounds from speaking any other language but German "so that we would integrate better." My mother nevertheless spoke some Dutch with me and I picked up even more from my family and playmates during my frequent holi-stays in the Netherlands. My father tried his best to speak German with me, although many of the words in his vocabulary were evidently of Yiddish origin. Real Yiddish was reserved for conversations with his friends. Who knows if this insistence on German represented an added barrier between the two of us?

Why am I putting these parts of my vita in an essay? You see, some of my German journalistic colleagues had been complaining that my German is not as sufficiently perfect as that of others they work with. I seem to make some language and grammar mistakes from time to time, and Anglicisms creep in on top of that. Working for a left-wing newspaper that endorses people of migratory and minority background, that surprised me.

I am certain that there are people in Germany with migrant backgrounds, including Jewish authors, whose German is absolutely flawless. Yes, there were even some among the generation of survivors. My father, for example, was one of the most fervent admirers of the Jewish-German "Literaturpapst" (literature pope) Marcel Reich-Ranicki. He had travelled a similar path to my father. There are also authors like Henryk Broder or Michael Wolfson, who never really left Germany. They are a legitimately admirable group of Jewish writers

For others, people like Micol, Awi, Deborah, Kalmon, Shirly, Pnina, Leon and me, life in Germany was too oppressive, too entangled with the history of the Shoah.

Our parents wanted the best, indeed they had somewhat forgiven Germany. My father had always said that the postwar generation had nothing to do with the murderers, except for those who followed right-wing ideologies.[191] *Many of our parents hoped that we would somehow put down roots in Germany, while they were also berating Germans, talking about their experiences and, somewhere in the back of their minds, hoping that their children might perhaps move to Israel after all.*

My father had a lifelong relationship with Israel, but he preferred the more temperate climate in Germany and ran a successful restaurant there. What he earned there sometimes was enough to also help his two brothers in Israel.

Postwar Germany came with its own challenges. In 1972, he had to witness what happened at the Olympic Games. We lived just ten minutes from the Olympic site. There was a terror attack at Munich Airport, and the Jewish retirement home was also attacked once, a few years earlier.

Family feuds split the family. The topic of disagreement? Germany in the light of the Shoah. My father perceived the fall of the Berlin Wall as unsettling. The guilt had not yet been cleared up, Germany had not yet earned the right to be great and self-confident again, in his view.

The schizophrenic life in the Federal Republic, the often unexpected confrontation with history, people who stood in front of us as if we had fallen from the sky because we were Jewish or those days when we encountered an old drunk Nazi (it were mostly men) on public transport or had to witness how right-wing parties sprung up, or violent attacks were carried out in Germany, for example by the NSU terror group, and those Wehrmacht demonstrations, all of these were moments of losing the sense that this is our country.

In the UK, on the other hand, I often had to fight to be understood as the son of a Holocaust survivor. British Jews were

---

[191] Note: He would have been very upset about the success of the AFD in February 2025.

largely unharmed by the suffering of the Shoah, and those who had something to do with it were to a large extend refugees or families of refugees, and not people or their families who had gone through the grinding wheels of the German mass murder machinery, like my father, and who managed to survive it against all odds. On the other hand, that also gave me degrees of freedom in London, because the Third Reich history was not omnipresent.

And yet surprisingly perhaps, something rather positive from Germany accompanied me in England. The kind of politicised and critical anti-authoritarian postwar education that I experienced in Germany had had a huge impact on me, and I am grateful for that, because it was mostly absent here in England.

In this respect, and this is my real point for writing this, I consider myself to be the missing part of the postwar generation of German Jews. I am one of the many Jewish people who saw the home our parents -people who were born outside of Germany – had built, as not an easy or simple placement, who preferred to try living elsewhere because, we felt both at home and not at home in Germany.

The fact that we, who should have been the first or second German-born generation after the war, became migrants again and did not take advantage of our childhood that had started in Germany, put many of us at an initial disadvantage in the countries we found ourselves in, be it Israel, Great Britain or the USA. We had to perfect another language and commute between these new shores and Germany, where our parents were now left behind without us. What must they have thought?

I am one of the few who had the fortune to be able to write in German day in, day out, since 2012. However, we are part of the wider spectrum, and as the Great Britain correspondent for the taz and sometimes the smaller Jüdische Allgemeine, I found myself in the vocation I had aspired to at the age of 20. Moreover, I can be German and Jewish and in London at the same time.

However, this privilege apparently comes without flawless mastery of German. I think that this would be understandable given the journey and turns my life and that of my parents took. You would think that it is perhaps something that the language puritans amongst my colleagues should have to learn to deal with. You see, it is not just about people like myself. There may be similar experiences among other minorities in Germany, especially from the Turkish-speaking regions of the world, and increasingly Arab speaking areas.

There are certainly standards in the German language, and I agree that one should at least attempt to push oneself towards these. However, it is important to ensure that the drive towards perfection does not become an exercise of marginalisation. I believe that in the interests of unity, even from the distance of London, and some people live much closer to the editorial offices in Germany, that those who have the privilege of "German parents" and a "German" and "perfect" upbringing or a life in German, with German-speaking friends and German-speaking life partners, or who are otherwise more linguistically adept, should stand by those, who, due to their background and location may produce linguistic deviations or make the cardinal sin of that occasional or even repeated habitual grammatical error.

Many of us have already been excluded during our school education, with some of us shunted off to lower and intermediate secondary schools. The proportion of people with a migrant background in these "lower schools" is enormous due to the tough examinations after the fourth grade that often disadvantage people of recent migratory experiences from countries where the language was anything but German.

Against that background, I would argue that our voices are actually extremely important, not the least because some of us have experienced Germany in ways that are slightly different from the majority. Allowing people like us to write should not constitute a burden but should be seen as a contribution to plurality and to insights that would otherwise remain hidden. Journalists and publishers like to be a little elitist about their trade, even in the UK. But it is important for them to keep the gates open. What I mean by this is to put in that bit of extra work and time for our way of speaking and writing, otherwise everyone is missing out on entire sections of society in all contemporary discourses.

As a Jewish person living in London, whose parents came from Poland and Holland and lived in Germany, and, although I only lived in Germany for a total of 18 years of my life (but those mostly in the elementary childhood years), people like myself belong to the German linguistic diversity, even if we sometimes do not express ourselves as well or as elaborately as others.

It was Jhumpa Lahiri, an author whose parents come from Bangladesh, who speaks Bengali, grew up in the USA, has a Spanish-speaking Guatemalan husband and who writes in Italian, who confirmed that she is not completely at home in any language. If this kind of writing from the margins can lead to a Pulitzer Prize, then all voices of dissent towards linguistic variations due to unorthodox backgrounds should also fall silent in Germany!"

This letter was responded to with some direct and supportive letters from some of my colleagues. I was very grateful for them. Similarly, when, some years later, I put together a few informal words along these lines for a workshop on the topic of discrimination in the media for the course leader, she felt it was so important, that she asked me if she could pass these on to the course participants anonymously. I was surprised and very pleased to receive encouraging feedback and expressions of thanks after the workshop had ended. They largely agreed with me and reiterated that the original story and original research was the most important factor in writing.

Some others remain silent to this day, perhaps stuck in notions of a past glory of undiluted German, who knows. What should be my right to write in English publications, or the lack of it, after 30 years in Britain, is another matter, I should perhaps write an essay on, one day.

76

Educational Dances

I spent many years with my daughter at some of the finest children's playgrounds that London has to offer. I did my best to actively be there for her as a father. We went to all kinds of children's groups, including special playgroups for fathers and their children. With our transport bike, we got further than most and visited almost all playgrounds within a radius of around five kilometres. Many days, weeks and years went by. We even travelled to school on this bike until Shifrah was about seven or eight years old and outgrew the bike.

Like many parents, my wife and I were looking for the ideal school for our daughter right from the start. Not the least as migrants to Britain we did not quite trust the English school system. It is politicians who in the devolved nations of the UK decide what pupils have to learn about history, identity and nationhood.[192] We considered alternatives for our child, be it Montessori or other progressive schools. In the end, it was the offer of a Waldorf playgroup for small children, once a week, which we attended regularly that impressed us. The original approaches used here we witnessed nowhere else. The nursery teachers packed a whole repertoire into just under two hours, that varied with the season. It included

---

[192] For examples, see Higgins (2011) and Heath (2018), Okolosie (2020)

everyday relevance, play elements, as well as baking and eating. The bread dough had to be passed from hand to hand, which was impressive because young children usually want to keep everything for themselves. Cleo Lane, the main educator at the time, had an enchanting voice when she sang the children's songs, as she was also a professional singer. The ability to create fantastic worlds of imagination through simple puppets and role play, a world that stimulated the imagination only existed in this Waldorf group.

Nevertheless, Shifrah started nursery and school at the nearest state nursery, because we actually listened to our newly made British friends, all parents with little children of the same age and whom we had met on one or the other the playground. They said that in England, it was the way things were done. What choice do you have as a migrant, than to listen to well-meaning locals? But the more we saw how the education system in England worked, the less we were impressed by the methods employed.

Looking back on my own school experiences, especially at my secondary school years in Munich, but also Claudia's experiences with nuns in a Catholic school in Freetown, who had used brutal methods that jeopardised children's health, we wanted something better for our child.[193] The fact that we would probably have to pay for what we had in mind was a problem, but compared to other British public schools, often very English and very elitist, the Steiner-Waldorf school in the London Borough of Islington, which had also co-ordinated the playgroup that I have mentioned, was also one of the most affordable independent schools in the wider area.

In what way did we think it could be better? For one thing, the education was seemingly more "child friendly." The change from the stage of playful child to learning-obsessed teenager was age-appropriate. In

---

[193] After Claudia had once been cheeky at school, a teacher, who was also a nun, asked her to look directly at the sun. When Claudia's grandfather, who was a judge, heard about this, he immediately made a personal complaint in the sternest tone.

Educational Dances

state schools, the school day lasted from 9 a.m. to 3.30 p.m. right from the start, at the Waldorf School it was 8.30 a.m. to 1 p.m. It scheduled in much more play, theatre, dance, music, art, crafts, gardening and lots of time spent outdoors. In year one of Shifrah's state school, a school awarded the mark of outstanding, and regarded as one of the best in the area, everything was statistically standardised and failure to achieve high success rates meant that teachers would be paid less. In theory that was a good thing, but the delivery was in parts quite tough on the still young children. Shifrah, had developed wrist pain by April in her reception year due to the school's obsessive attempt to meet statutory guidelines in writing.

When we finally decided to move our daughter out of the state school into the nearest Steiner-Waldorf school in 2014, it was not done in a haste. I saw it as my duty to examine Rudolf Steiner (1861-1925) and his anthroposophical approach first, as this founder of all Steiner-Waldorf schools had flirted with racist theories.[194] Unlike the excuses of some, Steiner was not a victim of his time. Franz Boas (1858-1942), the father of modern anthropology, for example, had written at the same time as Steiner and famously rejected racial theories.[195] Steiner was well read, and it is unconceivable he had not also heard of Boas.

This fact forced us to expose ourselves to a critique of Waldorf schools and approaches. A racist or anti-Semitic school, in which our daughter also learnt nothing, as some people claimed about Waldorf Schools, would not have been an option for us. So being a critical journalist, I read every negative and positive criticism I could get my hands on regarding Waldorf schools and of Rudolf Steiner and ordered many books on the subject, including a German book that was known to be very critical.[196] This book reported even fascist German nationalist undertones in some schools, and a lack of safeguarding and organisation

---

[194] Steiner (1966)
[195] Boas, 1904, p. 243
[196] Sybille-Christin Drewes (2001)

in others. Other books praised and extolled Waldorf education but lacked sufficient references to comparative education studies.[197] On the other hand, I learnt from my extensive reading that even some of the educational programmes and methods used in the British state system were not always based on sound evidence, such as the introduction of the phonetic reading system in England. When this was introduced in all of England, there were initially only a few studies available, although these had praised the system.[198] But they were in luck. As it happened, phonics ended up being quite successful.

In the end we decided to send our daughter to the Steiner-Waldorf School and which she attended until 2022. It turned out to be a mostly wonderful education, even if there were some problems here and there (all of which we communicated to the school's leadership). Shifrah developed excellently academically, and the school also developed and nurtured her artistic side. In addition to textile work, she loved theatre. However, being based in a city in which diversity was very evident everywhere else, the school's intake was largely white, even though diverse at that, and its religious references were mainly Christian orientated. Instead of just complaining about the problem, I decided to take responsibility and ownership of it and try to initiate change. I not only started a joint initiative of parents and teachers but eventually became elected school trustee for diversity, later changed to diversity, equality and inclusion, the first the school ever had.

And change there was! The teachers publicly distanced themselves collectively from some of Rudolf Steiner's texts, which had shown clear racial thinking. They introduced globally orientated education, with German abolished as a compulsory subject (though continued for those who wanted it, like multi-lingual families who had a German parent, us included). By the time that I left the board position, the school celebrated the Jewish harvest festival of Sukkot, Islamic Ramadan and

---

[197] Clouder & Rawson (2003)
[198] Gibbons (2020)

the Chinese New Year, as well as Christian and secular holidays, and allowed for gender diversity and for diversity of sexual identities, while continuing to protect spaces reserved for cisgender women and girls. Due to my journalistic experiences during Brexit, I invited teachers to teach the United Kingdom from more in-depth regional, social, and cultural backgrounds. I called for better evidence that neurodiverse children were making progress at school and insisted from the outset that the school think more about accessibility. Interestingly, it was not a run to the bottom, as critics of DEI claim. For many children of minority background a school they trusted had a guarantee of excellent outcomes. Only then many parents of Black children and Children of Colour were prepared to take on the expense. This was somewhat different to what other parents, wanted, who were more relaxed about outcomes, but excited about promises of a child sensitive pedagogy, the art curriculum, the commitment to the outdoors education, a less tech obsessed way of learning, community, and for some, an openness to a sense of a spiritual feel. Whilst I was DEI trustee, we started after-school provision, important for working parents, carers and guardians, up-kept discounts for children from less well off backgrounds and had for the first time some fully funded bursaries.

After Shifrah left her School, she went on to a state school in Bethnal Green, Tower Hamlets, where she completed her GCSEs in most subjects, plus a performing arts diploma and after an audition went on to be accepted at one of London's best performing arts colleges.

It seems like our decision to send Shifrah to the more art oriented and child-friendly Waldorf school worked for us. Shifrah had been given the chances in arts that were denied to me 30 years earlier. That too was rectifying something, and whilst she attended the school, I fixed some of its weaknesses.

77

Becoming British

This chapter, abbreviated for this book, was published on 7ᵗʰ March 2019 as part of a special edition on Brexit in the German language version of LeMonde Diplomatique. It was adapted here for the English edition. Some of the issues this chapter mentions are summaries of episodes already mentioned in greater depth in earlier chapters of the book-series. They were kept in, as the chapter can stand on its own with these summary paragraphs, which may be helpful in educational settings.

It was a sunny Sunday in Fitzrovia, London, back in 1992. Of course, I would later raise a complaint about what happened on that day and I would even receive an apology in the post. You see, there were some old shabby and worn-out furniture items standing next to some offices on the street for days. For me, then a student with few resources, these could still be of great use. With difficulty, being on my own, I shleppt an old worn-out office chair and an old table towards my flat five minutes away.[199] Suddenly a police car stopped next to me. A police-officer got out and asked what I was doing with the stuff I carried. I was surprised but

---

[199] Yid. dragged

simply informed the officer of my intention to put seemingly unwanted furniture chucked out on the street to a new lease of life. He asked me where I was from, and I replied, Germany. "We don't need furniture thieves here, go back to your bloody Germany." The officers demanded access to my flat, found nothing there, then ordered me to carry all the furniture back. The furniture remained on the street for days thereafter, until it had been removed by the rubbish collection.

I had flashbacks to that Sunday, when I went through the pages of the application for my second citizenship. I had persuaded myself to become British after having lived in London for 28 years without this step, as a safeguard against the possible consequences of Brexit. What's more, if I hurried and applied before March 2019, I wouldn't have to submit a special additional application to keep my German citizenship.

I was born in Munich. My mother migrated to Germany from Holland, whilst her father was a German-Jewish refugee to Amsterdam, who had moved back to Germany after the war. My own father, who is a Jewish Holocaust survivor from Poland, and who had moved to Germany after the war, refused German citizenship until he was in his 70s. As migrants who felt foreign, mum and dad wanted me to integrate into the "new Germany." I attended a Catholic kindergarten, the local state primary school and the arch-conservative Maximiliansgymnasium. It was the Erasmus student programme that would eventually allow me to travel to British Isles for university studies.

For me, London not only represented the chances of a good academic education; the city also offered me a vibrant music culture and a common ground with people from all over the world. In 1995, I married the woman, I still love and share my life with today. My wife grew up in Freetown, Sierra Leone, and is in part a descendant of freed or runaway formerly enslaved Africans from the Caribbean and the USA, who returned to West Africa. She came to live in the UK at the age of 16 through the former English partner of her mother.

During visits in Bavaria, Germany, my wife perceived that country as somewhat oppressive, especially in the 1990s and 2000s. Only recently

(2018) some idiot tried to push her off a park bench in Munich that he claimed to be reserved for unemployed, white Bavarians only. Britain seems to be better in this regard, but in truth the UK is the place where she and I have both encountered fully fledged and violent racism. Those who once ruled the world with their Empire are now struggling to come to terms with the world's presence in their own backyard. Jamaican-born sociologist Stuart Hall once labelled Britain as the last colony to still decolonise. He meant a state of mind. Brexit proves that this process of decolonialisation has not yet been achieved.

To make Brexit sound good, some people talk about the British tradition of trade. They don't talk about the enslavement that fed that trade. And those who had believed the self-important chatter of the British in their overseas colonial outposts, who had become Christians, paid homage to Her Majesty the Queen, spoke English, drank tea, indeed, who had fought or even fallen for King, Land and Country, were made to understand after 1945 that there was a difference between darker and lighter skin colour shades and that privileges were attributed by the chance of birth.

For us, my wife and I, this thinking was reflected by two blatant racist attacks: in Brighton in 1995, we had been assaulted as a "mixed couple." The British police and the Crown Prosecution Service investigated so superficially that the two perpetrators got away with what they had done. In London in 2001, two racist men attacked my wife brutally out of the blue. One of them ended up behind bars.

At about the same time, when the police had stopped me about that furniture I had been carrying, I had been told by an ultra-left-wing student group that they would "not support a Nazi organisation at the university." I had been trying to establish a pan-academic German Language Project. In fact, I was considered to be a Nazi twice over because I had also "lived as a Zionist in Israel." Unjustified hatred in London didn't always have to come from the right.

My daughter cried after she had learnt of the result of the Brexit vote. In her innocence, she was only eight years old, she thought the

British no longer wanted her German dad to stay. I, on the other hand, didn't believe that we EU-citizens would be deprived of our right to stay, if only because of the many Britons who live in many EU-countries. That assumption changed in April 2018 with the Windrush scandal, when British nationals, mostly from the Caribbean, but also some other Commonwealth countries, who had been living in the Britain legally, suddenly had to prove their right to citizenship. I concluded that if people who had spent a lifetime working on the island and whose identity was so closely linked to Britain through colonialism and slavery were suddenly treated shamefully and as apparent illegals, my own residency status could also potentially be quite fragile. I better arranged everything I could to secure, or rather to document my right to be in Britain.

With the shift to the political far right in Germany and the AfD Party entering the Bundestag and similar trends elsewhere in Europe, I realised that my family – Jewish and West African, German and British – could not assume that we would be able to live in the EU as unquestioned and undisturbed as others. On the other hand, in the UK, it is still said that respect and tolerance are key cultural values. In cities like London, Manchester and Birmingham, families like us are the norm.

A Jewish friend, a human rights lawyer whose parents were Shoah survivors, suggested in a casual conversation concerning the acquisition of British nationality, that for Jewish people, there could not be enough passports, just in case bad times came over us again. This is why I eventually ordered the book that prepared applicants for the British citizenship test. This test had been the first step towards citizenship since 2005. The presentation of British history in the book was however so bad that I started to highlight all the weak points. There was no mention of the Holocaust in the section on the Second World War and the colonial period was treated completely uncritically, not even emphasising Britain's role as the birthplace of progressive movements such as co-operatives. Black people were only mentioned as athletes. I complained to the Citizenship Select Committee of the House of Commons.[200] Months later, Home Secretary Sajid Javid said he would have the book, and the test overhauled, not because of me of course, but because a report by the committee had come to a similar conclusion

I had no other option but to memorise by heart historically inaccurate answers, as the "right answers" for the purposes of passing the test. It took me no more than 15 minutes to answer the 24 questions inside a shabby East London computer centre and was informed that I had answered all correctly. An Indian woman who had completed the test just before me burst into tears in despair instead, after learning that she had failed the test. I felt sorry for her. If she could afford it, she could re-sit the test at extra expense. At the end of October 2018, I sent off my application for British citizenship and waved Good Bye to £1330 of hard-earned cash for the application fee. Within a week, various original documents had to be submitted by post, including biometric data.

On my way to the Post Office, I met two middle-aged women, who were evidently Labour supporters. They spotted my large application files and commented that with Corbyn as Prime Minister, I would not have to become British. I pointed to his lukewarm stance on the EU and mentioned that I was Jewish and that I no longer liked him because of all the antisemitic incidents in the party and Corbyn's curious closeness to Israel haters. One of the ladies reacted hysterically and declared that Israel had no right to exist and was a Nazi-state. Doubts arose in my mind. Should I really go ahead and become a British national, given there were people like that about with whom I would have to share my right to be British? But the momentary doubts ebbed away soon. I paid my fee, had my fingers scanned and submitted the file. It took three weeks for my documents to come back, along with a letter from the Home Office. I would be granted citizenship as soon as I had taken an oath of allegiance

---

[200] Daniel Zylbersztajn: Open Letter to Lord Hodgson on the citizenship test. 18.07.2018 https://dzx2.net/2018/07/04/open-letter-to-lord-hodgson-on-uk-citizenship-test/ (accessed 10.11.2024)

to Her Majesty the Queen, according to a law passed in 2004. In the past, such an oath had only been required of special civil servants or soldiers.

For me as a journalist, this is now something that conflicts with my press-freedom. If I would like to write something against the monarchy, or ever said anything at all against the British royals, would that constitute a breach of the oath? I asked my local MP, who happens to be (the now Prime Minister and Labour Leader) Keir Starmer, to check the legal position for me and others with the Home Office and he answered it should not matter.

For a faster and personal oath ceremony I coughed up an additional £160 Pound to the London Borough of Camden, as I wanted to get the thing over and done with. The ceremony began with a 24-minute delay, as the responsible officer was nowhere to be found. Eventually he came and led us through a maze of offices, to the room where the ceremony was to be carried out. On a small table stood two items that gave the impression that they would disappear into the cupboard straight afterwards: They were a Union Jack and a picture of Her Majesty. The clerk read out a long-winded introduction on the history and advantages of the borough that felt a bit insulting. I knew Camden inside out, as I had lived there for over 20 years. Finally, he came to the matter of the Oath of Allegiance, the playing of the national anthem and the presentation of my naturalisation certificate. The clerk lacked true conviction and seemed not really interested in the procedure, totally failing to appreciate the mental wranglings and bureaucratic hurdles that had to be overcome to get to this point. I would therefore describe it as a ceremonial entry into British citizenship in name only.

Of course I wrote a complaint to the council about the shabbiness of the ceremony – a sign perhaps that, after all, I was still German. However, during my next visit to Munich in January 2019, I was quite annoyed by the inability of my German compatriots to be able to wait patiently in a queue. How uncivilised, I thought! Oops, in some respects, I appear to have become quite British now.

78

Forty-Five Years to Justice

The end of the chapter regarding the Munich Terror of 1972 reached me just as unexpectedly and in the same way as the announcement that terrorists had stormed the Israeli quarters of the Munich Olympic Village on 5th of September 1972, namely via television. It was the 5th of September 2017 and Claudia, Shifrah and I were in Munich visiting my mother to celebrate her 79th birthday in Munich's former Olympic Village. Because Shifrah started school the next day, we had to travel back to London later in the afternoon. It was late morning, and I went to fetch our rental car. As I drove around the Olympic Village, I saw that all the access roads to the Olympic Park had been closed off by the German police. I assumed there probably had been an accident and thought nothing more of it.

In the rush of our imminent departure, Shifrah asked if she could watch German children's television one last time. Whilst flicking through the TV channels on the search for a children's programme, I spotted something unusual but oddly familiar instead. Three weeks earlier, I had walked past the then still unfinished memorial site that would document for all who bothered to go there the 1972 terror attack on the Israeli Olympic team. Then, plastic tarpaulins still covered everything. The familiar sight on TV was in fact a live broadcast of the opening of

Forty-Five Years to Justice

the memorial site on Bavarian television, taking place no more than a 10-to-20-minute walk from where we were, with political representatives and invited honourable guests. So that was the reason why the roads were closed. The police had secured all roads around it.

My growing up in the Olympic Village, my identification with what had happened there on that fatal day in 1972, the ever-present contradiction that so personally affected not only my life in the Olympic Village, but also my mother's birthday, were all marginal phenomena to us, if you compared it to the true loss and suffering of the survivors of that day and the relatives of the murdered athletes, people who had campaigned for most of their lives for a memorial site like this to be erected. In 2015, when the representatives of residents of the Olympic village opposed a plan by the Bavarian State Government to finally build such a memorial site, they argued that it would interfere with their "Rodelberg" – their snow-fun-hill. I asked the *Jüdische Allgemeine* to be allowed to write an opinion piece that would reflect on my experiences and perspective on the matter. My request was granted. I wrote how my personal perception of the village and its history, and that of my family was totally different to that of the non-Jewish inhabitants of the village. The piece ended with the following words:

> *No one can bring the dead back to life. But the memory of the murdered Israeli athletes will weigh on the Olympic Village forever. It is about more than a memorial plaque or a monument, whether on the grounds of the old bus station or on the tip of the snow-fun-hill opposite the apartments that housed the Israeli Olympic Team in Connollystraße or a few hundred metres further to the East, as has recently been under consideration. The Olympic Village in Munich not only stands for "lightness" and "cheerful games", as it was so beautifully called in 1972, but also for the literally blood-drenched seriousness of history.*
>
> *This should be as much a part of the upbringing of children growing up in the village as carefree fun in the snow during the winter months. All those who live in the Olympic Village today can*

enjoy their lives in this particularly friendly place, a location without cars, with a shopping centre, artificial fountains and lots of greenery. However, they should also bear in mind that for many people, the 1972 Olympic Village is also something else – the site of a terrible, unforgotten massacre.[201]

A few months after the opinion piece, I was invited by a friend, a history professor at Edgehill University, to give a lecture as part of the faculty's history seminar on Memory and Repression, which was later published on YouTube by the faculty.[202] Here, too, I strongly argued that a memorial site in Munich's Olympic Village was absolutely essential, whereby I argued in favour of an alternative location, near the former bus station and the former apartment of the Israeli athletes as possible and suitable locations for the remembrance.

At the opening ceremony, Ankie Spitzer, the widow of the murdered Andre Spitzer, summed it all up by asking the residents of Munich's Olympic Village who had initially been so very much opposed to its construction to visit this memorial and explain it to their children. I felt that the speech of Rachel Salamander, the owner of a famous Jewish bookshop in Munich, was however a touch exaggerated. Rachel Salamander was a woman I admired in my youth, after she had started her bookshop in a quiet backstreet in the centre of Munich. When the new Munich (conservative orthodox) synagogue opened its doors, her bookshop moved into the attached Jewish cultural center there, and not only that, but offshoots of her shop also came to life in Berlin and other cities. This is why Salamander had been invited to speak. She had become a kind of cultural and literary spokeswoman and organiser. In any case, in her speech on the opening of the memorial site in Munich, she described the terror of 1972, indeed Palestinian terror, as the forerunner of all terror today. I felt that was taking it slightly too

---

[201] Zylbersztajn (2015a), adapted for English.
[202] EdgeHist (2018)

far. Contemporary Palestinian terror was part of a much older ideology that was inspired by the struggle of militant anti-colonial movements, especially in Algeria, but also elsewhere. Terrorism had even been part of the Jewish freedom movement in Palestine, if you count in the actions of groups such as Etzel and the Irgun against the British in particular. Perhaps Salamander had just been a little imprecise. What the Black September Movement and the PLO and affiliated organisations brought into the world was a spectacular terrorist attack during international events broadcasted live worldwide.

In spite of all the quarrelling there was now finally a memorial site on the edge of the Olympic Village. My involvement ended with an e-mail to Ankie, in which I explained to her how I had followed the opening ceremony from a distance and yet from close by and that I was glad that it had come that far.

In 2022, during the 50th anniversary of that fateful day, the 5th of September 1972, I was not even in Munich, but I know that there were many events remembering both the Olympics and the terrorism attack. More significantly, it was in the same year, that the families of the victims finally received compensation totalling 28 million Euros, for the failure of Germany to protect the athletes.

One year and one month later, the Palestinian Hamas carried out the largest terrorist bloodbath against Jews since the end of the Shoah. Not only had people been murdered and burned to death, but many had also been raped or mutilated before being killed. Their actions triggered a foreseeable response. The fact that Hamas hid behind the civilian population and operated from within civilian infrastructure cost many more people their lives when Israel responded. The waste-land and destruction and loss of life of so many will remain a stain of darkness. It is so much more preferable to compromise and practice acceptance and degrees of self-limitation and humility.

It seemed though as if there are not enough memorials against terror and hate against Jews, and not enough institutions that teach the reduction of conflict and how to try to handle conflict without resorting to violence, surely worthy lessons for all without exception.

The analysis of this conflict, which fuelled hatred of Jews worldwide, provides material for another book. But in the example of Wahat-Al – Salam-Neve Shalom I at least saw and witnessed a small lived reality, that things could be different to what they have been for so many years.

My daughter protested, when she noticed that I was not keeping my promise of a bit more German children's-TV. Maybe the residents of the Olympic Village were right. Children's programmes and winter snow-fun are also actually quite important, and in the Olympic village such activities can now run concurrently with suitable remembrance of the 5th of September 1972 and a sense of closure from that terrible historic event.

79

End of an Era

The Bruno Lewandowski shop at Sendlingerstraße 62 was for decades the last small remnant of the grand Lewandowski family history. In 2016 it too shut its door for the final time. The shop had been run since 1975 by Adelinde Dilz, one of Bruno Lewandowski's former employees. In the small shop, bras and ladies' underwear were closely arranged according to colour, style and in shop-counters and shelves.

After the shop closed, not all was lost. The City of Munich decided to protect the old sign in the style of the 1950s or 1960s that advertised the Bruno Lewandowski shop. It still hangs there today, even though the shop has since become a café.

Zol Zayn Shulem II: Faroys

The remaining shop sign in Sendlingerstraße in Munich.

80

Bat Mitzvah with a Surprise

My daughter was due to have her bat mitzvah in June 2021 (Jewish year 5781), but the world was still in the midst of the coronavirus pandemic.[203] My mother had always wished to be able to attend her granddaughter's bat mitzvah. From the perspective of 2020 when we had to start planning, it was safer to postpone the bat mitzvah and hope that the risk of the infectious illness had decreased by then.

That time had come 17 months later, and we set her day of religious maturity finally for Saturday the 5th of November 2022. Shifrah started preparing for her first public Torah reading some six months earlier.[204] Not only did we have to book rooms, invite guests and make sure they were entertained and catered for, but hotels also had to be rented for some of our foreign guests. My uncle and my mother had to be picked up by me personally in Germany because, given their ages, neither had enough confidence to travel on their own. We had to organise food, including kosher food, and drinks for the celebration in the synagogue and for the second celebration, the party in the evening in a rented

---

[203] Bat Mitzvah, acceptance of girls into the adult community, equal to Bar mitzvah for boys in progressive Jewish communities (e.g. Liberal, Reform, Masorti)
[204] Shifrah read Parasha (Chapter) Lech Lecha (Genesis 12:1-17:27)

community café near where we lived. A DJ had to be found to entertain the teenagers, while our friend "Sunshine", a British Jazz singer of Jamaican-Philippian family background and her band would play jazz and soul numbers for the older guests. Invitations had to be sent out. Shifrah went with me to a mikveh (Jewish ritual bath) and prepared her *Dvar Torah*, the analysis of the chapters she had to read out in Hebrew, whilst I also prepared a dedication in her honour. The whole family bought new clothes for the day. My late cousin's husband in Israel also said that he would come all the way from Jerusalem together with Itai, one of his sons. Claudia, her cousin Christiana from Wales and her aunt Kathleen (Anjabi) from Hamburg cooked through two nights. Just the normal chaos.

On the morning of 5th November 2022, or 11 Cheshvan 5783, the time had come. Everyone was excited. Shifrah's nerves fluttered the night before and there were tears, but by the morning she had calmed down and was all ready. I loaded up our car with the snacks to be eaten after the end of service at the synagogue. I drove with Claudia's cousin Christiana, two of her children and Shifrah to the East London area of Stoke Newington, where our then (the liberal progressive) synagogue was located. They held their synagogue service in a room of one of the local landmarks, St Mary's Church. We arrived there at 10.00 a.m. one hour before the start of the service.

I wanted to park the car in front of the community centre to unload all the stuff. There was usually a free space for such purposes on the side, but on that day I found a small white transport lorry standing there. A slim man of around 20 years of age loaded stuff into it, which he brought out from an adjacent house that belonged to the church grounds. He was wearing a grey track suit, had a cap on and a loose haired beard. Having arrived, the first thing I did, was to send Shifrah to the centre, as she was expected there to prepare for her reading. Then, I turned to the man loading the lorry and asked him if he would be here for much longer. I told him I had quite a few things to unload. He replied taciturnly, almost angrily: "All day!" When I spoke to him again in a friendly manner, we

Bat Mitzvah with a Surprise

were met with a "Fuck off!." Claudia's cousin now addressed the man and noted that it wasn't helpful and his attitude was unnecessarily unfriendly. But that only made the man angrier. He told us that he wouldn't move anything for us here because he had seen what kind of people those in the centre, were. What kind of people? "Murderers of Palestinian children!", who had falsified "the Book." I explained to him in a calm manner that Jewish people from North Africa and the Middle East for example had been expelled or had been forced to flee. But I had totally misread the situation. The man didn't want to discuss particulars. He let me know that he had heard what I said by replying that the expulsions had been justified because they, the Jews, had done something. And he did not stop there. He crowned his quickly developing speech with a declaration: "Hitler was right!" I still didn't realise that I wasn't dealing with a normal person here, that this was not a normal exchange over the specifics of the Middle East conflict but one filled with real hatred projected against Jews. This is why I explained to him that my father was a survivor and that most of my family had been murdered in the Holocaust. Did I really imagine that he would cease to make his angry and racist remarks because of this? How could I be so naïve? He now deliberately repeated that Hitler had been right and that my family members had also done something for which they had been justifiably murdered.

After I saw the CCTV years later, I saw that at this moment I drove the car off the yard, parked it and walked towards the centre. Yet he kept shouting "Hitler was right!" again. I suddenly appeared to change course and walked directly towards him and then pushed him away from me. At that moment I did not think clearly, and I was in a state of intense provocation and humiliation. I was outraged that he shouted all of that, and I wanted to defend myself, and protect the name of my murdered ancestors. Objectively speaking, certainly with the benefit of hindsight, I could have walked to the hall instead and get help, but in that moment the world was reduced between him and me. The pushing away did nothing good. He responded with several repeated strong blows that landed in my face and on my head. All had suddenly become violent, and

Zol Zayn Shulem II: Faroys

I hastily managed to punch him back once with a defensive side swing, but after the third blow or so to my head, I tumbled to the ground.

As he punched me, both my legs and my arms refused to move, and that was not out of fear or inability, but because all I could think of was Shifrah and her big bat mitzvah day, my mum, our guests, yes, the state of my new suit. The last thing I wanted to do here in front of the synagogue was to be involved in a fight or be injured. Should I really engage? Before I had come up with an answer I was on the floor.

As soon as I got back on my feet, I walked into the hall at pace and warned everyone: "There is an antisemite outside, call the police!" Various people alerted the police, including Christiana and my daughter. With a bleeding lip and swollen face, I sat on a chair and collapsed in tears. One of the congregants by the name of Simon, I am eternally grateful, sat with me and calmed me. The police arrived a few minutes later. They took care of the man, who continued to be aggressive and shout. The emergency services rushed over and examined me. I was "lucky" they said and judged I did not require hospital treatment. By the time the police and emergency services had finished, and the man had been taken away, the synagogue service had already started. I realised immediately that as far as we could, I had to get on with my duties. I would not let the incident ruin our long hoped for and prepared celebration for anything in the world. I went to the bathroom, refreshed myself and looked in the mirror. Quietly, I sat down on a chair in the front row, next to Shifrah and we hugged each other and that was that.

Shifrah read her Torah portion excellently in Hebrew. Relatives and friends took on their various roles in the service. Then Shifrah gave her speech about the name changes in the Old Testament from Abram to Abraham and the different names of G-d, Elohim, HaShem and El-Shadai, and spoke about her additional Yoruba name and the fact that I had added my mother's surname Lewandowski to my father's name later in life (in fact, because of the things I discovered whilst researching and writing this book). She spoke about how we had become members of this Jewish community. Her speech was well received. Now it was my turn to give my speech, as I had been planning for days. I wanted to read it quickly and only parts of it. However, nerves got hold of me after all that happened, and it took me twice as long as planned. Finally, Claudia followed. She was the only one who mentioned to the congregation that something had happened in the morning and, turning to Shifrah, emphasised that whatever happened, she should stay on her path.

This we did. In the evening, we continued the party as planned. When our friend Sunshine finally sang "*Simcha tov u'mazel tov*", the whole room danced, Jews, Christians, Muslims and others all united. Shifrah had a wonderful, unforgettable bat mitzvah. We had managed to put the violence of the morning behind us, as something to be dealt with later. Luckily, I had not been injured to a degree that made that impossible.

Now, as I write these lines, I remember the theatre and music stage of Factory C in the Hasag forced labour camp in Skarżysko-Kamienna, where the incarcerated Jews, including my father and grandfather, by virtue of these performances gave each other courage week on week in the midst of the terrible degrees of violence, dehumanising torture and starvation they were exposed to.

Many people let us know how brave we were by carrying on with the celebration.

The *Jewish Chronicle* decided to write about the incident a few days later, while the police investigated.[205] I did have a few days of a persisting headache and slight pain where the man had hit me, but after a week or so it healed.

Three years before the incident, I had written to the then chairman of the synagogue. I told him that I believed that there should be security outside the synagogue. At the time, I often had to write about antisemitism and terrorist attacks, and it was this, that prompted my warning. My knowledge of the attacks at the 1972 Olympic Games in Munich was also in the background. In his reply, the then chairman wrote that

---

[205] Jewish Chronicle (2022)

the majority of synagogue members rejected this. The synagogue, which had undergone some changes in the spiritual leadership after Rabbi Shulamit had left a few years earlier, was at that time one of the few synagogue communities in London, perhaps even the UK, without any adequate security. Only one member of the synagogue had undergone full security training and at one point, I learned, the Jewish safety group Community Security Trust had come around to discuss the security of the building but there were no major measures in place, certainly no outside guards or anything of the kind. Now I think it was an irony or the mysterious nature of higher powers that made me, of all people – the person who had requested security – the victim of the first serious and violent anti-Jewish incident of hate the synagogue had encountered.

And that was not all. Shortly after the Jewish Chronicle had published their report, a prominent member of the synagogue even reproached me for daring to talk to the newspaper about security and "without approval of the committee." The truth was, the editor was an acquaintance, and he contacted me after he saw me posting something on my social media regarding what happened.

A few months later, I decided to leave the congregation and join another synagogue community. It did not come out of the blue. I had already visited that synagogue before Shifrah's bat mitzvah. I liked the more traditional prayer services, the social commitment and explorative attitude that synagogue had towards Torah. This egalitarian Masorti community was not just nearer to us, it had a proper fenced synagogue building with real security measures in place, taking the risk of antisemitism much more seriously.[206]

---

[206] I will say a few more words about this community, as there is no space later. The founding ethos of the Masorti movement, established by Rabbi Jacob Louis was also amongst the most revolutionary I encountered. It did not go as far as the Jewish Humanist Society founded by Rabbi Sherwin Wine in abandoning the concept of a G-d and prayer to G-d, Masorti Judaism kept the idea of a G-d alive, alongside the traditions. The revolutionary thing they say, is that the Thora could not have been written in total by G-d, but that it was written by fallible humans about G-d

After years of being with my family in Stoke Newington I had to meet new people and the process of being seen as a member by most took a good two years. As I write, I still do not know everyone's names, and I also have to learn some of the traditions they uphold.

Was I shocked, traumatised about the attack? After many years of working on this book with all its bitter and brutal facts, after a decade as the Great Britain correspondent for the German *taz*, I cannot claim that I was surprised or shocked in terms of things like that happening. Of course, I could never have imagined that it would involve my family on my own daughter's bat mitzvah, that I would be beaten to the ground, that 77 years after the end of the Shoah I would be attacked in England by a man to whom I was nothing more than a figure of abstract hate. The fact that I had worked for peace, fought for equal rights and, just a few days before the attack, had publicly declared my displeasure on social media regarding Benjamin Netanyahu's re-election in coalition with far-right politicians, such things were completely irrelevant to the attacker, as was the fact that my daughter, who was indirectly victimised, counts amongst her best friends people whose parents come from Muslim majority countries in the Middle East.

That is how it is when fanaticism possesses and blinds people. I was lucky, because I know that acts and anger that arise out of such blind hatred sometimes also kill.

And it was lucky too, that my daughter remained the centre of attention on that day and so it must remain, even if the introduction to her life as a religious adult in Judaism was challenged in that way. What happened will always be part of her and our story.

---

or their experience of G-d This honesty amounts to endless debates about meanings and contexts. Masorti is at the same time conservative when it comes to changing the sound and meaning of prayers and of halacha. Masorti was late with its egalitarianism compared to the liberal and reform movements, but had sorted itself out by the time it caught my attention again with women and LGBTQIA+ members given equal status and one of its senior rabbis, Jonathan Wittenberg had founded the green synagogue movement. So from all these perspectives it was not the end of the world to switch.

Zol Zayn Shulem II: Faroys

Almost three years later the trial against the perpetrator was finally held in front of a jury of twelve. My wife's cousin was witness together with myself and the information of the police. Days before I had learned that the defendant was a Muslim man. His full name suggested that he or his parents had links to an Arab country adjoining Israel, with which Israel had forged peace. He himself had lived or grew up in Italy. The state prosecution barrister did not take time to talk to me beforehand. On my way to the court building I listened to Matisyahu "One Day" trying to organise my thoughts to a positive and reconciliatory outlook. I was determined to request that the perpetrator should not go to prison to avoid him getting more radicalised.

The jury was the usual London mix. As far as I could see there was no religious Jewish person amongst them. The defendant had no longer a beard but was clear shaven and wore a shirt. He was in his late 20s slightly bolding. For a moment I studied him, looking at him directly, as he starred back. The state barrister asked numerous questions, but the recollection three years on was not totally clear. By the time the defence lawyer cross-examined me, the judge insisted that the time delay that had occurred due to the pandemic meant, that no-one should expect a second to second account from witnesses three years on.

One of the things the jury was however asked to examine and I was questioned about was the CCTV recording. It showed how my daughter walked first to the community centre wearing a kippa, and then the man talking with us. To my surprise I saw how the man hit me again after I had fallen to ground and was trying to get up, a fact I had not remembered. But the video lacked a crucial piece of evidence! There was no sound recording, that would give credence to the antisemitic and Jew hating abuse.

Before I left the witness-stand, I informed the judge and jury that it was my wish for the man to go on a programme and not to prison, if he were held to be guilty. The man gestured thanks to me.

When we left the court building, it so happened that the defendant and his female translator stood in front of it. He said: "How can I repay you?" It was not clear if he meant this with regard to the attack, or my demand that he should not go to prison. My wife's cousin, who is a deep believing Christian, answered, he should just work on his heart and hugged him briefly. I stretched out my hand and said, I do hope you have a chance and gave him a brief forgiving hug too. I thought of the words of one of our Rabbis who kept reminding the congregation in the months after the 7th of October, that all are created in the image of G-d, in other words, there is humanness in all people, even bad people – a call for respect and dignity. It felt like making amends right there between a Jewish person, a Christian and a Muslim, the three Abrahamic cousins and I went on to write a statement on my social media about that, as it felt empowering. I was no longer only a victim.

Only later through a court report in a Jewish newspaper did I learn that on the very next day the defendant and his defence lawyer had constructed a complete lie in spite of that moment. They argued I was but a mad man angry over not being able to park my car. He alleged that I had abused him with foul language – some of the words he attributed to me, I had not used in 30 years since coming to Britain – and that I then proceeded to attack him. He had further claimed to never have made any remarks about Palestine or Jews. The prosecutor asked him however why he made a remark on changes of the book and religion, as there was a 999-call on which he can be heard shouting this later. He answered that all religions were the same to him. What a lie.

Yet the jury concluded that either they did not believe me, and believe the accused, or that the evidence before them was not sufficient enough for a safe conviction. He was thus declared not guilty. Friends told me that the Scottish system has a better verdict to that with "not proven." But in England he basically was free to go.

Today I feel that I was lucky that the man had no weapons. I also hope that the scene in front of the court sits on the man's conscience. We tried to meet him with humanity. He not only abused me on the day of my daughter's Bat Mitzwah, he also fabricated a lie and was not honest about his past before the court and before G-d, which allowed him to get away without any blemish.

A senior authority on antisemitism in the UK commented on hearing about the outcome, that it was not unheard of, that Jews are not believed in this country when they get attacked. Others commended me on the attempt to make peace with the man. I may not have gotten justice, but I walked towards peace, said one observer.

During the Amidah one of the key Jewish prayers, there is a line that reads quietly: Hold my tongue from speaking evil, and keep my soul at peace, whilst others curse me. That line has a special meaning to me these days, and I advise others, that their first defence is to walk away from danger and provocation, that Jewish centres account for security arrangements, and that people do not forget, that with their mobile phone they have a powerful tool in their pocket. Had I had the presence of mind and switched on my phone's recording, the case would have ended with a guilty verdict, of that I am sure.

In October 2025 it fell to me to report on the terror attack on Yom Kippur in front of a synagogue in Manchester. I interviewed traumatized Jewish congregants and attended a funeral. Two men had lost their lives. Memories of the assault on me in 2022 reemerged, whilst I had stood in front of my current London synagogue for a shift as a security volunteer when the synagogue in Manchester was attacked.

Yom Kippur 1942 (5703) my father's community was summoned violently and deported to be murdered. In 1973 multiple Arab forces attacked Israel on Yom Kippur. The 7th of October 2023 (5784) was both Shabbat and a holiday. It is clear, we have to be on guard and ready to defend ourselves, even as we celebrate our festivals.

The Amidah Prayer I mentioned earlier, also read on Yom Kippur ends however with a prayer for hope and peace. There are two separate calls. Sim Shalom and Ose Shalom. The latter reads:

Ose shalom bimrovav hu yase shalom aleynu, we al kol Israel. Some add: *we al kol ha olam.* **"He who makes peace in high places, may He make peace for us and for all Israel - and for the whole world."** Amen!

81

German, Jewish, Mizrachi, British, Dutch, Human. Call to Confront Self-Destruction

The question of humaneness, we call it *Menschlichkeit* in German, of belonging and not belonging, of pseudo-racial categorisation, classification and identification, questions of trauma, the quest for a life without trauma, all these facets have played a role in my life. The construction of my own identity lies in the shadow of great catastrophes, and antisemitism, anti-Jewish hate, is omnipresent. I have encountered it myself in different guises. My wife Claudia has also repeatedly experienced discrimination and racism because of the colour of her skin and her accent.

Science, once also at the very heart of racializing doctrines, today bears witness to our shared common universal belonging to one single human race. I wish for my daughter, those who come after her and all other people that the recognition of this *Mensch-sein* (to be a human) and *Menschlichkeit* will triumph, not to eradicate local traditions or cultures, instead it shows that the apparent borders we set between us, transition into each other. All of us human beings must count as much as any other, or as one of the Rabbis of my synagogue states, we are all created in the image of G-d equally. Some parts of Germany are closer to this process than other societies. History well taught and documented concerning the Third Reich Era, but also concerning the Stasi rule of the GDR, have led many people in the Western part of Germany to deeply consider questions of identity and *Menschlichkeit*. It does not mean that you would not find negative types of behaviour or Germans that are not problematic – we all know that there continue to be neo-Nazis, racists and Holocaust deniers in Germany. But there is also a more open, and more self-reflective Germany, taking true account of difficult chapters of its history, in whose centre one finds sincere concern for the dignity of each individual person. In contrast to the United Kingdom or the USA, amongst others, concepts of racial differentiation and race-(pseudo)-science are completely rejected on account of German Third Reich history. Still, sadly, some people in Germany fell down the dark holes of antisemitism after the tragic events that occurred on 7th of October 2023. Antisemitism and hatred of Jewish people have paradoxically increased since the greatest mass murder of mostly Jewish people since the Shoah that occurred on that day. Noteworthy is also the sad fact of one fifth of Germans, mostly in the Eastern parts, where for decades the official dogma was, that they were apparently not part of National Socialism, because "they were the communists", became enthused by the far right AfD. Yes real communists suffered under Hitler, but that part of society was only a small part of the population.

In Britain, inhibitions about being honest concerning the past persist. The great achievements of the Allies in the Second World War still give British people legitimate reasons to be proud and celebrate, but it is sometimes at the expense of a deeper, more soul-searching examination of the past. There are indications that this is slowly changing too.

In Germany, the UK and other countries, education against antisemitism and hatred of Jewish people needs to become more robust so that it also reaches Muslim minorities and left-wing circles, beside the far-right, and in Germany only, it must also reach the Eastern part.

Call to Confront Self-Destruction

I wrote this book in recognition of my ancestors, above all their stories as human beings. The right of many of them to continue living as *Mitmenschen* (co-humans, co-citizens) was taken from them by brutal force in gigantic and immense undertakings, driven by racism and hate of Jews. The consequences of this dehumanisation continue in part into the generation of their descendants. It is not only insulting, but also nonsense, when some Germans demand that descendants of the victims of the Third Reich should no longer talk about what happened between 1933 and 1945, and to some extend in the years and decades before and after, because our whole lives were strongly impacted by these events, even all those years later, to greater or lesser degrees.

This book provides testimony to that. Contrary to the fact that many people had been voids in my life, there are now two books. Jewish people have always understood the symbol of life in writing, albeit in very specific forms to do with G-d.

I felt constricted and deprived of my rights and voice during the protests in autumn 2023 and all that followed. The protests where everything was the fault of Israel and the Jews, in deafening simplicity, made me uneasy and I felt like I was watching a modern version of the mass events of the Third Reich. "*Der Jude trägt an allem schuld*", was the consensus of that era.[207] Today it is still the Jew, or the word is surrogated with Zionists, Israel or the short of that "small powerful elite." I feel certainly less safe than ever before, and I cannot say if my feelings of relative safety before were an illusion or truth. Statistics show that hate is consistently on the rise with record numbers of incidents.

May this book series, with the insights into the history of a family, my family, heal wounds. *Le Refua Schlema!*[208] Through my research, I have already contacted cousins and relatives with whom there was either no contact or where nobody knew about each other. Perhaps other diaries of my grandfather, which he is said to have written, and

---

[207] German, The Jew is to blame for everything.
[208] Hebr. trad. to wholesome healing

Zol Zayn Shulem II: Faroys

other things will come to light, which can then provide further details for the second edition.

Survivors of the Shoah, like my father or my Aunt Ruszke and others who played such a fundamental role in my life, often spoke of a wish. "*Zoll shoin Zayn shulem!*" – may there be finally peace. But they didn't just talk about such hope regarding the fate of Jewish people in general or specifically, for example when something bad happened again in Israel in the conflict with the neighbours. The word *shulem* – peace – also stood for the longing for tranquillity and the return to a calm, good and peaceful life, without the all-pervasive fears, hardships or nightmares. Nothing more than that is also my own wish for the future. So, when these people raised a glass to a *l'chaim* – to life – it could not have had a deeper meaning to anyone else in the world in that moment.

> *La Chaim Toivim we Shulem …*
> *Lomir alle frejlach sein,*
> *lomir trinken La Chaim!*
> *Kein Zures soll schoin mehr nicht sein!*
> *La Chaim, for a Leben a naijen!*
> *Zures wird schoin mehr nicht sein,*
> *La Chaim, for a Leben a naijen!*

After Ben-Zion Witler (1907-1961)[209]

---

[209] To a good life and peace. Let us all be merry, let us drink to life, Let there be no more sorrows, To life, a new life. There will be no more worries. To life, a new life. Lomir Ale Freilich Sein · Ben-Zion Witler, Hed-Arzi Orchestra, Marcel Kreisler Lomir Ale Freilich Sein (Original Album), 1.8.2015 Listen for example here: https://open.spotify.com/track/5cSmXLmdbajD9HoPnfn78F?si=20e68b9103114fd9 (accessed 27.10.2024)

My mother Corrie, Claudia, Shifrah and myself
in London Hampstead, c.a. 2016.

82

Epilogue Following the 7th October 2023

A much longer version of this epilogue appeared in the German original. For the English version I have satisfied myself with but 2 pages.

Have we really done enough against the growth of hatred? Have we done enough for the building of peace, in an age where the polarised, and often limited, opinions and world views of too many can follow us everywhere at the touch of a button?

If more than one fact can be part of the whole truth, if there is more than one context, and different interests can exist in the same place, don't we need to learn how to deal with that diversity and find a way through, to make important compromises?

I finished this book with a chapter on hope. Even before it went to print very dark clouds arose on the horizon. For one moment, I stood with others protesting for democracy in Israel, a few weeks later, we stood united in shattered silence inside our synagogues. It was Shabbat, it was the 7th of October 2023, a sombre day.

Over the bodies of our murdered, tortured and abducted on that very day the marching season was rekindled, and to date, as the number of those who survived the Third Reich, and those who defeated the

German national-socialist state dwindle rapidly from amidst our communities, the marching has not ceased.

History obliges, or so we thought.

Those who indulge in the hatred of everything Jewish are wading in the historic footsteps of the Roman destruction, Arab and Christian "holy" conquests, the persecutions in England and other places in Europe during the Middle Ages, the Spanish inquisition, the Pogroms of the East, the Shoah and Ha Gerush.[210]

The terms of reference through which, after the horrors of the Shoah, Israel became a modern Jewish majority state amongst the families of nations again, demanded a compromise from the onset. Whilst Jewish rights to the land were acknowledged, the non-Jewish population that had settled there over time was to be accounted for too. The suggested two state solution was rejected at the outset with an annihilation plan "from the river to the sea" by a total of five armed forces. Fighting with heavy losses, Israel prevailed. Displaced people and those who had fled bemoaned the losses of their homes and called it the Nakba.

We woke up to more war, more terrorist acts, assassinations and too many devastating fields of destruction and hate. In the depth of despair some courageous attempts in peace-making succeeded nevertheless, while other, bolder opportunities for a more enduring and comprehensive peace were shunned and violently trampled upon. This only lead to more tragic events. Ideology drove crude opportunism, blind hatred and gruesome violence.

Hard-earned and precious freedom and security gained or aspired to, must not just be guarded and fought for. It cries out for the upkeeping of responsibilities, obligations, self-imposed limits, both towards oneself and others, respect and humility before the Law, our many traditions and writings, and last but not least, before G-d.

The instructions could not be clearer and yet remain unheard. Amid tribulations, I pledge not to give up hope. I will stand upright as a Jew and as a human being to be counted in on the call and ask the same from others.

---

[210] Ha Gerush, the expulsion of Jews from Muslim majority lands in the 20th Century.

Pursue nothing but justice and peace!

Justice: *Deut 16:20,*
Quran 5:8,
Matthew 5:6-7,
Peace: *Psalm 34:14,*
Surah Al-Baqarah (8:61),
1 Peter 3:11

Literature, Sources and Archives

Videos, Films and DVDs

Ruth Boronow Danson and Leslie Brent Talk at St. Paul's Steiner School (2016) *https://www.youtube.com/watch?v=7eC5hYSTTg8* and *https://www.youtube.com/watch?v=vHPanFrtI4o*

(Abgerufen 27.3.2021)

Lemer, Shulem & Shira Choir (2015). Avinu Malkenu,, Sirreel Productions.,LLC, *https://www.youtube.com/watch?v=anPJFBzVC2c* (accessed on 26.3.2021)

Loipedinger, Martin: Julius Pinschewer. Klassiker des Werbefilms, Absolut Medien GMBH, Berlin, 2012

Robinson, Ken (2006). Do Schools kill creativity? Tedtalk Februar 2006, *https://www.ted.com/talks/sir_ken_robinson_do_schools_kill_creativity?language=en* (accessed on 26.3.2021)

Samura, Sorious (2000). Cry Freetown, Insight News TV. First shown on CNN, 3.2.2000

CUnorthodox (2020). Netflix Serie, Anna Winger & Alexa Karolinski

USC Schoah Foundation:

Rozah Zylberstayn, Interview 33278, 8th Sept.1997

Wolf Zylbersztajn, Interview 51541, 21.2.2001

Yale University Library (1983). Holocaust Testemonies, Leon S., Edited Testimony (HVT-8025) *https://www.youtube.com/watch?v=ErtPjsisYLg* (accessed am 18.8.2020)

Zol Zayn Shulem II: Faroys

In Germany

Archiv der Gedenkstätte KZ Sachsenhausen
Arolsen Archives
Bayerisches Staatsarchiv
Berliner Stadtarchiv
Frohburger Kommunalarchiv
Gedenkstätte für Zwangsarbeit Leipzig
Staatsarchiv Landshut
Staatsarchiv Sachsen
Stadtarchiv große Kreisstadt Borna
Stadtarchiv der Landeshauptstadt München

In Israel

Yad Vashem

In the Netherlands

Delfer Nationaal Archief (NA),
Nederland Stadsarchief Amsterdam

In Poland

City Archive Szczekociny, Polen

In USA

New York State Archives
United States Holocaust Museum

Other Sources

Hedges, Chris (1993). New York Times 30. Juli 1993, Acquittal in Jerusalem; Israel Court Sets Demjanjuk Free, But He Is Now Without a Country, *https://www.nytimes.com/1993/07/30/world/acquittal-jerusalem-israel-court-sets-demjanjuk-free-but-he-now-without-country.html* (accessed am 8.7.2020)

Lewandowski, Alfred (1981). 125 Jahre 1856-1981. Das Haus Lewandowski, Jubiläumsschrift

Mythos Erwin Rommel. Der Wüstenfuchs als Wegbereiter des Holocaust, Der Spiegel, 27.08.2007, *https://www.spiegel.de/geschichte/mythos-erwin-rommel-a-946888.html*, (accessed on 05.07.2020)

My Heritage, Website

The Record from Hackensack (2011). New Jersey (Hackensack), 18.11.2011, S. L4

Zylbersztajn, Daniel

    (1995). Wolf Zylbersztajn interviewed by his Son Daniel Zylbersztajn (privat, unpublished)

    (1997). London Back Radio & The Community, MA Dissertation, Goldsmiths College, University of London

    (2004). The Effectiveness of Imagery Facilitated Instructions / Idiokinesis for Improved Performance Outcomes from (in) Pilates Novices, MA Dissertation, Brunel University, West-London

Internet Pages /Online

ADL (2019). ADL Global Survey of 18 Countries Finds Hardcore Anti-Semitic Attitudes Remain Pervasive. 15.11.2019 *https://www.adl.org/news/press-releases/adl-global-survey-of-18-countries-finds-hardcore-anti-semitic-attitudes-remain* (accessed on 2.9.2022)

Avraham, Alexander (2010). Sephardim. YIVO Encyclopedia of Jews in Eastern Europe. *https://yivoencyclopedia.org/article.aspx/Sephardim* (accessed on 4.4.2021).

Barakat, Amiran (2004). Poland to Remove Public Toilets Built on Jewish Cemetery, in Haaretz, 22. November 2004 online *https://www.haaretz.com/1.4763449* (accessed on 26.2.2021).

Barne, Donna, Pirlea, Florina. (2019). Money sent home by workers now largest source of external financing in low- and middle-income countries (excluding China), World Bank, 2.7.2019, *https://blogs.worldbank.org/opendata/money-sent-home-workers-now-largest-source-external-financing-low-and-middle-income* (accessed on 22.11.2020).

Bonikowsky, Laura N. (2013). Editorial: The Arrival of Black Loyalist in Nova Scotia, The Canadian Enyklopedia, updated 2020, *https://www.thecanadianencyclopedia.ca/en/article/black-loyalists-feature* (accessed on 14.5.2022).

Bryc, Katarzyna, Durand, Eric, Macpherson, Michael, Reich, David,and Mountain Joanna (2015). The Genetic Ancestry of African Americans, Latinos, and European Americans across the United States. In *American Journal of human Genetics*, 2015 Jan 8; 96(1). 37–53. (accessed on 3.2.2021).

Campbell, Lucy (2021). David Lammy praised for Response to radio caller who Said he was ‚not Englisch', The Guardian, 29.2.2021 *https://www.theguardian.com/world/2021/mar/29/david-lammy-praised-for-response-to-lbc-caller-who-said-he-was-not-english* (accessed on 30.3.2021).

Caroll, Rory (2000). Pope says sorry for sins of Church. Guardian 13.3.2000 *https://www.theguardian.com/world/2000/mar/13/catholicism.religion* (accessed on 2.9.2022).

Central Bureau of Statistics (2023). Israel in Figures – Rosh Hashana Selected Annual Data 2023, 13.9.2023 *https://www.cbs.gov.il/en/mediarelease/Pages/2023/Israel-in-Figures-Rosh-Hashana-Selected-Annual-Data-2023.aspx* (accessed on 15.3.2024).

Cole, Michael (2020). Holy war in the city of knives: anti-semitism and football on the streets of Krakow. In Open Democracy, 17.9.2020 *https://www.opendemocracy.net/en/countering-radical-right/holy-war-city-knives-anti-semitism-and-football-streets-krakow/* (accessed on 2.9.2020).

CST (2024). Antisemitic Incidents 2023, 15.2.2024, *https://cst.org.uk/public/data/file/9/f/Antisemitic_Incidents_Report_2023.pdf* /accessed on 10.3.2024).

Curry, Andrew (2019). Parents' emotional trauma may change their children's biology. Studies in mice show how. In American Association for the Avancement of Science (AAAS), doi:10.1126/science.aay7690, 18.8.2019, *https://www.sciencemag.org/news/2019/07/parents-emotional-trauma-may-change-their-children-s-biology-studies-mice-show-how* (accessed on 11.4.2021).

Daniel Counter Blog (2008). Leon Zelman „Shoa survivor „extraordinaire" *https://danielscounter.blogspot.com/2008/01/leon-zelman-sa-shoa-survivor.html* (accessed on 28.2.21).

Daniel Counter Blog (2009). „Untermenschen" and „Asylum Seekers": 8.1.2009, *https://danielscounter.blogspot.com/2009/12/london-refugee-conference-in-january.html* (accessed on 28.2.2021).

Daramy, Ade (2016). Remittances are three times greater than aid – how can they go even further? The Guardian, 11.5.2016, *https://www.theguardian.com/global-development-professionals-network/2016/may/11/remittances-three-times-greater-aid-sdgs* (accessed on 22.11.2020).

Dayan, Linda (2023). Thousands Attend Funeral of Slain Canadian-Israeli Peace Activist Vivian Silver, Haarez, 16.11.2023, *https://www.haaretz.com/israel-news/2023-11-16/ty-article/.premium/thousands-attend-funeral-of-slain-canadian-israeli-peace-activist-vivian-silver/0000018b-d9cd-d423-affb-fbef6e360000* (accessed on 15.3.2024, paywall).

DeCelles, Katherine (2016). Minorities Who ‚Whiten' Job Resumes Get More Interviews, Havard Business Schoo , *https://hbswk.hbs.edu/item/ minorities-who-whiten-job-resumes-get-more-interviews* (accessed on 30.10.2020).

Departament Badań Demograficznych (2012). Raport z wyników Narodowy Spis Powszechny Ludności i Mieszkań 2011 (accessed on 2.9.2022).

https://stat.gov.pl/cps/rde/xbcr/gus/lud_raport_z_wynikow_NSP2011.pdf

Devlin, Hannah (2015). Genetic study reveals 30% of White British DNA has German ancestry. The Guardian, 18.3.2015, *https://www. theguardian.com/science/2015/mar/18/genetic-study-30-percent-white-british-dna-german-ancestry* (accessed on 30.3.2021).

Devlin, Hanna (2018). First modern Britons had ‚Dark to black' skin, Cheddar Man DNA Analysis reveals. The Guardian 7.2.2018, *https:// www.theguardian.com/science/2018/feb/07/first-modern-britons-dark-black-skin-cheddar-man-dna-analysis-reveals* (accessed on 30.3.2021).

Doktor, Lara (2008). Liebestöter ziehen noch, in Süddeutsche Zeitung, 16.09 2008, *https://www.sueddeutsche.de/muenchen/adelinde-dilz-liebestoeter-ziehen-noch-1.690968*, (accessed on 3.7.2020).

Dollinger, Hans (2004). Schwarzbuch der Weltgeschichte. 5000 Jahre der Mensch des Menschen Feind, Erfstadt: Area Verlag.

Duffel, Nick (2014). Why Boarding schools produce bad Leaders, in The Guardian, 9.6.2014, *https://www.theguardian.com/education/2014/ jun/09/boarding-schools-bad-leaders-politicians-bullies-bumblers* (accessed on 27.3.2014).

Ebbighausen, Rodion (2016). Erfolgreich an deutschen Schulen: vietnamesische Kinder, 05.05.2016 *https://www.dw.com/de/erfolgreich-an-deutschen-schulen-vietnamesische-kinder/a-19237644* (accessed on 30.3.2021).

EdgeHist (Youtube Kanal der Fakultät für Geschichte an der Edgehill University), Daniel Zylbersztajn: On the Difficulties of Memorialising Jewish Victims in Europe: Munch, 1972. *https://www.youtube.com/ watch?v=iAEnz9yJUfI&t=1s* (accessed on 19.9.2023).

Engel, David (1998). Patterns Of Anti-Jewish Violence in Poland, 1944-1946, Yad Vashem Studies Vol. XXVI, Jerusalem 1998, S. 43-85, Online *https://www.yadvashem.org/articles/academic/patterns-of-anti-jewish-violence.html* (accessed on 12.4.2021).

Enthoven, Victor (2016). Slavery in Dutch America and the West Indies, Oxford Bibliographies, DOI: 10.1093/OBO/9780199730414-0230 *https://www.oxfordbibliographies.com/display/document/obo-9780199730414/obo-9780199730414-0230.xml* (accessed on 24.2.2023).

Filkins, Dexter (2015). Shot in the Heart, in The New Yorker, 19.10.2015, *https://www.newyorker.com/magazine/2015/10/26/yitzhak-rabin-assassination-israel-oslo-peace-accords* (accessed on 15.3.2024).

Frankel, Leora (1992). Out There: Israel; Pilgrimages With Reggae. New York Times 11.10. *1992/ https://www.nytimes.com/1992/10/11/style/out-there-israel-pilgrimages-with-reggae-beat.html* (accessed on 17.2.2022) .

Francis-Tan, Andrew and Mialon, Hugh. M (2014). 'A Diamond is Forever' and Other Fairy Tales: The Relationship between Wedding Expenses and Marriage Duration (September 15, 2014). Zugang: SSRN: *https://ssrn.com/abstract=2501480* or *http://dx.doi.org/10.2139/ssrn.2501480* (accessed on 23.1.2022).

Grant, John N (2015). Jamaican Maroons in Nova Scotia, Canadian Enyklopedia, updated 2019, *https://www.thecanadianencyclopedia.ca/en/article/maroons-of-nova-scotia* (accessed on 14.5.2022).

Gilad, Elon (2014). What does your Jewish Name mean? in Haaretz, *https://www.haaretz.com/jewish/.premium-what-does-your-name-mean-1.5244607* (accessed in 2021).

Gritz, Linda & Michael Katz (2020). Boston Workers Circle, Arbeter Ring Yiddish Sing, 22.6.2020 *https://circleboston.org/sites/www.circleboston.org/files/event_files/Yiddish%20Sing%20booklet%20 06_22_20-comp_Part1.pdf* (accessed on 2.4.2021).

gov.uk (2018). Ethnicity Facts and Figures: Population of England and Wales. Updated 2020. *https://www.ethnicity-facts-figures.service.gov.uk/uk-population-by-ethnicity/national-and-regional-populations/population-of-england-and-wales/latest* (accessed on 20.2.2022).

gov.uk (2020). Ethnicity Facts and Figures. Renting Social Housing. Erneuerte Version 4.4.2021 *https://www.ethnicity-facts-figures.service.gov.uk/housing/social-housing/renting-from-a-local-authority-or-housing-association-social-housing/latest* (accessed on 20.2.2022).

Heath, Deana (2018). British Empire is still being whitewashed by the school curriculum – historian on why this must change, in The Conversation, 2.11.2018, *https://theconversation.com/british-empire-is-still-being-whitewashed-by-the-school-curriculum-historian-on-why-this-must-change-105250* (accessed on 27.2.2021).

Higgins, Charlotte (2011). Historians say Michael Gove risks turning history lessons into propaganda classes, in Guardian, 17.8.2011 *https://www.theguardian.com/politics/2011/aug/17/academics-reject-gove-history-lessons* (accessed on 27.03.2021).

Hilgert, Romain (2018). Aberglaube mit Pressehilfe, in d'Lëtzebuerger Land, 29.06.2018 https://www.land.lu/page/article/408/334408/DEU/index.html (accessd on 28.3.2021)

Hope not Hate (2016). Cable Street, *http://www.cablestreet.uk/* (accessed on 14.8.2020).

House of Commons Library (2020). Research Briefing, 2.12.2020, *https://commonslibrary.parliament.uk/research-briefings/sn06077/#:~:text=in%20the%20year%20ending%20December,other%20EU%20countries%20excluding%20Ireland* (accessed on 18.3.2021).

House of Commons Library (2023). Constituency data: Ethnic groups, 2021 census, 29.3.2023, *https://commonslibrary.parliament.uk/constituency-statistics-ethnicity/#:~:text=Across%20England%20and%20Wales%2C%2082,20%20constituencies%20by%20ethnic%20group* (accessed on 15.2.2024).

Literature, Sources and Archives

Houston, Peter (2022). The Week Junior, keeping children reading with magazines they want to read. In Whats New in Publishing? *https://whatsnewinpublishing.com/the-week-junior-keeping-children-reading-with-magazines-they-want-to-read/* (accessed on 14.11.2022).

Janes, Jerome (2013). Pope John Paul II's Divided Loyalties to Jews. Forward 17.7.2013 (accessed on 2.9.2022).

Janzen, Cornelius (2023): Antisemitismus-Vorwürfe: Offener Brief an Roger Waters: „Unmoralisch," in ZDF Heute, 21.11.23, *https://www.zdf.de/nachrichten/politik/pink-floyd-roger-waters-antisemitismus-vorwuerfe-israel-100.html,* (accessed on 10.3.2024).

Jerusalem Post (2020) Arson feared after second fire in a week at Neve Shalom, Jerusalem Post, 7.9.2020 *https://www.jpost.com/israel-news/arson-feared-after-second-fire-in-a-week-at-neve-shalom-641346* (accessed on 15.3.2024).

Jewish Agency (2023). Jewish Population Rises to 15.7 Million Worldwide in 2023, 15.9.2023, *https://www.jewishagency.org/jewish-population-rises-to-15-7-million-worldwide-in-2023/* (accessed on 15.3.2024).

Jewish Chronicle (2022). Man arrested on suspicion of religiously aggravated assault on father of batmitzvah girl, 8.11.2022 *https://www.thejc.com/news/news/man-arrested-on-suspicion-of-religiously-aggravated-assault-on-father-of-batmitzvah-girl-2P44Ztf4vk2I3Kl7NGXI41* (accessed on 17.12.2022).

Jewish Policy Institute (JPR) (2011). Key trends in the British Jewish community: A review of data on poverty, the elderly and children. *https://www.jpr.org.uk/documents/Key%20trends%20in%20the%20British%20Jewish%20community.pdf* (accessed on 20.2.2022).

Jewish Policy Institute (JPR) (2024). Jews in the UK today: Key findings from the JPR National Jewish Identity Survey, 8.2.24. *https://www.jpr.org.uk/reports/jews-uk-today-key-findings-jpr-national-jewish-identity-survey* (accessed on 10.3.24).

Jiao-Yang Tian, wie Wang, Yu-Chun Li, Wen Zhang, Yong-Gang Yao, Jits van Straten, Martin B. Richards & Qing-Peng Kong (2015). A genetic contribution from the Far East into Ashkenazi Jews via the ancient Silk Road. In nature Briefing, Scientific Reports, Scientific Reports Vol 5, Article Nr. 8377, 11.2.2015 *https://www.nature.com/articles/srep08377* (accessed on 8.3.2021).

Kaldor Mary and Vincent, James (2006). United Nations Development Programme Evaluation Office: Case Study Sierra Leone. Evaluation of UNDP Assistance to Conflict Affected Countries. New York, United Nations. *http://web.undp.org/evaluation/evaluations/documents/thematic/conflict/SierraLeone.pdf* (accessed on 22.1.2023).

Kaufman, Lissy (2018). Das Cafe mit der Hausnummer 70. Jüdische Allgemeine, 26.4.2018 https://www.juedische-allgemeine.de/israel/das-cafe-mit-der-hausnummer-70/ (accessed 8.8.2025)

Kessler, Danna (2015): Tel Aviv's Café Tamar Closing After 74 Years, in *Tablet,* 19.5.2015, https://www.tabletmag.com/sections/news/articles/tel-avivs-cafe-tamar-closing-after-74-years accessed 7.08.2025

King, Susan (2015). HBO's 'Night Will Fall' chronicles making of WWII Holocaust film, in Los Angeles Times,25 Jan 2015, Online *https://www.latimes.com/entertainment/tv/la-et-st-hbo-night-will-fall-alfred-hitchcock-20150126-story.html* (accessed on 17.3.2021).

Klären, Jutta (Red.) Bundeszentrale für Politische Bildung (Herausg.). (2010). Jüdisches Leben in Deutschland *https://www.bpb.de/izpb/7643/juedisches-leben-in-deutschland* (accessed on 10.8.2020).

Kotkowsky, Charles (ohne Datum) Memoirs of A Survivor, in Mervin Butovsky und Kurt Jonassohn (red). Memoirs of Holocaust Survivors in Canada, Concordia University Chair in Canadian Jewish Studies *http://migs.concordia.ca/memoirs/kotkowsky/kot_mem.html* (accessed on 10.8.202).

Kruse, Jürn (2016). Nachruf auf Peter Lustig, in taz, die Tageszeitung, 24.2.2016, https://taz.de/Nachruf-auf-Peter-Lustig/!5278185/ (accessed 17.2.2025)

Lewis, Paul (1991). U.N. Repeals ist '75 Resolution Equating Zionism With Racism in New York Times, 17.12.1991. https://www.nytimes.com/1991/12/17/world/un-repeals-ist-75-resolution-equating-zionism-with-racism.html (accessed on 15.3.2024).

Lori, Aviva (2007). Is there a doctor in the House? in Haaretz, 11.10.2007 *https://www.haaretz.com/1.4984036* (accessed on 17.2.2022).

Luh, Jürgen (2022). Schlagwort: Novembertage. T-RECS #51: Ein öffentlicher Mann. Der deutsche Kronprinz Wilhelm 1930 bis 1934. Recs, Research Center Sanssouci. Für Wissen und Gesellschaft. 15.8.2022 *https://recs.hypotheses.org/tag/novembertage#_ftn61* (accessed on 4.9.2022).

Marks, Joshua Robbin (2019). Sephardic and Mizrahi Jews in Ashkenazic Lands, The Times of Israel, *https://blogs.timesofisrael.com/sephardic-and-mizrahi-jews-in-ashkenazic-lands/* (accessed on 4.4.2021).

Matiluko, Seun (2021). Census 2021: Why we need to acknowledge the differences between black people in Britain, The Voice online, 22.3.2021, *https://www.voice-online.co.uk/opinion/2021/03/22/census-2021-why-we-need-to-acknowledge-the-differences-between-black-people-in-britain/* (accessed on 30.3.2021).

Mcpherson, William (1999). The Stephen Lawrence Inquiry. *https://assets.publishing.service.gov.uk/government/uploads/system/uploads/attachment_data/file/277111/4262.pdf* (accessed on 7.4.2023).

Neuer, Hillel C (2023). Antisemitism and Discrimination Against Israel at the United Nations. UN Watch, 22.6.2023, *https://docs.house.gov/meetings/FA/FA06/20230622/116138/HHRG-118-FA06-Wstate-NeuerH-20230622.pdf* (accessed on 15.3.2024).

Ohio, Margaret Amaka (2017). Racism in Public Discourse in Poland. A Preliminary Analysis. In Edutainment, 01 (2016). *https://www.asc.uw.edu.pl/wp-content/uploads/2020/06/RACISM-IN-PUBLIC-DISCOURSE-IN-POLAND.-A-PRELIMINARY-ANALYSIS.pdf* (accessed on 2.9.2022).

Okolosie, Lola (2020). White guilt on its own won't fix racism': decolonising Britain's Schools, in The Guardian, 10.7.2020 https://www.theguardian.com/education/2020/jun/10/white-guilt-on-its-own-wont-fix-racism-decolonising-britains-schools (accessed on 27.3.2020).

Olusoga, David (2016). Black and British a forgotten History. Part 2. Freedom. BBC Documentary *https://www.bbc.co.uk/iplayer/episode/b083bv43/black-and-british-a-forgotten-history-2-freedom* (accessed 20.2.2025), also available in book form.

O'Malley, JP (2020). Historian: Polis society shunned Jewish survivors returning from Nazi camps, in The Times of Israel, 19.12.2020, *https://www.timesofisrael.com/historian-polish-society-shunned-jewish-survivors-returning-from-death-camps/* (accessed on 12.4.2021).

Parker, Fiona & Murphy, Michael (2023). Jewish families leaving synagogue 'targeted' by pro-Palestinian Demonstrators, Daily Telegraph, 11.11.2023, *https://www.telegraph.co.uk/news/2023/11/11/protesters-extreme-anti-semitic-signs-pro-palestinian-march/* (accessed on 15.3.2023, Paywall).

Peters, Freia (2011). Die besten deutschen Schüler stammen aus Vietnam. Die Welt, 6.2.2011 *https://www.welt.de/politik/deutschland/article12458240/Die-besten-deutschen-Schueler-stammen-aus-Vietnam.html* (accessed on 30.3.2021).

Pew Research Centre (2016). Israel's Identity, 8.3.2016, *https://www.pewresearch.org/religion/2016/03/08/identity/#:~:text=Israeli%20Jews%20are%20nearly%20evenly,associated%20with%20their%20ancestral%20roots* (accessed on 15.3.2024).

Priddy, Sarah & Torrance, David (2919). Contribution of the Jewish community to the UK. House of Commons Library Debate Pack. *https://researchbriefings.files.parliament.uk/documents/CDP-2019-0149/CDP-2019-0149.pdf* (accessed on 20.2.2022).

Literature, Sources and Archives

Pullan-Sheffield, Amy (2018). DNA suggests Yiddish began on the Silk Road, in Futurity, 20.4.2016 *https://www.futurity.org/yiddish-ashkenazic-jews-1143632-2/* (accessed on 8.4.2021).

Pybus, Cassandra, Candlin Kit & Petterd Robin (2009). BlackLoyalists.info (Australian Research Council, Univ. of Sydney), Internetseite ist archiviert unter *https://web.archive.org/web/20150905172923/http://www.blackloyalist.info/about/* (accessed on 15.5.2022).

Reuters & Times of Israel (2024). UNRWA report claims some agency employees admitted Hamas ties under Israeli coercion, Times of Israel, 9.3.2024, *https://www.timesofisrael.com/unrwa-report-claims-some-agency-employees-admitted-hamas-ties-under-israel-coercion/* (accessed on 17.3.2024).

Roumani, Mourice M (2020). First, Libya's Jews Were Deported. Then the S.S. Stepped in, Haaretz, 8.08.2020. *https://www.haaretz.com/world-news/2020-02-08/ty-article-magazine/.premium/first-libyas-jews-were-deported-then-the-s-s-stepped-in/0000017f-f7ed-d2d5-a9ff-f7ede3b30000*, (accessed on 15.9.2023).

Samuels, Ben (2023). Too Little, Too Late | Eight Weeks After Oct 7 Massacre, UN Women Condemns Hamas' Use of sexual Violence Against Israeli Women, Haaretz, 2.12.2023, *https://www.haaretz.com/israel-news/2023-12-02/ty-article/.premium/after-eight-weeks-un-women-condemns-hamas-use-of-sexual-violence-on-oct-7/0000018c-2b09-dc03-a9ec-3f7ba0190000* (accessed on 15.3.2024).

Sidiqque, Haroon (2019). Minority ethnic Britons face ‚shocking' job discrimination, The Guardian, 17.01.2017. *https://www.theguardian.com/world/2019/jan/17/minority-ethnic-britons-face-shocking-job-discrimination* (accessed on 28.2.2021).

Stichting voor Wetenschappelijk Onderzoek van Nationaal-Socialistische Misdrijven (2021). Justiz und NS-Verbrechen, Deutsch/deutsche Verfahren (JuNSV – Deutsch/deutsche Verfahren *https://junsv.nl/junsv-01/junsv/inhvzbrdddr.htm* (accessed on 28.12.2022).

Taylor, Diane (2018). It was like a family: Remembering the Mangrove, Notting Hill's Caribbean Haven. The Guardian 15.9.2018. *https://www.theguardian.com/uk-news/2018/sep/15/remembering-the-mangrove-notting-hill-caribbean-haven* (accessed on 18.2.2022).

The Baroness Casey Review. (2023). *https://www.met.police.uk/police-forces/metropolitan-police/areas/about-us/about-the-met/bcr/baroness-casey-review/* (accessed on 7.4.2023).

The Guardian Editorial (2019). The Guardian View on creativity in Schools: a missling ingredient, 18.10.2019, *https://www.theguardian.com/commentisfree/2019/oct/18/the-guardian-view-on-creativity-in-schools-a-missing-ingredient* (accessed on 26.3.2020).

The Sutton Trust and The Social Mobility Commission (2019). Elitist Britain, *https://assets.publishing.service.gov.uk/government/uploads/system/uploads/attachment_data/file/811045/Elitist_Britain_2019.pdf* (accessed on 26.3.2021).

Times Educational Supplement (2020). ‚Little or no evidence' that phonics improves reading, in Times Educational Supplement (TES), 22.01.2020, *https://www.tes.com/news/little-or-no-evidence-phonics-improves-reading* (accessed on 27.3.2021).

Travis, Alan (2017). Number of Romanians and Bulgarians in UK rises to 413,000: The Guardian, 11.10.2017 (accessed on 18.3.2020).

Trepka, Tomasz (2016). Potworne tajemnice skarżyskiej fabryki,Echodnia, 18.09.2016 *https://echodnia.eu/swietokrzyskie/potworne-tajemnice-skarzyskiej-fabryki/ar/c3-10528324* (accessed on 28.05.2020).

Van Dam, Andrew, (2022). People from elite backgrounds increasingly dominate academia, data Shows first-generation academics were always rare. Now they're vanishing. In Washington Post, 8.7.2022 *https://www.washingtonpost.com/business/2022/07/08/dept-of-data-academia-elite/* (accessed on 25.1.2023).

Vyas, Shekha (2014). East End producer Rockboi turns his hand to being a rapper, Hackney Gazette, 9.1.2014, *https://www.hackneygazette. co.uk/news/east-end-producer-rockboi-turns-his-hand-to-being-a-rapper-1-3838532*, (accessed on 10.11.2020).

Wikipedia: Blooms Restaurant *https://en.wikipedia.org/wiki/Bloom%27s_ restaurant* (accessed on 16.8.2020).

Williams, Len (2020). Inside Brick Lane's Mosque That Was A Synagogue That Was A Church, in Londonist, 17.2.2020, *https://londonist.com/london/history/brick-lane-mosque-east-london-church-synagogue-hugenots* (accessed on 16.8.2020).

Wolke, Karol (2020). The liberation of the german concentration camp in Holýšov, Czech Republic, by the Polish Armed Forces in The Warsaw Institute Review, *https://warsawinstitute.review/issue-2-2020/the-liberation-of-the-german-concentration-camp-in-holysov-czech-republic-by-the-polish-armed-forces/* (accessed on 26.4.2022).

Yad Vashem: Anti-Jewish Violence in Poland After Liberation, *https://www.yadvashem.org/articles/general/anti-jewish-violence-in-poland-after-liberation.html* (accessed on 1.3.2021).

Yad Vashem: Names of Righteous by Country *https://www.yadvashem.org/righteous/statistics.html* (accessed on 28.2.21).

Youth Against Racism in Europe: Stopping the BNP in Tower Hamlets, *http://www.yre.org.uk/towerhamlets.html* (accessed on 16.8.2020)

Zeleznice v Prorektoratu (Eisenbahnen im Vizerektorat) *https://www.fronta.cz/utoky-na-zeleznice-v-protektoratu* (accessed on 24.6.2020)

Yoman: Szczekociny – Jewish Cemetery & Gravestones, in Hebrew, Israelische Nachrichtensendung, Channel One, *https://www.youtube.com/watch?v=huiYtzrAwmg* hochgeladen auf Youtube oYossi Bornstein 21 März 2007 (accessed on 28. Februar 2021).

Wade, Lizzie (2018). Genetic study reveals surprising ancestry of many Americans, Science Mag18.12.2018 *https://www.sciencemag.org/news/2014/12/genetic-study-reveals-surprising-ancestry-many-americans* (accessed on 30.3.2021).

*h*ttps://www.zeeuwsarchief.nl/en/themepage/slave-voyage-aboard-the-unity/the-voyage-history/ (accessed on 11.11. 2022).

Zylbersztajn-Lewandowski, Daniel

(2008). School of Peace in Oasis of Peace, by Daniel Zylbersztajn for Oasis of Peace UK, Internet Archive *https://archive.org/details/Mp3SchoolInOasisFinal1* (accessed on 19.11.2020).

(2011), The possibilities and impossibilities of being a neighbour, Open Democracy, 4.11.2011, *https://www.opendemocracy.net/en/possibilities-and-impossibilities-of-being-neighbour/* (accessed on 25.6.2020).

(2012a). That's The Way to do it. Punch and Judy Turns 350, DW Online, *https://www.dw.com/en/thats-the-way-to-do-it-punch-and-judy-turns-350/a-15707807* (accessed on 24.2.2021).

(2012b). Großkonzerne bei Olympia: „Gesund, nachhaltig, zertifiziert", taz, die Tageszeitung, 29.7.2012 *https://taz.de/Grosskonzerne-bei-Olympia/!5087971/* (accessed on 24.2.2021).

(2012c). A Better Way? What can food co-operatives offer in the Age of the Supermarket? London Resoance FM 103.4 *https://archive.org/details/ABetterWayWhatCanFoodCo-operativesOfferInTheAgeOfTheSupermarket* (accessed on 24.2.2021).

(2012d) Nappy Change, The Challanges of contemporary fatherhood (as broadcasted on London Resonance FM 104.4, March 2012 (accessed on 24.2.2021). *https://archive.org/details/NappyChangeTheChallangesOfContemporaryFatherhoodasBroadcastedOn(2012e)*. Lieber rot als britisch, taz, die Tageszeitung: 2.9.2012, *https://taz.de/!571166/* (Tazarchiv, accessed on 18.3.2021).

(2012f). Ernüchternd und erleichternd: taz, die Tageszeitung, 13.8.2012, *https://taz.de/Kolumne-London-Eye/!5086649/* (accessed on 18.3.2021).

(2012g). Genetischer Reduktionismus ist falsch, in taz, die Tageszeitung, 9.8.2012 *https://taz.de/US-Forscher-ueber-Rassismus-im-Sport/!5086963/* (accessed on 30.3.2021).

(2013). Die Macht der Pedale, Zeit Online, 7.8.2013 *https://www.zeit.de/reisen/2013-08/london-fahrradrennen* (accessed on 24.2.2021).

(2013a). Wahlerfolge britischer Rechtspopulisten. Ukip on the Block, taz, die Tageszeitung, 14.5.2013 *https://taz.de/!5067407/* (accessed on 18.3.2021).

(2013b). Nach dem Mord in London:„England, England, EDL! EDL!", taz, die Tageszeitung, 23.5.2013 *https://taz.de/Nach-dem-Mord-in-London/!5066858/* (accessed on 18.3.2021).

(2015). Die Überlebende *https://taz.de/!215237/*, taz die Tageszeitung, (accessed on 24.2.2021).

(2015a). Haltestelle Olympiapark, Jüdische Allgemeine. Haltestelle Olympiapark, 15.1.2015 *https://www.juedische-allgemeine.de/kultur/haltestelle-olympiapark/* (accessed on 19.9.2023).

(2016). Zwischen den Welten, taz die Tageszeitung *https://taz.de/Nach-dem-Grossbrand-im-Grenfell-Tower/!5436291/* (accessed on 24.2.2021).

(2016a). Wahlkampf um Parlamentssitz von Jo Cox: Eine Schauspielerin soll's richten: taz, die Tageszeitung, 18.10.2016, *https://taz.de/!5345863/* (accessed on 18.3.2021).

(2016b). Eine Schwäbin in Kent, Jüdische Allgemeine, 10.05.2016, *https://www.juedische-allgemeine.de/?p=25477* (accessed on 23.3.2021).

(2016c). Arm aber erfolgreich, taz, die Tageszeitung, 25.6.2016 *https://taz.de/Migrantenkinder-in-Tower-Hamlets/!5303675/* (accessed on 26.3.2021).

(2017). Im Schatten der Strahlen, taz die Tageszeitung, 21.2.2017, *https://taz.de/Atomkraft-im-Nordwesten-Englands/!5382462/* (accessed on 24.2.2021).

(2017a). Nach Anschlag auf Londoner Moschee :„Jetzt könnt ihr mich umbringen", taz die Tageszeitung, 19.6.2017, *https://taz.de/!5418939/* (accessed on 18.3.2021).

(2017b). Die Auswirkungen des Terrors: Manchester United?, taz die Tageszeitung, 28.5.2017, *https://taz.de/!5409852/* (accessed on 18.3.2021).

(2017c). Nach dem Anschlag von London nicht nachgeben, taz die Tageszeitung, 4.6.2017 *https://taz.de/!5417678/* (accessed on 18.3.2021).

(2017d). Couscous & Co: Jüdische Allgemeine, 15.6.2017, *https://www.juedische-allgemeine.de/juedische-welt/couscous-co/* (accessed on 29.3.2021).

(2018). Als Austauschjude in Belsen, Jüdische Allgemeine, 29.11.2018 *https://www.juedische-allgemeine.de/?p=2009487*, (accessed on 9.1.2022).

(2019a). Mayday, Mayday, taz die Tageszeitung, 24.3.2019 *https://taz.de/Brexit-Demos-in-Grossbritannien/!5582690/* (accessed on 23.3.2021) .

(2019b). 15.5.2019: Brexit Reloaded *https://taz.de/!5592134/* (accessed on 23.3.2021).

(2019c). Im Armenhaus der Brexiteers: taz, die Tageszeitung, 17.10.2019 *https://taz.de/Grossbritannien-und-die-EU/!5629650/* (accessed on 23.3.2021).

(2020). I was there, A rare photo from the hell of the Schoa, Medium, 21. April 2020 *https://link.medium.com/p2TiT9xmU6* (accessed on 30.5.2020).

(2020a). Labour suspendiert Corbyn, taz die Tageszeitung, 29.19.2020 *https://taz.de/!5724684/* (accessed 10.1.2026)

(2020b). Die Türsteher vom Ärmelkanal, taz, die Tageszeitung, 20.9.2020, *https://taz.de/!5711448/* (accessed on 23.3.2021).

(2020c). Labour suspendiert Corbyn, taz, die Tageszeitung, 29.10.2020 *https://taz.de/!5724684/* (accessed on 23.3.2021).

(2021). Große Herzen, harte Fäuste, taz, die Tageszeitung, 23.11.2021 *https://taz.de/Juedischer-Antifaschismus-in-England/!5814040/* (accessed on 23.11.2023).

(2022). Antisemitismus in Großbritannien. Bundeszentrale für politische Bildung. *https://www.bpb.de/themen/antisemitismus/dossier-antisemitismus/* (abgerufen 10 April 2022).

(2023). Mahnwache für alle Toten in Nahost: Gegen den Hass, in taz, die Tageszeitung, 4.12.2023, *https://taz.de/Mahnwache-fuer-alle-Toten-in-Nahost/!5978206/* (accessed on 10.2.23).

Literature

Adorno, Theodor (1994). The Stars down to Earth, Abingdon, Oxon: Routledge Classics

Ahmed, Imitaz (2022). Recognising the 1991 Bangladesh Genocide. An Appeal for Rendering Justice. Public Diplomacy Wing, Ministry of Foreign Affairs, Government of the Peoples Republic of Bangladesh, Dhaka: Nymphea Publication.

Ali, Shahrazad (1992). The Blackwoman's Guide to Understanding the Blackman, Philadelphia: Civilized Publications

Arad, Yitzhak (1999). Belzec, Sobibor, Treblinka. The Operatioon Reinhard Death Camps, Boomington: Indiana University Press

Bajohr, Frank (2002). Aryanisation in Hamburg, New York Oxford: Berghan Books

Bookbinder, Susan (2013). Izyk cheated Death many Times, but died before his Son restored Jewish History to Szczekociny, in Jewish Telegraph (Großbritannien), 16.8.2013

Baddiel, David (2021). Jews Don't Count, London: TLS Books

Bakó, Tihamér & Zana, Katalin (2020). Transgenerational Trauma and Therapy, London & New York: Routledge

Bauer, Hannah (2014). Vom Korsett zum Büstenhalter. Einfluss gesellschaftlicher Extremsituationen am Beispiel der zwei Weltkriege auf den Unterwäschemarkt Norderstedt: Grin Verlag

Baumann, Angelika (Red.) (1995). Jüdisches Leben in München, München: Buchenberger Verlag

Baumann, Angelika & Heuslert, Andreas (2004). München arisiert. Entrechtung und Einteignung der Juden in der NS-Zeit München: C. H. Beck

Baumann, Zygmund (1991). Modernity and Holocaust, Cambridge: Polity Press

Barbier, Muriel & Boucher, Shazia (2005). Die Dessous, Berlin – New York: Parkstone

Beimler, Hans (2019). Im Mörderlager Dachau, Köln: PappyRossa Verlag

Boas, Franz (1904). Some Traits of primitive Culture: *Journal of American Folclore, 17*: 243-254

Bornstein, Izyk Mendel (2009). B-94, The Spirit of the Survivor, Rosh ha-ayi, Reborn Roots

Bornstein Yossi, Piskiewicz, Angnieszka, Skrzypzyk, Miroslav & Wieczorek, Anna (2017). Szckeocinski Festiwal Kultur Zydowskiej YAHAD-RAZEM. 10 lat, Wloszczowa: Drukania Kontur

Brenner, Michael (1995). Nach dem Holocaust. Juden in Deutschland 1945–1950. München: C. H. Beck

Brenner, Michael, Jersch-Wenzel, Stefanie & Meyer Michael A. (1996). Deutsch-Jüdische Geschichte in der Neuzeit, 4 Bde., Bd.2, Emanzipation und Akkulturation 1780-1871, München: C. H. Beck

Brenner, Michael (2019). Der lange Schatten der Revolution. Juden und Antisemiten in Hitlers München 1918-1923, Berlin: Jüdischer Verlag im Suhrkamp Verlag

Brooke, Kevin (2003). Russian History, Spring-Summerr 2003 / Printemps-Ete 2003, Vol. 30, S. 1-22

Campbell, Mavis C. (1990). The Maroons of Jamaica, 1655–1796. Trenton, NJ: Africa World Press

Cleaver, Eldridge (1968). Soul on Ice. New York: Dell Publishing

Clouder, Christopher & Rawson, Martyn (2004). Waldorf Education, Edinburgh: Floris Books

Cohen, Mark (2014). Prologue. The "Golden Age" of Jewish-Muslim Relations: Myth and Reality, in Meddeb, Abdelwahab and Stora, Benjamin. A History of Jewish-Muslim Relations: From the Origins to the Present Day, Princeton: Princeton University Press

Cziborra, Pascal (1996). KZ Venusberg. Der verschleppte Tod, Bielefeld: Lorbeer Verlag

Cziborra, Pascal (2015). KZ Freiberg, Geheime Schwangerschaft, Bielefeld: Lorbeer Verlag

Dachauer Hefte 21 (2005). Häftlingsgesellschaft, Dachau: Verlag Dachauer Hefte

Darke, Diana (2020). Stealing from the Saracens: How Islamic Architecture Shaped Europe, London: Hurst

Dollinger, Hans (2002). Schwarzbuch der Geschichte, Köln: Area Verlag

Drukier, Manny (1996). Carved in Stone, Holocaust Years – A Boys Tale, Toronto: University of Toronto Press

Epstein Helen (1995). Die Kinder des Holocaust. Gespräche mit Söhnen und Töchtern von Überlebenden. München: H. C. Beck.

Fanizadeh, Andreas (2021). Die Deutschen vor El Alamein, in taz, am Wochenende, 27/28 März, S.12

Feldman, Deborah (2012). Unorthodox, New York: im Orginal bei Simon & Schuster, als Übersetzung bei Secession Verlag, 2016

Frey, Hans, (1949). Die Hölle Kamienna, Die Hölle von Kamien, unter Benutzung des amtlichen Prozessmaterials zusammengestellt, Berlin Potsdam: VVN

Garwood, Aldred (2021). Holocaust Trauma and Psychic Deformation, London &New York: Routledge

Gibaszewski, Krzysztof (2015). Hasag. Historia obozu pracy przymusowej w Skarżysku-Kamiennej, Skarżysko-Kamienna, Krzysztof Gibaszewski & PjS Agencja Wydawniczo-Poligraficzna

Gilman, Sander (1991). The Jew's Body, London: Routledge

Gilroy, Paul (1987). The Cultural Politics of Race and Nation, London: Hutchinson

Gilroy, Paul (1993). The Black Atlantic – Modernity and Double Consciousness. London: Verso Books

Gilroy Paul (2000). Between Camps: Nations, Cultures and the Allure of Race. London: Allen Lane, Penguin Press, 2000

Goldhagen, Daniel (1996). Hitler's Willing Executioners. Ordinary Germans and the Holocaust. London: Little, Brown and Co.

Gundel, Kay (1986). Reborn, Memoirs of a Camp Survivor, (unpublished), copy available in USHMM, 1986.019.2 | RG Number: RG-02.004.0

Haikal, Mustafa (2002). Einige Bemerkungen zur Auseinandersetzung mit der Geschichte der Hugo Schneider Aktiengesellschaft (Hasag). In fremd- und Zwangsarbeit in Sachsen 1939-1945. Beiträge eines Kolloquiums in Chemnitz am 16. April 2002. Herausgeber sächsisches Staatsministerium des Inneren. Halle (Saale), Dresden: Mitteldeutscher Verlag. S. 81-88

Hansen, Valerie (2016). The Silk Road: A New History with Documents, Oxford: Blackwell

Harari, Yuval (2014). Sapiens, London: Penguin Press

Haus der Geschichte Baden-Würtemberg (Hrsg.) (2008). Mythos Rommel, Ulm: Süddeutsche Verlagsgesellschaft

Herbert, Ulrich (1991). Europa und der Reichseinsatz ausländischer Zivilarbeiter Kriegsgefangene und KZ-Häftlinge und Deutschland 1938-1945, Essen: Klartext Verlag

Hoberman, John (1997). Darwin's Athletes: How Sport Has Damaged Black America and Preserved the Myth of Race. Boston: Houghton Mifflin

Hooks, Bell (1992). Black Looks: Race and Representation. Boston, MA: South End Press

Jacob, Sybille-Christin & Drewes, Detlef (2001). Aus der Waldorfschule geplaudert: warum die Steiner-Pädagogik keine Alternative ist. Aschaffenburg: Alibi Verlag

Karay, Felicja (2004). Death Comes in Yellow: Skarżysko Kamiennna Slave Labour Camp, Abingdon, Oxfordshire: Routledge

Klein, Tobias (2009). Fremd- und Zwangsarbeit im Raum Leipzig 1939-1945, zum Forum Geschichtswerkstatt Europa 1938-1949 – Dekade der Gewalt, Nordted: Grin Verlag

Knigge, Volkhard (2020). Buchenwald. Ausgrenzung und Gewalt 1937 bis 1945. Göttingen: Druckhaus Gera

Knobloch, Charlotte (2012). In Deutschland angekommen – Erinnerungen München: Deutsche Verlags-Anstalt

Krystal, Henry (1968). Massive Psychic Trauma. New York: International University Press

Krzyzanowski, Lukas (2020). Ghost Citizens. Jewish Return to a Postwar City, Cambridge MA: Harvard University Press

Lee, Thomas H. C. (1991). China and Europe. Images and Influences in Sixteenth to Eighteenth Centuries. Hongkong. The Chinese University Press

Levy, Primo (1988). Drowned and Saved. New York: Summit Books

Linebaugh, Peter (1991). The London Hanged. London: Verso

Maier, Lily (Hg.) (2018). Die Möhlstraße – ein jüdisches Kapitel der Münchner Nachkriegsgeschichte. Münchner Beiträge zur jüdischen Geschichte und Kultur, Jg. 12 Heft 1, München

Marcus, Paul & Rosenberg, Alan (1989). Healing their wounds. Psychotherapy with Holocaust survivors and their families., New York: Praeger Publishers

Martin, Ben L. (1991). From Negro to Black to African American: The Power of Names and Naming. In Political Science Quarterly Vol. 106, No. 1 (Spring, 1991), S. 83-107, The Academy of Political Science

Maurer Zenck, Claudia, Petersen, Peter & Fetthauer, Sophie (Hg.) (2017). Lexikon verfolgter Musiker und Musikerinnen der NS-Zeit, Hamburg: Universität Hamburg

Morgan, David (1991). The Mongols. Hobroken: Wiley-Blackwell

Niederland, William G. (1961). The Problem of the Survivor, *Journal of the Hillside Hospital*, 10, 233-247

Niederland, William G. (1981). The Survivor Syndrome: Further Observations and Dimensions., *Journal of the American Psychoanalytic Association* 29.2 413-325

Nordau, Max (1909). Zionistische Schriften. Köln und Leipzig: Jüdischer Verlag

Neuman-Nowicki (1998). Struggle for Life During the Nazi Occupation of Poland. Lewiston NY: Edwin Mellen press

Owusu, Kwesi (red.) (2000). Black British Culture and Society, Routledge, London, 2000.

Paterson, Tony (2011). Was the Desert Fox an honest soldier or just another Nazi?, The Independent, 04.12.2011

Rao, Zhen, Fink, Elian & Gibson, Jenny (2020). Dyadic association between aggressive pretend play and children's anger expression, in British Journal of Developmental Psychology, 5.10.2020

Richardi, Hans-Günther (1986). Schule der Gewalt. Das Konzentrationslager Dachau 1933-1934, München: C. H. Beck

Reuth, Ralf Georg (2005). Rommel, the end of a legend. London: Haus Publishing

Rose, Susan and Garske, John (1987). Family Environment, Adjustment and Coping among Children of Holocaust Survivors. A Comparative Investigation, *American Journal of Orthopsychiatry* 57, 3, 322-344

Rost, Christian (2010). Ausverkauf beim König der Pelze, Aufstieg und Fall eines Münchner Unternehmens: Die Geschichte der Firma Rieger, die ihr Geschäft jetzt schließen muss, Süddeutsche Zeitung, 23. März 2010, *https://www.sueddeutsche.de/muenchen/insolvenz-der-firma-rieger-ausverkauf-beim-koenig-der-pelze-1.13367* (accessed on 06.07.2020)

Schiller, Kay & Young Christopher (2012). München 1972. Olympische Spiele im Zeichen des modernen Deutschland, Göttingen: Wallstein Verlag

Schriftreihe des Museums der Stadt Borna,(2007). Band 2, das Jahr 1945 in Borna, Borna: Druckhaus Borna

Schreiber, Gerhard (1996). Deutsche Kriegsverbrechen in Italien: Täter, Opfer, Strafverfolgung, München: C. H. Beck

Singer, Peter (1975). Animal Liberation, New York: Harper Collins

Sofsky, Wolfgang (1997). Der Orden des Terrors: Das Konzentrationslager. (Übersetzt von William Templer) Princeton University press

Steiner, Rudolf (1966). Die Welträtsel und die Anthroposophie, GA 54. Dornach: Rudolf Steiner Verlag

Strigler, Mordechai (1949). in di Fabrikn Fun toyt, Buenos Aires: Union Central Israelit Polaca en la Argentina

Strigler, Mordechai (2017). In den Fabriken des Todes (deutsche Ausgabe), Springe: zu Klampen Verlag

Strigler, Mordechai (2019). Werk-C, ein Zeitzeugenbericht aus den Fabriken des Todes, Springe: zu Klampen Verlag

Sussman, Robert (2014). The Myth of Race: Cambridge (MA). Harvard University Press

Szwajcer, Isroel (Ben-Awrom) (2010). Pinkes Szczekocin Księga Pamięci Szczekocin, Tel Aviv, [5720 – 1959]: polnische Ausgabe, Marek Tuszewicki, Szczekociny

Terezinska Pametni Kniha, Terezinska Iniciativa, vol. I-II Melantrich, Praha 1995, vol. III Academia Verlag, Prag 2000

Tyson, B. Timothy (2000). Radio Free Dixie, Robert F. Williams and the Roots of Black Power, Chapel Hill, N. C.; London: University of North Carolina Press

Verein Gedenkstätte KZ-Außenlager Schlieben-Berga. Ev (2001). Schlieben Force Labour Camp. Memorial Association Schlieben. Schlieben

Westphal, Uwe (1992). Berliner Konfektion und Mode: die Zerstörung einer Tradition, 1836-1939, Berlin: Edition Henrich

Williams, Robert F. (1962). Negroes with Guns, NY: , Marzani & Munsell, Inc.

Wardi, Dina (1992). Memorial Candles, Children of the Holocaust, London: Routledge

Watt, W Montgonery (1994). Influence of Islam on Medieval Europe, Edinburgh University Press

Williams, Eric (1944) Capitalism and Slavery: Chapel Hill, University of North Carolina Press. worldcat.org

Yehuda, Rachel, Lehrner, Amy & Rosenbaum, Tali (2015). PTSD and Sexual Dysfunction in Men and Women, Journal of sexual Medicine, Sex Med 2015;12: S. 1107–1119

Zelman, Leon (1995). Ein Leben, nach dem Überleben, Wien: Verlag Kremayr &Scheriau

Zylbersztajn, Daniel (1997). Hey Jude. ‚in *Jewish Socialist* 39, Winter 1998, S. 14-15

Abbreviations

DZL – Daniel Zylbersztajn-Lewandowski

DP – Displaced Person / Displaced Persons

SOAS – School of Oriental and African Studies

SPD – Sozialdemokratische Partei Deutschlands

UCL – University College of London

Z"L – hebräische Abkürzung für Zikarohn le Bracha. Trad Namen einer of a passed waay person,"May is memory be a blessing"

ZLB – Zentral – und Landesbibliothek Berlin

Literature, Sources and Archives

Geographical Map.

Zol Zayn Shulem II: Faroys

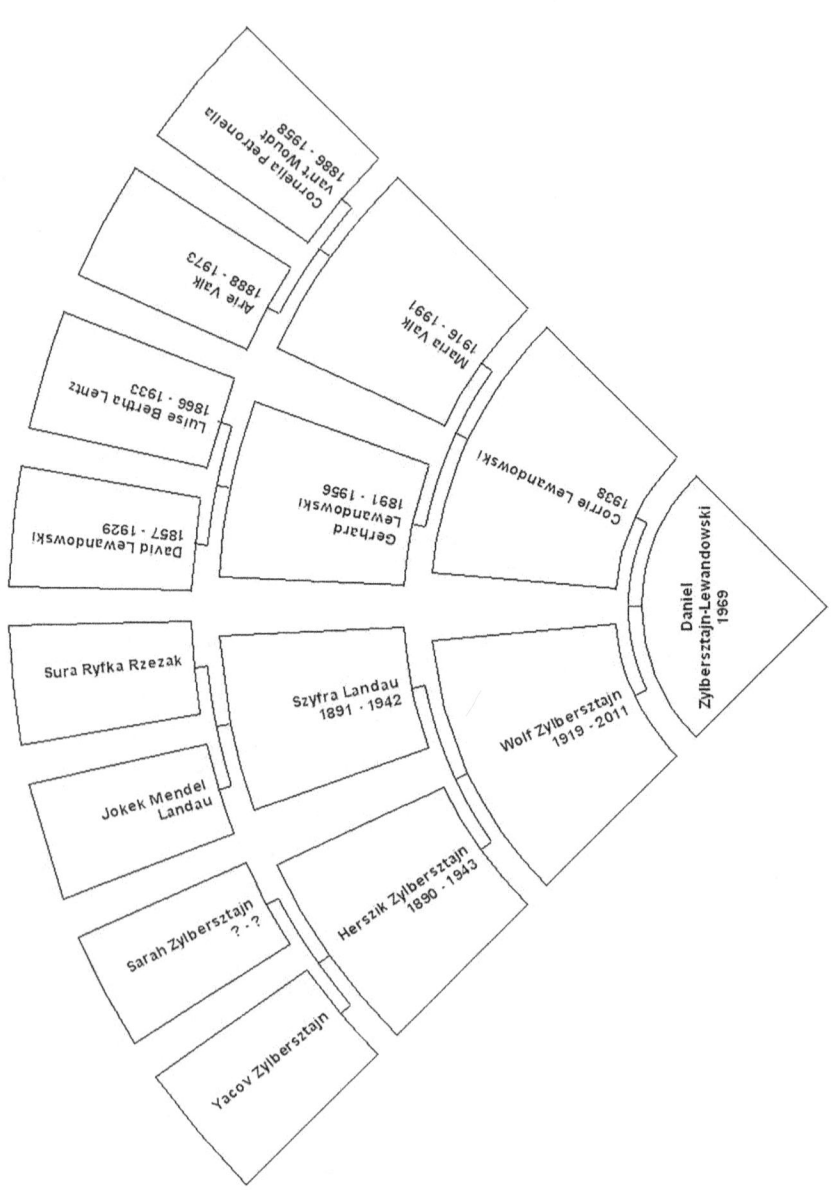

Daniel Zylbersztajn-Lewandowski: Ancestors of the last three generations.

Index

7 Oktober 234, 393, 405f, 412
1860 München 23, 48
1938 184, 234
1969 2f
1972 7-10, 149f, 368f, 375, 390-394, 401
Abberton
    Ishmael & Jasyl 243
    Michael 238
Abendzeitung 40
Aberystwyth 238, 243, 312
AHRC 284
Aliyat-ha-Noar 125-127, 133, 139, 175f
Alonei Yitzhak 125, 128-145
Althoff, Patrizia 186
Ambalu, Shulamit, Rabbi 270
Amsterdam 16, 363
ANC 136
Angelou, Maya 254
Anti-Authoritarian 57, 64, 103, 157, 176, 313, 376
Antisemitism 41, 50, 61, 121, 126, 149, 188, 194, 305, 342, 348-350, 369, 371, 401f, 406-408
Apartheid 250
Apeldoorn 15, 77, 317
Arabic 61, 202, 230f, 299
Arafat 225f
ARD 244

Arts and Humanities Research Board 284
Asemonim 165
Arazi Yardena 61
Atari, Gali 61
Auschwitz / Auschwitz-Birkenau xi. 61, 335, 246, 349, 351-357
Bad Wiessee 22
Bagrut 161f, 179
Bangladesh 105, 234f, 378
Bar Meisel, Rabbi Dov 337
bar mitzvah /bat mitzvah 87-91, 247, 397-406
Bauman, Zygmund 267, 284
Bayerischer Rundfunk 190
BBC 267, 271f, 295, 365, 366
Bei Mir Bist Du Shayn 95
bell hooks 255
Benedict Anderson 129
Bergen Belsen xi, 61, 93, 95
Biderman, Moshe 344
Birkbeck College 265, 290
Black Community 293, 267f
Black Cultural Studies Group 312
Black Loyalists 238f
Black Panther 284
Black Power 267f
Blair, Tony 369, 372
Blaszczyk, Henryk 342
BMW 183

443

Zol Zayn Shulem II: Faroys

Bornstein
   Agnieszka xii, 333, 341, 343, 345
   Yossi xii, 333-345, 349
Brauer-Kvam, Ruth 160
Brexit 369f, 384f, 386
British Library 223
Brit Mila 1, 3, 90
Brown, James 153
Brunel University 295f
Burden, Janet, Rabbi 314
Burton-Trust 283
Caesarea 154, 166
Canada 239
Carell, Rudi 61
Caribbean 213f, 224f, 235, 238, 240f, 248, 357, 371, 387
Casagrande Claudius and Vittorio 148
Cavallini (-Gross) Family 317
   Claudia 15, 255, 317f, 328
   Gerda 12, 13, 15, 19, 54, 194, 255, 317, 328
   Marcello 12-15, 54f, 194, 317, 328
   Salvatore 14
Christian 14, 23, 54, 83, 88, 102, 181, 185, 220, 240, 249, 284, 288, 355, 382f, 405 413
Cohen, Itzar 61
colonialism 191, 215, 224, 229, 240f, 284, 387
conversion 22, 27, 36, 44, 90
co-op 218, 220, 256, 265, 277
Corbyn, Jeremy 371, 389
cougar 231
Curacao 235
Dachau xiv, 58, 353, 184, 353
D.A.F. 110, 204
Daffarn, Eddie 370

Dalli Dalli 60
Dalston Youth Project 268
Dana International 61, 131
Dan Fodio, Usman 250
Damari, Shulamit 95
Darling, Alistair 272
Das feuerrote Spielmobil 63f
Davidson, Nico 242
Davis, Miles 154
Day of Unity (Tag der Einheit) 197-199
Dege, Erik 205
dehumanisation 401, 409
democracy 65, 234, 345, 349, 412
Depeche Mode 109, 136
Depression 272, 274, 276
Deutsche Welle/DW 276, 279, 365, 367
Dilz, Adelinde 395
discrimination 283, 287, 323, 378, 407
Dresden 22
drugs 106, 148
Du Bois, W.E.B. 268
Duran Duran 123
Dvar Torah 91, 398
Edgehill University, 392
Egypt 40f, 177, 188, 225
Eilat 123f
el-Shabazz, El-hadjj Malik 268
England 46, 65, 234, 282, 286, 293, 369, 376, 380, 413
   Batley 371
   Brighton 252, 258-265, 386
   Epping 257
   Luton 280-282
Erasmus 191, 286f, 385
Etzel 393
Eurovision 61
Fanon, Frantz 254

Index

far-left 10, 82, 224, 386
far-right 112, 190, 282, 292 348, 371, 387, 403, 408
Farage, Nigel 370
FC Bayern x, 23, 28, 36, 46-53
Flößberg xiii, 259
Frankenwarte Nürnberg 190
Freetown xii, 239-249, 289, 319, 380, 384
Frojmovic, Eva 284
Frühschoppen 38
Fulani 250
football x, 25, 28, 36, 43, 46-53, 59, 68, 147, 266. 282, 330, 348
forced labour x, xiii, 37, 69, 251, 401
Galloway, George 370
Gambia, The 227f
Garvey, Marcus 268
Garwood, Alfred 89
Gaza 159
GDR 112, 116, 408
Geneva 276
Genocide 234, 266
George
    Aloysius 242
    Bola 249
    Sissi 242, 249
German Jews 97, 126, 161, 201, 376
German Language 63, 187, 224, 266f, 325, 377, 386
German Primary School 56f, 66
German Writing Society 224f, 266
Gibaszewski, Krzysztof xii, 346, 350
Gidley, Ben 264, 279, 287, 312
Gilroy, Paul 237f, 248, 250, 254, 264, 276, 284
Givat Ada 128f, 141, 144
Glassman, Gaby 206, 304f, 315, 330

Goldhagen, Daniel 266f
Goldfarb Henrik 22-26, 47-49, 193
Goldfarb Edith 22, 24-27, 193
Goldsmiths College 224, 237f, 248, 265, 269, 288, 279. 285, 287
Gottlieb, Freddy 169
Goodman, Tony 290
Grenada 357, 367. 371
GTZ 22
Guinea Bissao 289
Grönemeyer, Herbert 65
Gross, Mendel 27, 332
Gwinne Anijabi 242, 258
Gwinner Joost xv, 242
Habeck, Michael 64
Ha Gerush 413
Hall, Stuart 237, 254, 284, 386
Hanukkah 88, 143, 314, 348
Hamas 393
Hamilton, Jackie 245
Hammer, Motti 140
Hasag xiii, 33, 71, 346, 401
Haza, Ofra 61, 189. 216
Haverkampf, Christian 114f, 127, 187
Hebrew 46, 80, 87, 89. 91, 132, 155, 156, 158, 160, 231, 267, 270, 299, 310. 312-314, 398, 400
Hegel 265f
Hehner, Kalmon 122, 146, 203, 375
Herdman, Alan 296
Hezbollah 226
Hiz-but-Tahrir 234
Holocaust Deniers 408
Holocaust Survivors xii, xiii, 20, 27-29, 44, 46, 47, 50, 52, 55, 68, 89, 96, 207, 253, 274, 315, 318, 333, 337-345, 366, 370, 374, 387, 410

445

Humanist Judaism 314, 402
Ice-Hockey World Championship 1983 33
Imafidon, Chris 370
Immigrants 46, 122, 133-134, 272, 323, 340 371
Infil Housing 218f, 232f, 237, 256, 258, 271
Iraq War 188f
Irgun 393
Islamist organisation 226, 234, 393
Islamist Terror 282, 371, 393
Israel
    Ben-Gurion-Airport 93, 128
    Hadera 128, 160
    Haifa 123-125, 131, 140, 160, 190
    Jerusalem 100, 123, 131, 161, 333
    Kafr Qara 128, 163-165
    Kfar Glikson 129, 164
    Masada 123
    Music 190
    Rosh-ha-Nikra 123
    Sde Boker 159
    Tel Aviv see Tel Aviv
Jäger, Alexander 103, 107
Jamaica 239, 242
Jew Hate 393
Jewish Cooking 25f, 94, 100
Jewish North African 100, 132, 135, 138, 177
Jewish-Orthodox 13, 27, 46-48, 49, 80, 225, 273, 303, 313, 355, 392
Jewish Socialist 273
Jhumpa Lahiri 378
Joan Baez 112
Johnson, Boris 309
Johnson, Dominic 368
journalism 177, 181, 188, 190f, 201, 223, 267, 368, 276, 278, 325, 364-372

Jüdische Allgemeine 177, 368. 376, 391
justice xvi, 64, 137, 198f,, 219, 235, 263, 270, 390, 406, 414
Kaddish xiii, 45, 315, 353f. 356
Kahane, Meir 190, 283, 288
Karstadt Oberpollinger 183
Kasperle-Theater 367
Kennedy, Helena 261
Kielce 342
Kindertransport 306
King, Michael 290
Kli Kla Klawitter 63
Kollmar, Gregor xv, 114, 116, 257, 279, 306f, 328
Kosher 25, 27, 48, 96, 204, 216
Kozott, Klaus-Peter 205
Krakow 56, 338f, 341, 343, 347, 351
Kress, Kai 327f
Krio 238, 259, 258
Kucharski 27
Kulp, Kai 114-117, 146
Kung Fu 136-138
Kuwait 184f
Kwaśniewski, Aleksander 336
Labour Party 321, 369
Labrana Alarcón, Carlos 324f
la chaim 410
Lanzmann, Claude 63
Latin 80-85, 88, 101-104, 108, 111
Laue, Karl-Friedrich 103
La Vie en Rose 95
Lawrence, Stephen 219, 262f
Lebanon War 1982 61
Lelow xiv, 344
Levi, Dan 144
Levy, Primo 266
Lewandowski

Index

Bruno 13, 395
Eddie 16f, 363
Eugen 255
Gerhard xi, 13, 58, 184, 409
Louise, see Zierer, L.
Sonia 16, 255
Lewitan, Louis 27, 332
LGBTQIA+ 131, 219, 226, 259, 268, 403
liberal politics 180, 321
Liberal Judaism 46f, 116, 269f, 314, 321, 353f, 397f, 403
Litvinenko, Marina 370
London
   Belsize Square Synagogue 304
   Bloomsbury 273, 325
   Cable Street 234
   Café 'O'Porto 213
   Camden 219, 277, 292, 389
   Coram's Field 325
   Clapton 268
   Docklands 253
   East End 234
   East London Central Synagogue 234
   Euston Station 246
   Finsbury Park 278
   Fitzrovia 384
   Goldborne Road 213
   Golders Green 204, 233
   Great Titchfield Street 219, 233
   Grenfell Tower 69f
   Hampstead Heath 308, 411
   Happening Bagels 204
   Hyde-Park 218, 254
   King's Cross 204, 212
   Ladbroke Grove 212, 219
   Latimer Road 213, 215
   Café Lisboa 213
   North Kensington 212, 214, 233
   Notting Hill 312f
   Olympic and Paralympic Games 368
   Piccadilly Circus 123
   Portobello Road 212-215
   Shadwell 233, 235, 256, 258, 299
   Stamford Hil 273l
   St Ethelburga's Church 299
   Stoke Newington 398, 403
   Watney Markt 234
London Jungle Music Scene 245
Löwenzahn Children Programme 63
LSE 205f, 224, 244
Luftwaffe (Third Reich) 84
Lustig, Peter 64
Maafa 264, 371
Malamud, Bernard 158
Malcolm X, see el-Shabazz
Mapam 189, 321
Mandy, Clarrie 370
Mansfield, Michael 261
Maroons (Jamaican) 239
Masorti (Judaism) 46, 91, 270, 397, 402f
mass murder 352, 376, 408.
Maurer, Lisbeth, Oleg & Freddie 24
Maximiliansgymnasium (The "Max") 81-85 88f, 101-105, 107, 127, 118, 385
Menschlichkeit 407f
Mercury, Freddy 111
Meredith Christiana 243, 312, 398, 400
Meredith Mark 343
Meretz (Zionist Party and Movement) 159, 177, 321, 322, 323, 324
Metropolitan Police 219, 263
Mesko xiv
Miller, Laura 311, 314
Middlesex University 265, 290

447

Zol Zayn Shulem II: Faroys

mikwe 90, 344, 398
minyan 45, 48, 50, 333
Mugabe, Robert 283
Munich
    Alabamahalle 111
    Connollystraße 149
    Funkerstraße. 5, 22
    Herzog-Max-Straße 184
    Hofbräuhaus 278
    Hurler 33
    Kaufingerstraße 146
    Leopoldstraße 27, 29, 30, 31, 33f, 108
    Milbertshofen 57, 185
    Möhlstraße 146
    Münchner Freiheit 108
    Nymphenburger Schloss (Palace) 8
    Olympic Games 6-10, 375, 401
    Olympic Park 6f, 21, 59, 65, 114, 118, 390
    Olympiastdium 36, 47, 112
    Olympic Village (Olympiadorf) 10f, 20, 23, 54, 56f, 59, 64, 66, 82, 103, 108, 114f, 121, 149f
    Pizzeria bei Harry 30
    Reichenbachstr. 44
    Rotkreuzplatz 104
    Schwabing 110
    Schwabylon 31-33
    Sendlingerstraße 13, 395
    Unterfahrt 112
    Munich Synagogue 27, 24, 46f, 48, 83, 89-91, 184
Munich Night-Life:
    Café Reitschule 109
    Jazz Café 147
    Mirage 110
    P1 110, 147f

Parabel 109f
Park-Café 110, 147
Muskeljudentum / Muscle Jews 281
Muslims 78, 235, 240. 300, 355, 401.
Morawiecki, Mateusz 348
National Socialism 204, 348, 408.
Nation of Islam 284
Nakba 300, 413
nazis 112, 225, 353
Netanyahu, Benjamin 403
Neo-Nazis 50, 110, 348, 376, 408
Neu-Ulm 148
Netherlands
    Amsterdam 16, 363
    Apeldoorn 15, 77, 317
    Beekbergen 77, 318
    Dalfsen 75-79, 301, 374
    Ommen 75
    Ugchelen 15, 77, 78
    Zwolle 76
New Wave (style) 109
Nihilism 109
Nihola 325
Nova Scotia 239
Operation No Living Thing 289
Oskar-von-Miller-Gymnasium 104, 119, 182
Palestinian Terror 7-10, 164, 392f, 413
Palestinians 8, 98, 101, 128, 163-165, 190. 224, 234, 299, 300, 355, 365, 392f, 399
PLO 393
Passau 148
Passover 22-26, 88, 90, 312
Peabody 233
peace 254, 298f, 321, 355, 403, 406, 410, 411-415

Index

Peace Now 159
Pfaffing 17
Pilates 58, 69, 290f, 294-297, 298-300, 311, 324f
Piśkiewicz, Agnieszka xii, 333, 350
Plaszow 355
pogrom 341f
Poland 338, 342, 343, 346-351, 356, 366
Pollock, Grieselda 284, 288
Pöring 13
Postwar-Generation 51, 61, 64, 375, 376
progressive education 64f, 157, 176, 313, 379
Prozac 272, 274
psychological 55, 72, 73, 142, 169, 194-196, 253, 274, 304, 307
PTSD 74, 274f, 304, 305
punk 106, 110, 131, 163
Punch and Judy 267
Queen (Band) 111
Queen Elizabeth II 386, 389
Rabin, Yitzhak 190, 224, 226, 283
racism 50, 52, 122, 208f, 213f, 217, 237f, 246, 264f, 293, 348f, 350, 371. 386, 407, 409
Rappelkiste 63, 65
Raz (Israeli Party) 159, 189, 203, 221
reconciliation 340, 349f, 404
Reich-Ranicki, Marcel 50, 374f
refugees 96f, 100, 133, 155, 199, 322, 366, 370, 376
Reggae 153, 214, 216, 245, 348, 350. 367
Rene Cassin 276, 285
Renton, James 287
Rieger Hertz / Pelze 134
Rieger Micol 134f, 136, 160, 164, 169, 203, 206, 375

Rita 189
rotmoffen 78
Rolling Stones 31, 112
Roma and Sinti 340, 347, 354f
Romans 251
Rosenthal, Hans 60
Rotstein, Arminio 63
Rottach-Egern 22
royal
Ruïtenauer, Andreas 368
Santana, Carlos 112
Salamander, Rachel 392f
Shma Israel 150
Schmid, Claudia 225
Schmidt, Renate 186, 206
Schönhuber, Franz 112f
Sholem Alejchem 302
Schutt Evert & Jenni 70, 77, 194, 317
Second Generation 55, 89, 109, 122, 196, 207, 253, 254, 274f, 304, 345
Sendung mit der Maus 63
Sephardi 133, 144, 177
Shabbat 22, 36, 53, 92, 96, 140, 144, 234, 269, 412
Shalom Achshav 159
Shalvata 274, 304, 315
Shapira, Shahak 357
Shiva 332f
Shma Israel 150
Shoa Survivors xii, 20-25, 46f, 89, 196, 207, 304, 318, 387
Shushan:
   Awi 100, 209, 398
   Hannah (Hanni) xii, 99f, 195, 209, 333, 362
   Idan 100
   Itai 100, 398

449

Sierra Leone 238-243, 248, 289, 385
Silberschatz 27
Sister Orli 153
Skarżysko-Kamienna x, xi, xiii, 346, 352, 359, 401
Skrzypczyk, Beata und Mirek 350
Slavery xii, 387, 229, 266, 277, 283
Soas 191, 205f, 222, 224-230, 248-251, 254f, 272
Social Democracy 185
Solingen 97
Sonnenbichl 22
SOS-Sahel 230
South Arfrica 250, 288, 136, 157
SPD 185, 186. 188f, 199, 206
Spitzer Andre & Ankie 8, 392
Sportschau 53
Springsteen, Bruce 112
Srebrenica 78
Starmer, Keir 389
Straw, Jack 260
Steiner, Rudolf 381
Strauß., Franz Josef 186
Stern-Gang 283
Suriname 235
swastica 41, 147
Szczekociny xii, xiii, xiv, 89, 334-344, 349, 352
Szwarcbojm Hanka und Cella 97
Talking Afrika 279
Tavistock Clinic 305f, 308
taz 50, 177, 189, 364, 368-372, 376, 403
Tel Aviv 12f, 22, 26f, 61, 88-90, 93-100, 124, 142, 152f, 163, 179f, 188, 190, 373
    Allenby Street 96
    Beach 96, 123, 153

Boy Shop 153
Café Mersand, 96
Café Tamar 180
Dan Hotel 89
Dizengoff 125
Frishman Street 153
Ha-Osem-Ha-Shlishi 180
Ichilov-Hospital 142
Shuk-ha-Carmel 96
Shenkin Street 180
Soweto Club 152f
tolerance 351, 387
Toussaint Louverture 284
Torah 2, 87, 91f, 345, 397, 400, 402
Trauma ix, 3, 20, 62, 194, 208. 220, 253, 265 275, 307, 319, 320, 370, 403, 407
Trzaskowski, Rafal 347
Treblinka 2, 61, 352, 353
Trevelyan 371
Tumbalalaika 95, 118
Turner, Nat 284
Ukraine xiv, 348
Ulpan 155
University College London (UCL) 224f, 229, 298, 315
University of Bedfordshire 277, 280, 282
University of Birmingham 251f, 260, 264
University of Leeds 63, 276, 281, 284, 298f
University of London 191, 224, 265, 271
University of Sussex 259f, 263
van Veen, Herman 61, 65
Valk Arie 77
Valk Martha 15f, 77f, 318
Vaterstetten 15, 17
Waldenfels, Titus 119
Waffen-SS 112

Index

Wahat al-Salam-Neve Schalom 177, 299, 321, 340, 355, 394
Waldorf School 179, 379-383
Wales 238, 243, 370
Wehrmacht 266, 376
West Africa xii, 227-229, 240, 248, 250-252
West Bank 159, 190
Wiedervereinigung (reunification) 192f, 197-19
Wilberforce, William 239
Witler, Ben-Zion 410
Wolffsohn, Michael 190
Wojcik, Stanislaw 345
yake 96
Yiddish 13, 22-26, 37, 43, 47f, 49, 63, 69, 89, 92, 94, 96, 98-100, 118, 125, 128, 201f, 208, 313, 353f, 374
YMCA-England 287, 288
Yolocaust 357
Yom Kippur 22, 44, 46f, 90, 98
Yom-Kippur-War 41
Yoruba 240, 401f, 250, 311
Zelman, Leon 334
Zierer Georg & Louise 13, 17f
Zierer Markus & Family 15, 18, 363
Zimbabwe 250, 289, 315
Zionism 121, 125, 146, 185, 202, 282, 321f, 355, 386, 409
ZJD 146
Zorneding 13
Zylbersztajn
    Abraham xi, 4, 9, 16, 63, 73, 88. 90-100, 142, 333f, 400
    Bracha 4, 73, 95, 98, 100
    Chaftje xii, 16 26, 91, 100
    Claudia xii, xv, 220, 238f, 242-265, 270-272. 277, 289-295, 298, 301, 307, 309-314, 317, 319, 323-327, 343
    355, 360, 362f, 380, 390, 398, 401, 407, 411
    Corrie x, xii, 3, 15, 22, 26, 28, 43f, 51, 5f, 61 66, 70f, 75-80, 90-95, 98, 115, 141, 143, 193f, 207, 209, 247 254f, 301f, 313, 318, 320, 327, 330-333, 338f, 341, 343, 362f, 374, 385, 390, 397, 411
    Dowid (David) xi
    Fiszl xi, 341
    Herszik ix, x, 2, 5
    Leah 98
    Moisze 16, 37, 91, 99f, 333, 341
    Ruszke 4, 26, 61, 88, 93, 95, 97f, 100, 142 346, 359, 410
    Shifrah xi, xv, 310- 317, 319, 324-328, 343, 360, 362-364, 379-383, 390, 397-401
    Szyfra ix, xi
    Yaron & Rinat 95, 98
    Wolf ix, x, 1-5, 7, 9, 11f, 16, 21-56, 60-63, 66-80, 86-91, 95, 96, 98-100, 113, 115, 119, 123, 126, 133
    138, 141, 143, 146, 167, 193f, 197, 200f, 207-209, 247, 252, 254f, 260, 266, 267, 270, 275, 301-303 312, 315, 318-320, 327, 329--353, 355, 358-360, 374-376, 399, 401, 410
    Zwika 4, 93f, 97f, 100, 128, 255

www.ingramcontent.com/pod-product-compliance
Lightning Source LLC
Chambersburg PA
CBHW050829230426
43667CB00012B/1934